National
Geographic
Society

Field Guide to
the Birds of
North America

D0401852

National
Geographic
Society

Field Guide to the

Birds
of North America

Published by
The National
Geographic Society

Gilbert M. Grosvenor
President

Melvin M. Payne
Chairman of the Board

Owen R. Anderson
*Executive
Vice President*

Robert L. Breeden
*Vice President,
Publications and
Educational Media*

Prepared by
National Geographic
Book Service

Charles O. Hyman
Director

Ross S. Bennett
Managing Editor

*Consultants
for this book*

Jon L. Dunn
Eirik A. T. Blom
Chief Consultants

Dr. George E. Watson
General Consultant

Dr. John P. O'Neill
Consultant on Songbirds

Staff for this book

Shirley L. Scott
Editor

Lise M. Swinson
Associate Editor

Mary B. Dickinson
Catherine Herbert Howell
Assistant Editors

David M. Seager
Art Director

Thomas B. Allen
Wayne Barrett
Seymour L. Fishbein
Philip Kopper
Edward Lanouette
David F. Robinson
Robert D. Selim
Jonathan B. Tourtellot
Writers

Paul A. Dunn
Martha B. Hays
Feroline B. Higginson
Diane S. Marton
Maura J. Pollin
Penelope A. Timbers
L. Madison Washburn
Jayne Wise
Researchers

Charlotte J. Golin
Design Assistant

Georgina L. McCormack
Teresita Cóquia Sison
Editorial Assistants

Robert C. Firestone
Production Manager

Karen F. Edwards
Richard S. Wain
*Assistant Production
Managers*

John T. Dunn
David V. Evans
Ronald E. Williamson
Engraving and Printing

John D. Garst, Jr.
Virginia L. Baza
Peter J. Balch
Joseph F. Ochlak
Publications Art

Teresa S. Purvis
Index

Contributions by
Caroline Hottenstein
Robert M. Poole
Deborah Robertson
Margaret Sedeen

First Edition
250,000 copies

Library of Congress
CIP data page 463

Contents

Introduction

More than 800 species of birds breed in North America, or visit the continent regularly, or drop in occasionally. This is a daunting number for a beginning bird watcher who is merely trying to identify a newcomer at the feeder. But no one person has seen all these birds. Many species are found only in certain regions or specialized habitats. And some species are extremely rare.

Bird watching—nowadays more frequently called birding—is a fascinating pastime enjoyed by millions of people. The challenge lies not only in finding birds but in accurately identifying each bird seen, and this requires both preparation and experience.

Some birders want only to become better acquainted with the neighborhood birds. Others try to see as many species as possible. For every level of interest, the first place to use a field guide is at home. Leaf through it often to become familiar with the wonderful variety of birds that inhabit or visit our continent.

Species

This guide includes all species known to breed in North America—defined for this book as the land extending northward from the northern border of Mexico, plus adjacent islands and seas within about a hundred miles of the coast. Also included are species that breed in Mexico or Central America or on other continents but are seen in North America when they spend the winter here or pass through on regular migration routes.

And we include species that are seen in North America only when they wander off course or are blown in by storms. Our standard requires that they have been seen at least three times in the past five years or five times in this century. A few species that fail to meet this standard are nevertheless included because of a strong likelihood that they will be seen again, especially if watchers are looking for them.

We have also included *exotic* species, birds from other continents that have been introduced into North America as game, park, or cage birds and are now often seen in the wild. A number of these species have established wild breeding populations here; a few, such as the House Sparrow, are abundant in the wild.

The sequence in this guide follows only generally that of the American Ornithologists' Union (A.O.U.) 1983 Check-list, which places species in the sequence of their presumed natural relationships. We departed from that sequence where it seemed more useful for field reference to group together the species that share similar life-styles or look somewhat alike.

The A.O.U. Check-list is the standard for species classification, scientific names, and common names. Many names have been changed in the latest edition of the Check-list. Some birds once classified as separate species are now regarded as different forms of a single species. Such changes are incorporated in this field guide and cross-referenced under the old names. Veteran bird watchers looking in the index for the Sparrow Hawk, for example, are directed to the American Kestrel; those searching for the Slate-colored Junco will learn that it has been combined with two other former species, all now called Dark-eyed Junco.

Families

Ornithologists organize the species into family groups that share certain structural characteristics. Some families have more than a hundred members; others have only one. Family resemblance is often helpful in identifying birds in the field. Members of the family Picidae (page 264), for example, are quickly recognizable as woodpeckers, narrowing the identification problem down from 800 possibilities to 21.

You will find brief family descriptions at the beginning of each group in this field guide. They contain information applicable to all members of the family. You will also find within some family sections a description of distinctive smaller groups such as the sapsuckers (page 268), three species that share some traits unique among woodpeckers.

Scientific Names

Each kind of bird, or species, has a two-part Latin scientific name. The first part, always capitalized, indicates the genus, a group of closely related species. Nine members of the family Picidae are placed in the genus *Picoides*. The second part of the name, not capitalized, indicates the species. *Picoides pubescens* is the name of one specific kind of woodpecker (commonly known as the Downy Woodpecker). *Picoides tridactylus* (or *P. tridactylus*) is the Three-toed Woodpecker. No two species share the same two-part scientific name.

Species are sometimes further divided into subspecies, when populations in different geographical regions show recognizable differences. Each subspecies bears a third Latin name. *Picoides tridactylus bacatus* (*P.t. bacatus*) identifies the dark-backed form of the Three-toed Woodpecker that inhabits eastern North America. *P.t. dorsalis* is the paler-backed form found in the Rockies. (In this book, "form" is synonymous with "subspecies.") We have endeavored to illustrate or describe each form or geographic variation that looks different from other forms and thus might cause confusion. Latin names are used for subspecies that cannot easily be described by color or range.

Plumages

How much easier identification would be if every bird of each species always looked the same! But it is not enough for us to know what a bird's plumage—its overall feathering—looks like in only one season or sex or at one age. Most species undergo a complete molt in late summer or early fall, replacing all their feathers. This plumage is usually held through the fall and winter. Often the molt occurs before the birds migrate, and thus we see the birds in this plumage even if they spend the winter outside North America. In late winter or early spring, the birds undergo a partial molt to the plumage we see in spring and summer. Fall and winter plumage may vary considerably from spring and summer plumage, and a bird in the process of molting can confound even expert birders.

In many species the male and female look quite different, and the young birds unlike either parent. And we must also keep in mind that some species of the same genus occasionally breed with other species, producing *hybrid* offspring that look partly like one parent, partly like the other. Subspecies also interbreed, producing *intergrade* populations.

Some species have two or more *color phases*, occurring regionally or within the same population. Female Spruce Grouse, for example, can be reddish or gray.

Where adult males and females are similar, we show only one illustration. When male (δ) and female ($\circ$) look different, we show both. If spring and fall, or breeding and nonbreeding, plumages differ only slightly, or if only one of these plumages is usually seen in North America, we show only one figure. Juvenile and immature birds are illustrated when they hold a different-looking plumage after they are old enough to be seen away from their more easily recognizable parents.

Plumage Sequence

In general, nestlings wear fluffy *down*. The first coat of true feathers, acquired before the bird leaves the nest, is worn by the *juvenile* and may show some traces of down. In many species, juvenile plumage is replaced in late summer or early fall by a *first-fall* or *first-winter* plumage that usually more closely resembles the adult. First-fall and any subsequent plumages that do not resemble the adult are termed *immature* plumages and

8

may continue in a series that includes *first-spring* (when the bird is almost a year old), *first-summer,* and so on, until it attains *adult* plumage. When birds take more than one and a half years to reach adult plumage, we have labeled the interim plumages as *subadult* or with the specific year or season shown.

Some species wear colorful plumage in the breeding season and molt to duller colors for fall and winter. In some songbirds, the bright plumage of spring appears with the gradual wearing away of dull tips on the feathers of their winter plumage, with very little actual molting involved. By late summer, feathers become worn and faded; fresh fall plumage can be brighter than the colors of August.

In some species, breeding plumage looks much like winter plumage. Some changes are evident only during the brief period of courtship. In herons, for example, the colors of bill, lores, legs, and feet may change or deepen. When these colors are at their height, the birds are said to be in *high* breeding plumage.

Male ducks, after courtship, molt into an *eclipse* plumage that resembles the dull colors of the female. In most species, eclipse plumage is held only for a few weeks, when another molt begins. All the flight feathers are lost simultaneously during eclipse; the ducks are unable to fly until new flight feathers grow in.

Field Marks

More often than not, there are good clues to a bird's identity in every plumage. These *field marks* are what birders must look for—the extent of yellow on a bird's sides, the color of its head in contrast to its back, the shape of the bill, the length of the tail. A field mark can be as obvious as the Killdeer's double breast bands (see page 107) or as subtle as the difference in head shape between Greater and Lesser Scaups (page 81). Some field marks are plainly visible only in strong light or from a certain angle or when the bird is in flight. Not every bird seen can be identified, even by experts.

It is important to become familiar with the terms commonly used in describing the parts of a bird. You will find these terms illustrated on pages 10-11.

The most distinctive field marks for each species in each plumage are usually listed first in our text descriptions, for quick reference. But few birds will hold still long enough for you to study your field guide. Instead you must study the bird, noting its overall size, shape, and colors and such details as eye ring, bill shape, and wing bars. After the bird has flown you can turn to your field guide or jot down notes for later review.

Parts of a Bird

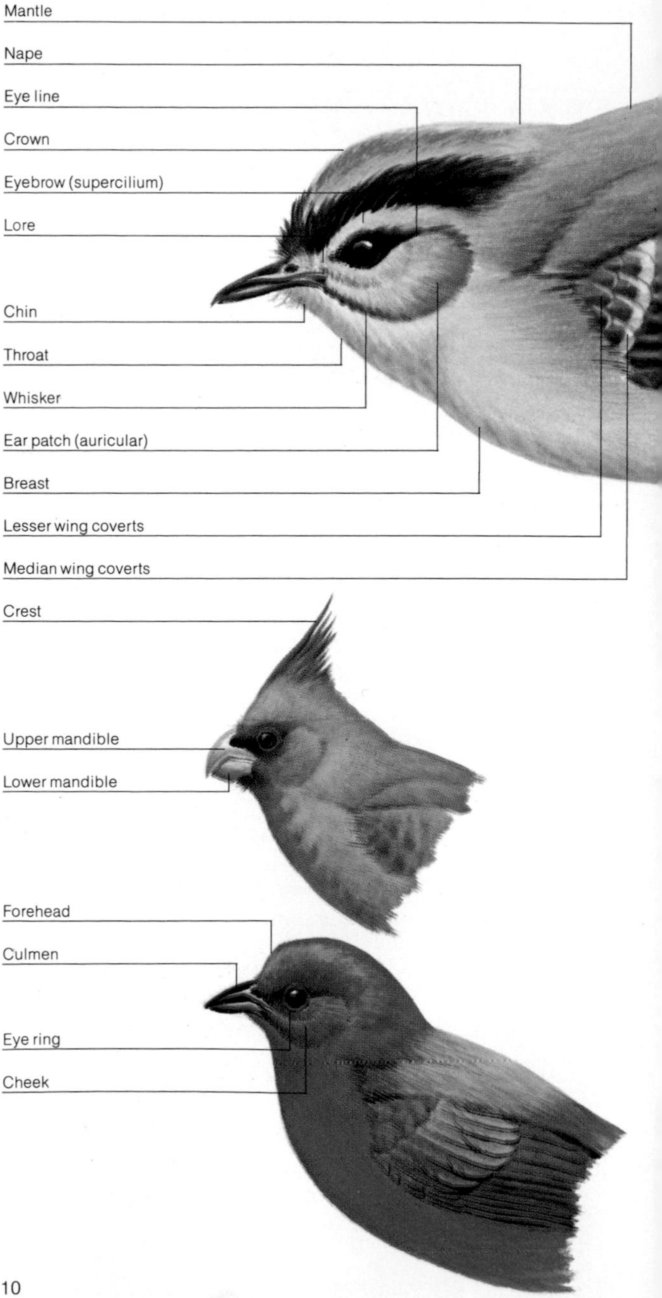

Mantle

Nape

Eye line

Crown

Eyebrow (supercilium)

Lore

Chin

Throat

Whisker

Ear patch (auricular)

Breast

Lesser wing coverts

Median wing coverts

Crest

Upper mandible

Lower mandible

Forehead

Culmen

Eye ring

Cheek

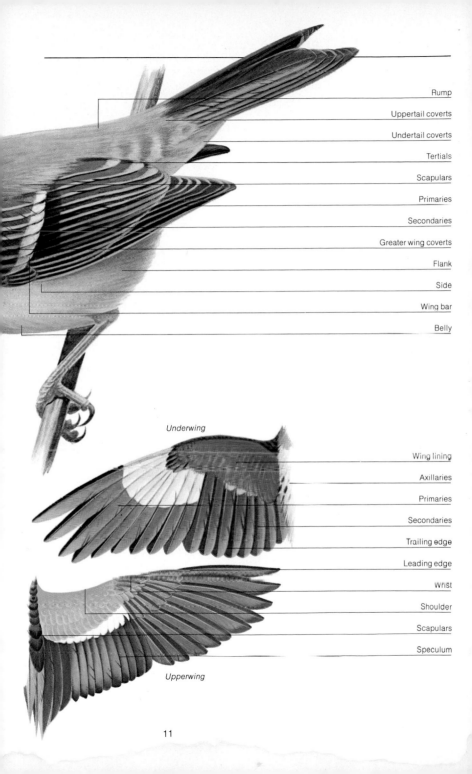

Rump

Uppertail coverts

Undertail coverts

Tertials

Scapulars

Primaries

Secondaries

Greater wing coverts

Flank

Side

Wing bar

Belly

Underwing

Wing lining

Axillaries

Primaries

Secondaries

Trailing edge

Leading edge

Wrist

Shoulder

Scapulars

Speculum

Upperwing

11

Successful birding requires that you recall and recognize quickly what field marks identify which species, and this ability comes with experience. Study more closely the familiar birds that you can identify without even trying. What is distinctive about them? Get help from experts by joining outings sponsored by local clubs and nature centers.

Measurements

If you are searching for a kinglet, it helps to know that the bird is only about four inches long. Relative size is also important. Downy Woodpeckers are readily distinguished from the similar Hairy Woodpeckers, even at some distance, by their smaller size.

The figures in this book, compiled from standard sources, represent measurements of museum study skins. The difficulty of accurately measuring a living and lively bird justifies the use of skin measurements at least as a general guide.

Average length (L) from tip of bill to tip of tail is given for each species. If males and females differ markedly in size, average length for each sex is given. Where size varies greatly within a species (chiefly among the raptors), a range of smallest to largest is provided. And for large birds that you will most often see in flight, we indicate the average wingspan (W), measured from wing tip to wing tip.

Voice

Just as field marks and size help to identify a bird, so do range, habitat, behavior, and voice. A bird's songs and calls not only reveal its presence but also, in many cases, provide instant identification. Some species—particularly nocturnal or secretive birds such as owls, nightjars, and rails—are more often heard than seen. A few species, such as some of the flycatchers, are most reliably identified by voice, even when seen.

Our text describes distinctive songs and calls. In addition, the recordings that accompany this guide include many of the songs and calls most important in field identification. A musical note (♪) next to the name of the bird indicates that its voice is included on the National Geographic records. The index entry refers you to the specific record.

Behavior

Behavioral traits also provide clues to identification. Is the bird's flight direct or undulating? Does it beat its wings rapidly or slowly? Does it forage on the ground or high in the treetops? Is the bird shy or bold? The Limpkin's peculiar gait leaves no doubt as to its identity, even at a distance. Some species of warblers walk rather than hop. Turkey Vultures often soar with their wings held slightly raised; Black Vultures soar on level wings. Black-and-white Warblers climb up and down and around tree trunks; the similar Blackpoll Warbler does not. Such distinctive behavior is not only useful for identification but fascinating to watch.

Abundance and Habitat

Abundance must be considered in relation to habitat. A species that is *common* in one part of its range is sure to be only *fairly common* or even *uncommon* in other parts of that range. The House Sparrow is plainly *abundant*. The California Condor is just as plainly *rare*. But from certain mountaintops in California, you are much more likely to see a Condor than a House Sparrow.

Habitat information included in the text will help you find a particular species within its range. Some species are highly *local*, found only in a very specialized habitat. Bank Swallows, for example, are fairly common in summer, but only near the steep sandy or gravelly banks they require for nesting.

Seasons of the year also affect abundance. White-throated Sparrows are common in the northern half of eastern North America in summer but almost entirely absent during the winter, while the opposite is true in the southern half of the continent. In the central part of North America, Whitethroats are seen only during migration.

Birders call *casual* the species that turn up irregularly in small numbers in areas outside their normal range. Casual occurrences are not unexpected but neither are they annual, or *regular*. A *vagrant* is a bird that has strayed off its usual migration route. A *visitor* is generally just passing through on its usual migration route and occurs regularly enough to be expected.

Some birders and texts use the term "accidental" for species that have been seen only a few times in an area far out of their normal range. Such sightings may never again occur. We have instead alerted you to the rarity of these sightings. Any species can show up unexpectedly almost anywhere, but we must be doubly cautious about the identification of such surprises.

Range Maps

Maps are provided for all species except those with very limited ranges, which instead are described in the text, and those species that do not ordinarily breed or winter in North America. Range boundaries are drawn where the species ceases to be regularly seen. Every species is rare at the edges of its range. The sample map on page 15 explains the colors and symbols used.

Range information is based on actual sightings and therefore depends upon the number of knowledgeable and active birders in each area. There is much to learn about bird distribution in every part of North America. One of the pleasures of birding is the discovery of expanding ranges. Breeding-bird surveys undertaken by federal and state governments and by birding clubs make a vital contribution to the general fund of information about each species.

Our maps were compiled by Eirik A. T. Blom especially for this guide and reflect his interpretation of the best information currently available. Data were obtained from published sources and from consultation with birders and ornithologists across the continent. Extensive help was provided in particular by Danny Bystrak, Jon L. Dunn, Kim Eckert, Kenn Kaufman, Dr. John P. O'Neill, Robert F. Ringler, Dr. William B. Robertson, Dr. John Trochet, Peter Vickery, and Dr. George E. Watson.

Birds are not, of course, bound by maps. Ranges continually expand and contract, making any map a tool rather than a rule. The Northern Cardinal, for instance, is steadily expanding its range in the northeast.

Irruptive species, such as the Snowy Owl, move southward in some years in large or small numbers and for great or small distances. These irregular movements are generally but not specifically predictable; certainly they cannot be precisely mapped.

Among herons and some other groups, juveniles leave the nesting grounds in late summer and scatter northward. These *postbreeding wanderers* do not remain in their newfound lands but migrate southward with the winter. In the following spring, some of them may return to the new area to breed.

Range maps of *pelagic* species, birds that spend most of their time over the open sea, are of course somewhat conjectural, because seabird observers are few.

Birding

Time spent at home with your field guide will be repaid when you go out into meadows and woodlands, deserts and mountains, looking for birds. But much is also learned only from experience. When you have seen the Northern Harrier many times, for instance, its distinctive flight pattern signals its identity for you long before you can see its facial disk or white rump.

Experienced birders know how to move quietly and to stand patiently still. They know that a sudden riot of scolding songbirds may mean that an owl is roosting nearby; that a flock of familiar Ring-billed Gulls should

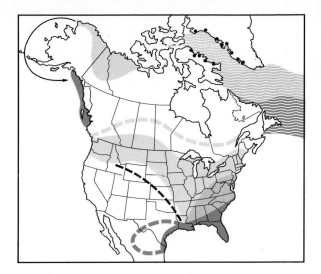

Range Map Symbols

 Breeding range, generally in spring and summer.

 Summer seabird range. *(Includes winter range of Southern Hemisphere species)*

 Year-round range.

 Year-round seabird range.

 Winter range. *(If no winter or year-round range is shown, winters outside North America)*

 Winter seabird range.

 Extent of post-breeding dispersal in summer.

 Species migrates chiefly east of this line.

 Extent of irregular or irruptive range in some winters.

 Direction of migration route.

Breeding colonies.

be studied closely to determine whether one or two other gull species might also be present.

The rule of quietness has an exception: If you make squeaking or "pishing" noises or imitate an owl's call, an inquisitive bird may come to investigate.

A rule that has no exceptions: Take care not to disturb either the birds or their habitats. Take particular care not to frighten parent birds away from nests.

The bird life of our continent has, on the whole, declined with the advance of human population and technology. Many local and national organizations, such as the National Audubon Society and The Nature Conservancy, work tirelessly toward the preservation of habitat and the protection of individual species. These and other such organizations welcome your support and active participation.

Binoculars

Expert birders sometimes leave their field guides at home. But no birder would leave behind the binoculars, essential equipment even for backyard birding.

Try several kinds before deciding what to buy. The best choice for most birding, and relatively inexpensive, is 7x35 binoculars with coated lenses and center focusing. The "7" indicates power of magnification; a bird will appear seven times closer. The "35" is lens size in millimeters. A ratio of 1 to 5 between power and lens size is generally considered ideal for light-gathering capability; that is, the lens is large enough in relation to the magnification power to admit sufficient light for distinguishing colors in poor light conditions.

Coated lenses reduce glare and the "halo" effect common in uncoated lenses. Center focusing is convenient when speed is important.

Using binoculars efficiently takes practice. Try them first on a stationary object to learn to locate and focus on it quickly. Then practice with any moving object—car, airplane, a bird in your backyard. You will soon form the habit of keeping your eyes on the bird while raising the binoculars.

Telescopes

If you spend much time watching shorebirds or waterfowl, a telescope is particularly useful. Scopes are made in a variety of styles. You will need to decide whether you want one with a fixed eyepiece or a zoom lens and, if it is important to you, whether the scope is adaptable for photography. You will need a tripod; be sure that it has a center brace and that it can be raised high enough for you to use the scope comfortably. In places where a tripod isn't practical, or when you want to follow a moving bird, a shoulder mount (often called a gunstock mount) will help steady the scope. Useful also is a mount that clamps onto a car window. Cars, where permitted, make fine birdwatching blinds; birds will often allow a car to approach them more closely than people on foot. You can sit comfortably in your car, put the scope on the window mount, and get excellent views.

Checklists

Most birders make lists of the birds they see. Some keep several lists, ranging from birds seen in a certain area to all birds ever seen—a *life list*. In addition to being a source of pride, such lists are a source of great pleasure, enabling you to look back and remember the first time you saw a bluebird or an eagle.

The index in this guide includes check-off boxes beside the common-name entry for each species; you can use this for your life list. Better still, keep a notebook in which to record not only the name of the bird you see but also the date and place and notes about field marks, behavior, voice. Such information, reviewed over the years, will help you remember when and where to expect each species and how to identify it.

The Illustrations

Over a period of more than three years, thirteen artists painted the 220 plates in this field guide, using museum study skins and photographs and working meticulously under the guidance of our consultants. You will find on page 464 a list of these artists and the plates that each painted. Other artists made last-minute changes and additions reflecting new information as the plates were readied for the printer.

It would have been impossible to produce this field guide without the use of extensive collections of study skins available in major museums. Such collections are the only way to confirm details of plumage variation and subtle field marks.

The following museums generously lent study skins from their collections: the National Museum of Natural History, Smithsonian Institution, Washington, D. C.; the Museum of Natural Science, Louisiana State University, Baton Rouge; the Museum of Vertebrate Zoology, University of California at Berkeley; the Denver Museum of Natural History, Colorado; the Museum of Natural History, Santa Barbara, California; and the Natural History Museum, San Diego, California.

We were also assisted by photographs provided by our consultants and by Stephen Bailey, Jen and Des Bartlett, Robert F. Ringler, Richard A. Rowlett, Lawrence Sansone III, Claudia P. Wilds, and others.

Loons (Family Gaviidae)

All four members of this family occur in North America. Loons ride low on the water. Legs set well back make travel on land difficult. In all species, juvenile plumage is held through the first winter and first summer; they resemble adults but have more white on upperparts, giving them a scaly look.

Common Loon *Gavia immer* L 32" (81 cm)
Large, thick-billed loon with black bill in breeding season. Bill is grayer in winter plumage; crown and nape darker than back; dark nape borders white throat in an irregular line, but note especially the white indentation at mid-neck. Many birds show a pale area encircling the eye. Forehead is steep, crown peaked at front; culmen is rounded, making bill look straight. Holds head level. In flight, large head and feet help distinguish Common from Arctic and Red-throated Loons. A few Commons are almost as small as Arctic Loons. Fairly common; nests on large lakes. Migrates over land as well as coastally. Winters mainly on coastal waters, casually inland. Loud yodeling calls are heard chiefly on breeding grounds; also in migration; rarely in winter.

Yellow-billed Loon *Gavia adamsii* L 34" (86 cm)
Breeding adult has straw yellow bill; culmen is straight, giving bill a very slightly uptilted look. Bill is duskier or paler in winter and immature plumages. Note also pale face and distinct dark mark behind eye. Bill is usually paler and longer than in Common Loon; back is browner; head is paler than back; crown is peaked at front and rear, giving a subtle double-bump effect. Tends to hold head slightly uptilted. Rarest of our loons, breeding on tundra lakes and rivers; replaces Common Loon in the high Arctic. Calls similar to Common Loon but rarely heard south of breeding grounds. Migrates coastally; very rare inland; rare south of Canada.

Arctic Loon *Gavia arctica* L 26" (66 cm)
In breeding adult, head and nape are pale gray; throat shows purple patch. Patch is dark green in the slightly larger form breeding in Siberia and perhaps on the west coast of Alaska; the two forms are indistinguishable in winter plumage; throat patches look black under most circumstances. Winter bird's crown and nape are paler than back; cap extends to eye. Neck is three-toned: front white, bordered by a thin, dark line; rear pale gray. Distinctive on many birds is a thin row of brown spots forming a chin strap. In all plumages, note that bill is slim and straight; head is smoothly rounded and held level. In flight, resembles Common Loon but head and feet are smaller. Nests on large lakes. A coastal migrant, casual inland throughout the west; very rare on east coast.

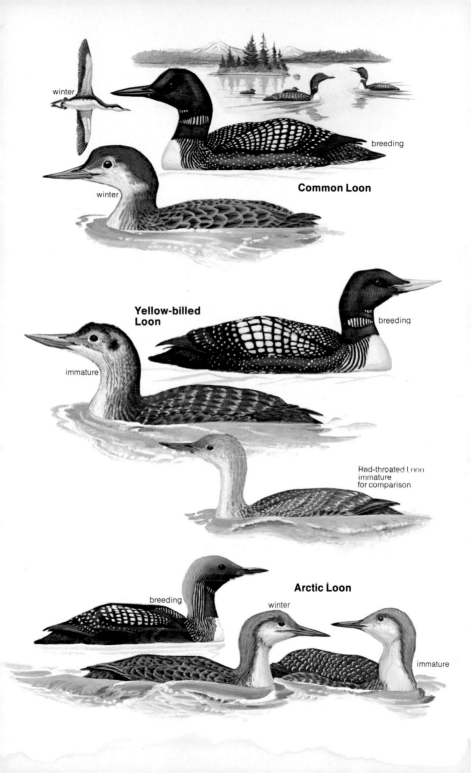

winter

winter

breeding

Common Loon

Yellow-billed Loon

breeding

immature

Red-throated Loon
immature
for comparison

breeding

winter

Arctic Loon

immature

Red-throated Loon *Gavia stellata* L 25" (64 cm)

In breeding plumage, distinguished by striped nape and pale gray face and neck, with dark red patch on throat, and by lack of white on upperparts. Winter bird has extensive white spotting on back; head is paler than back and paler than other winter loons, often blending into white of throat. Forehead is sometimes white. In all plumages, note thin, slightly upturned bill; head smooth and rounded. Tends to hold head tilted up slightly. In flight, shows smaller head and feet than Common Loon (preceding page); wingbeat is quicker; holds head below line of body, giving a hunchbacked look. Migrates coastally; also over land in the east. Winters along coasts; casual in the interior during winter.

Grebes (Family Podicipedidae)

A worldwide family; six species occur in North America. Lobed toes make them strong swimmers. Grebes are rarely seen on land or in flight.

♪ Western Grebe *Aechmophorus occidentalis* L 25" (64 cm)

Our largest grebe, strikingly black-and-white, with a swanlike neck and long, thin bill. In dark-phase bird, black cap extends to include eyes and lores; bill is yellow-green; back and flanks are darker. Black cap is less extensive in light-phase bird; bill yellowish-orange; back and flanks slightly paler. A very few intermediate birds are seen, usually with orange bills and dark lores. Dark-phase birds predominate in the north and east, light-phase in the south. In flight, both phases show long, white wing stripe. Calls of the two phases are distinct: dark birds give a two-note courting call; light birds' call is a longer single note. Gregarious; breeds on broad, open, freshwater lakes edged with reeds. Dramatic courtship ritual involves sprinting across the water with necks kinked. Winters on sheltered bays, protected coastal areas, and large inland bodies of water. Casual during winter and migration in the east; almost all records are of dark-phase birds.

Red-necked Grebe *Podiceps grisegena* L 20" (51 cm)

Large grebe with heavy, tapered, yellowish bill almost as long as the head. Breeding adult has striking whitish throat and cheeks, reddish foreneck. In winter plumage, throat is mottled, white of chin extends onto rear of face in an ill-defined crescent. First-winter bird has rounder head, paler eye; lacks strong facial crescent. Juvenile has striped head. In flight, Red-necked Grebe shows a white leading and trailing edge on inner wing; thick neck is often held slouched down. Generally solitary. Breeds on shallow lakes; winters mostly along coasts. Casual in winter along Gulf coast and inland.

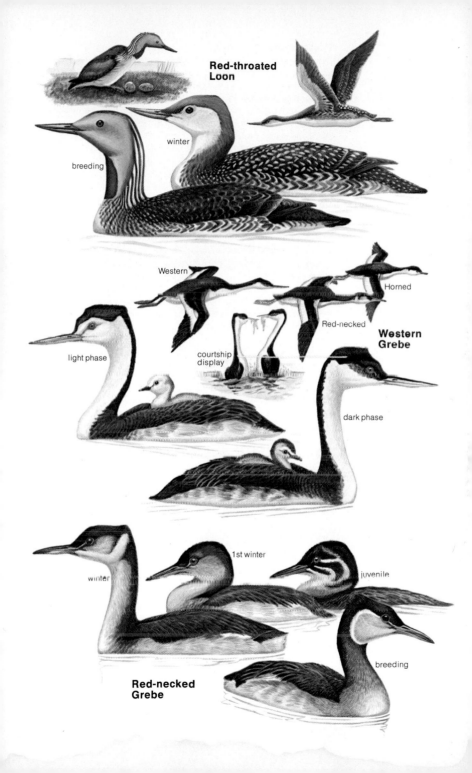

Red-throated Loon

breeding

winter

Western

Horned

Red-necked

Western Grebe

courtship display

light phase

dark phase

winter

1st winter

juvenile

breeding

Red-necked Grebe

Horned Grebe *Podiceps auritus* L 13½" (34 cm)

Breeding adult has chestnut throat, golden "horns." In winter plumage, white cheeks and throat contrast sharply with dark crown and nape; a few birds show some dusky on lower neck. Black on nape narrows to a thin stripe. Most birds show a pale spot in front of eye. In flight (preceding page), white secondaries show as patch on trailing edge of wing; note also the inconspicuous white patch at shoulder. Bill is short and straight, with pale tip; thicker than Eared Grebe's. Crown is flatter than in Eared Grebe. Size and short, dark bill most readily separate Horned from Red-necked Grebe. Tends to leap forward when diving. Breeds on sheltered freshwater lakes and ponds. Winters mostly on salt water; a few winter inland.

Eared Grebe *Podiceps nigricollis* L 12½" (32 cm)

Breeding adult has blackish neck, golden "ears" fanning out behind eye. In winter plumage, throat is washed with dusky; cheek dark; whitish on chin extends up as a crescent behind eye; compare with Horned Grebe. Note also the Eared Grebe's longer, thinner bill, with lower mandible angled upward; thinner neck; more peaked crown. Lacks pale spot in front of eye. Generally rides higher in the water than Horned Grebe, exposing fluffy white undertail coverts. In flight, white secondaries show as white patch on trailing edge of wing. Usually nests in large colonies on freshwater lakes. Winters inland and along coast. Rare but regular in Gulf coast states; casual along the Atlantic coast south of New York.

Pied-billed Grebe *Podilymbus podiceps* L 13½" (34 cm)

Breeding adult is brown overall, with black ring around stout, whitish bill; black chin and throat; pale belly. Winter birds lose bill ring; chin is white, throat tinged with pale rufous. Juveniles resemble winter adult but throat is much redder, eye ring absent, head and neck streaked with brown and white. First-winter birds lack streaking; throat is duller. A short-necked, big-headed, stocky grebe. In flight, shows almost no white on wing. Nests around marshy ponds and sloughs; tends to hide from intruders by sinking until only its head shows. Common but not gregarious. Winters in fresh or salt water.

Least Grebe *Tachybaptus dominicus* L 9¾" (25 cm)

A small, short-necked grebe with golden yellow eyes and a slim, dark bill. Breeding adult has blackish crown, hindneck, chin, and back. Winter birds have white chin, paler bill, less black on crown. In flight, shows large white wing patch. Uncommon and local; usually stays hidden in thick vegetation near shores of ponds, sloughs, ditches. May nest at any time of year on any quiet inland water. Rare straggler to extreme southern Arizona and upper Texas coast.

Horned Grebe
breeding
winter

Eared Grebe
winter
breeding

Pied-billed Grebe
breeding
winter

Least Grebe
breeding
winter

Albatrosses (Family Diomedeidae)

Gliding on incredibly long, narrow wings, these largest of seabirds spend most of their lives at sea, alighting on the water when becalmed or to feed on squid, fish, and refuse. Rarely do they come close enough to be seen from the shore. Albatrosses nest in large colonies on remote oceanic islands.

Short-tailed Albatross *Diomedea albatrus*
L 36" (91 cm) W 83" (211 cm) Now extremely rare off west coast. Large size, massive pink bill, and pale feet distinctive in all plumages. Adult is mostly white, with golden wash on head. First-year bird is dark brown; gradual molt to adult plumage produces a patchy coloration easily confused with some older Black-footed Albatrosses or with Blackfoot-Laysan hybrids (not shown). Short-tailed subadult always has some white on upper surface. Entire world population of Short-taileds numbers about 250 but may be increasing. Breeds only on Japanese island of Torishima.

Black-footed Albatross *Diomedea nigripes*
L 32" (81 cm) W 89" (226 cm) Mostly dark in all plumages. White area around dark bill is more extensive on old birds, barely visible on immatures. Undertail coverts are pale or white; a few older birds have pale bellies. Smaller dark bill and lack of white on back distinguishes them from subadult Short-tailed Albatross. Seen year round off west coast; common in summer. Often follows ships, feeding on garbage.

Laysan Albatross *Diomedea immutabilis*
L 32" (81 cm) W 82" (208 cm) Dark above except for white flash in primaries. Underwing is mostly white, with irregular black margins. Blackfoot-Laysan hybrid (not shown) resembles larger subadult Short-tailed Albatross but lacks white on back and has smaller bill. Rare but regular far off California. More numerous off Alaska.

Yellow-nosed Albatross *Diomedea chlororhynchos*
L 32" (81 cm) W 80" (203 cm) Casual off the Atlantic coast; rare off Gulf coast. Often confused with Black-browed Albatross. Yellow-nosed is slimmer and longer necked; bill is dark; predominantly white underwing has a narrow dark border. Yellow ridge on top of adult's bill is visible only at close range.

Black-browed Albatross *Diomedea melanophris*
L 35" (89 cm) W 88" (224 cm) Rare off New England and northeastern Canada in summer. May be confused with Yellow-nosed Albatross. Black-browed is chunkier; adult's bill is pale and underwing has a much broader dark margin on leading edge. Immature has dark bill and dusky collar; underwing is almost entirely dark.

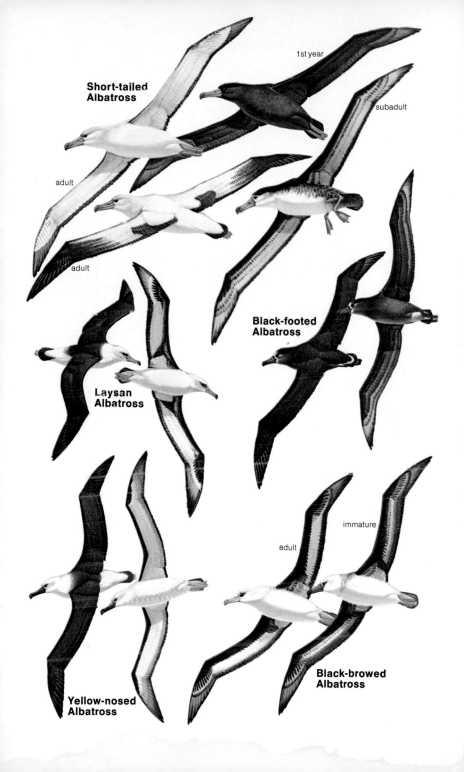

Short-tailed Albatross

1st year

subadult

adult

adult

Black-footed Albatross

Laysan Albatross

Yellow-nosed Albatross

adult

immature

Black-browed Albatross

Shearwaters, Petrels (Family Procellariidae)

These gull-size seabirds have longer wings than gulls; bills are topped with large nostril tubes. Rapid wingbeats alternating with stiff-winged glides present a distinctive flight pattern as these birds skim the waves in search of food. Highly pelagic; most species are rarely seen from shore.

Northern Fulmar *Fulmarus glacialis*

L 19" (48 cm) W 42" (107 cm)   In most phases, color is nearly uniform overall, without strong contrast between upperparts and underparts. Light phase predominates in Atlantic; dark phase more common in Pacific. Intermediates of all shades are also seen; all appear uniform in color. Distinguished from gulls by nostril tube and stiff-winged glides; from shearwaters by thick, yellow bill and stockier head and neck. Common and sometimes abundant, Northern Fulmars gather in large flocks near fishing boats. Wander north into Bering Strait in summer. In the Atlantic, winter north to limits of open water.

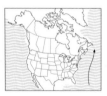

Flesh-footed Shearwater *Puffinus carneipes*

L 19½" (50 cm) W 43" (109 cm)   Entirely dark above and below except for paler flight feathers, pale base of bill, pale feet. Compare especially with Sooty Shearwater, which has whitish wing linings, darker legs. Breeds on islands off Australia and New Zealand. Winters (our summer) in North Pacific; rare but regular off west coast. Formerly called Pale-footed Shearwater.

Sooty Shearwater *Puffinus griseus*

L 19" (48 cm) W 43" (109 cm)   Whitish underwing coverts contrast with overall dark plumage; bill entirely dark. Otherwise resembles Flesh-footed Shearwater, but has a faster wingbeat, shorter glides. Almost identical to the smaller Short-tailed Shearwater. Fairly common off east coast. Abundant off west coast; often seen from shore. Dark shearwaters seen off Oregon and California in summer are invariably Sooties rather than Short-taileds.

Short-tailed Shearwater *Puffinus tenuirostris*

L 14" (36 cm) W 38" (97 cm)   Dark overall, sometimes with pale wing linings; bill entirely dark. Almost identical to Sooty Shearwater. Note Short-tailed's smaller size; steeper forehead; and, usually, the more uniform color of wing linings and flight feathers. Breeds off Australia. Winters (our summer) in North Pacific. Seen along west coast from British Columbia to California during southward migration in fall and winter. Some nonbreeding birds remain off California during our winter. Formerly called Slender-billed Shearwater.

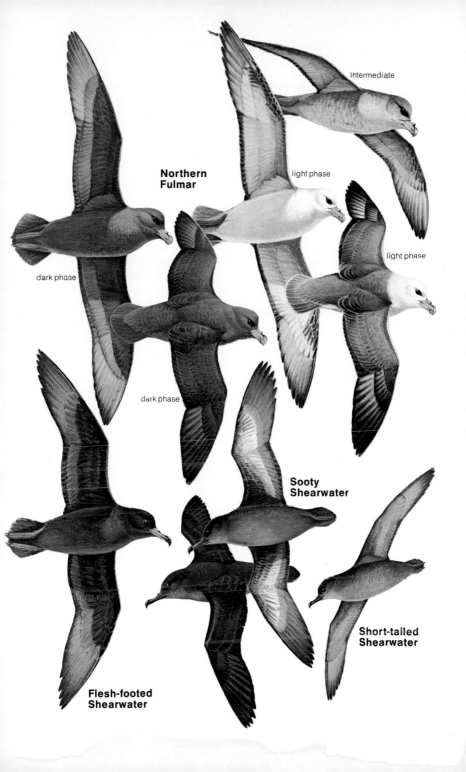

Intermediate

**Northern
Fulmar**

light phase

light phase

dark phase

dark phase

**Sooty
Shearwater**

**Short-tailed
Shearwater**

**Flesh-footed
Shearwater**

Cory's Shearwater *Calonectris diomedea*

L 18" (46 cm) W 44" (112 cm) Grayish-brown upperparts merge into white underparts without sharp contrast; bill is yellowish. Similar Greater Shearwater has dark cap, dark bill. Flight of Cory's Shearwater is more leisurely and buoyant than that of other shearwaters, with slower, less frequent wingbeats. Breeds in eastern Atlantic and in the Mediterranean. Seen off east coast primarily in summer and fall. Generally uncommon in the Gulf of Mexico.

Greater Shearwater *Puffinus gravis*

L 19" (48 cm) W 44" (112 cm) Dark brown cap contrasts with grayish-brown upperparts and white cheeks. Bill is dark; underparts white with indistinct dusky patch on belly. Compare with Cory's Shearwater's whiter underparts, pale bill, lack of dark cap. Some Greater Shearwaters have a white nape, may be confused with Black-capped Petrel, but lack white forehead and wide black bar on leading edge of underwing. Greater Shearwater breeds in South Atlantic. Fairly common off east coast during migration, chiefly in spring.

Manx Shearwater *Puffinus puffinus*

L 13¹/₂" (34 cm) W 33" (84 cm) Blackish above, white below, with gleaming white wing linings. White undertail coverts extend to end of short tail. Breeds on islands from Azores to Iceland; one colony nests in Newfoundland. Winters off eastern South America. Fairly common off northern Atlantic coast from June to October; less common farther south. Wanders rarely to Florida coast. The Black-vented Shearwater (next page) of the Pacific was formerly considered a form of this species.

Audubon's Shearwater *Puffinus lherminieri*

L 12" (31 cm) W 27" (69 cm) Dark brown above, white below, with long tail, dark undertail coverts; undersides of primaries dark. Breeds on Caribbean islands. Common off southern Atlantic coast, chiefly from May to December; casual wanderer as far north as New York.

Little Shearwater *Puffinus assimilis*

L 11" (28 cm) W 25" (64 cm) Very rare vagrant off Atlantic coast in summer and fall. Resembles Manx Shearwater but is smaller, blacker above, with more white on face. Wings are very short; undersides of primaries pale. Flies with fast, whirring wingbeats, seldom gliding. Breeds on islands in eastern Atlantic.

Cory's
Shearwater

Black-capped Petrel
for comparison

Greater
Shearwater

Manx
Shearwater

Audubon's
Shearwater

Little
Shearwater

Pink-footed Shearwater *Puffinus creatopus*
L 19″ (48 cm) W 43″ (109 cm)   Uniformly blackish-brown above; white wing linings and underparts are extensively mottled; pink bill and feet distinctive at close range. Flies with slower wingbeats and more soaring than Sooty Shearwater (page 26). Breeds on islands off Chile; winters (our summer) in the northern Pacific, generally far offshore. Common in summer; rare throughout rest of year.

Streaked Shearwater *Calonectris leucomelas*
L 19″ (48 cm) W 48″ (122 cm)   An Asian species, seen very rarely off California in fall. Pale, finely streaked head looks all-white at a distance. White head and underparts distinguish Streaked from other Pacific shearwaters; compare also with light-phase Northern Fulmar.

Buller's Shearwater *Puffinus bulleri*
L 16″ (41 cm) W 40″ (102 cm)   Gleaming white below, including wing linings. Gray above, with a darker cap and a long, dark, wedge-shaped tail. Dark bar across leading edge of upperwing extends across back, forming a distinct M. Flight is graceful and buoyant, with long periods of soaring. Breeds on islands off New Zealand. Irregular off west coast during southward migration. Most common from Washington to central California; rarer north and south along west coast. Formerly called New Zealand Shearwater and Gray-backed Shearwater.

Black-vented Shearwater *Puffinus opisthomelas*
L 14″ (36 cm) W 34″ (86 cm)   Dark brown above, white below, with dark undertail coverts. Dusky mottling on sides of breast, often extending across entire breast. Seen off California from August to January; sometimes visible from shore. Nests chiefly on islands off Baja peninsula. Formerly considered a subspecies of Manx Shearwater (preceding page) of the Atlantic. The Manx-type shearwaters, with white undertail coverts, reported several times off California, are of unknown origin and species.

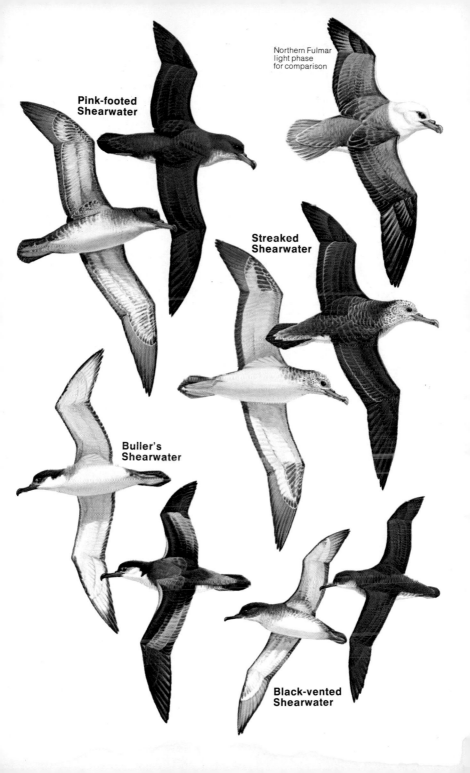

Pink-footed Shearwater

Northern Fulmar light phase for comparison

Streaked Shearwater

Buller's Shearwater

Black-vented Shearwater

Storm-Petrels (Family Hydrobatidae)

Sprightly fliers, these small seabirds hover close to the water. Pattering or hopping across the wave tops, they pluck small fish and plankton from the surface. Some species follow ships. Storm-Petrels are most easily identified by differences in their flight patterns, but flight can vary deceptively depending on weather.

Band-rumped Storm-Petrel *Oceanodroma castro*
L 9" (23 cm) Rare off Gulf and Atlantic coasts. Deep wing strokes are followed by stiff-winged glides, like the flight of a shearwater but unlike the swooping, erratic flight of Leach's Storm-Petrel and fluttery, skimming flight of Wilson's. White band crosses rump but is not as bold and broad on undertail coverts as in Wilson's. Tail squarish or slightly forked. Band-rumped is larger and slightly paler than Wilson's; stouter and darker than Leach's. Breeds on tropical islands. Formerly called Harcourt's Petrel.

Wilson's Storm-Petrel *Oceanites oceanicus*
L 7¹/₄" (18 cm) Skims across the water with shallow, fluttery wingbeats. Flight similar to that of a swallow. Wings short and rounded; in flight, feet trail behind tip of squarish or rounded tail. Often hovers to feed. Bold, white, U-shaped band crosses rump and extends onto undertail coverts; white flanks conspicuous even on sitting bird. Brownish-black overall with pale wing patch. Smaller than Leach's and Band-rumped. Yellow webbing between black toes is sometimes visible at close range. Common off Gulf and Atlantic coasts from May to September; rare off California coast from August to October, annual in Monterey Bay. On west coast, compare with Wedge-rumped Storm-Petrel (opposite and on next page).

Leach's Storm-Petrel *Oceanodroma leucorhoa*
L 8" (20 cm) Distinctive erratic flight like that of a bat or butterfly, with deep strokes of long, pointed wings. Does not patter like Wilson's; wings are narrower and more sharply angled. Dusky line divides white rump band; no white visible on flanks of sitting bird. Blackish-brown overall, with pale wing stripes and long, forked tail. Amount of white on rump varies; birds off southern California may have brown rump. Fairly common off the Pacific coast; uncommon south of breeding range along the Atlantic coast.

White-faced Storm-Petrel *Pelagodroma marina*
L 7¹/₂" (19 cm) Casual vagrant off Atlantic coast from North Carolina to Massachusetts. Flies low, dangling its feet and bounding over the waves. Sometimes swings from side to side like a forward-moving pendulum. Distinctive white underparts, wing linings, and face. Dark eye stripe, crown, and upperparts; paler rump. Breeds throughout the Atlantic and in southern Pacific, Indian Ocean.

Band-rumped Storm-Petrel

Wilson's Storm-Petrel

Leach's Storm-Petrel

White-faced Storm-Petrel

Leach's west coast

Wilson's   Band-rumped   northern   intermediate   southern   Wedge-rumped

Black Storm-Petrel *Oceanodroma melania* L 9" (23 cm)
Deep, languid wing strokes, graceful flight. Largest of the all-dark storm-petrels. Blackish-brown overall with pale bar on upper surface of wing. Tail forked and fairly long. Bill, legs, and feet black. Slow, deep wingbeats distinguish Black from brown-rumped variation of Leach's Storm-Petrel (preceding page). Breeds from May to December on Santa Barbara Island off southern California coast. Common off California coast in spring, summer, and fall.

Ashy Storm-Petrel *Oceanodroma homochroa*
L 8" (20 cm) Fluttery wingbeats, but flight fairly direct; not as swallowlike as flight of Wilson's Storm-Petrel (preceding page). Gray-black overall, darkest on crown, leading edge of wings, and upper surface of flight feathers. Pale mottling on underwing coverts may be visible at close range. Viewed from the side, Ashy appears long-tailed. Distinguished from Black Storm-Petrel by rapid, shallow wingbeats; and overall paler, grayer appearance. Fairly common. Breeds on islands off central and southern California.

Fork-tailed Storm-Petrel *Oceanodroma furcata*
L 8½" (22 cm) Wingbeats shallow, rapid, often followed by glides. Looks fairly long-tailed in flight. Occasionally makes shallow dives for food. Distinctively bluish-gray above, pearl gray below; undertail coverts and flanks sometimes white. Note also dark gray forehead and eye patch, dark wing linings. Now rare off California coast; progressively more abundant farther north.

Least Storm-Petrel *Oceanodroma microsoma*
L 5¾" (15 cm) Smallest of the storm-petrels, the size of a sparrow. Swift, indirect flight, low over the water, with deep wingbeats like the much larger Black Storm-Petrel. Blackish-brown above; slightly paler below. Short-tailed; appears almost tailless in flight. Irregularly fairly common to abundant off the coast of southern California.

Wedge-rumped Storm-Petrel *Oceanodroma tethys*
L 6½" (17 cm) Very rare off California coast from August to January. Very small, with distinctive bold white wedge-shaped patch on tail that gives the appearance of a white tail with dark corners. Compare rounded rump band of Wilson's Storm-Petrel (preceding page). Brownish-black overall. Almost as small as Least Storm-Petrel, with similar deep wingbeats. Breeds on the Galapagos Islands and on islands off Peru. Formerly called Galapagos Petrel.

**Black
Storm-Petrel**

**Ashy
Storm-Petrel**

**Fork-tailed
Storm-Petrel**

**Least
Storm-Petrel**

**Wedge-rumped
Storm-Petrel**

Frigatebirds (Family Fregatidae)

These large, dark seabirds have the longest wingspan, in proportion to weight, of all birds. Seafarers named these aerial predators for a swift warship.

Magnificent Frigatebird *Fregata magnificens*
L 40" (102 cm) W 90" (229 cm) Long, forked tail; long, narrow wings. Male is glossy black overall; orange throat pouch becomes bright red when inflated in courtship display. Female is blackish-brown, with white at center of underparts. Young birds show varying amount of white on head and underparts; require four to six years to reach adult plumage. Frigatebirds skim the sea, snatching up food from the surface; also harass other birds in flight, forcing victims to disgorge food. Generally seen offshore, but also stray inland. Breed on Marquesas Key off south Florida; casual wanderer north along Atlantic coast.

Tropicbirds (Family Phaethontidae)

Long central tail feathers identify adults. These seabirds are usually seen far out at sea, diving for fish or resting on calm waters, streamers held high.

White-tailed Tropicbird *Phaethon lepturus*
L 30" (76 cm) W 37" (94 cm) Tropical species, rare but regular in summer along Gulf and Atlantic coasts to North Carolina. Smaller and slimmer than Red-billed Tropicbird; wings show distinctive black stripes; primaries show less black than in Red-billed. Bill varies from yellow to red-orange. Immature lacks tail streamers; bill is yellow, upperparts boldly barred.

Red-billed Tropicbird *Phaethon aethereus*
L 40" (102 cm) W 44" (112 cm) Tropical species, casual well off-shore on coast of southern California; very rare off Atlantic coast to North Carolina. Adult has red bill, black primaries, barring on back and wings, white tail streamers. Immature lacks streamers; tail is tipped with black; barring on upperparts is finer than in other young tropicbirds; note also black collar on nape; bill color varies from yellow to orange.

Red-tailed Tropicbird *Phaethon rubricauda*
L 37" (94 cm) W 44" (112 cm) South Pacific species, very rare off southern California coast. Flight feathers mostly white. Adult has red bill; red tail streamers, narrower than in other tropicbirds. Juvenile lacks streamers; tail is all-white; upperparts barred; bill black, gradually changing to yellow and then red. Note also lack of black collar on nape.

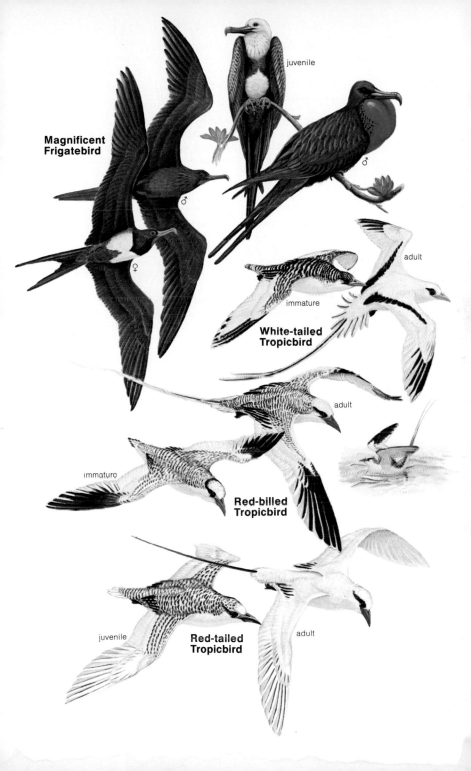

Magnificent Frigatebird

juvenile

♂

♂

♀

White-tailed Tropicbird

immature

adult

Red-billed Tropicbird

immature

adult

Red-tailed Tropicbird

juvenile

adult

Pelicans (Family Pelecanidae)

Large, heavy water birds with massive bills and huge throat pouches used as dip nets to catch fish. In flight, pelicans hold their heads drawn back.

American White Pelican *Pelecanus erythrorhynchos*
L 62" (158 cm) W 108" (274 cm) White, with black primaries and outer secondaries. Breeding adult has pale yellow crest; bill is brighter orange, with a fibrous plate on upper mandible. Plate is shed after eggs are laid; crown and nape become grayish. Juvenile is dusky overall. Immature is mostly white but wing coverts are mottled, head and neck grayish. Usually seen in flocks, White Pelicans do not dive for food but dip their bills into the water while swimming. Nonbreeding birds are seen in summer throughout area enclosed by dashed line on map. Breeding birds may fly 150 miles from nest to feed. In fall and winter, vagrants may appear almost anywhere, increasingly in the east.

Brown Pelican *Pelecanus occidentalis*
L 48" (122 cm) W 84" (213 cm) Nonbreeding adult has white head and neck, often washed with yellow; grayish-brown body; blackish belly. In breeding plumage, hindneck is dark chestnut; yellow patch appears at base of foreneck. Molt during incubation and chick-feeding produces creamy-white head and foreneck. Juvenile is grayish-brown above, tipped with pale buff; underparts whitish. First-year bird is browner overall; acquires adult plumage by third year. Dives from the air after prey, capturing fish in its pouch. Rare inland, Brown Pelicans prefer saltwater habitats year round. Wanderers are seen at any time of year to limit of dashed line on map.

Gannets and Boobies (Family Sulidae)

High-diving seabirds noted for their sudden, headlong plunges after prey. All have long, narrow wings, tapered tail, and tapered bill. Species vary in the color of facial skin, bill, and feet. All are gregarious, nesting in colonies on small islands. The rest of the year, gannets roost at sea, boobies on land.

Northern Gannet *Sula bassanus*
L 37" (94 cm) W 72" (183 cm) Large, white seabird with long, black-tipped wings, pointed white tail. Spectacular high dives also aid identification. Juvenile is blackish above, with pale speckling; grayish below. First-year birds are whiter below; distinguished from juvenile and immature Masked Booby (next page) by lack of white patch on upper back. Full adult plumage is acquired in third year. Common; breeds in large colonies on rocky cliffs; winters at sea. Often seen from shore during migration, flying in long lines.

American White Pelican

immature

nonbreeding

chick-feeding adult

breeding

nonbreeding

Brown Pelican

1st year

chick-feeding adult

juvenile

nonbreeding

breeding

Northern Gannet

juvenile

adult

adult

1st year

2nd year

Brown Booby *Sula leucogaster* *L 30" (76 cm) W 57" (145 cm)*
Dark brown, with sharply contrasting white underparts and
wing linings. Western form has whitish head and neck. Bill
and feet yellow to gray-green. Juvenile is also dark, but underparts and wing linings are pale brown, bill and face dark
grayish-blue. Gradually acquires adult plumage over more
than two years. The Brown Booby is casual at the Salton Sea,
and along the Colorado River Valley, mostly in late summer.
Fairly common in the Gulf of Mexico, but rarely seen from
land. Very rare along Atlantic coast to New Jersey. Dives from
air or surface to catch fish. Often follows ships. Also fishes
close to land, may roost in trees, buoys, oil rigs.

Red-footed Booby *Sula sula* *L 28" (71 cm) W 60" (152 cm)*
Tropical species; casual on Florida's Dry Tortugas; very rare
on Gulf coast and in California. Bright red feet adorn both adult
phases; one phase is brown with a white tail, the other white
with black primaries and secondaries and a black patch on the
underside of the outer wing. In both phases, note bright pink
base of bill. All young birds are brown, usually with dark feet;
adult plumage is gradually acquired over three years. Smallest
of the boobies, the Redfoot flies with grace and speed, chasing
flying fish and catching them in the air. Follows ships for days,
sometimes perching in the rigging.

Masked Booby *Sula dactylatra* *L 32" (81 cm) W 62" (158 cm)*
Adult similar to Northern Gannet (preceding page) but readily
distinguished by yellow bill and extensive black facial skin,
black tail, black secondaries. Immature has yellowish bill; upperparts brown, with white on wing coverts, white patch on
upper back; underparts white; underwing mostly white. Gradually acquires adult plumage over two years; rump stays
brown longest. The Masked Booby hunts from high in the air,
bill pointing straight down; dives deeper and straighter than
other boobies. Feeds mainly on flying fish. Rests on sandy
atolls. Rarely seen from land, but fairly common in the Gulf of
Mexico in summer. Formerly called Blue-faced Booby.

Blue-footed Booby *Sula nebouxii*
L 32" (81 cm) W 62" (158 cm) Feet bright blue; bill dark bluish-
gray; white nape patch and white on rump are also distinctive.
Adults have streaked pale heads. Juveniles have brown head
and neck and white lower breast and belly; gradually acquire
adult plumage in about three years. Blue-footed Boobies
tend to fish in clear, shallow waters close to shore, working
in small flocks. Like other boobies, they are pursued by Frigatebirds and harassed until they disgorge food. Closest breeding grounds are arid islands in the Gulf of California. Irregular
wanderer in late summer and fall to inland waters of the
southwest, particularly the Salton Sea, occasionally to the
Pacific coast.

Brown Booby

western

eastern

eastern

western

Red-footed Booby

white-tailed dark phase

white-tailed dark phase

white phase

Masked Booby

adult

immature

Blue-footed Booby

♂

♀

immature

adult

immatures

Northern Gannet

Masked Booby

Blue-footed Booby

Brown Booby

Red-footed Booby

Anhingas (Family Anhingidae)

Long, slim neck and long tail distinguish Anhingas from cormorants. They often swim submerged to the neck, spearing fish with their sharply pointed bills.

Anhinga *Anhinga anhinga* *L 35" (89 cm) W 45" (114 cm)*
Black above, with green gloss; silvery-white spots and streaks on wings and upper back. During breeding season, male acquires pale, wispy plumes on upper neck; bill and bare facial skin become brightly colored. Adult female has buffy neck and breast; immatures are browner overall. Anhingas prefer freshwater habitats; often seen perched on branches or stumps with wings spread to dry. In flight, their profile looks headless. Slow, regular wingbeats alternate with long glides. Rare postbreeding wanderer well north of breeding range and to Arizona and California.

Cormorants (Family Phalacrocoracidae)

Large water birds with setback legs, long necks, and long, hooked bills. Dark plumage sets off colorful facial skin and throat pouches. They often swim submerged to the neck, and dive from surface for fish.

Olivaceous Cormorant *Phalacrocorax olivaceus*
L 26" (66 cm) W 40" (102 cm) A small, long-tailed cormorant with pale-bordered yellow-brown throat pouch. In breeding plumage, adult acquires short white plumes on sides of neck; border around throat pouch becomes pure white and tapers to sharp point behind bill. Compare with Double-crested Cormorant which has shorter tail and larger, more rounded throat pouch (see also next page). Olivaceous immatures are browner overall than adults, particularly on underparts; paler and smaller overall than young Double-cresteds. A fairly common species, found at marshy ponds or shallow inlets near perching stumps and snags. Formerly called Neotropic Cormorant.

Great Cormorant *Phalacrocorax carbo*
L 36" (91 cm) W 63" (160 cm) A large, short-tailed cormorant with small yellow throat pouch broadly bordered with white feathering. In breeding plumage, adult shows white flank patches and wispy white plumes on head. Similar Double-crested Cormorant has orange throat pouch and no flank patches. First-year birds are brown above; on underparts, white belly contrasts with streaky brown neck, breast, and flanks. During second year, immatures resemble nonbreeding adults more closely but have a brown tinge on upperparts. Compare to young Double-crested which has a slimmer bill and, often, a darker belly. Generally rare in winter south of Chesapeake Bay but seen with increasing frequency as far south as Florida.

breeding ♂

Anhinga

♀

♀

Great
2nd year

Double-crested
2nd year

Olivaceous
immature

breeding

immature

nonbreeding

2nd year

Double-crested
eastern
for comparison

Olivaceous
Cormorant

Great
Cormorant

breeding

1st year

Double-crested Cormorant *Phalacrocorax auritus*

L 32" (81 cm) W 52" (132 cm) Large, rounded throat pouch is orange year round. Breeding adult shows double crest of two tufts curving back from behind eyes. Tufts are partly white in western birds, dark and less conspicuous in eastern birds (preceding page). First-year birds are brown above, variably pale below, but palest on upper breast and neck. Among western cormorants, Double-crested's kinked neck is distinctive in flight. Common and widespread; found on rocky coasts and beaches as well as inland lakes and rivers. Breeding populations in the interior are local and irregular.

Brandt's Cormorant *Phalacrocorax penicillatus*

L 35" (89 cm) W 48" (122 cm) A band of pale buffy feathers bordering the throat pouch identifies all ages of this species. Dull blue throat pouch becomes bright blue in breeding plumage; head, neck, and scapulars show fine, creamy-white plumes. First-year birds are dark brown above; underparts paler, but not as pale as in young Double-crested Cormorant. In flight, Brandt's is distinguished by fairly large head and bill. Common and highly gregarious; often fishes in large flocks and flies in long lines between feeding and roosting grounds.

Pelagic Cormorant *Phalacrocorax pelagicus*

L 26" (66 cm) W 39" (99 cm) Dark overall, with green and purple gloss. Smaller and slenderer than other cormorants. Breeding adult shows tufts on crown and nape; fine white plumes on sides of neck; white patches on flanks. Distinguished from Red-faced Cormorant by absence of yellow in bill or contrast between colors of wings and upperparts. First-year bird is uniformly dark brown; closely resembles young Red-faced. Pelagics are distinguished in flight by straight profile of small head and slender, outstretched neck. Less gregarious than other species; breed in smaller colonies. Feed near cliffs and rocky shores, in tidal rips and surf.

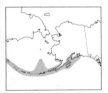

Red-faced Cormorant *Phalacrocorax urile*

L 31" (79 cm) W 46" (117 cm) Partly yellow bill best distinguishes this species from the very similar Pelagic Cormorant. In adult, dull brown wings contrast with glossy upperparts. Throat pouch is bluish; dull red facial skin becomes brighter in breeding season. First-year bird is uniformly dark brown; closely resembles young Pelagic. More gregarious than Pelagics, Red-faced Cormorants nest on the wider ledges of steep cliffs; also on rocky sea islands alongside gulls, murres, and auklets.

1st year

breeding

western

Double-crested Cormorant

Double-crested

Pelagic

Brandt's

Brandt's Cormorant

nonbreeding

nonbreeding

Pelagic Cormorant

breeding

1st year

1st year

breeding

Red-faced Cormorant

1st year

breeding

Herons (Family Ardeidae)

Wading birds; most have long legs, neck, and bill for stalking food in shallow water. Graceful crests and plumes adorn some species in breeding season.

Least Bittern *Ixobrychus exilis* L 13" (33 cm) W 17" (43 cm)
Buffy wing patches identify this small, secretive heron as it flushes briefly from dense marsh cover. When alarmed, may freeze with bill pointing up. In male back and crown are black; in female they are browner. Juvenile resembles female but has more prominent streaking on back and breast. Rare dark phase (not shown) of eastern populations is russet where typical plumage is pale. Least Bittern's calls include a series of harsh *tut* notes. Fairly common in the east; less common in western portion of range. May breed sporadically beyond mapped range in west.

American Bittern *Botaurus lentiginosus*
L 28" (71 cm) W 42" (107 cm) Ground-dwelling species. When alarmed, freezes with bill pointing up, or flushes with rapid wingbeats and nasal *haink* call. Adult's rich brown upperparts set off by black neck streaks. Contrasting dark flight feathers are conspicuous in flight; note also that wings are somewhat pointed, not rounded as in night-herons. Juvenile lacks neck patches. Distinctive song, *oonk-a-lunk,* most often heard at dusk as the Bittern skulks in dense marsh reeds. Fairly common within range; casual breeder south of range.

Black-crowned Night-Heron *Nycticorax nycticorax*
L 25" (64 cm) W 44" (112 cm) Stocky heron with short neck and legs. Breeding adult identified by black crown and back with white hindneck plumes. Juvenile distinguished from juvenile Yellow-crowned Night-Heron by browner upperparts with bolder white spotting; thicker neck; paler, less contrasting face; longer, thinner bill with mostly pale lower mandible. In flight, legs barely extend beyond tail. Full adult plumage is not acquired until third year. Calls include a low, harsh *woc,* more guttural than in Yellowcrown. Nocturnal feeder. Roosts in trees. Fairly common but local.

Yellow-crowned Night-Heron *Nycticorax violaceus*
L 24" (61 cm) W 42" (107 cm) Breeding adult has buffy-white crown, black face with white cheek, and long plumes. Juvenile distinguished from juvenile Black-crowned Night-Heron by grayer upperparts with less prominent white spotting; thinner neck; stouter, all-dark bill; and, in flight, by legs extending well beyond tail and by contrastingly darker flight feathers and trailing edge on wings. Full adult plumage is not acquired until third year. Calls include a short *woc,* higher and less harsh than call of Blackcrown. Yellowcrown roosts in trees in wet woods or swamps. Casual in California.

Least Bittern

♂

♀

juvenile

American Bittern

juvenile

2nd spring

breeding

Black-crowned Night-Heron

1st spring

juvenile

juvenile

breeding

juvenile

breeding

Yellow-crowned Night-Heron

Green-backed Heron *Butorides striatus*

L 18" (46 cm) W 26" (66 cm) Small, chunky heron with short legs. Back and sides of adult's neck are deep chestnut; green on upperparts is mixed with blue-gray; throat is white. Greenish-black crown feathers, sometimes raised to form shaggy crest. Legs are usually dull yellow but in male turn bright orange in high breeding plumage. Immature is browner above; white throat and underparts heavily streaked with brown. Generally solitary; found in a variety of habitats, but prefers streams, ponds, marshes with woodland cover; often perches in trees. Common call is a sharp *kyow*. When alarmed, raises crest and flicks tail; alarm call is a distinctive, piercing *skeow*. Common, but rare in some parts of western range; a few winter north of resident limit. Formerly known as Green Heron.

Tricolored Heron *Egretta tricolor*

L 26" (66 cm) W 36" (91 cm) White belly and foreneck contrast with mainly dark blue upperparts. White throat is tinged with chestnut; bill long and slender. Immature has chestnut hindneck and wing coverts. Common inhabitant of salt marshes and mangrove swamps of the east and Gulf coasts. Generally rare inland, but has bred in North Dakota and Kansas. Formerly known as Louisiana Heron.

Little Blue Heron *Egretta caerulea*

L 24" (61 cm) W 40" (102 cm) Slate blue overall. In nonbreeding plumage, head and neck are dark purple, legs and feet dull green. In breeding plumage, head and neck become reddish-purple, legs and feet black. Immature is easily confused with immature Snowy Egret (next page); note Little Blue Heron's dull yellow legs and feet; thicker, two-toned bill with gray base and dark tip; and, in most birds, dusky primary tips. By first spring, immature's white plumage is splotched with blue-gray. Little Blue Herons are slow, methodical feeders in freshwater ponds, lakes, and marshes, as well as coastal saltwater wetlands. Common. Large numbers, mostly white immatures, disperse widely after breeding season. Casual as far as northern California coast.

Reddish Egret *Egretta rufescens*

L 30" (76 cm) W 46" (117 cm) While feeding, this heron "dances," dashing about with wings spread in a canopy. Breeding adult has shaggy plumes on bright rufous head, neck. Bill is pink with black tip; legs are cobalt blue. Nonbreeding plumage varies, but in general is duller, plumes shorter. Immature is gray with some pale cinnamon on head, neck, inner wing; bill is dark. Compare with adult Little Blue Heron. Rare white-phase adult resembles immature Little Blue Heron or Snowy Egret (next page), but note pink-and-black bill, shaggy plumes, dark legs. Uncommon, the Reddish Egret inhabits shallow, open salt pans. Wanders along Gulf coast in post-breeding dispersal; casual to southern California.

Green-backed Heron

immature

immature

Tricolored Heron

breeding

molting immature

Little Blue Heron

breeding

immature

nonbreeding

white phase breeding

immature

Reddish Egret

breeding

Cattle Egret *Bubulcus ibis* *L 20" (51 cm) W 36" (91 cm)*
Small, stocky heron with large, rounded head. Breeding adult's white body is adorned by orange-buff plumes on crown, back, and foreneck. At height of breeding season, bill is bright red-orange, lores purplish, legs dusky-red. Nonbreeding adult has shorter, whitish plumes, bill is yellow, legs yellowish. Immature lacks plumes but otherwise resembles nonbreeding adult. Often seen among livestock in pastures or open fields, feeding on insects stirred up by hooves or by tractors; also perches on animal's back and picks off insects. In flight, resembles Snowy Egret but is smaller, with more rapid wingbeats. An Old World species, the Cattle Egret spread from populations introduced in South America, became established in Florida in the early 1950s, and expanded its range as far as California by mid-1960s. Range continues to expand rapidly throughout North America. In summer, postbreeding wanderers reach far north of mapped breeding range.

Snowy Egret *Egretta thula* *L 24" (61 cm) W 41" (104 cm)*
Snow white heron with slender black bill, yellow eyes, black legs, and bright yellow feet. Graceful plumes on head, neck, and back, where they curve upward, are striking in breeding adult. In high breeding plumage, lores turn red, feet bright orange. In nonbreeding plumage, bill, leg, and eye colors are duller, plumes shorter. Immature lacks plumes and sometimes shows a bit of bluish-gray at base of black bill. Back of leg is yellow-green, but remainder is dark and feet are yellow as in adult. Can be confused with immature Little Blue Heron (see also preceding page); note young Snowy Egret's predominantly dark legs; slimmer, mostly black bill; and usually paler wing tips. Snowy Egrets move briskly in the water, stirring up prey with their feet, stabbing repeatedly to catch it. Common in marshes, ponds, mangrove swamps; occasionally found in dry fields. In summer, postbreeding wanderers reach far north of mapped breeding range. This species was once hunted extensively for plumes. Now protected, populations have recovered; range is expanding.

Great Egret *Casmerodius albus* *L 39" (99 cm) W 51" (130 cm)*
Large white heron with heavy yellow bill, blackish legs and feet. In breeding plumage, long plumes trail from back, extending beyond tail. In immature and nonbreeding adult, bill and leg colors are duller, plumes absent. Distinguished from most other white herons by large size; from white form of larger Great Blue Heron by black legs and feet. Common in marshes, mangrove swamps, mud flats. Partial to open habitats for feeding; stalks prey slowly, methodically. Great Egrets may breed far beyond usual range limits. Population was greatly reduced by plume hunters at the turn of the century; now mostly recovered and is expanding in some parts of range. Formerly called Common Egret and American Egret.

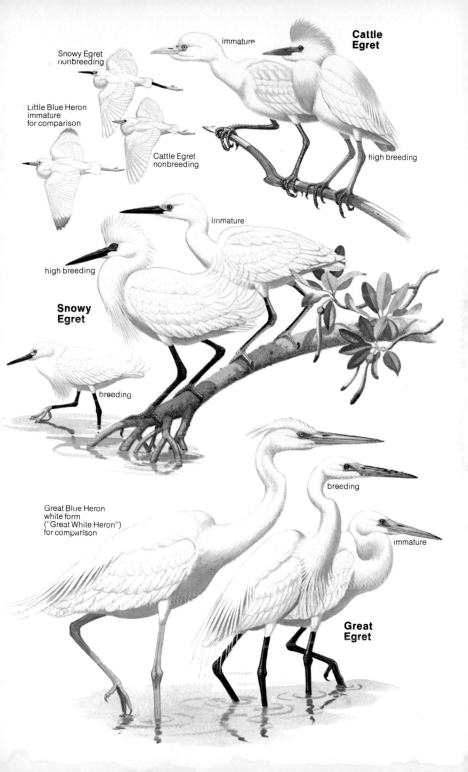

Snowy Egret
nonbreeding

immature

**Cattle
Egret**

Little Blue Heron
immature
for comparison

Cattle Egret
nonbreeding

high breeding

immature

high breeding

**Snowy
Egret**

breeding

breeding

immature

Great Blue Heron
white form
("Great White Heron")
for comparison

**Great
Egret**

Great Blue Heron *Ardea herodias*

L 46" (117 cm) W 72" (183 cm) Large, slate blue heron with white head; black stripe extends above eye; white foreneck streaked with black. Breeding adult has yellowish bill and ornate plumes on head, neck, and back. Nonbreeding adult lacks plumes; bill is yellower. Juvenile has black crown, no plumes. All-white form found in southern Florida was formerly considered a separate species, "Great White Heron" (preceding page). In the "Wurdemann's Heron" phase found chiefly in the Florida Keys, head is all-white. The Great Blue Heron is common but breeds sporadically across large parts of range. A few birds winter far north into breeding range.

Storks (Family Ciconiidae)

Large, tall, cranelike birds that walk sedately and fly with slow, deliberate beats of their long, broad wings, soaring and circling like hawks over open wetlands.

Wood Stork *Mycteria americana*

L 40" (102 cm) W 61" (155 cm) Black flight feathers and tail contrast with white body. Adult has bald, blackish-gray head; thick, dusky, downcurved bill. Immature's head is feathered and grayish-brown; bill is yellow. Wood Storks inhabit wet meadows, swamps, muddy ponds, coastal shallows. A few birds wander beyond normal range in postbreeding dispersal; very rare as far north as Maine and British Columbia.

Jabiru *Jabiru mycteria* *L 52" (132 cm) W 90" (229 cm)*

Huge stork of Central and South America, rare straggler in south Texas. Distinguished from Wood Stork by larger size; large bill, slightly upturned; and all-white wings and tail. Immature is patchy brown-gray; head is feathered with blackish-brown. Usually sighted with flocks of Wood Storks.

Flamingos (Family Phoenicopteridae)

Large waders with big, bent bills, used to strain food from the waters of shallow lakes, lagoons.

Greater Flamingo *Phoenicopterus ruber*

L 46" (117 cm) W 60" (152 cm) Caribbean species, rare vagrant to south Florida. Note pink legs, black flight feathers, tricolored bill. Immature is grayer, with pink wash below; paler bill. Many sightings in Florida and elsewhere are of escaped zoo birds, which are usually duller pink than wild birds. Other similar escapes include a European subspecies with pink-and-black bill; Chilean Flamingo (*P. chilensis*), which has grayish legs with pink joints; and Lesser Flamingo (*Phoeniconaias minor*), with dark red bill, blotchy red wing coverts and axillaries. Very rare wanderer along Atlantic and Gulf coasts.

breeding

Great Blue Heron

"Wurdemann's Heron"

juvenile

Wood Stork

immature

immature

Greater Flamingo

Jabiru

immature

Ibises, Spoonbills (Family Threskiornithidae)

Gregarious, heron-like birds, these long-legged waders feed with long, specialized bills: slender and curved downward in ibises, wide and spatulate in spoonbills.

Glossy Ibis *Plegadis falcinellus* L 23" (58 cm) W 36" (91 cm)
Breeding adult's chestnut plumage is glossed with green or purple on head and upperparts; looks all-dark at a distance. Distinguished from White-faced Ibis by brownish-olive bill, brown eye, gray-green legs with red joints, and lack of white, feathered border to facial skin. In Glossy Ibis, pale edge to gray facial skin does not extend behind eye or under chin; turns cobalt blue at height of breeding season. Winter adult closely resembles winter White-faced Ibis but usually retains a short, pale line from eye to bill. First-fall bird is indistinguishable from immature White-faced Ibis. By late winter resembles winter adult, but adult breeding plumage is not acquired until second spring. Glossy Ibises inhabit freshwater and saltwater marshes. Fairly common but local. Range is expanding north along the east coast.

White-faced Ibis *Plegadis chihi* L 23" (58 cm) W 36" (91 cm)
Breeding adult's chestnut plumage is glossed with green or purple on head and upperparts; looks all-dark at a distance. Distinguished from Glossy Ibis by reddish bill, red eye, all-red legs, and white, feathered border around red facial skin; border extends behind eye and under chin. Winter adult plumage is like Glossy, but lacks pale line from eye to bill. Immature plumages are indistinguishable from Glossy. White-faced prefers freshwater marshes but also frequents brackish areas. Uncommon, but breeding range is expanding east.

White Ibis *Eudocimus albus* L 25" (64 cm) W 38" (97 cm)
Adult's white plumage and pink facial skin are distinctive. In breeding adult, facial skin, bill, and legs turn scarlet. Dark tips of primaries visible only in flight. Immatures have white underparts and wing linings, pinkish bill; gradually molt into white adult plumage by second spring. Locally abundant in coastal salt marshes, swamps, mangroves. Closely related Scarlet Ibis (*Eudocimus ruber*), a South American species introduced or escaped in Florida, hybridizes with White Ibis; offspring are various shades of pink or scarlet.

Roseate Spoonbill *Ajaia ajaja* L 32" (81 cm) W 50" (127 cm)
Adult has pink body with red highlights; spatulate bill; unfeathered greenish head. Head may become buffy during courtship. First-fall bird has white feathering on head; body is mostly pale pink. Spoonbills feed in shallow waters, swinging their bills from side to side. Fairly common locally on Gulf coast; very rare north to Maryland. Strays are occasionally seen as far west as California.

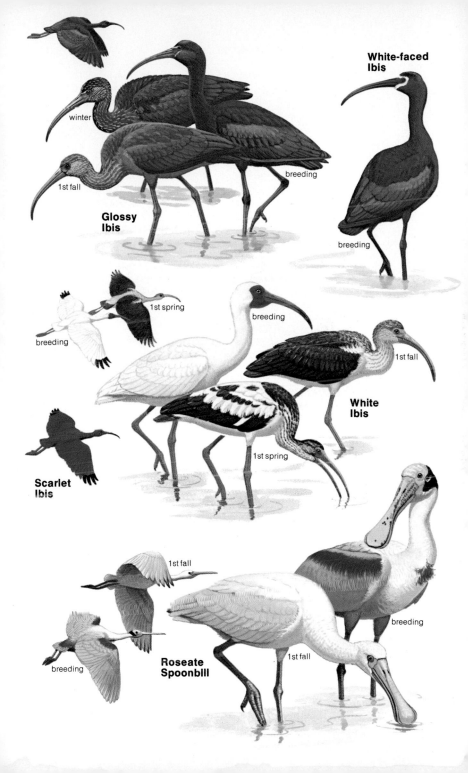

White-faced
Ibis

winter

1st fall

Glossy
Ibis

breeding

breeding

1st spring

breeding

breeding

1st fall

White
Ibis

Scarlet
Ibis

1st spring

1st fall

breeding

1st fall

Roseate
Spoonbill

breeding

1st fall

Cranes (Family Gruidae)

Tall, stately birds with long necks and legs and fairly long, heavy bills. Tertials droop over the rump in a "bustle" that distinguishes cranes from herons. Cranes fly with their necks and legs fully extended. Courtship rites include a frenzied, leaping dance.

Sandhill Crane *Grus canadensis*
L 41" (104 cm) W 73" (185 cm) Adult is gray overall, with dull red skin on the crown and lores; whitish chin, cheek, and upper throat; and blackish primaries. Immatures lack red patch; head and neck vary from pale to tawny; gray body is irregularly mottled with brownish-red. Full adult plumage is reached after two and a half years. Similar Great Blue Heron (page 54) lacks bustle. Preening with muddy bills, cranes may stain the feathers of upper back, lower neck, and breast with ferrous solution contained in the mud. Locally common; breeds on tundra and in marshes and grasslands. In winter, regularly feeds in dry fields, returning to water at night. Resident along parts of the Gulf coast; other populations highly migratory. Casual during fall and winter on east coast from Massachusetts south. Migrating flocks fly at great heights, sometimes too high to be seen from the ground. Common call is a trumpeting, rattling *gar-oo-oo*, audible for more than a mile.

Common Crane *Grus grus* *L 44" (112 cm) W 75" (191 cm)*
Eurasian species, very rare vagrant to the Great Plains, western Canada, and Alaska, almost always with migrating flocks of Sandhill Cranes. Adult distinguished from Sandhill Crane by blackish head and neck marked by broad white stripe. Immature bird resembles immature Sandhill; may show trace of white head stripe in spring. In flight, in all ages, black primaries and secondaries show as a broad black trailing edge on gray wings.

Whooping Crane *Grus americana*
L 52" (132 cm) W 87" (221 cm) Endangered; breeds in freshwater marshes of Wood Buffalo National Park, Alberta, and Grays Lake National Wildlife Refuge, Idaho; winters in Aransas National Wildlife Refuge on Gulf coast of Texas and in refuge areas in New Mexico. Adult is white overall, with red facial skin; black primaries show in flight. Immature bird is whitish, with pale reddish-brown head and neck and scattered reddish-brown feathers over the rest of its body; begins to acquire adult plumage after first summer. Call is a shrill, trumpeting *ker-loo ker-lee-loo*. Breeding population currently numbers about a hundred birds. Intensive management and protection programs seem to be slowly succeeding.

immature

Sandhill Crane

stained

immature

Common Crane

Whooping Crane

immature

Swans, Geese, Ducks (Family Anatidae)

Worldwide family: aquatic, web-footed, gregarious birds, ranging from small ducks to large swans. Most feed on water, but geese are primarily land grazers.

♪ **Tundra Swan** *Cygnus columbianus* L 52" (132 cm)
In adult, black facial skin tapers to a point in front of eye and cuts straight across forehead; many birds have a yellow spot in front of eye. Head is rounded, bill slightly concave. In Eurasian form, "Bewick's Swan," seen casually on the west coast, facial skin and base of bill are yellow, but usually only above the nostril; compare with Whooper Swan. Immature Tundra Swans molt earlier than immature Trumpeters and Whoopers; appear much whiter by late winter. Even when relaxed, Tundra Swan usually holds neck straight up from breast. Call is a noisy, high-pitched whooping. Nests on tundra or sheltered coastal marshes; winters in flocks on shallow ponds, lakes, coastal estuaries. Uncommon and local in winter throughout interior U.S. North American subspecies was formerly called Whistling Swan.

♪ **Trumpeter Swan** *Cygnus buccinator* L 60" (152 cm)
Black facial skin tapers to a broad point at the eye, dips down in a V on forehead. Adult's forehead slopes evenly to straight bill. Immatures retain gray-brown plumage through first spring. At rest, Trumpeters often hold neck kinked back at base. Most common call is a sonorous single or double honk. Once common on sheltered freshwater or brackish lakes, marshes. Now rare over most of range, but slowly recovering and being reintroduced in some old breeding areas.

Whooper Swan *Cygnus cygnus* L 60" (152 cm)
Eurasian species closely related to Trumpeter Swan. Regular winter visitor to outer and central Aleutians. Large yellow patch on lores and bill usually extends to the nostrils; compare with "Bewick's Swan." Forehead slopes evenly to straight bill. When relaxed, often holds neck kinked back. Most common call is a bugle-like double note. Immatures retain dusky plumage through first winter, when bill turns white with a yellow wash. Whooper Swans are found on shallow freshwater ponds and lakes and in sheltered brackish and salt water.

Mute Swan *Cygnus olor* L 60" (152 cm)
Prominent black knob at base of orange bill. Juvenile plumage may be white or brownish; bill gray with black base. Darker juvenile begins to molt to white plumage by midwinter; bill becomes pinkish. Mute Swan usually holds its neck in an S-curve, with bill pointed down. Often swims with wings arched over back. Gives a variety of hisses and snorts, but generally silent. An Old World species, introduced in U.S. Commonly seen in parks; wild populations on east coast growing, most others not yet fully self-sustaining.

immature

"Bewick's Swan"

Tundra Swan

Trumpeter Swan

Whooper Swan

immature

Mute Swan

juvenile

Greater White-fronted Goose *Anser albifrons*

L 28" (71 cm) Named for the distinctive white band at base of bill. Medium-size, grayish-brown goose, with irregular black barring on underparts. Bill pink or orange, with whitish tip. Legs and feet orange. In flight, note grayish-blue wash on wing coverts, white U-shaped rump band. Young birds lack white front and bill tip until first winter; acquire black belly markings by second fall; distinguished from similar Bean Goose by bill color; from Pink-footed Goose by bill and leg color; from immature blue-phase Snow Goose (next page) by bill and leg color and rump band. Color and size vary in adults: small, pale arctic tundra birds have heavy barring; taiga breeding birds are larger, darker, with less heavy barring; Greenland's intermediate-size tundra form is grayer, with the heaviest barring and distinctive orange bill. Vagrant Greenland birds are seen on the east coast. Whitefronts prefer to breed and feed near fresh water. Seen in migration and winter west of the Mississippi Valley in wetlands, grassy fields, grainfields. Flocks may number in the thousands. V-formations resemble Canada Geese, but flight is more agile, call a laughing *kah-lah-aluck*. Casual winter visitor on east coast from Quebec to Georgia; occasional winter visitor outside mapped range in all western states and north into southern Canada. Breeding distribution in Canada may be more extensive than shown.

Bean Goose *Anser fabalis L 31" (79 cm)*

Eurasian species; casual spring migrant on western and central Aleutians, very rare in western Alaska. Grayish-brown goose with plain underparts, orange legs and feet; darker head and neck noticeable in flight. Similar to plain-bellied immature White-fronted Goose; best distinguished by different bill color: black with yellow, orange, or pink midsection, usually without white area at base. Of the two Siberian forms shown here, *A.f. serrirostris* is seen more often; *middendorffii* has a longer, narrower bill and a longer, thinner neck. Generally silent; call is a low, reedy *ung-unk*.

Pink-footed Goose *Anser brachyrhynchus L 26" (66 cm)*

East coast vagrant from breeding grounds in eastern Greenland. Several records between Newfoundland and Long Island; future sightings possible in the Maritime Provinces. May be confused with plain-bellied immature White-fronted Goose; distinguished by pink legs and dark base and tip to pinkish bill; bill is also stubbier, neck shorter than Whitefront. In flight, Pinkfoot shows extensive area of bluish-gray on mantle and wing coverts that turns brownish with wear; darker head and neck contrast with grayish body. Considered by some authorities a small Bean Goose subspecies.

Greater White-fronted Goose

1st winter

taiga

tundra

Greenland

Bean Goose

middendorffii

serrirostris

Pink-footed Goose

Snow Goose *Chen caerulescens* L 28" (71 cm)

Two color phases. All adults distinguished from smaller Ross' Goose by larger, pinkish bill with black "grinning patch," longer neck, flatter head. In flight, less agile than Ross', with slower wingbeat; rusty stains often visible on face in summer. White phase has black primaries; immature is grayish above, with dark bill. Blue phase formerly considered a separate species, Blue Goose. Adult has mostly white head and neck, brown back, variable amount of white on underparts. Primaries and secondaries are black, wing coverts bluish-gray. Immature has dark head and neck; distinguished from White-fronted Goose (preceding page) by dark legs and bill, lack of white front and white rump band. Intermediates between white and blue phases have mainly white underparts and whitish wing coverts. Immatures of both phases resemble adults by first spring. Abundant. Breeds on high Arctic tundra; seen in winter in grasslands, grainfields, coastal wetlands. Occasionally hybridizes with Ross' Goose. Larger form, "Greater Snow Goose," breeds around Baffin Bay, winters only along mid-Atlantic coast; blue phase almost unknown. Smaller form, "Lesser Snow Goose" (different phases shown here), winters casually outside mapped range throughout interior U. S. and in southern Canada. Blue phase abundant on Gulf coast; extremely rare in winter on west coast, uncommon in east.

Ross' Goose *Chen rossii* L 23" (58 cm)

A smaller edition of Snow Goose, but stubby, triangular bill lacks Snow's "grinning patch" and shows warty bluish or greenish base at close range; neck shorter, head rounder. In flight, more agile than Snow Goose, with faster wingbeat; white head generally lacks rusty stains. Ross' has two color phases. White phase has black primaries; immature has grayish wash on head, back, and flanks, but far less than immature white-phase Snow Goose. Extremely rare blue phase has white face and belly. Compare with blue-phase Snow Goose. Ross' Goose nests typically on lake islands on high Arctic tundra; occasionally hybridizes with Snow Goose at eastern edge of range. Seen during migration and winter in grasslands, grainfields. Casual winter visitor to much of west outside mapped range; very rare visitor to mid-Atlantic states.

Emperor Goose *Chen canagica* L 26" (66 cm)

Fairly stocky, small goose with short, thick neck. Head and back of neck white; chin and throat black; face often stained rusty in summer. Bill pinkish or purplish; lower mandible sometimes black. Black-and-white edging to silvery gray plumage creates a scaled effect below; upperparts appear barred. Juvenile has dark head and bill. During first fall, immature acquires white flecking on head; resembles adult by first winter. Emperor Goose breeds in tidewater marsh and tundra; winters on seashores, reefs. Casual south on Pacific coast to central California and inland to northeastern California.

Snow Goose

blue phase

blue phase variant

white phase immature

white phase

blue phase immature

Ross' Goose

white phase immature

white phase

blue phase

Emperor Goose

immature

Canada Goose *Branta canadensis*

L 25"-45" (64 cm-114 cm) Our most common and familiar goose. Black head and neck marked with distinctive white "chin strap" stretching from ear to ear. In flight, note large, dark wings, white undertail coverts, and white U-shaped rump band. Subspecies vary geographically in breast color, ranging from pale *B.c. canadensis* of the eastern seaboard to dark *occidentalis* of southern Alaska. Size decreases northward, with the smallest forms breeding on the high Arctic coastal tundra: pale-breasted *hutchinsii* in central and western Canada, and Mallard-size *minima,* smallest of all, in western Alaska. Endangered Aleutian subspecies, *leucopareia,* is distinguished from *minima* by slightly larger size, paler breast, and often a broad white neck ring; *minima* may show a very narrow ring. Canada Geese breed in open or forested areas near water. Flocks usually migrate in V-formation, stopping to feed in wetlands, grasslands, or cultivated fields. Call is a deep, musical *honk-a-lonk* in larger forms, a rapid, high-pitched cackle in smaller ones. Breeding programs have produced expanding populations south of mapped range and along the Atlantic and Pacific coasts.

Brant *Branta bernicla* *L 25" (64 cm)*

A small, dark, stocky goose with black head, neck, and breast and whitish patch on either side of neck. Extensive white uppertail coverts almost conceal black tail. White undertail coverts conspicuous in flight. Wings comparatively long and pointed, wingbeat rapid. Immature birds show bold white edging to wing coverts and secondaries, and fainter neck patches than adults. Juveniles are brownish; usually lack neck patches entirely. In eastern subspecies, *B.b. hrota,* pale belly contrasts with black chest, and neck patches do not meet in front. Western *nigricans,* formerly the Black Brant, has dark belly, and neck patches meet in front. Primarily a sea goose; rare inland, but a few eastern birds are sighted during migrations through the Great Lakes region. Flocks fly low in ragged formation; feed on aquatic plants of shallow bays and estuaries. Call, a low, hoarse *cronk.* Locally common; both forms casual in winter on opposite coasts and south of their mapped range.

Barnacle Goose *Branta leucopsis* *L 27" (69 cm)*

Breeds in northeastern Greenland, casual vagrant in Maritime Provinces. Distinctive head pattern: white or creamy face with black streak extending from bill to eye; rest of head, neck, and breast black. Bluish-gray upperparts, barred with black, and white U-shaped rump band formed by uppertail coverts. Silver gray wing linings show in flight. More of a land goose than the Brant, feeding in fields near the ocean. Fairly common in captivity. East coast sightings south of the Maritime Provinces may be either wild or escaped birds; those in the interior are more likely to be escapes.

Canada Goose

canadensis

occidentalis

leucopareia

minima

hutchinsii

hrota

nigricans

Brant

hrota immature

Barnacle Goose

Dabbling Ducks

The familiar "puddle ducks" of freshwater shallows and, chiefly in winter, salt marshes. Seldom diving, dabblers feed by tipping tail-up to reach aquatic plants, seeds, snails. They require no running start to take off but spring directly into flight. In most species, a distinguishing swatch of bright color, the speculum, marks the trailing edge of the secondaries. Many species are known to hybridize.

Mallard *Anas platyrhynchos* L 23" (58 cm)
Male readily identified by metallic green head and neck, yellow bill, narrow white collar, chestnut breast. Black central tail feathers curl up. Both sexes have white tail, white underwings, bright blue speculum with both sides bordered in white (see page 93). Female's mottled plumage resembles other *Anas* species; look for orange bill marked with black. Juvenile and eclipse male resemble female but bill is dull olive. Abundant and widespread. Mallards in Mexico, formerly considered a separate species, Mexican Duck, are darker, lack distinctive male plumage; intergrades occur in southwestern U.S.

Mottled Duck *Anas fulvigula* L 22" (56 cm)
Both sexes resemble female American Black Duck but body is paler, bill is yellower. Differs from female Mallard by darker plumage; greener speculum, bordered in black; and absence of white in tail or black on bill. Common year round in coastal marshes. Begins pairing in January or February, much earlier than the migratory American Black Ducks and Mallards. Some authorities consider the Mottled Duck to be a subspecies of the Mallard.

American Black Duck *Anas rubripes* L 23" (58 cm)
Blackish-brown, paler on face and foreneck. In flight (page 92), white wing linings contrast with otherwise dark plumage. Violet speculum is bordered in black, may show a thin white trailing edge. Male's bill is yellow; female's dull green, may be flecked with black. Nesting pairs favor woodland lakes and streams, freshwater or tidal marshes. In many parts of range, especially deforested areas, Mallards are replacing American Black Ducks; Mallard-Black Duck hybrids are increasingly common. Black Ducks seen in the west may be captive birds released by hunting clubs rather than true vagrants.

Spot-billed Duck *Anas poecilorhyncha* L 22" (56 cm)
Asian species, casual vagrant in Aleutians and Kodiak Island. Dark bill's pale tip, visible at some distance, sets this species apart from similar American Black Duck and female Mallard. Folded wing's thin white streak shows in flight as white patch on inner wing. The subspecies seen in North America lacks the red spots at base of bill for which this duck is named.

eclipse ♂

Mallard

juvenile

♀

♂

Mottled Duck

"Mexican"-Mallard Intergrade

American Black-Mallard Hybrid

♂

American Black Duck

Spot-billed Duck

Gadwall *Anas strepera* L 20" (51 cm)

Male is mostly gray, with white belly, black tail coverts, pale chestnut on wings. Female's mottled brown plumage resembles female Mallard (preceding page), but belly is white, forehead steeper; upper mandible is gray with orange sides. Both sexes have white inner secondaries that show as small patch on swimming bird and identify the species in flight (page 93). Fairly common in the west, less so in the east. Widespread range appears to be expanding eastward.

Falcated Teal *Anas falcata* L 19" (48 cm)

Asian species, rare visitor to western Aleutians. Named for male's long, falcated—sickle-shaped—tertials that overhang tail. Both sexes are chunky, with large head. Female's all-dark bill distinguishes her from female wigeons (next page) and Gadwall. In flight (page 93), both sexes show a broad, dark speculum bordered in white. Birds sighted on U. S. west coast may be escapes from captivity rather than true vagrants.

Green-winged Teal *Anas crecca* L 14^1/$_2$" (37 cm)

Our smallest dabbler. Male's chestnut head has dark green ear patch outlined in white. Female distinguished from other female teals (see also page 74) by smaller bill and by largely white undertail coverts that contrast with mottled flanks. A fast-flying, agile duck. In flight (page 92), shows green speculum bordered in buff on leading edge, white on trailing edge. In the subspecies seen in most of North America, *A.c. carolinensis,* male has vertical white bar on side. Larger *nimia,* resident on Aleutians and probably on Pribilofs, lacks vertical bar but has white stripe along scapulars. Eurasian form, *crecca,* resembles *nimia* in pattern, *carolinensis* in size; casual vagrant in western Alaska; rare but regular on east and west coasts. Eurasian *crecca* and *nimia* were formerly considered a separate species, Common Teal.

Baikal Teal *Anas formosa* L 17" (43 cm)

Asian species, casual vagrant in Alaska. Rare elsewhere on west coast; birds seen may be escapes from captivity rather than true vagrants. Adult male's intricately patterned head is unmistakable. Long, drooping dark gray scapulars are edged in rufous and white. Gray sides are set off front and rear by vertical white bars. Female similar to female Green-winged Teal; note white spot outlined in dark brown at base of bill; second white area below eye. On a few females, face has bridle marking. In flight (page 92), Baikal Teal's underwing shows less extensive white than in Green-winged Teal. Green speculum has a cinnamon buff inner border.

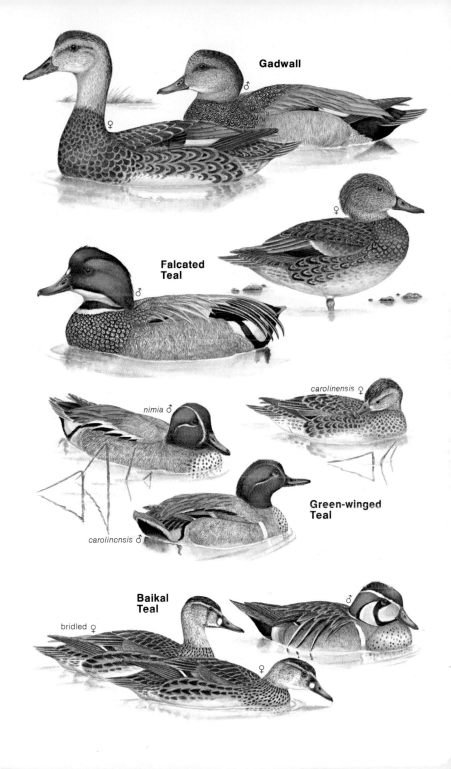

Gadwall

♀

♂

Falcated Teal

♂

♀

nimia ♂

carolinensis ♀

carolinensis ♂

Green-winged Teal

Baikal Teal

bridled ♀

♂

♀

American Wigeon *Anas americana* *L 19" (48 cm)*
Male's white forehead and cap are conspicuous in mixed flocks foraging in fields, marshes, and shallow waters. In flight (page 92), identified by white axillaries and large white patches on upperwing. Female closely resembles female of gray-phase Eurasian Wigeon; white axillaries are the best distinguishing field mark. Wing patches are grayish on adult female and immatures. A recently established breeder on east coast; casual during winter north to the Aleutians and the Great Lakes. Also called Baldpate.

Eurasian Wigeon *Anas penelope* *L 20" (51 cm)*
Male's creamy forehead and cap crown reddish-brown head and neck; green speckling surrounds eye in some birds. Many fall males retain some brown eclipse feathers but show distinctive reddish head. Immature male begins to acquire adult head and breast color but retains some brown juvenile plumage. In flight (page 92), Eurasian Wigeon's large white upperwing patches are like American Wigeon, but axillaries are grayish, not white. Female has two color phases: gray phase closely resembles female American Wigeon, but is distinguished by gray axillaries; rufous phase has reddish head. The Eurasian Wigeon is a regular winter visitor along both coasts, more common in the west; very rare inland. Regular migrant and winter visitor on western and central Aleutians.

Northern Pintail *Anas acuta* *♂ L 26" (66 cm) ♀ L 20" (51 cm)*
Male's chocolate brown head tops long, slender white neck, the white extending in a thin line onto head. Black central tail feathers extend far beyond rest of long, wedge-shaped tail. In both sexes, flight profile (page 92) shows long neck; slender body; long, pointed wings; dark speculum bordered in white on trailing edge. In flight, female's mottled brown wing linings contrast with white belly; tail long and wedge-shaped but lacks male's extended feathers. An abundant and widespread duck, common in marshes and open areas with ponds, lakes; in winter often feeds in grainfields. Much more common in west than in east. Casual in winter north to the Aleutians and the Great Lakes.

White-cheeked Pintail *Anas bahamensis* *L 17" (43 cm)*
Casual vagrant to southern Florida and Gulf coast from the West Indies. White cheeks and throat contrast with dark forehead and cap; blue bill has red spot near base. Long, pointed tail is buffy; tawny or reddish underparts are heavily spotted. Female is paler than male; tail slightly shorter. In flight, both sexes reveal green speculum broadly bordered on each side with buff. Most sightings of this species other than in Florida and along Gulf coast are probably birds escaped from captivity.

**American
Wigeon**

♂

eclipse ♂

♀

rufous phase ♀

gray phase ♀

♂

**Eurasian
Wigeon**

immature ♂

♀

♂

**Northern
Pintail**

♂

**White-cheeked
Pintail**

Northern Shoveler *Anas clypeata* L 19" (48 cm)
Large, spatulate bill, longer than head, identifies both sexes. Male distinguished by green head, white breast, brown sides. Most immature males have a white crescent on each side of face, like Blue-winged Teal. Female's grayish bill is tinged with orange on cutting edges and lower mandible. In flight (page 93), both sexes show blue forewing patch. Common in the west; increasing in the east. Found in ponds, marshes, bays.

Blue-winged Teal *Anas discors* L 15¹/₂" (39 cm)
Lead gray head with white crescent on each side identifies male. Female distinguished from female Green-winged Teal (page 70) by larger bill, spotted undertail coverts, yellowish legs. In comparison with female Cinnamon Teal, look for Bluewing's grayer plumage, bolder facial markings, and smaller bill. Male in eclipse plumage resembles female; distinguished from eclipse Cinnamon by dark eye. In flight (page 93), in both sexes, wing patterns match those of Cinnamon Teal. Blue-winged Teal is fairly common on marshes, ponds, and lakes in open country. Casual on west coast.

Garganey *Anas querquedula* L 15¹/₂" (39 cm)
Old World species, regular migrant to Alaska, chiefly in western Aleutians; casual elsewhere along west and east coasts; rare in midwest. Male's bold white eyebrows separate dark crown, red-brown face. In flight (page 93), shows gray-blue forewing and green speculum bordered fore and aft with white. Wing pattern is retained when male acquires female-like eclipse plumage, held well into fall. Female has strong facial pattern: dark crown, pale eyebrow, dark eye line, white lore spot bordered by a second, fainter dark line; note also dark bill and legs, dark undertail coverts. Larger and paler overall than female Green-winged Teal (page 70). Female in flight (page 93) shows gray-brown forewing, dark green speculum bordered in white. Note also pale gray inner webs of primaries, visible from above.

Cinnamon Teal *Anas cyanoptera* L 16" (41 cm)
Cinnamon head, neck, and underparts identify male. Female closely resembles female Blue-winged Teal but plumage is a richer brown, lore spot and eye line less distinct, bill longer and more spatulate. Young birds and males in eclipse resemble female. Males more than eight weeks old have red-orange eyes; Blue-winged Teal's eyes are dark. Cinnamon Teal's yellowish legs distinguish all ages, plumages, from Garganey and Green-winged Teal (page 70). Wing pattern (page 93) is almost identical to Blue-winged Teal. Common in marshes, ponds, lakes. Casual sightings in east may be escaped birds. Cinnamon Teal is known to interbreed with Blue-winged Teal.

Northern Shoveler

immature ♂

♀

♂

Blue-winged Teal

♀

♂

Garganey

♀

fall ♂

♂

Cinnamon Teal

♀

♂

Stiff-tailed Ducks

Long, stiff tail feathers serve as a rudder. When alarmed, these ducks often dive rather than fly. In both species, male's bill is blue in breeding season.

Ruddy Duck *Oxyura jamaicensis* L 15" (38 cm)
Chunky, thick-necked duck with large head, broad bill, long tail, often cocked up. Male's white cheeks are conspicuous both in breeding plumage, generally held April to August, and in dull winter plumage. In female, single dark line crosses cheek. Young resemble female through first winter. Common; nests in dense vegetation of freshwater marshes, lakes, ponds. During migration and winter, found on large lakes, shallow bays, salt marshes. Shown in flight on page 92.

Masked Duck *Oxyura dominica* L 13½" (34 cm)
Tropical species, rare visitor to southern Texas and along Gulf Coast to Florida. Male's black face on reddish-brown head is distinctive. In female, winter male, and juvenile, two dark stripes cross face. Secretive; found in small, densely vegetated ponds. Unlike Ruddy Duck, Masked Duck launches vertically into flight without a running start. In all plumages, white wing patches are conspicuous in flight (page 93).

Whistling-Ducks

Named for their whistling calls, these gooselike ducks have long legs, long necks. Wingbeats are slower than ducks, faster than geese. Formerly called Tree Ducks.

Fulvous Whistling-Duck *Dendrocygna bicolor*
L 20" (51 cm) Overall a rich tawny color; back darker, edged with tawny. Dark stripe along hindneck is continuous in female, usually broken in male. Bill and legs dark. Whitish band on rump conspicuous in flight. Distinctive call, a loud, squealing *pe-chee*. Forages in rice fields, marshes, shallow waters; more active at night than during day. Irregular wanderer in any season north to dashed line on map; casual farther north. Declining in the west. Formerly called Fulvous Tree Duck, this species seldom perches in trees.

Black-bellied Whistling-Duck
Dendrocygna autumnalis L 21" (53 cm) Gray face with white eye ring, reddish bill. Legs vary from red to pink. Belly, rump, and tail black; lacks the whitish rump band of the Fulvous Whistling-Duck. White wing patch shows as broad white stripe in flight. Juvenile is paler, with gray bill. Call is a high-pitched, four-note whistle. Inhabits woodland streams, ponds, marshes; nests in trees. Breeds irregularly in southeast Arizona. Formerly called Black-bellied Tree Duck.

Ruddy Duck

breeding ♀

breeding ♂

winter ♂

winter ♀

Masked Duck

breeding ♂

winter ♀

winter ♂

breeding ♀

juvenile

Fulvous Whistling-Duck

Black-bellied Whistling-Duck

juvenile

Perching Ducks

These woodland ducks, equipped with sharp claws, sometimes perch on snags, stumps, or branches. Nests are made in tree cavities or nest boxes.

Wood Duck *Aix sponsa* L 18¹/₂" (47 cm)
Male's glossy, colorful plumage and sleek crest are unmistakable. Head pattern and bill colors are retained in drab eclipse plumage. Female identified by short crest and large, white, teardrop-shaped eye patch; compare with female Mandarin Duck (page 90). Juvenile resembles female but is spotted below. In all plumages, flight profile (page 92) is distinctive: large head with bill angled downward; long, squared-off tail. Female's squealing flight call also distinctive: a loud, rising *oo-eek*. Fairly common in open woodlands near ponds or rivers. Casual during winter throughout most of breeding range, especially in mild winters.

Pochards

Legs are set far back and wide apart, which facilitates diving but makes walking awkward. Heavy bodies require a running start on water for take-off.

Canvasback *Aythya valisineria* L 21" (53 cm)
Forehead slopes to long, black bill. Male's head and neck are chestnut, back and sides whitish. Female and eclipse male have pale brown head and neck, pale brownish-gray back and sides. In flight (page 94), whitish belly contrasts with dark breast, dark undertail coverts. Wings lack the contrasting pale stripe of Common Pochard and Redhead. Locally common in open lakes, marshes; feeds in large flocks. Migrating flocks fly in irregular V's or in lines.

Common Pochard *Aythya ferina* L 18" (46 cm)
Eurasian species, rare migrant to Pribilofs and to western and central Aleutians. Resembles Canvasback in plumage and head shape. Bill similar to Redhead's but dark at base and tip, gray in center. In flight (page 94), wings show gray stripe along trailing edge.

Redhead *Aythya americana* L 19" (48 cm)
Rounded head and shorter, tricolored bill separate this species from Canvasback. Bill is mostly pale blue or slate, with narrow white ring bordering black tip. Male's back and sides are smoky gray. Female and eclipse male are brown overall, with darker crown, buffy patch at base of bill; compare with female scaups (next page). Redheads in flight (page 94) show gray stripe on trailing edge of wings. Locally common in marshes, ponds, lakes. May be expanding breeding range eastward.

Wood Duck

juvenile ♂

♂

Canvasback

♀

♂

Common Pochard

♂

♀

Redhead

♂

♀

Ring-necked Duck *Aythya collaris* L 17" (43 cm)

Peaked head; bold white ring near tip of bill. Male has second white ring at base of bill; white crescent separates black breast from gray sides. Cinnamon collar is very hard to see in the field. Female has dark crown, white eye ring; may have a pale line extending back from eye; face is mottled with white. In flight (page 94), all plumages show a gray stripe on secondaries. Fairly common on freshwater marshes, woodland ponds, small lakes; in winter, found also in southern coastal marshes. Range is variable; may breed south or winter north of mapped range. Rare but regular breeder in Alaska.

Tufted Duck *Aythya fuligula* L 17" (43 cm)

Old World species; regular visitor to western Alaska. Rare winter visitor along east coast as far south as Maryland, casual on west coast to southern California. Head is rounded; crest distinct in male, smaller in female and immatures; may be absent in eclipse male. Gleaming white sides further distinguish male from male Ring-necked Duck. First-winter male has gray sides but lacks the white crescents conspicuous in male Ringneck. Female is blackish-brown above; lacks white eye ring and white bill ring of female Ringneck. Some females have small white area at base of bill. In flight (page 94), all plumages show broad white stripe on secondaries and extending onto primaries. Found on ponds, rivers, bays, often with Ringnecks and Scaups.

Greater Scaup *Aythya marila* L 18" (46 cm)

Smoothly rounded head helps distinguish this species from Lesser Scaup. In close view, note Greater Scaup's larger bill with wider black tip. In good light, male's head may show a green gloss. In both species, female has bold white patch at base of bill. Some female Greater Scaups have a paler head with a distinct whitish ear patch. In flight (page 94), Greater Scaup shows a bold white stripe on secondaries and well out onto primaries. Locally common; found on large, open lakes, bays. Breeds irregularly as far south as Michigan and Nova Scotia. Migrates and winters in small or large flocks, sometimes with Lesser Scaups. Slightly larger size helps distinguish Greater Scaup in mixed flocks. Rare but regular winter visitor throughout Gulf states.

Lesser Scaup *Aythya affinis* L 16¹/₂" (42 cm)

Peaked crown distinctive from rounded head of Greater Scaup. In close view, note Lesser Scaup's smaller bill with smaller black tip. In good light, male's head may show a purple gloss, sometimes mixed with green. Female is brown overall, with bold white patch at base of bill. In some females, head is paler, with whitish ear patch less distinct than in female Greater Scaup. In flight (page 94), Lesser Scaup shows bold white stripe on secondaries only. Common; breeds in marshes, small lakes, ponds. In winter, found in large flocks in sheltered bays, inlets, lakes, sometimes with Greater Scaups.

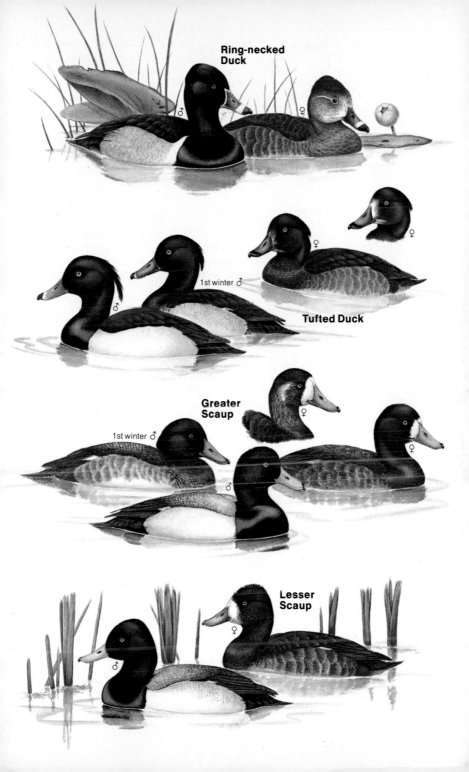

Ring-necked Duck

♂

♀

1st winter ♂

♀

Tufted Duck

♂

Greater Scaup

1st winter ♂

♀

♂

♀

Lesser Scaup

♀

♂

Eiders

Large, bulky diving ducks with dense down feathers that help insulate them from the cold northern seas. Females pluck their own down to line nests.

Common Eider *Somateria mollissima* L 24" (61 cm)
Female distinguished from female King Eider by evenly barred sides and scapulars, sloping forehead. Feathering extends along sides of bill to or beyond nostril, with minimal feathering on top of bill. Females vary in overall color from rust to gray. Eastern *S.m. dresseri* is reddish-brown. Western *v-nigra* is duller brown; eclipse plumage paler. Male's head pattern is distinctive. Most western and a few eastern males show a thin black V on throat; *v-nigra* male has orange-yellow bill. Eclipse and first-winter males resemble female, except that first-winter has white on breast; full adult plumage is attained by fourth winter. In flight (page 94), adult male shows white upperparts with black tail, black primaries and secondaries. Locally abundant; inhabits shallow bays, rocky shores.

King Eider *Somateria spectabilis* L 22" (56 cm)
Female distinguished from female Common Eider by crescent or V-shaped markings on sides and scapulars, more rounded head. Feathering extends only slightly along sides of bill but extensively down the top, making bill look stubby. Male's red bill and orange frontal shield are distinctive; in flight (page 95), shows black back, black wings with large white patches. First-winter male has brown head, pinkish or buffy bill, buffy eye line; lacks white wing patches. Full adult plumage is attained by fourth winter. A common species on tundra and coastal waters in northern part of range; winters casually on west coast and on east coast to Virginia; rare elsewhere.

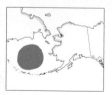

Spectacled Eider *Somateria fischeri* L 21" (53 cm)
Green head with white, black-bordered eye patches and orange bill make male unmistakable. In flight (page 95), black breast distinguishes adult male from other eiders. Drab female has paler spectacle pattern outlined in brown; bill is gray-blue; feathering extends far down upper mandible. Uncommon; found on coastal tundra, usually near lakes and ponds. Winter range poorly known; rare to southeast Alaska and British Columbia.

Steller's Eider *Polysticta stelleri* L 17" (43 cm)
Greenish head tufts, black eye patch, chin, and collar identify male. Female is dark cinnamon brown with distinct pale eye ring, unfeathered dark bill. In flight (page 95), shows blue speculum bordered fore and aft in white. Female has white wing linings, unlike females of other eider species. Steller's Eider is uncommon in North America, found along rocky coasts; nests on inland grassy areas or tundra. Winters casually south to British Columbia. May breed in coastal Yukon.

v-nigra eclipse ♂

v-nigra eclipse ♀

Common Eider

dresseri ♀

dresseri ♂

dresseri 1st winter ♂

v-nigra ♂

1st winter ♂

King Eider

♂

♀

♂

Common Eiders in flight

Spectacled Eider

♀

Steller's Eider

1st winter ♂

♀

♂

Sea Ducks

Stocky, short-necked diving ducks. Most species breed in the far north and migrate in large, compact flocks to and from their coastal wintering grounds.

Black Scoter *Melanitta nigra* L 19" (48 cm)
Male is black overall, with conspicuous orange-yellow knob at base of dark bill. Female's dark crown and nape contrast with pale face and throat; feathering does not extend onto bill. In both sexes, forehead is strongly rounded; feet and legs are dark. In flight (page 95), blackish wing linings contrast with paler flight feathers. Immatures resemble females but are whitish below. Fairly common; nests along tundra and woodland rivers, lakes, ponds. Winters on coastal waters. Formerly called Common Scoter.

White-winged Scoter *Melanitta fusca* L 21" (53 cm)
White secondaries, conspicuous in flight (page 94), may show as a small white patch on swimming bird. Forehead slightly rounded. Feathering extends almost to nostrils on top and sides of bill. Female and immatures lack contrasting dark crown and paler face of other scoters; white facial patches are usually distinct on immatures, often indistinct on adult female. Immatures are whitish below. Adult male has black knob at base of colorful bill; white crescent-shaped patch below white eye. Fairly common on inland lakes and rivers in breeding season, coastal areas in winter. Small numbers winter on the Great Lakes each year.

Surf Scoter *Melanitta perspicillata* L 20" (51 cm)
Male's overall black plumage sets off colorful bill, white eye, white patch on forehead and nape. In all birds, note that forehead is sloping, not rounded. Female is brown, with dark crown; usually has two white patches on each side of face; sides of bill are not feathered. Female and first-winter male may have whitish nape patch. All immatures have whitish underparts, may have white face patches. In flight (page 94), more uniform color of underwings helps distinguish Surf Scoter from Black Scoter; note also orangish legs and feet. Common; nests on tundra and in wooded areas near water. Winters on coastal waters.

Harlequin Duck *Histrionicus histrionicus* L 16½" (42 cm)
A small duck, with steep forehead, rounded head, stubby bill. Male's colorful plumage appears dark at a distance. Female has three white spots on each side of head; belly is pale. Juveniles resemble adult female; young male begins to acquire some adult plumage by late fall. Locally common along rocky coasts; moves inland along swift streams for nesting. Flight is rapid, low. Compare female in flight (page 95) with female Bufflehead. Male's call is a high-pitched nasal squeaking.

Black Scoter

1st winter ♂

♂

♀

White-winged Scoter

1st winter ♂

1st winter ♀

♂

♀

Surf Scoter

1st winter ♀

♂

♀

1st winter ♂

Harlequin Duck

♀

1st winter ♂

♂

Oldsquaw *Clangula hyemalis* ♂ *L 22" (56 cm)* ♀ *16" (41 cm)*
Male's long tail is conspicuous in flight, may be submerged in swimming bird. Male in winter and spring is largely white; breast and back dark brown, scapulars pearl gray; stubby bill shows pink band. In partial eclipse plumage, acquired in late spring, male becomes mostly dark, with pale facial patch, bicolored scapulars. Molt into full eclipse plumage continues until early fall. Female lacks long tail; bill is dark; plumage whiter overall in winter, darker in summer. First-fall birds are even darker (see page 95). Common, active, and noisy, Oldsquaws are identifiable at some distance by their swift, careening flight and loud, yodeling, three-part calls. Both sexes show uniformly dark underwings.

Barrow's Goldeneye *Bucephala islandica* *L 18" (46 cm)*
Male has white crescent on each side of face; white patches on scapulars show on swimming bird as a row of spots; dark color of back extends forward in a line partially separating white breast from white sides. Female and male in eclipse plumage closely resemble Common Goldeneye. Puffy, oval-shaped head, steep forehead, and stubby triangular bill help identify Barrow's. Adult female Barrow's head is slightly darker than female Common; bill mostly yellow, except in eastern birds and young females, which may have only a yellow band near tip of bill. In all plumages, white wing patches visible in flight (page 95) differ subtly between the two species. Both species summer on open lakes and small ponds, often near woodlands where nest holes are available; winter in sheltered coastal areas, inland lakes and rivers.

Common Goldeneye *Bucephala clangula* *L 18½" (47 cm)*
Male has round white spot on each side of face; scapulars are mostly white. Female and eclipse male closely resemble Barrow's Goldeneye. Head of Common Goldeneye is more triangular; forehead more rounded; bill longer. Female's head is slightly tawnier than female Barrow's; bill generally all dark or with yellow near tip only; rarely all yellow. In all plumages, white wing patches visible in flight (page 95) differ subtly between the two species. Both species summer on open lakes, often near woodlands where nest holes are available; winter in sheltered coastal areas, inland lakes and rivers.

Bufflehead *Bucephala albeola* *L 13½" (34 cm)*
A small duck with a large, puffy head, steep forehead, short bill. Male is glossy black above, white below, with large white patch on head. Female is duller, with small, elongated white patch on each side of head. Young male and male in eclipse resemble female. In flight (page 95), males show white patch across entire wing; female has white patch only on inner secondaries. Fairly common, Buffleheads nest in woodlands near small lakes, ponds. During migration and winter, found also on sheltered bays.

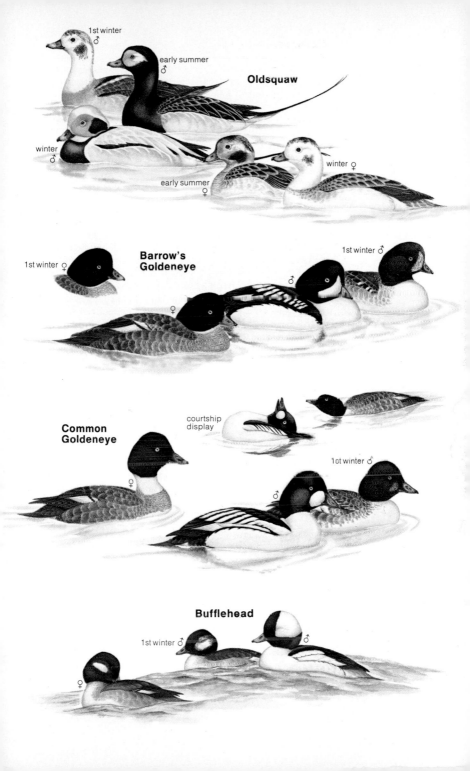

1st winter ♂

early summer ♂

Oldsquaw

winter ♂

early summer ♀

winter ♀

1st winter ♀

Barrow's Goldeneye

1st winter ♂

♂

♀

Common Goldeneye

courtship display

1st winter ♂

♂

Bufflehead

1st winter ♂

♂

♀

Mergansers

Long, thin, serrated bills help these divers catch fish, crustaceans, and aquatic insects. Mergansers usually fly fast and low over water in single file.

Common Merganser *Mergus merganser* L 25" (64 cm)
Large duck with long, slim neck and thin, hooked, red bill. White breast and sides and lack of crest distinguish male from similar Red-breasted Merganser. Female's bright chestnut, crested head and neck contrast sharply with white chin, white breast. Adult male in flight (page 94) shows white patch on upper surface of entire inner wing, partially crossed by a single black bar. Eclipse male resembles female but retains wing pattern. Female has white inner secondaries, partially crossed by black bar. First-winter male resembles adult female. Common Mergansers nest in holes and crevices in woodlands near lakes and rivers; in winter, may also be found on brackish water.

Red-breasted Merganser *Mergus serrator* L 23" (58 cm)
Shaggy, double crest, white collar, and streaked breast distinguish male from Common Merganser. Female's head and neck are paler than in female Common Merganser; chin and foreneck white. Adult male in flight (page 94) shows white patch on upper surface of entire inner wing, partially crossed by two black bars. Eclipse male resembles female but retains wing pattern. Female's white inner secondaries are crossed by a single black bar. First-winter male resembles adult female. Red-breasted Mergansers nest in woodlands near lakes and rivers or in sheltered coastal areas. Much more likely to be found on brackish or salt water year round than the Common Merganser.

Hooded Merganser *Lophodytes cucullatus* L 18" (46 cm)
Puffy crest; thin bill. Male's white head patches are fan-shaped and conspicuous when crest is raised; bill is dark. Compare with male Bufflehead (preceding page). Female brownish overall; upper mandible dark, lower mandible yellowish. First-winter male resembles adult female. In flight (page 95) both sexes show black-and-white inner secondaries. Crest is flattened in flight, so that male's white head patch shows only as a white line. Uncommon. In breeding season, found on woodland ponds, rivers, sheltered backwaters; less often on large lakes. Winters chiefly on fresh water.

Smew *Mergellus albellus* L 16" (41 cm)
Eurasian species, rare vagrant in Aleutians; very rare elsewhere on west and east coasts. Bill is dark, relatively short. In female, white throat and lower face contrast sharply with reddish head and nape. Adult male is mostly white; black markings more visible in flight (page 95).

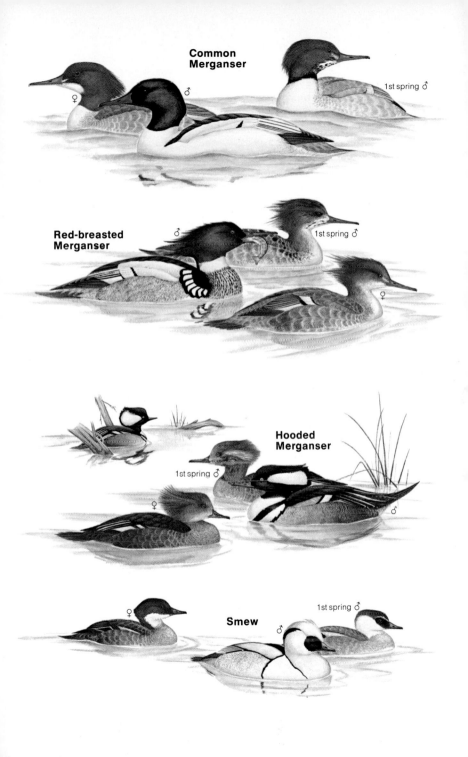

**Common
Merganser**

1st spring ♂

♀

♂

**Red-breasted
Merganser**

♂

1st spring ♂

♀

**Hooded
Merganser**

1st spring ♂

♀

♂

Smew

1st spring ♂

♀

♂

Exotic Waterfowl

Many waterfowl species are brought into North America from other continents for zoos, farms, parks, and private collections. These birds occasionally escape from captivity. The species shown here are among those most often seen; none has become established in the wild.

Black Swan *Cygnus atratus* L 60" (152 cm)
The dark beauty of this Australian species makes it a popular addition to parks, zoos, and estates, primarily on the east coast. Also popular is the South American Black-necked Swan, *C. melancoryphus*, with a white body, black head and neck.

Red-breasted Goose *Branta ruficollis* L 22" (56 cm)
Popular in private collections, chiefly on the east and west coasts. Breeds in Siberia.

Greylag Goose *Anser anser* L 34" (86 cm)
Eurasian species, progenitor of most domestic geese. May be confused with immature Greater White-fronted Goose or Bean Goose (page 62).

Bar-headed Goose *Anser indicus* L 30" (76 cm)
Asian species, common in zoos and private waterfowl collections across the continent.

Muscovy Duck *Cairina moschata* L 28" (71 cm)
A common domestic duck in parks and farms across the continent. Varies from glossy purplish to black-and-white to all-white. In the wild, found from Mexico to South America.

Chinese Goose *Anser cygnoides* L 45" (114 cm)
Asian species, domesticated in many variations. Wild form is slimmer, has long, swanlike bill lacking knob at base. Also called Swan Goose.

Domestic Goose *Anser "domesticus"* L 22-45" (56-114 cm)
Common on farms. Individuals sometimes desert the barnyard to join a flock of wild geese or ducks.

Northern Shelduck *Tadorna tadorna* L 25" (64 cm)
Eurasian species, common in North American zoos and private collections. Female is smaller, lacks knob on bill. Also called Shelduck or Common Shelduck.

Ruddy Shelduck *Tadorna ferruginea* L 26" (66 cm)
Afro-Eurasian species, common in zoos and private collections. Compare with Fulvous Whistling-Duck (page 76).

Mandarin Duck *Aix galericulata* L 18" (46 cm)
Asian species, common in zoos and private collections. Female closely resembles female Wood Duck (page 78).

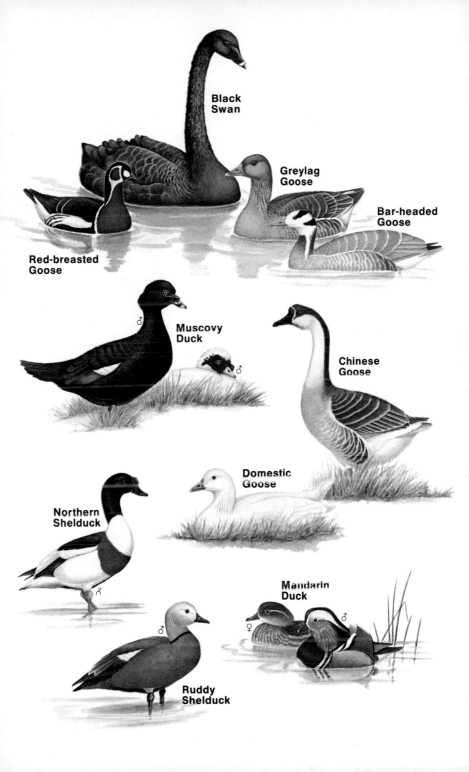

Black
Swan

Greylag
Goose

Bar-headed
Goose

Red-breasted
Goose

Muscovy
Duck

Chinese
Goose

Domestic
Goose

Northern
Shelduck

Mandarin
Duck

♀   ♂

Ruddy
Shelduck

Ducks in Flight

Northern Pintail ♂

♀

American Black Duck ♂

Eurasian Wigeon ♂

gray phase ♀

American Wigeon ♂

♀

Baikal Teal ♂

♀

Wood Duck ♂

♀

carolinensis ♂ Green-winged Teal

carolinensis ♀

Ruddy Duck ♂

♀

Mallard ♂ ♀

Gadwall ♂ ♀

Northern Shoveler ♂ ♀

Falcated Teal ♂ ♀

Cinnamon Teal ♂

Blue-winged Teal ♂ ♀

Garganey ♂ immature ♂ ♀

Masked Duck ♂ ♀

Ducks in Flight

Common Merganser ♂ ♀

Common Eider *dresseri* ♂ *dresseri* ♀

White-winged Scoter ♂ ♀

Red-breasted Merganser ♂ ♀

Surf Scoter ♂ ♀

Canvasback ♂ ♀

Common Pochard ♂ ♀

Redhead ♂ ♀

Lesser Scaup ♂ ♀

Greater Scaup ♂ ♀

Tufted Duck ♂ ♀

Ring-necked Duck ♂ ♀

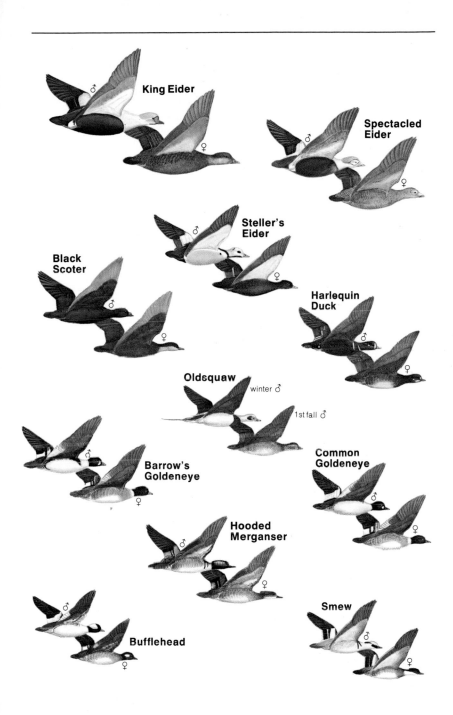

Limpkin (Family Aramidae)

Large, long-necked wading bird, named for its unusual limping gait. Once hunted nearly to extinction, this bird is again common in southern swamps, marshes.

Limpkin *Aramus guarauna* L 26" (66 cm)
Chocolate brown overall, densely streaked with white above. Bill long and slightly downcurved. Long legs and large, webless feet are dull grayish-green. Juvenile resembles adult but is paler. Locally common in swamps and wetlands, where it wades or swims in search of snails, frogs, insects. Call, heard chiefly at night, is a wailing *krr-oww*.

Rails, Gallinules, Coots (Family Rallidae)

Small swimming and diving birds with short tails, short legs, and short, rounded wings. Most species are solitary and secretive. Some, especially the rails, are distinguished chiefly by call and habitat.

♪ **King Rail** *Rallus elegans* L 15" (38 cm)
Large freshwater rail with long, slightly downcurved bill. Much larger than similar Virginia Rail (next page). Black above, with olive or tawny streaks; head slate, with brown cheeks, buffy eyebrow; underparts cinnamon; flanks strongly barred black and white. Juvenile is darker above, paler below. Common in freshwater swamps and marshes but seldom seen. Most often heard at dusk and dawn. Some birds winter in coastal marshes with Clapper Rails. Hybridizes with Clapper Rail in narrow zone of overlap; some authorities consider them to be one species. Some calls of the two are identical. Usually distinctive in King Rail is a series of less than ten *kek kek kek* notes, fairly evenly spaced.

♪ **Clapper Rail** *Rallus longirostris* L 14½" (37 cm)
A common rail of coastal salt marshes; also found along lower Colorado River and Salton Sea. Much larger than Virginia Rail (next page). Slightly smaller and usually duller than King Rail. Plumage variable. East coast forms such as *R.l. crepitans* are gray-brown above, buffy-cinnamon below; cheeks are gray; flanks less strongly barred than in King Rail. Gulf coast forms such as *scottii* are brighter cinnamon below. West coast forms such as *levipes* and the inland *yumanensis* are brighter below than east coast birds; cheeks brownish-gray. Clapper Rails hybridize with King Rails in narrow zone of overlap. Some calls of the two species are identical; usually distinctive in Clapper Rail is a series of ten or more dry *kek kek kek* notes, accelerating and then slowing. More often heard than seen, Clappers call chiefly at dusk and dawn.

Limpkin

**King
Rail**

juvenile

crepitans

yumanensis

scottii

levipes

**Clapper
Rail**

♪ Virginia Rail *Rallus limicola* *L 9¹/₂″ (24 cm)*

Smaller than King Rail (preceding page); cheeks bluish-gray; wings and underparts richer chestnut; legs and bill often redder than in King Rail. Juvenile is blackish-brown above, mottled black or gray below. Common but secretive; found in freshwater marshes and wetlands. Also winters in brackish or saltwater marshes. Some calls are similar to those of King Rail. Distinctive call is a series of *kid kid kidick kidick* phrases. Also gives a descending series of *oink oink* notes.

♪ Sora *Porzana carolina* *L 8³/₄″ (22 cm)*

Short, thick bill, yellow or greenish-yellow. Breeding adult is brownish-olive above, with coarse black streaks, fine white ones. Face and center of throat and breast are black. Female is duller than male. In winter adults, black throat is somewhat obscured with gray edgings. Juvenile lacks black on face and throat; underparts are paler. Compare with Yellow Rail. Juvenile Sora is not as black; upperparts are streaked, not barred, with white. Common in freshwater and brackish marshes, rice fields, grainfields. Also in saltwater marshes during migration and winter. Calls include a plaintive *ker-wee* and a descending whinny. Common winter call is a descending *wee-ker.*

♪ Yellow Rail *Coturnicops noveboracensis* *L 7¹/₄″ (18 cm)*

A small rail, deep tawny-yellow above with wide dark stripes marked by white crossbars. In flight, shows a large white patch on trailing edges of wings. Bill is short and thick; color varies from yellowish to greenish-gray. Juvenile is darker than adult. Extremely secretive. Breeds in grassy marshes, boggy swales, damp fields; not found in deepwater marshes or swamps. Winters in fresh, brackish, or salt marshes, rice fields, dry fields. Calls include a variety of grunts, squeaks, cackles; typical call is a four- or five-note *tick-tick, tick-tick-tick,* in alternate twos or twos and threes, like the sound made by tapping two pebbles together.

♪ Black Rail *Laterallus jamaicensis* *L 6″ (15 cm)*

A very small, extremely secretive rail. Blackish above, with white speckling, chestnut nape. Bill short, black. Underparts grayish-black, with narrow white barring on flanks. Inhabits fresh, brackish, and salt marshes, grassy swamps, wet meadows. Male's distinctive call, a repeated *kik-kee-do.* Female's call is a soft *hoo-hoo-hooo.*

Corn Crake *Crex crex* *L 10¹/₂″ (27 cm)*

European species, formerly casual along east coast in fall but not seen in recent years. European populations are seriously declining. A rail of damp, grassy fields, croplands; not found in marshes. Dull buffy-yellow overall, with short, thick, brownish bill; distinctive large chestnut wing patch.

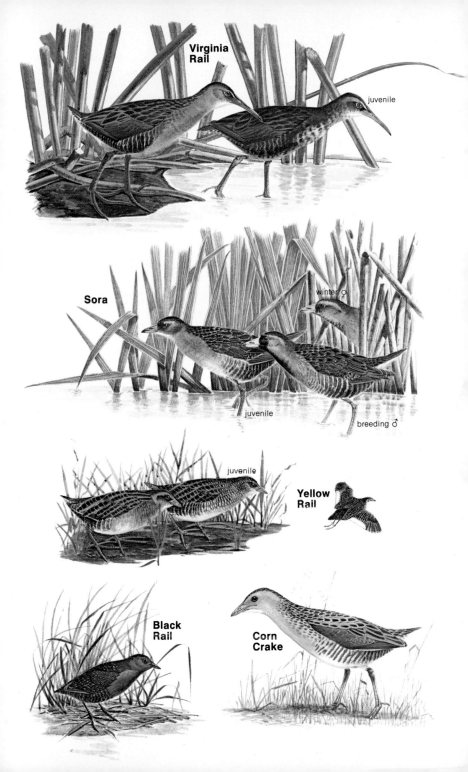

Virginia Rail

juvenile

Sora

winter ♀

juvenile

breeding ♂

juvenile

Yellow Rail

Black Rail

Corn Crake

Purple Gallinule *Porphyrula martinica* L 13" (33 cm)
Bright purplish-blue head, neck, and underparts, with pale blue forehead shield, red and yellow bill. Back is brownish-green, legs and feet yellow. Juvenile is buffy-brown overall, with brownish-olive back, greenish wings; forehead dark brown, bill mostly dark olive, legs and feet dull olive. Molts into winter plumage after fall migration but may retain traces of juvenile plumage into first spring. In all ages, all-white undertail coverts are conspicuous. Fairly common in overgrown swamps, lagoons, marshes. Highly migratory; winters from southern Florida to Argentina. Wanderers are seen in all seasons far north of mapped range; frequently breeds north of area shown, occasionally far north.

Common Moorhen *Gallinula chloropus* L 14" (36 cm)
Black head and neck, with red forehead shield, red bill with yellow tip. Back brownish-olive; underparts slate, with white streaking on flanks that shows as a thin white line. Outer undertail coverts are white, inner ones black. Legs and feet yellow. Juvenile is paler, browner; whitish throat is flecked with black; bill and legs dusky. Distinguished at all ages from Purple Gallinule and coots by white line along side, just below wing. Winter adult has brownish facial shield, brownish bill with dusky-yellow tip. Common in freshwater marshes, ponds, placid rivers. Formerly called Common Gallinule.

American Coot *Fulica americana* L 15½" (39 cm)
Blackish head and neck, with small reddish-brown forehead shield, whitish bill; body slate; paler below; outer feathers of undertail coverts are white, inner ones black. Leg color ranges from greenish-gray in young birds to yellow or orangish in adults. Toes are lobed, unlike gallinules. Juvenile is paler than adult, with whitish feather tips, especially below. In a flying bird, white trailing edge on most of wing is distinctive. Common to abundant; nests in freshwater marshes, wetlands, or near lakes or ponds; winters in both freshwater and saltwater habitats, usually in large flocks.

Caribbean Coot *Fulica caribaea* L 15½" (39 cm)
Casual in southern Florida, chiefly in Miami area. Resembles American Coot but forehead shield is broader and white, sometimes tinged with yellow. A few American Coots may show extensively white facial shields. Identification requires extreme caution and may not always be possible. The Caribbean Coot is considered by some authorities to be a subspecies of the American Coot.

Eurasian Coot *Fulica atra* L 15¾" (40 cm)
Very rare straggler to Newfoundland, Labrador, and the Pribilofs. Slightly larger and darker than American Coot; undertail coverts all-black. Forehead and bill entirely white.

Purple Gallinule

juvenile

Common Moorhen

winter

juvenile

breeding

American Coot

juvenile

Caribbean Coot

Eurasian Coot

Jacanas (Family Jacanidae)

Extremely long toes and claws allow these tropical birds to walk on lily pads and other floating plants.

Northern Jacana *Jacana spinosa* L 9¹/₂″ (24 cm)
Mexican and Central American species, rare visitor to ponds and marshes in southern Texas. Frequently raises its wings, revealing greenish-yellow flight feathers.

Oystercatchers (Family Haematopodidae)

These chunky shorebirds have laterally flattened bills that can reach into mollusks, then pry the shell open; also probe sand for worms and crabs.

American Black Oystercatcher
Haematopus bachmani L 17¹/₂″ (45 cm) Resident on rocky shores and islands along the Pacific coast from the Aleutians to Baja California. Large red-orange bill, all-dark body. Immatures are browner; outer half of bill is dusky during first year.

American Oystercatcher *Haematopus palliatus*
L 18¹/₂″ (47 cm) Large red-orange bill. Black head and dark back cloak white wing and tail patches, white underparts. Juvenile is scaly-looking above; dark tip on bill is kept through first year. Oystercatchers feed in small, noisy flocks on coastal beaches and mud flats. Range is expanding northward in the east. Casual in southern California.

Stilts and Avocets (Family Recurvirostridae)

Sleek and graceful waders with long, slender bills and spindly legs. Two species inhabit North America.

American Avocet *Recurvirostra americana* L 18″ (46 cm)
Black and white above, white below; head and neck rusty in breeding plumage, gray in winter. Juveniles have cinnamon wash on head and neck. Fairly common on shallow ponds, marshes, lakeshores. Avocets feed by sweeping their bills from side to side through the water. Male's bill is longer, straighter, than female's. Common call is a loud *wheet*.

Black-necked Stilt *Himantopus mexicanus* L 14″ (36 cm)
Male's glossy black back and bill contrast sharply with white underparts, long red or pink legs. Female is brownish above. Juveniles have buffy edgings on upperparts. The Stilt breeds and winters in a wide variety of wet habitats. Rare breeder on the east coast; very local in the interior. Common call is a loud *kek kek kek*.

American Black
Oystercatcher

Northern
Jacana

immature

juvenile

American
Oystercatcher

juvenile

winter ♂

American
Avocet

breeding ♀

juvenile

Black-necked
Stilt

♂

Plovers (Family Charadriidae)

These compact birds dart across the ground, stop suddenly, then sprint off again. Shape and behavior identify plovers in general; species are more difficult. All juveniles resemble adults but backs look scaly.

Snowy Plover *Charadrius alexandrinus* L 6¼" (16 cm)
Pale above, very pale in Gulf coast birds; thin dark bill; dark or grayish legs; partial breast band; dark ear patch. Females and juveniles may be confused with Piping Plover; note much thinner bill, darker legs. Inhabits barren sandy beaches and flats. Uncommon and declining. Calls include a low *krut* and a soft, whistled *ku-wheet*.

Piping Plover *Charadrius melodus* L 7¼" (18 cm)
Very pale above; orange legs; white rump conspicuous in flight (page 138). In breeding plumage, shows dark narrow breast band, sometimes incomplete, especially in females. In winter, bill is all-dark. Distinguished from Snowy Plover by thicker bill, paler back; legs are brighter than in Semipalmated Plover. Distinctive call, a clear *peep-lo*. Found on sandy beaches, lakeshores, dunes. Uncommon; rare breeder in the midwest; rare vagrant in California.

Wilson's Plover *Charadrius wilsonia* L 7¾" (20 cm)
Long, very heavy, black bill; broad neck band is black in male, brown in female; legs grayish-pink. Juvenile resembles adult female but note scaly-looking upperparts. Breeding male may have cinnamon buff ear patch. Fairly common on barrier islands, sandy beaches, mud flats. Casual to New England and California. Call is a sharp, whistled *whit*.

♪ **Semipalmated Plover** *Charadrius semipalmatus*
L 7¼" (18 cm) Dark back distinguishes this species from Piping and Snowy Plovers; bill much smaller than in Wilson's Plover. (All shown in flight on page 138.) At very close range, Semipalmated shows partial webbing between toes. Juvenile has darker legs, scaly-looking back. Winter plumage is browner overall, bill darker. Common on beaches, lakeshores, tidal flats; seen throughout the continent in migration. Distinctive call is a whistled, upslurred *chu-weet*.

♪ **Common Ringed Plover** *Charadrius hiaticula*
L 7½" (19 cm) Almost identical to Semipalmated Plover; best distinguished by call, a soft, fluted *pooee*. Breast band is usually broader in center than Semipalmated's, extending farther up toward throat. White eyebrow is usually more distinct, especially in male. Webbing between toes is less extensive. Bill is slightly longer than in Semipalmated. Generally seen in North America only in breeding season and within breeding range; identification should be made with caution.

Snowy Plover

Gulf coast ♂

♀

♂

juvenile

Piping Plover

winter

breeding ♂

breeding ♂

breeding ♀

juvenile

Wilson's Plover

♂

♀

winter

breeding ♂

Semipalmated Plover

juvenile

breeding ♀

breeding ♂

breeding ♀

Common Ringed Plover

Killdeer *Charadrius vociferus* *L 10¹/₂" (27 cm)*

Double breast bands are distinctive, as is this plover's loud, piercing call: *kill-dee* or *dee-dee-dee*. Bright reddish-orange rump is visible in flight (page 138). Common in meadows, farm fields, airfields, lawns; also on shores and riverbanks. Feeds almost entirely on insects, worms, grubs. Nests on open ground, usually on gravel. Skilled actor; will feign a broken wing or leg to lead intruders away from the nest. Generally seen singly or in pairs; in winter, may form loose flocks. In mild winters a few birds are seen north into summer range. Vagrant north of breeding range in summer.

Mongolian Plover *Charadrius mongolus* *L 7¹/₂" (19 cm)*

Asian species, casual migrant to Aleutians and western Alaska. Rare in summer in western and northwestern Alaska, where it may breed. Bright rusty-red breast; black-and-white facial pattern. Females are duller. Winter birds lack reddish tones; underparts are white except for broad grayish patches on sides of breast.

Eurasian Dotterel *Charadrius morinellus* *L 8¹/₄" (21 cm)*

Eurasian species, uncommon, sporadic breeder in highlands and tundra of northwestern Alaska; vagrant along west coast south to Washington. Narrow whitish band on lower breast in all plumages, somewhat obscured in young and winter birds. Bold white eyebrow extends around the entire head. Unlike other plovers, females are brighter than males. In juvenile, upperparts are edged with cinnamon buff; underparts extensively buff. A chunky bird; generally unwary, it can often be closely approached.

Mountain Plover *Charadrius montanus* *L 9" (23 cm)*

In breeding plumage, unbanded white underparts separate this plover from all other brown-backed plovers. Buffy tinge on breast is more extensive in winter plumage; may be confused with winter Lesser Golden-Plover (next page), but has paler, unspotted upperparts, paler legs. In flight, Mountain Plover shows white underwings; Lesser Golden-Plover's are grayish. Calls vary from low, drawn-out whistles to harsh, shrill notes. Common in small flocks in dry upland habitats, high plains, semidesert, often far from water; in winter usually found on bare dirt fields. Larger flocks, sometimes more than a hundred birds, may form in winter.

Killdeer

Mongolian Plover

breeding

juvenile

winter

Eurasian Dotterel

winter

juvenile

breeding ♀

Mountain Plover

winter

juvenile

breeding

♪ **Black-bellied Plover** *Pluvialis squatarola* L 11¹/₂" (29 cm)
In black-and-white breeding plumage, white stripe extends across forehead, around crown and nape and down sides of breast; undertail coverts white. Winter and juvenile birds distinguished from Lesser Golden-Plover by larger size, larger bill, grayer plumage. Distinguished in flight in all plumages by white uppertail coverts, barred white tail, black axillaries, bold white wing stripe (see also page 138). Nests on arctic tundra. Migrates chiefly along coasts, but a few travel inland. Winters on sandy beaches, marshes. Usually seen singly or in small flocks. Typical call is a drawn-out, mournful, three-note whistle, the second note lower pitched.

♪ **Lesser Golden-Plover** *Pluvialis dominica* L 10¹/₂" (27 cm)
Breeding adults entirely black below; black upperparts speckled with gold and white; white stripe extends from forehead to sides of neck and breast. Juvenile and winter adult of the widespread subspecies, *P.d. dominica,* distinguished from Black-bellied Plover by smaller size, smaller bill, darker plumage. Juvenile and winter *fulva,* the subspecies that breeds in western Alaska, are much brighter above and below. All winter sightings of Lesser Golden-Plover have been *fulva.* In all plumages, distinguished in flight by uniformly dark upperparts (see page 138), grayish underwing and axillaries. Nests on arctic tundra; winters chiefly in Southern Hemisphere. Small numbers of *fulva* winter locally along Pacific coast. Fall migration is mostly over oceans. Spring migration crosses central plains; seen in large flocks in fields, less often on tidal flats. Call note is a loud, whistled *chu-weet,* the second note higher in pitch. Formerly called American Golden Plover.

♪ **Greater Golden-Plover** *Pluvialis apricaria*
L 11¹/₂" (29 cm) Eurasian species, seen regularly in Greenland, casually in spring in Newfoundland. Distinguished in all plumages from *dominica* subspecies of Lesser Golden-Plover by brighter upperparts and, in flight, by pale underwing with white axillaries (see also page 138). In breeding plumage, white stripe usually extends continuously from forehead to flanks. Calls are mournful single- and double-note whistles.

Northern Lapwing *Vanellus vanellus* L 12¹/₂" (32 cm)
Eurasian species, rare straggler in late fall to northeast coast of North America. All sightings have been immature birds. First-winter plumage is dark and green-glossed above, white below, with black breast; wispy but prominent crest. Wings broad and rounded, with white tips, white wing linings. Flight call is a whistled *pee-wit.*

Black-bellied Plover

juvenile

winter

breeding ♂

dominica juvenile

dominica winter

fulva winter

Lesser Golden-Plover

fulva juvenile

dominica breeding ♂

Greater Golden-Plover

1st winter

winter

Northern Lapwing

Northern Lapwing 1st winter

breeding ♂

Lesser Golden-Plover *dominica* winter

Greater Golden-Plover early spring

Black-bellied Plover winter

Sandpipers *(Family Scolopacidae)*

Rising in unison, wheeling, settling back on the sand, flocks of shorebirds are a joy to watch—and hard to identify. Most species have at least three distinct plumages. Juveniles and breeding adults may migrate separately. Molt to winter plumage usually begins as they near or reach their winter grounds.

Marbled Godwit *Limosa fedoa* L 18" (46 cm)
Long bicolored bill, usually upcurved, sets all godwits apart from other large shorebirds. The buffy-brown or tawny-brown Marbled Godwit is mottled with black above, barred below. Barring is much less extensive on winter birds and juveniles. In all birds, bill and legs are longer than in Bar-tailed Godwit. In flight (page 136), cinnamon wing linings and cinnamon on primaries are distinctive. Nests on grassy meadows, near lakes and ponds. Common on west coast in winter, fairly common on Gulf coast; rare in the east.

Bar-tailed Godwit *Limosa lapponica* L 16" (41 cm)
Long bicolored bill, slightly upcurved. Male in breeding plumage is reddish-brown below; lacks heavy barring of Black-tailed Godwit. Female is larger and much paler than male. In winter plumage, adults resemble Marbled Godwit but lack cinnamon tones. Note also shorter bill, shorter legs. Black-and-white barred tail distinctive but hard to see. Juvenile resembles winter adult but is buffier overall. Two subspecies of this Eurasian godwit occur in North America. *L.l. baueri,* shown opposite, breeds in Alaska, appears in migration along Pacific coast; rump is heavily mottled, wing linings brown with white barring. European *lapponica,* casual along Atlantic coast, has white rump, white wing linings, brown-barred axillaries. Both forms are shown in flight on page 136.

Black-tailed Godwit *Limosa limosa* L 16¹/₂" (42 cm)
Eurasian species, spring migrant on western Aleutians; rare in winter along Atlantic coast. Long bicolored bill is straight or slightly upcurved. Tail is black, uppertail coverts white. In breeding plumage, shows chestnut head and neck and heavily barred sides and flanks. Winter birds are plain gray above, whitish below. In all plumages, white wing linings and bold white wing stripe are conspicuous in flight (page 136).

Hudsonian Godwit *Limosa haemastica* L 15¹/₂" (39 cm)
Long bicolored bill, slightly upcurved. Tail is black, uppertail coverts white. Breeding male is dark chestnut below, finely barred. Female duller, larger. Juvenile's buff feather edges give upperparts a scaled look. Winter adult resembles Black-tailed Godwit. In flight (page 136), dark wing linings and narrow white wing stripe are distinctive. Breeding range not fully known. Migrates through Great Plains in spring, primarily off the east coast in fall.

Marbled Godwit

breeding

winter

Bar-tailed Godwit

breeding ♂

winter

juvenile

Black-tailed Godwit

winter

breeding

Hudsonian Godwit

winter

breeding ♂

juvenile

Eskimo Curlew *Numenius borealis* *L 14" (36 cm)*

Nests on arctic tundra; winters in South America. Most sightings in this century have been along the Texas coast during migration. This species is almost extinct; identification must be made with great care. Resembles Whimbrel but is much smaller; upperparts darker; bill thinner and less curved; crown less strongly patterned; wing linings cinnamon. Calls are soft twittering whistles.

Bristle-thighed Curlew *Numenius tahitiensis*

L 17" (43 cm) Rusty-orange rump and tail distinguish this species from the Whimbrel. Stiff feathers on thighs and flanks not easily seen in the field. Typical call is a loud, whistled *chu-a-whit*. Only known breeding area is in western Alaska. Migrates directly across Pacific to and from its winter grounds on Pacific islands. Shown in flight on page 136.

Whimbrel *Numenius phaeopus* *L 17¹/₂" (45 cm)*

Grayish-brown above, whitish and streaked below; boldly striped crown; dark eye line; long, downcurved bill. Typical call is a series of hollow whistles on one pitch. Fairly common; nests on open tundra; winters on beaches, mud flats, wet fields. In flight (page 136), the North American subspecies, *N. p. hudsonicus,* shows dark rump and underwings. European *phaeopus*, rare vagrant to east coast, has white rump and underwings. Asian *variegatus,* regular migrant through western Alaska, shows whitish, streaked rump and underwings.

Long-billed Curlew *Numenius americanus* *L 23" (58 cm)*

Cinnamon brown above, buff below, with very long, strongly downcurved bill. Lacks dark head stripes of Whimbrel. Juveniles have shorter bill. Cinnamon buff wing linings, visible in flight (page 136) are distinctive in all plumages. Typical call is a loud, musical, ascending *cur-lee*. Fairly common; nests in both wet and dry uplands; in winter, found on coastal and lake beaches and salt marshes. Casual on east coast from Virginia south in fall and winter.

Far Eastern Curlew *Numenius madagascariensis*

L 17" (43 cm) Asian species, seen occasionally in spring and early summer on the Aleutians. Brown overall, with heavy streaking below; bill long and strongly downcurved. Wing linings (see page 136) are white with dark barring; note also that rump is same color as back.

Eurasian Curlew *Numenius arquata* *L 22" (56 cm)*

Shown in flight on page 136. Eurasian species, very rare visitor to east coast in fall and winter. Brown overall, heavily streaked below; bill long, strongly downcurved. Distinguished from Long-billed Curlew by white rump, white wing linings; from European subspecies of Whimbrel *(N. p. phaeopus)* by lack of dark stripes on head.

Eskimo Curlew

Bristle-thighed Curlew

Whimbrel

hudsonicus juvenile

hudsonicus

juvenile

Long-billed Curlew

Far Eastern Curlew

Willet *Catoptrophorus semipalmatus* L 15" (38 cm)
Large and plump; grayish-brown above, heavily mottled above and below; belly white. Bill is heavier than Greater Yellowlegs; legs are gray. Winter bird is uniformly pale gray above, whitish below. In flight (page 137), Willets show a striking black-and-white wing pattern. Nests in marshes, wet meadows, lakeshores; winters on coastal beaches and at Salton Sea, often in small, loose flocks. Fairly common; conspicuous and noisy; one call sounds like *pill-will-willet*.

♪ **Greater Yellowlegs** *Tringa melanoleuca* L 14" (36 cm)
Legs yellow to red-orange. Larger than Lesser Yellowlegs; bill longer, stouter, often slightly upturned. In breeding plumage, throat and breast are heavily streaked; sides and usually the belly are spotted and barred. In flight (page 137), shows pale spotting on inner primaries; white uppertail coverts are conspicuous on both yellowlegs species. Greater Yellowlegs' call is a loud, slightly descending series of three or more *tew* notes. Fairly common; nests on tundra, winters on coastal mud flats and marshes, inland lakeshores, in small, noisy flocks. Winter birds are best distinguished from Lesser Yellowlegs by overall size, bill size, and voice.

♪ **Lesser Yellowlegs** *Tringa flavipes* L 10¹/₂" (27 cm)
Legs yellow to orange. Smaller than Greater Yellowlegs; bill shorter, thinner, and straight. In breeding plumage, breast is finely streaked; sides and flanks show fine, short bars. In flight (page 137), shows all-dark primaries; white uppertail coverts are conspicuous in both yellowlegs species. Lesser Yellowlegs' call is higher, shorter than Greater Yellowlegs, usually one to three *tew* notes. Both species give a similar alarm call, a series of five to twenty loud *tew* notes. Common in east and midwest; uncommon in far west; nests on sheltered tundra or in open woodlands. Winters chiefly in South America; a few remain in U. S. Winter birds are best distinguished from Greater Yellowlegs by overall size, bill size, and voice.

Common Greenshank *Tringa nebularia* L 13¹/₂" (34 cm)
Eurasian species, regular migrant through Aleutians and Pribilofs. Similar to Greater Yellowlegs but less heavily streaked; legs are greenish. In flight (page 137), wings appear uniformly dark; white wedge extends up to middle of back. Typical flight call is a loud *chu-chu-chu*.

Spotted Redshank *Tringa erythropus* L 12¹/₂" (32 cm)
Eurasian species, rare spring and fall visitor to Aleutians and Pribilofs; casual on both coasts during migration and winter. Long bill droops at tip; base of lower mandible red. Breeding adult is black overall with white spots above; legs very dark red. Juvenile and winter adult paler, with orange or red-orange legs. In flight (page 137), shows white wedge extending up to middle of back; wing linings are white. Call, a loud rising *chu-weet*, similar to call of Semipalmated Plover.

114

Willet

breeding

winter

juvenile

Greater Yellowlegs

breeding

winter

juvenile

Lesser Yellowlegs

breeding

winter

juvenile

Spotted Redshank

juvenile

breeding

winter

Common Greenshank

juvenile

breeding

Solitary Sandpiper   *Tringa solitaria*   L 8¹/₂" (22 cm)

Dark brown above, heavily spotted with buffy-white. White below; lower throat, breast, and sides streaked with blackish-brown. White eye ring and shorter olive legs distinguish Solitary Sandpiper from Lesser Yellowlegs (preceding page). In flight (page 137), shows dark central tail feathers, white outer feathers barred with black. Underwing is dark. Fairly common at shallow backwaters, pools, small estuaries, even rain puddles. Often keeps wings raised briefly after alighting; on the ground, often bobs its tail. Generally seen singly or in small flocks. Calls include a shrill *peet-weet* and, in flight, a series of *weet* notes, higher pitched than calls of Spotted Sandpiper.

Spotted Sandpiper   *Actitis macularia*   L 7¹/₂" (19 cm)

Striking in breeding plumage, with barred upperparts, spotted underparts. Juvenile and winter birds lack spotting, resemble Common Sandpiper. In both species, white of underparts extends onto shoulder. Note Spotted's shorter tail; in flight, shorter white wing stripe, shorter white trailing edge. In juvenile and first-winter birds, barred wing coverts contrast with back. Both species fly with stiff, rapid, fluttering wingbeats. On the ground, both nod and teeter constantly. The Spotted Sandpiper is common and widespread, found at sheltered streams, ponds, lakes, or marshes. Generally seen singly; may form small flocks in migration. Most winter in Central and South America. Casual in winter to southern edge of breeding range. Calls include a shrill *peet-weet* and, in flight, a series of *weet* notes, lower pitched than calls of Solitary Sandpiper.

Common Sandpiper   *Actitis hypoleucos*   L 8" (20 cm)

Eurasian species, rare but regular migrant, usually in spring, through outer Aleutians, Pribilofs, St. Lawrence Island. Like Spotted Sandpiper, flies with stiff, rapid, fluttering wingbeats; on the ground, bobs and teeters constantly. Breeding adult is brown above with dark barring and streaking; white below; upper breast finely streaked. Juvenile and winter birds resemble Spotted Sandpiper. Note Common Sandpiper's longer tail, longer white wing stripe, longer white trailing edge. Call in flight is a shrill *twee-wee-wee*.

Terek Sandpiper   *Xenus cinereus*   L 9" (23 cm)

Eurasian species, casual migrant on Aleutians, St. Lawrence, and western Alaska coast. Note long, upturned bill, short orange-yellow legs. In breeding adult, dark-centered scapulars form two dark lines on back. In flight, shows distinctive wing pattern: dark leading edge, grayer median coverts, dark greater coverts, white-tipped secondaries. Flight call is a high, trilled *du du du du du*.

Solitary Sandpiper

breeding

juvenile

1st winter

juvenile

Spotted Sandpiper

juvenile

breeding

breeding

juvenile

Common Sandpiper

juvenile

breeding

Terek Sandpiper

breeding

juvenile

Wandering Tattler *Heteroscelus incanus* L 11" (28 cm)
Uniform dark gray above, with dark eye line; white eyebrow flecked with gray; bill is dark, legs dull yellow. In breeding plumage, underparts are heavily barred. Juvenile and winter birds have only a dark gray wash over breast and sides; juvenile has pale spots above. Closely resembles Gray-tailed Tattler; best distinguished by voice. Wandering Tattler's call is a rapid series of clear whistles, all on one pitch. Breeds chiefly on gravelly stream banks. Winters on rocky coasts. Teeters and bobs continuously as it feeds. Generally seen singly or in small groups. Casual inland during migration.

Gray-tailed Tattler *Heteroscelus brevipes* L 10" (25 cm)
Asian species, regular spring and fall migrant on Aleutians, Pribilofs, St. Lawrence Island; rare visitor to western Alaska mainland. Closely resembles Wandering Tattler; upperparts slightly paler; barring on underparts finer and less extensive; whitish eyebrows are more distinct and meet on forehead. Best distinction is voice. Gray-tailed Tattler's common call is a loud, ascending *too-weet,* similar to call of Lesser Golden-Plover. Formerly called Polynesian Tattler.

Green Sandpiper *Tringa ochropus* L 8 ³/₄" (22 cm)
Eurasian species, very rare spring migrant in outer Aleutians. Resembles Solitary Sandpiper (preceding page) in plumage, behavior, and calls. Note white rump and uppertail coverts, with less extensively barred tail; lacks solidly dark central tail feathers of Solitary Sandpiper; wing linings are darker. Similar Wood Sandpiper has more barring on tail, paler wing linings.

Wood Sandpiper *Tringa glareola* L 8" (20 cm)
Fairly common spring migrant on outer Aleutians; rare but regular on the Pribilofs and St. Lawrence Island; rare in fall. Dark upperparts heavily spotted with buff; prominent whitish eyebrow. In flight (page 137), distinguished from similar Green Sandpiper by paler wing linings, smaller white rump patch, more densely barred tail. Note also the proportionately shorter bill. Breeds in marshes and mud flats in northern Eurasia, occasionally on outer Aleutians. Common flight call is a loud, shrill three-note whistle similar to call of Long-billed Dowitcher.

Wandering Tattler

breeding

winter

juvenile

breeding

juvenile

Gray-tailed Tattler

juvenile

breeding

Solitary Sandpiper

Green Sandpiper

Green Sandpiper

breeding

juvenile

Wood Sandpiper

breeding

Phalaropes

These elegant shorebirds have partially lobed feet and dense, soft plumage. Feeding on the water, they sometimes spin like tops, stirring up larvae, crustaceans, and insects. Females, larger and more colorful than the males, do the courting; males incubate the eggs and care for the chicks.

♪ Wilson's Phalarope *Phalaropus tricolor* L 9¹/₄" (24 cm)

Long, thin bill; bold blackish stripe on face and neck. Female is richly colored; male duller, smaller. In winter plumage, upperparts are gray, underparts white. Briefly held juvenile plumage resembles winter adult but back is browner and mottled, breast buffy. In flight (page 137), white uppertail coverts, whitish tail, and absence of white wing stripe distinguish juvenile and winter birds from other phalaropes (page 139). Fairly common, Wilson's Phalarope is primarily an inland bird, nesting on the grassy borders of shallow lakes, marshes, reservoirs. Feeds as often on land as on water. Calls include a hoarse *wurk* and other low, croaking notes. Range is expanding in eastern Canada. Uncommon migrant on east coast.

♪ Red-necked Phalarope *Phalaropus lobatus*

L 7³/₄" (20 cm) Chestnut on front and sides of neck distinctive in breeding female, less prominent in male. Both have dark back with bright buff stripes along sides. Bill is shorter than in Wilson's Phalarope, thinner than in Red Phalarope. Winter birds are blue-gray above with whitish stripes; underparts and front of crown white; dark patch extends back from eye. In flight (page 139), shows white wing stripe, whitish stripes on back, dark central tail coverts. Juvenile resembles winter adult but is browner above, buffier below. Red-necked Phalaropes breed on arctic and subarctic tundra and winter at sea in the Southern Hemisphere. Over much of North America they are common only during migration; seen well offshore or in coastal areas, occasionally at inland lakes and marshes. Call, a high, sharp *whit,* often given in a twittering series. Formerly known as Northern Phalarope.

Red Phalarope *Phalaropus fulicaria* L 8¹/₂" (22 cm)

Bill shorter and much thicker than in other phalaropes; yellow with black tip in breeding adult, all-dark in juvenile and winter adult. Female in breeding plumage has black crown, white face, chestnut red underparts. Male is duller, smaller. Briefly held juvenile plumage resembles male but is much paler. Winter birds distinguished by bill shape and uniformly pale gray back. In flight (page 139), shows white wing stripe and dark central tail coverts. Uncommon; breeds on arctic shores, islands; winters at sea. Seen occasionally on both coasts during migration; rarely on inland lakes, ponds.

Wilson's Phalarope

juvenile

winter

breeding ♀

breeding ♂

Red-necked Phalarope

breeding ♀

winter

juvenile

breeding ♂

Red Phalarope

winter

breeding ♂

juvenile

breeding ♀

Dowitchers

Medium-size, chunky, dark shorebirds with long, straight bills and distinct pale eyebrows. Feeding in mud or shallow water, they probe with a rapid jabbing motion. Dowitchers in flight (page 137) show a white wedge from barred tail to middle of back. Distinguishing the two species is easiest with juveniles, difficult with breeding adults, and usually impossible in winter except by voice.

♪ Short-billed Dowitcher *Limnodromus griseus*

L 11" (28 cm) Call is a mellow *tu tu tu,* repeated in a rapid series as an alarm call. Central tail feathers have white or, on some breeding birds, reddish bars wider than or the same width as the black bars, making the tail look paler than tail of Long-billed Dowitcher. In breeding plumage the three subspecies vary widely, with the more widespread *L.g. hendersoni* most closely resembling Long-billed Dowitcher. *L.g. caurinus* breeds on the west coast; *hendersoni* in western and central Canada; *griseus* in the northeast. Most birds show some white on belly, especially *griseus,* which also may have heavily spotted breast and densely barred flanks. In *hendersoni,* which may be entirely reddish below, foreneck is much less heavily spotted than in Longbills; sides of breast generally have little or no barring. Juvenile is brighter above, redder below than juvenile Longbill; back and scapular feathers have broad reddish-buff edges; tertials are similar, with reddish-buff internal markings, giving a tiger-striped appearance. Winter birds are gray above, white below, with gray breast. Common in migration along the Pacific coast *(caurinus),* along the Atlantic coast *(griseus),* and from the eastern plains east *(hendersoni).* Over much of North America, migration begins earlier in fall than Long-billed Dowitcher, generally in late June or early July. Juveniles migrate later than adults and are most common in August and September.

♪ Long-billed Dowitcher *Limnodromus scolopaceus*

L 11½" (29 cm) Call is a sharp, high-pitched *keek,* given singly or in a short, rapid series. Adult female's bill may be very long, up to twice the length of her head. In both sexes, central tail feathers generally have white or reddish bars narrower than the black bars, making the tail look dark. Breeding adult is entirely reddish below; foreneck heavily spotted; sides generally barred. Juvenile is darker above, grayer below, than juvenile Shortbill; back and scapular feathers have thin reddish edges; tertials are usually plain, with narrow reddish edges and, on some birds, two pale spots at the tips. Winter birds are gray above, white below, with gray breast. Common in migration in the west and midwest; less common in the east in fall, rare in spring. Migration generally begins later in fall than Short-billed Dowitcher, usually in late July or early August. Juveniles migrate later than adults, are rare before mid-September.

juvenile

winter

winter

griseus breeding

caurinus breeding

hendersoni breeding

**Short-billed
Dowitcher**

winter

breeding

juvenile

**Long-billed
Dowitcher**

breeding

Stilt Sandpiper *Calidris himantopus* L 8¹/₂" (22 cm)

In breeding plumage, striped crown, chestnut stripes on sides of head; slender, slightly downcurved bill, drooped at the tip in some birds; and heavily barred underparts distinguish this species from dowitchers (preceding page) and Lesser Yellowlegs (page 114). Winter adult grayer above, whiter below; lacks strong markings. Juvenile is like winter adult but has streaked crown, more sharply patterned upperparts, and more prominent eyebrow; often shows some chestnut on sides of face and buffy wash on breast. Juvenile and winter adult resemble Curlew Sandpiper (page 128), but note straighter bill, yellow-green legs, and, in flight (page 137), lack of prominent wing stripe, slightly different tail pattern. Sometimes seen feeding with dowitchers; feeding styles are similar. Breeds on tundra. Rare in spring on east coast; common in fall. Rare but regular migrant on west coast. Small numbers often winter at the Salton Sea.

Common Snipe *Gallinago gallinago* L 10¹/₂" (27 cm)

Stocky, with short legs, long bill. Boldly patterned above and below, with white belly; distinctive striped head and rusty tail. Fairly solitary and secretive, usually seen only when flushed. Takeoff is explosive; flight rapid and zigzagging on pointed wings, accompanied by a distinctive alarm call, a harsh *skipe*. Fairly common. On breeding grounds in marshes and bogs, often perches in the open. During erratic, swooping display flight, vibrating tail feathers make an eerie fluttering sound. Casual in winter in southern part of breeding range. Formerly called Wilson's Snipe.

American Woodcock *Scolopax minor* L 11" (28 cm)

Very chunky, short-necked and short-legged, with long bill, barred crown, large eyes set far back in large head. Wings rounded. Nocturnal, solitary, and secretive; seldom seen until flushed. Flies up abruptly, outer primaries making a twittering sound. Call is a nasal *peent,* heard mostly in spring but also at other times of year, most often on warm winter nights at dusk and dawn. In elaborate flight display, male circles high in the night sky giving a constant twittering call, then plummets to earth in a series of zigzags, wings whistling. Woodcocks are fairly common in moist woodlands and thickets. During mild winters, a few birds are found in the breeding range.

Stilt
Sandpiper

juvenile

winter

molting fall

breeding

Common
Snipe

American
Woodcock

♪ Ruddy Turnstone *Arenaria interpres* L 9½" (24 cm)

Striking black-and-white head and bib, black and chestnut back, and orange legs mark this stout bird in breeding plumage. Female is duller than male. Bib pattern and orange leg color are retained in winter plumage. Juvenile resembles winter adult but back has a scaly appearance. In flight, complex pattern on back and wings identifies both turnstone species; look for Ruddy's reddish coloring and bib. Distinctive call, a low-pitched, guttural rattle. Nests on coastal tundra. Turnstones use their slender bills to flip aside shells and pebbles in search of food.

♪ Black Turnstone *Arenaria melanocephala* L 9¼" (24 cm)

Black head, breast, and back in breeding plumage are marked by white eyebrow and lore spot, white mottling on sides of neck and breast. Legs dark reddish-brown. Juvenile and winter adult are slate gray, lack lore spot and mottling. Calls include a guttural rattle, higher pitched than call of Ruddy Turnstone. Breeds in coastal Alaska. Winters on rocky coasts.

Surfbird *Aphriza virgata* L 10" (25 cm)

Base of short, stout bill is yellow; legs yellowish-green. Breeding adult's head and underparts are heavily streaked and spotted with dusky-black; upperparts edged with white and chestnut; scapulars mostly rufous. Winter adults have solid dark gray head and breast. Juvenile's head and breast are flecked with white; back appears scaly. Black band at end of white tail and rump conspicuous in flight. Nests on mountain tundra; winters along rocky beaches and reefs.

Rock Sandpiper *Calidris ptilocnemis* L 9" (23 cm)

Black patch on lower breast in breeding plumage; compare with belly patch of Dunlin (next page). Crown and back are chestnut, streaked with black. Breeding birds on the Pribilofs have paler chestnut above and less black below. Long, slender bill, slightly downcurved; base is greenish-yellow. Winter birds distinguished from Surfbird by longer bill, smaller size, and more patterned upperparts and breast. In flight (page 139), shows white wing stripe and all-dark tail. Nests on tundra; winters on rocky shores, often with Black Turnstones and Surfbirds.

Purple Sandpiper *Calidris maritima* L 9" (23 cm)

Breeding adult has tawny-buff crown, streaked with black; back is edged with white and tawny-buff; breast and flanks spotted with blackish-brown. Long, slender bill, slightly downcurved; base is orange-yellow. Winter adult is dark gray-brown above and on breast; flanks are streaked and spotted with brownish-gray. In flight (page 139), shows white wing stripe and all-dark tail. Winters on rocky coasts, often with Ruddy Turnstones and Sanderlings.

juvenile

winter

Ruddy Turnstone

breeding ♂

Black Turnstone

winter

breeding

winter

winter

juvenile

Surfbird

breeding

Rock Sandpiper

winter

juvenile

Pribilofs breeding

breeding

juvenile

winter

breeding

Purple Sandpiper

Red Knot *Calidris canutus* *L 10¹/₂" (27 cm)*
One of the largest beach sandpipers, chunky and short-legged. Breeding adult is dappled gray and brown above, with reddish head and breast. In winter, back is pale gray; underparts white. Distinguished from dowitchers (page 122) by shorter bill, grayer back, paler head, and, in flight (page 137), by whitish rump finely barred with gray. Juveniles similar to winter adults, but have buffy wash on breast, scaly-looking upperparts. Feeds in huge flocks, often with dowitchers, along sandy beaches and on mud flats.

Great Knot *Calidris tenuirostris* *L 11" (28 cm)*
Asian species, casual spring migrant in western Alaska. Larger than Red Knot, with longer bill and less rufous on back, none on head and breast. Compare also with Surfbird (preceding page). In breeding plumage, shows black breast and bold black flank pattern. Juvenile has buffy wash and fine spots on breast; dark back feathers edged with rust. Resembles Red Knot in flight but wing bar is much less bold.

♪ **Dunlin** *Calidris alpina* *L 8¹/₂" (22 cm)*
Distinctive breeding plumage: reddish back; whitish, finely streaked underparts with conspicuous black belly patch; Rock Sandpiper (preceding page) has similar patch, but on chest. Note sturdy bill, curved at tip. Short-necked; appears hunchbacked. In flight (page 139), shows dark center on rump. In winter plumage, upperparts are grayish-brown; breast faintly streaked; belly white. Juveniles are rusty above, spotted below. Call, a harsh, reedy *kree*.

♪ **Sanderling** *Calidris alba* *L 8" (20 cm)*
Palest sandpiper of winter: pale gray above; white below; bill and legs black. Prominent white wing stripe shows in flight (page 139). In breeding plumage, head, mantle, and breast are rusty. Feeds on sandy beaches, sprinting just out of surf's reach to snatch up mollusks and crustaceans exposed by the retreating waves. Juveniles are similar to winter adults, but with more black and tawny-buff on upperparts. Call is a sharp *kip*, often given in a series.

Curlew Sandpiper *Calidris ferruginea* *L 8¹/₂" (22 cm)*
Eurasian species, casual migrant throughout North America, chiefly on Atlantic coast. Long, downcurved bill has whitish area at base. In breeding plumage, rich chestnut underparts and shoulders and mottled chestnut back are distinctive. Female is paler than male. Many sightings are of birds molting to winter plumage, showing grayer upperparts and patchy white underparts. Winter plumage mostly gray; compare with Dunlin. Curlew Sandpiper's bill is evenly curved, not drooped at tip. White rump is conspicuous in flight (page 137). Compare also with Stilt Sandpiper (page 124). Call is a soft, rippling *chirrup*. Very rare breeder in Alaska.

winter

Red Knot

juvenile

breeding

breeding

juvenile

Great Knot

winter

breeding

juvenile

Dunlin

juvenile

winter

breeding

Sanderling

molting fall adult

winter

juvenile

breeding

Curlew Sandpiper

Semipalmated Sandpiper *Calidris pusilla* L 6¹/₄″ (16 cm)

Black legs; tubular-looking, straight bill. Often confused with Western Sandpiper. In breeding birds, note that Semipalmated lacks spotting on flanks and rufous on scapular feathers; shows only a tinge of rufous on crown and ear patch. Juveniles are distinguished by stronger eyebrow, darker crown, and more uniform upperparts. Winter adults of these two species are almost identical (see also page 139), but Semipalmated is plumper than Western; bill is shorter. Call is a short *churk*. Abundant in wet habitats. A common migrant inland and on the east coast. Rare migrant in the west; very rare in winter in south Florida.

Western Sandpiper *Calidris mauri* L 6¹/₂″ (17 cm)

Black legs; tapered bill, sometimes slightly drooped at tip. Often confused with Semipalmated Sandpiper. In breeding plumage, Western has spotting along sides and rufous at base of scapulars; shows a bright rufous wash on crown and ear patch. Juvenile is distinguished by less prominent eyebrow, paler crown, and brighter rufous edges on back. Winter adult is almost identical to Semipalmated Sandpiper (see also page 139). Common in wet habitats. Call is a high, raspy *jeet*.

Least Sandpiper *Calidris minutilla* L 6″ (15 cm)

Smallest regularly occurring sandpiper. In all plumages, note short, thin bill, slightly downcurved and pale stripe on each side of brown back. In winter plumage (see also page 139), has a prominent brown breast band. Juvenile has strong buffy wash across breast. Legs are yellowish, but in poor light or when smeared with mud they appear dark. Very common in wet habitats. Call note, a shrill, high *kreeep*, unlike similar Temminck's Stint's dry rattle.

White-rumped Sandpiper *Calidris fuscicollis*

L 7¹/₂″ (19 cm) Long wings extend beyond tail in standing bird. Similar to Baird's Sandpiper but grayer overall; in breeding plumage, streaking extends to flanks. Note conspicuous white rump (see also page 139). Juvenile shows rusty edges on crown and back. Call note, a high-pitched, insectlike *jeet*. Fairly common; feeds in marshes and on mud flats.

Baird's Sandpiper *Calidris bairdii* L 7¹/₂″ (19 cm)

Long wings extend past tail in standing bird. Buff-brown above and across breast. Pale edgings on juvenile's back give a scaly appearance (see also page 139). Distinguished from Least Sandpiper by larger size, longer bill. Call is a low, raspy *kreeep*. Uncommon; found on upper beaches and inland on lakeshores, wet fields. Migration is through center of continent. Uncommon migrant, usually in juvenile plumage, on both coasts in fall.

Semipalmated Sandpiper

breeding

juvenile

winter

Western Sandpiper

breeding

winter

juvenile

Least Sandpiper

winter

breeding

juvenile

White-rumped Sandpiper

molting adult

juvenile

breeding

Baird's Sandpiper

juvenile

breeding

Long-toed Stint *Calidris subminuta* *L 6″ (15 cm)*
Asian species, rare migrant on St. Lawrence Island and the Pribilofs; can be fairly common on outer Aleutians. Distinguished in all plumages from the similar Least Sandpiper (preceding page) by dark forehead, more prominent eyebrow broadening behind eye; breeding adult lacks distinct dark necklace across breast.

Little Stint *Calidris minuta* *L 6″ (15 cm)*
Eurasian species, very rare on east coast and western Alaska coast in spring and fall. Breeding birds are brightly fringed with rufous above; throat and underparts are white, with bold spotting on sides of breast. Redder above than similar Western and Semipalmated Sandpipers (page 130). Compare also with Rufous-necked Stints, especially the paler birds. Juveniles of these two species are almost identical.

♪ Temminck's Stint *Calidris temminckii* *L 6¼″ (16 cm)*
Eurasian species, rare spring and fall migrant in western Alaska, Pribilofs, Aleutians, St. Lawrence Island. White outer tail feathers distinctive in all plumages. Breeding adult resembles the larger Baird's Sandpiper (preceding page), but generally has dull yellow or greenish-yellow legs. In juvenile, feathers of upperparts have dark subterminal edges and buffy fringe. Call is a repeated dry rattle, unlike similar Least Sandpiper's shrill call.

Rufous-necked Stint *Calidris ruficollis* *L 6¼″ (16 cm)*
Asian species, very rare migrant on both coasts; rare but regular on Aleutians. Breeding range in Alaska is conjectural. Rufous throat and upper breast of some breeding adults may be pale and indistinct, increasing their resemblance to Little Stint. Juveniles of the two species are almost identical.

Spoonbill Sandpiper *Eurynorhynchus pygmeus*
L 6″ (15 cm) Asian species, very rare migrant in British Columbia, Aleutians, and northern Alaska. In breeding plumage, may be mistaken for Rufous-necked Stint. Bill shape is distinctive but requires a close view.

Broad-billed Sandpiper *Limicola falcinellus*
L 7″ (18 cm) Eurasian species, very rare fall migrant on the Aleutians. All sightings so far have been of juveniles. Plump body, short legs, and long bill form a distinctive profile. Note that upper mandible droops at tip. Unusual marking above each eye looks like a forked eyebrow. In all plumages, head pattern and long bill suggest Common Snipe (page 124).

Long-toed Stint

juvenile

breeding

Little Stint

breeding

juvenile

Temminck's Stint

juvenile

breeding

juvenile

breeding

breeding

Rufous-necked Stint

Spoonbill Sandpiper

juvenile

breeding

breeding

Broad-billed Sandpiper

juvenile

Sharp-tailed Sandpiper *Calidris acuminata*

L 8¹/₂″ (22 cm) A Siberian bird, casual spring and fairly common fall migrant in western Alaska; scarce but regular in fall migration along entire Pacific coast. Very rare migrant across our continent. Most sightings are juveniles, distinguished from juvenile Pectoral Sandpiper by white eyebrow that broadens behind the eye; bright buffy breast lightly streaked on upper breast and sides; streaked undertail coverts; and brighter rufous cap and edging on upperparts (see also page 139). Adult in breeding plumage is similar to juvenile, but more spotted below. Call is a mellow, two-note whistle.

♪ Pectoral Sandpiper *Calidris melanotos* *L 8³/₄″ (22 cm)*

Prominent streaking on breast, darker in male, contrasts sharply with clear white belly. Juvenile has buffy wash on streaked breast. Compare especially with juvenile Sharp-tailed Sandpiper (see also page 139). Seen chiefly during migration, the Pectoral often feeds in wet meadows, marshes, pond edges. More common in east and interior than on west coast, where it occurs mainly in fall. Call is a rich, low *churk*.

Ruff *Philomachus pugnax* *L ♂ 12″ (31 cm); ♀ 10″ (25 cm)*

Old World species, casual migrant throughout North America but more often on coasts. Breeding males are unmistakable in their dramatic ruffs. Colors vary from black to red to white. Female, called a Reeve, lacks ruff, is smaller, has variable amount of black below. Both sexes have plump body, small head, white underwings. Leg color varies. Juvenile is buffy below, has prominently fringed feathers above. In flight (page 139), U-shaped white band on rump is distinctive in all plumages. Occasionally breeds in Alaska; may also breed elsewhere in North America.

Upland Sandpiper *Bartramia longicauda* *L 12″ (31 cm)*

Small head, with large, dark, prominent eyes; long, thin neck, long tail, long wings. Legs yellow. Prefers upland fields, where often only its head and neck are visible above the grass. Also perches on posts and stumps. In flight (page 137), blackish primaries contrast strikingly with mottled brown upperparts. Fairly common except in eastern range, where the species is declining. Casual on west coast in migration. Call is a rolling *pulip pulip*. Formerly called Upland Plover.

Buff-breasted Sandpiper *Tryngites subruficollis*

L 8¹/₄″ (21 cm) Face, throat, and breast are rich buff, much paler on belly and undertail coverts. In flight, in all plumages, shows white underwings. In mixed flocks of shorebirds, its longer, thinner neck, small head, and longer legs are distinctive. Prefers shortgrass fields, wet rice fields. Seen chiefly in migration in interior of continent. In fall, rare on the west coast, uncommon in the east; most sightings on coasts are of juveniles (see also page 137).

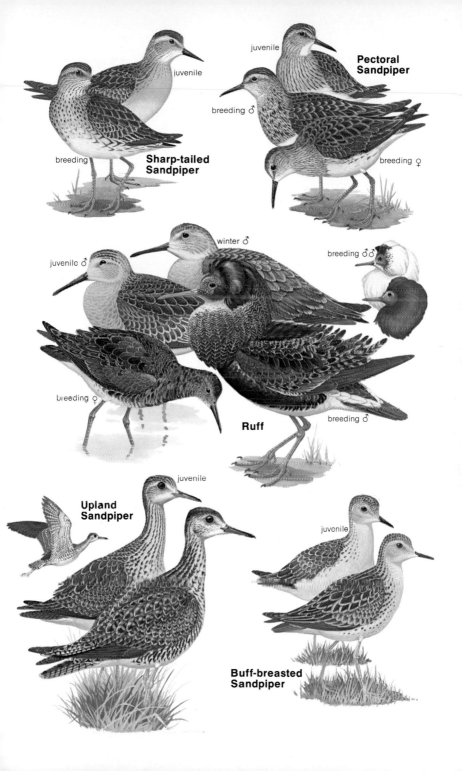

Sharp-tailed Sandpiper

juvenile

breeding

Sharp-tailed Sandpiper

Pectoral Sandpiper

juvenile

breeding ♂

Pectoral Sandpiper

breeding ♀

juvenile ♂

winter ♂

breeding ♂♂

breeding ♀

Ruff

breeding ♂

Upland Sandpiper

juvenile

juvenile

Buff-breasted Sandpiper

Shorebirds in Flight

Marbled Godwit
winter

Bar-tailed Godwit
baueri winter

Bar-tailed Godwit
lapponica winter

Hudsonian Godwit
winter

Black-tailed Godwit
winter

Far Eastern Curlew

Long-billed Curlew

Eurasian Curlew
juvenile

phaeopus juvenile

variegatus

hudsonicus

Whimbrel

Bristle-thighed Curlew

Eskimo Curlew

Willet
winter

Greater Yellowlegs
winter

Lesser Yellowlegs
winter

Green Sandpiper
juvenile

Wood Sandpiper
juvenile

Solitary Sandpiper
juvenile

Spotted Redshank
winter

Common Greenshank
juvenile

Short-billed Dowitcher
winter

Red Knot
winter

Curlew Sandpiper
juvenile

Stilt Sandpiper
juvenile

Wilson's Phalarope
juvenile

Upland Sandpiper

Buff-breasted Sandpiper
juvenile

Shorebirds in Flight

Snowy Plover ♀

Piping Plover winter

Common Ringed Plover juvenile

Mongolian Plover winter

Semipalmated Plover juvenile

Wilson's Plover ♀

Killdeer

Mountain Plover winter

Eurasian Dotterel juvenile

fulva juvenile

Lesser Golden-Plover

dominica juvenile

Greater Golden-Plover juvenile

Black-bellied Plover juvenile

Rock Sandpiper winter

Purple Sandpiper winter

Dunlin winter

Sanderling winter

Red Phalarope winter

Red-necked Phalarope winter

Western Sandpiper winter

Semipalmated Sandpiper winter

Least Sandpiper winter

Temminck's Stint juvenile

Baird's Sandpiper juvenile

White-rumped Sandpiper juvenile

Pectoral Sandpiper juvenile

Sharp-tailed Sandpiper juvenile

Ruff juvenile ♀

Skuas, Jaegers, Gulls,Terns (Family Laridae)

Large seabirds with strong wings, powerful flight. Some species are highly pelagic, spending most of their time over the open sea. Others are seen in coastal waters, and some frequent inland waters.

Great Skua *Catharacta skua* L 23" (58 cm) W 55" (140 cm)

Large, heavy, and barrel-chested; wings broader and more rounded than jaegers; tail shorter, broader. Both skua species show a distinctly hunchbacked appearance in flight and a large, conspicuous white bar at base of primaries; bill is heavier than in jaegers (next page). Great Skua is distinguished from South Polar Skua by overall reddish or ginger brown color and heavy streaking on back, wing coverts, and much of underparts; sometimes shows dark brown cap. Immature shows less streaking, especially on underparts. Uncommon; breeds in Iceland and northern Europe; winters in North Atlantic. Seen well offshore from November to April; very rare in summer off New England. Strong, powerful fliers, skuas pursue gulls and other seabirds and rob them of their prey.

South Polar Skua *Catharacta maccormicki*

L 21" (53 cm) W 52" (132 cm)   Large, heavy, and barrel-chested; wings broader and more rounded than jaegers (next page); tail shorter, broader. Slightly smaller overall than Great Skua; both species show a distinctly hunchbacked appearance in flight, a bold white bar at base of primaries, and a heavier bill than in jaegers. In all ages, South Polar Skuas show uniform back and wing color. In light-phase birds, contrastingly pale nape is distinctive. South Polar Skua lacks reddish tones and streaking on upperparts of Great Skua. Dark phase is uniformly blackish-brown across mantle, with golden hackles on nape; distinguished from subadult Pomarine Jaeger by larger size, broader and more rounded wings, more distinct white wing bar. Light phase has grayish head, nape, and underparts. Immatures of both color phases are darker than light-phase adults, ranging from dark brown to dark gray. In the field, birds under two years of age are generally indistinguishable from juveniles; birds over two years old are generally indistinguishable from full adults. The South Polar Skua breeds in the Antarctic; winters (our summer) in North Atlantic and North Pacific, usually from May to early November. Most numerous in spring and fall off west coast, in spring off east coast. Rare in Alaska. Very rare in Gulf of Mexico. Generally stays well offshore; seen casually from shore in the west.

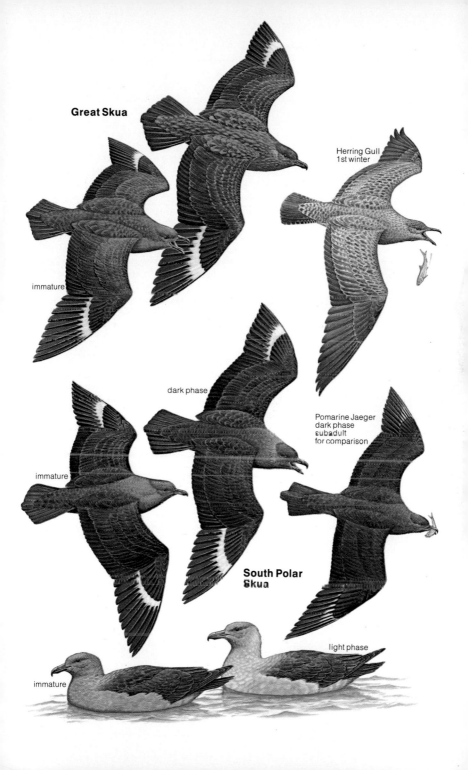

Great Skua

Herring Gull
1st winter

immature

dark phase

Pomarine Jaeger
dark phase
subadult
for comparison

immature

**South Polar
Skua**

immature

light phase

Jaegers

Predatory seabirds with strongly hooked bill and long, pointed, angled wings. Adult plumage and long central tail feathers take three or four years to develop. Identification of subadults is extremely difficult. Molt occurs after the fall migration.

Pomarine Jaeger *Stercorarius pomarinus*
L 21" (53 cm) W 48" (122 cm) Adult's tail streamers, twisted at ends, form long dark blobs when seen from side. Body bulkier, bill larger, than Parasitic Jaeger; compare also with South Polar Skua (preceding page). Wingbeats are deep and regular, slower than Parasitic. On light-phase bird, breast band is heavier than on other jaegers. May show distinctive second pale underwing patch at base of primary coverts; tail is broader than Parasitic Jaeger. Juvenile plumage varies: light phase (rare), or barred (shown), or dark phase; streamers are very short, squared-off, not yet twisted. Barred phase has more prominent barring below and on rump than Parasitic. In all ages, white at base of primaries is more extensive than in other jaegers. Breeds on low, swampy tundra, winters at sea; rarely seen from east coast, more commonly from west. Casual inland during fall migration.

Parasitic Jaeger *Stercorarius parasiticus*
L 19" (48 cm) W 42" (107 cm) Smaller, more slender than Pomarine Jaeger; wing stroke faster. Tail streamers pointed and shorter, white on wing less prominent than in Pomarine. Juvenile varies from light to dark, much like Pomarine. In all ages, note less white on upperwings, narrower tail. On light-phase juvenile, barring below is comparatively muted. Rufous-brown tint unique to Parasitic juvenile. Immature loses barring gradually with age. Fairly common; breeds on low tundra, stony areas. During fall migration seen casually on east coast, rarely inland, most often on west coast.

Long-tailed Jaeger *Stercorarius longicaudus*
L 22" (56 cm) W 40" (102 cm) Most lightly built jaeger, with proportionately long tail in all ages. Adult's very long, pointed tail streamers often flutter in flight. Flight is more graceful, tern-like. In all plumages, note distinctive contrast between grayish mantle and darker flight feathers. Adult lacks white on underwings; juvenile does have white there but is grayer overall than Parasitic Jaeger, with pale belly. In all ages, white at base of primaries is less extensive than in Parasitic. Juvenile tail streamers are more rounded than Parasitic; in older immatures they become pointed. Common in dry, upland-tundra breeding area; migration routes far offshore; migrating birds uncommon off west coast, very rare inland and off east and Gulf coasts.

Pomarine Jaeger

dark phase breeding

light phase breeding

light phase subadult

barred phase juvenile

Parasitic Jaeger

light phase breeding

dark phase breeding

light phase juvenile

dark phase juvenile

light phase subadult

Long-tailed Jaeger

light phase juvenile

dark phase juvenile

breeding

subadult

Gulls

A large, widespread group; often called "seagulls," but many species nest inland. Gulls take two, three, or four years to reach their first breeding plumage. Many are highly variable and hard to identify in subadult plumage. Most have a complete molt in fall and only a partial molt in spring.

Heermann's Gull *Larus heermanni*

L 19" (48 cm) W 51" (130 cm) Three-year gull. Adult distinctive with white head, streaked gray-brown in winter; red bill; dark gray body; black tail with white terminal band; white trailing edge on wings. Second-winter bird is browner, bill two-toned, tail band buff. First-winter bird has dark brown body, lacks contrasting tail tip and trailing edge on wing. Wings are long, flight buoyant. Common postbreeding visitor along west coast; uncommon at Salton Sea.

Franklin's Gull *Larus pipixcan* *L 14¹/₂" (37 cm) W 36" (91 cm)*

Two-year gull. In breeding plumage has black hood, white underparts variably tinged with pink, slate gray wings with white bar and black-and-white tips on primaries. Distinguished from Laughing Gull by white bar and large white tips on primaries; less extensive dark on underside of primaries; gray central tail feathers; and broader white eye crescents. All winter plumages have a dark half-hood, more extensive than in any winter Laughing Gull. First-summer bird is like adult but lacks white bar in primaries, hood is incomplete, bill and legs black. First-winter bird resembles immature Laughing Gull; note white outer tail feathers, half-hood, broader eye crescents (page 160). Juvenile is like first-winter bird but back is brown, head and underparts darker. In all ages, distinguished from Laughing Gull by smaller size, smaller bill with less prominent hook, rounder forehead, shorter legs and shorter wings, giving a stocky look when standing, and by more graceful flight. Casual migrant along both coasts; very rare in winter along Gulf coast and in southern California.

Laughing Gull *Larus atricilla* *L 16¹/₂" (42 cm) W 40" (102 cm)*

Three-year gull. Adult in breeding plumage has black hood, white underparts, slate gray wings with black outer primaries. In winter, shows light gray wash on nape; compare to dark half-hood of Franklin's Gull. Second-summer bird has partial hood, some spotting on tip of tail. Second-winter bird (page 160) is similar but has gray wash on sides of breast, lacks hood. First-winter bird has extensively gray sides, complete tail band, pale gray wash on nape, slate gray back, dark brown wings; compare with first-winter Franklin's Gull. Juvenile is like first-winter bird but brown on head and body. Common along coasts; casual inland throughout the east and midwest; rare in most of the west.

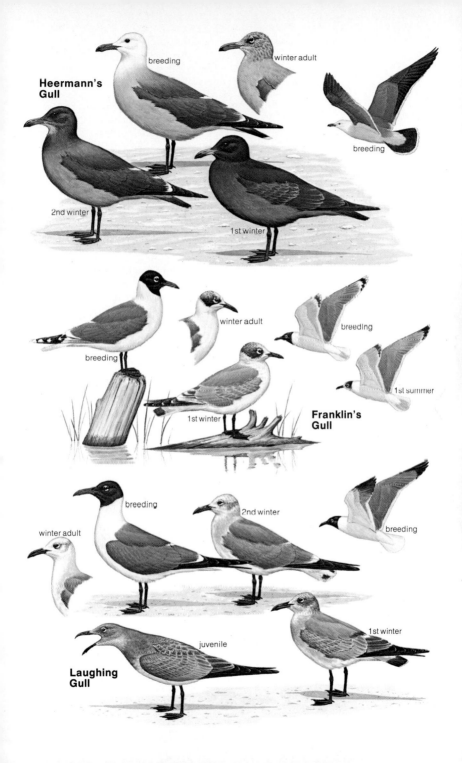

Heermann's Gull

breeding

winter adult

breeding

2nd winter

1st winter

breeding

winter adult

1st winter

Franklin's Gull

1st summer

winter adult

breeding

2nd winter

breeding

juvenile

1st winter

Laughing Gull

Bonaparte's Gull *Larus philadelphia*
L 13¹/₂" (34 cm) W 33" (84 cm) Two-year gull. Breeding adult has black hood, black bill, gray mantle with black wing tips that are pale on underside; white underparts, red legs. In winter, head is white with dark smudge behind eye. In flight, shows white wedge on wing. First-summer bird has partial hood; wings and tail are like first-winter. First-winter bird has a dark brown carpal bar on leading edge of wing, dark band on secondaries, black tail band (see also page 160); compare with immature Black-legged Kittiwake (page 158). Flight is buoyant, wingbeats rapid. Querulous, chattering call is distinctive. Uncommon inland migrant, common on the Great Lakes.

Common Black-headed Gull *Larus ridibundus*
L 16" (41 cm) W 40" (102 cm) Two-year gull. Breeding adult has dark brown hood; red bill and legs; mantle slightly paler gray than Bonaparte's Gull; black wing tips; white underparts. Head is white in winter, with dark spot behind eye. First-summer bird has incomplete hood; wings and tail are like first-winter. In flight, shows white wedge on wing; compare with Bonaparte's. Juvenile and first-winter birds have two-toned bill, pale legs, dark tail band, dark brown carpal bar (see page 160). Distinguished from Bonaparte's at all ages by larger size, bill color, darker underside of primaries. Recent colonizer from Europe, casual breeder in eastern Canada. Uncommon in winter on east coast, casual elsewhere in North America.

Little Gull *Larus minutus* *L 11" (28 cm) W 24" (61 cm)*
Two-year gull. Breeding adult has black hood, black bill, pale gray mantle, white wing tips, white underparts, red feet. Winter adult has dusky cap, dark spot behind eye. Wings are uniformly pale gray above, dark gray to black below, with white trailing edge. Second-winter bird is like adult but underwing pattern is incomplete; shows some black in primaries (see page 160). First-summer bird has partial hood, some brown in primaries and coverts, partial tail band. First-winter is like Bonaparte's but primaries are blackish above, lack white wedge; wing has strong blackish W pattern; crown shows more black. In all plumages, note short, rounded wings. An Old World species, now breeding around Great Lakes. Uncommon winter visitor and migrant on east coast, casual elsewhere in U.S.

Ross' Gull *Rhodostethia rosea* *L 13¹/₂" (34 cm) W 33" (84 cm)*
Old World arctic species, recently found breeding at three sites in northern Canada and Greenland. Common fall migrant along northern coast of Alaska; presumably winters at sea in the Arctic. Two-year gull. Adults variably pale pink to bright pink below; upperwing pale gray; underwing pale to dark gray. Black collar in summer; collar partial or absent in winter. First-winter bird has black at tip of tail, dark spot behind eye; in flight, shows strong black W pattern like Little Gull. In all plumages, note long, pointed wings; long, wedge-shaped tail; and broad, white trailing edge to wings.

Bonaparte's Gull

brooding

winter adult

1st winter

winter adult

Common Black-headed Gull

breeding

1st summer

winter adult

1st winter

winter adult

Little Gull

breeding

1st winter

breeding

winter adult

Ross' Gull

winter adult

1st winter

breeding

Ring-billed Gull *Larus delawarensis*

L 17¹/₂" (45 cm) W 48" (122 cm) Three-year gull. Typical of three-year gulls, acquires a new and different plumage in each of the first three winters; summer plumage varies only slightly from winter. Adult has pale gray mantle; white head and under-parts; yellow bill with black subterminal ring; pale eyes; yellowish legs; black primaries tipped with two white spots. Head streaked with brown in winter. Second-winter birds are like winter adult but bill has broader band, black of primaries is more extensive, tail has some brown terminal spots. First-winter bird has gray back, brown wings with dark blackish-brown primaries, brown-streaked head and nape; underparts mostly white, with brown spots and scalloping on breast and throat; tail has medium-wide brown band and extensive mottling above band; uppertail and undertail coverts are lightly barred; secondary coverts medium gray; wing linings mostly white, with some barring (see page 160). Distinguished from first-winter Mew Gull by white underparts spotted on breast and throat, tail pattern, darker primaries, heavier bill, paler back. Juvenile plumage is like first-winter but back is brown, spotting below more extensive, bill has more black. On east coast, compare with European form of Mew Gull. Common and widespread; winters casually outside mapped range.

Mew Gull *Larus canus* *L 16" (41 cm) W 43" (109 cm)*

Three-year gull. Adult has white head, heavily washed with brown in winter; dark gray mantle; primaries tipped with black and white; thin, unmarked yellow bill; large dark eye. Second-winter bird is like adult but bill is two-toned, brown on primaries more extensive; first primary has large white spot; spotty tail band. First-winter birds are heavily washed with brown below, almost solid brown on belly; spotted with white on breast. The head and nape are washed with soft brown; mantle dark gray; primaries light brown with pale edges. The tail is almost entirely brown, with heavily barred uppertail and undertail coverts; wing lining evenly pale brown (see page 160). Juvenile is like first-winter, but dark brown on the back and head, darker below. The Siberian form (not shown) recorded in the Aleutians is like American birds except that male is almost as large as Ring-billed Gull. European form has been seen on the east coast in winter. It is like American birds in second-winter and adult plumage but more like Ring-billed Gull in first-winter; note the mostly white tail with dark subterminal band, unbarred white uppertail and undertail coverts, darker gray back, pale brown secondary coverts, white wing linings mottled with brown. Winter adults sometimes have a faint dusky subterminal ring on the bill. All Mew Gulls are comparatively smaller than Ring-billed Gulls, with rounder heads, thinner bills, larger eyes. Adults in flight show much more white in primaries. Rare inland in winter.

Ring-billed Gull

winter adult

breeding

2nd winter

juvenile

1st winter

breeding

Mew Gull

breeding

winter adult

breeding

2nd winter

European 1st winter

juvenile

1st winter

Herring Gull *Larus argentatus* L 25" (64 cm) W 58" (147 cm)
Highly variable four-year gull. Adult has pale gray mantle;
white head, streaked with brown in winter; white underparts;
primaries black toward the tips; legs and feet pink; bill yellow
with red spot. Third-winter plumage is like adult but with
black smudge on bill, some brown on body. Second-winter bird
has gray back, brown wings, pale eye, two-toned bill; gray back
is distinctly paler than Lesser Black-backed and Western
Gulls (pages 154, 156), slightly paler than California Gull.

First-winter bird is brown overall, with dark brownish-black
primaries and tail band, dark eye, usually all-dark bill, sometimes with flesh-colored base; a very few can have bill like first-
winter California Gull; usually distinguished by all-dark bill,
usually paler face and throat, and, in flight (page 161), by pale
area at base of primaries and single dark bar on secondaries.
Distinguished from first-winter Western Gull by smaller bill,
paler body plumage, and in flight by paler wings and lack of
contrast between back and rump. Distinguished from first-
winter Lesser Black-backed Gull by generally darker, less contrasting body plumage, usually darker belly, and in flight by
pale primary and secondary coverts and less contrasting rump
pattern. A very few Herring Gulls in all ages can show yellowish legs. Abundant and spreading, the Herring Gull is the most
commonly seen gull in most coastal areas.

California Gull *Larus californicus*
L 21" (53 cm) W 54" (137 cm) Four-year gull, less variable than
larger species. Adult has dark gray mantle, darker than Herring Gull, paler than Lesser Black-backed Gull (page 154);
white head, heavily streaked with brown in winter; dark eye;
yellow bill with black and red spots, the black spot often reduced in breeding season; gray-green or greenish-yellow legs.
Bill is smaller, head rounder than in Herring Gull. Third-
winter plumage is like adult but bill is more extensively
smudged with black; wings show some brown; tail has some
brown spotting. Second-winter bird has gray back, brown
wings, grayish legs, two-toned bill. First-winter bird is brown
overall; not usually paler on face and throat as is Herring Gull;
legs pinkish; bill two-toned, the colors sharply defined. In
flight (page 161), first-winter birds show double dark bar along
trailing edge of wing, entirely dark primaries and primary
coverts; uppertail coverts more heavily barred than Herring
Gull. Distinctly smaller than Western Gull (page 156), with
much smaller bill. Common throughout most of range; rare on
the east coast and Gulf coast in winter. First-winter birds
should be compared carefully with first- and second-winter
Herring Gulls.

winter adult

juvenile

breeding

Herring Gull

3rd winter

2nd winter

breeding

1st winter

California Gull

breeding

breeding

winter adult

2nd winter

juvenile

1st winter

Glaucous Gull *Larus hyperboreus*
L 27" (69 cm) W 60" (152 cm)   Heavy-bodied four-year gull. In all ages, note translucent tips of white primaries. Adult has pale gray wings and mantle, yellow eye, yellow bill with red spot, pink legs. Head is streaked with brown in winter. Third-winter plumage is like adult but has dark smudge on bill, some buff on body. Late second-winter bird has gray back, pale eye. First-winter birds may be buffy or almost all-white; bill distinctly bicolored. Distinguished from Iceland Gull by larger size; heavier, longer bill; flatter crown; slightly paler mantle of adults (see also page 161); proportionately shorter wings, barely extending beyond tail at rest. At all ages, distinguished from Glaucous-winged Gull (pages 156, 161) by translucent primaries; in first-winter plumage, by two-toned bill. Rare in winter south to Gulf states and southern California. Birds in Alaska are slightly smaller and adults are slightly darker mantled than birds from eastern Canada.

Iceland Gull *Larus glaucoides*   *L22" (56 cm) W 54" (137 cm)*
Highly variable four-year gull. Adult has translucent white tips on primaries, occasionally marked with gray above; gray mantle, yellow bill with red spot, white head, streaked with brown in winter. Most adults have yellow eye; a few have brown. Late second-winter birds have pale eye, gray back, two-toned bill. First-winter birds are buffy to mostly white; bill black, thin, pointed; eye dark; wing tips white or irregularly washed with brown. Distinguished from first-winter Thayer's Gull by speckled tail, translucent primaries, usually paler body plumage (see also page 161). Distinguished from Glaucous Gull by smaller size, rounder head, all-dark bill; proportionately longer wings, extending well beyond tail at rest. Extremely rare south to Gulf states.

Thayer's Gull *Larus thayeri*   *L 23" (58 cm) W 55" (140 cm)*
Variable four-year gull. In most adults, eye is dark brown, mantle slightly darker than Iceland or Herring Gull (preceding page); bill yellow with dark red spot; legs darker pink than similar species. Primaries pale gray below, with dark tips forming a thin trailing edge; irregularly dark gray above. A few adults have yellow eye flecked with brown. Second-winter bird has gray mantle, contrasting gray-brown tail band, dark eye. First-winter birds are variable but primaries are always white below, darker than mantle above. Distinguished from Herring Gull by more uniform body plumage, shorter, stubbier bill, and lack of contrasting dark secondaries (pages 150, 161). Distinguished from Iceland Gull by smooth, unspeckled tail band, generally darker body plumage, and primaries darker above than mantle. On west coast, compare with similar Glaucous-winged Gull (page 156), which is larger, with larger bill, less speckling in subadult body plumage, and wing tips the same color as mantle. Casual winter visitor in the east and throughout the interior, but identification is extremely difficult. Formerly considered a subspecies of Herring Gull.

Glaucous Gull

breeding

2nd winter

winter adult

winter adult

1st winter

1st winter

Iceland Gull

1st winter

winter adult

breeding

winter adult

1st winter

2nd winter

Thayer's Gull

winter adult

winter adult

breeding

2nd winter

1st winter

1st winter

Slaty-backed Gull *Larus schistisagus*

L 25" (64 cm) W 58" (147 cm) Siberian species, uncommon summer and rare fall visitor to western Alaska and Aleutians, rare on north coast. Winters in Japan. A heavy, four-year gull only seen at sea and along the coasts. Adult has dark gray back and wings, black primary tips separated by a whitish bar. Underside of primaries gray, not black. Note broad white trailing edge to wings. Legs bright pink; eyes yellow. Third-summer bird is like adult but note brown primaries. Second-summer bird has dark back, very pale wings. First-summer bird (page 161) is quite pale and has dark bill, dark eyes. Similar Siberian form of Herring Gull (not shown), widespread in western Alaska, has dark back and wings but lacks broad white trailing edge; underside of primaries distinctly darker.

Lesser Black-backed Gull *Larus fuscus*

L 21" (53 cm) W 54" (137 cm) European species; casual to uncommon but increasing on Atlantic coast; casual throughout the east. A four-year gull. Adult has white head, streaked with brown in winter; white underparts; yellow legs. Third-winter bird has dark smudge on bill; yellow or, rarely, pink legs; some brown in wings. Second-winter plumage resembles second-winter Herring Gull (page 150) but note dark gray of back; legs are sometimes yellow. First-winter bird is very much like first-winter Herring Gull but head and belly are usually paler, upperparts more contrastingly black and white. Identified in flight (page 161) by the darker primary and secondary coverts, more extensively dark primaries, and paler rump showing more contrast to back. Much smaller than Great Black-backed Gull. Smaller on average than Herring Gull, with smaller bill, but note substantial range of overlap; also note longer wings, usually extending well beyond tail at rest. Scandinavian subspecies (not shown), reported from the northeast, has back as dark as in Great Black-backed Gull.

Great Black-backed Gull *Larus marinus*

L 30" (76 cm) W 65" (165 cm) Four-year gull. In all ages, huge size and massive bill are distinctive. Adult has white head, virtually unstreaked in winter; black upperparts; white underparts; pale eye; pink legs. Third-winter bird is like adult but shows some dark on bill, some brown in wings, sometimes dark in tail. Late second-winter bird has pale eye, black back; wings and tail are like first-winter. First-winter bird resembles Herring Gull (page 150) but head and body are much paler, back and wings have the checkered look of young Lesser Black-backed Gull; in flight (page 161), shows almost white rump, more diffuse tail band. Very uncommon on Great Lakes, casual inland throughout the east and on Gulf coast to Texas. Breeding range is expanding southward on the Atlantic coast.

Slaty-backed Gull

winter adult

breeding

3rd summer

1st summer

Lesser Black-backed Gull

breeding

winter adult

winter adult

2nd winter

1st winter

Great Black-backed Gull

breeding

3rd winter

winter adult

1st winter

2nd winter

Yellow-footed Gull *Larus livens*

L 27" (69 cm) W 60" (152 cm) Breeds in the Gulf of California. Increasingly common as a postbreeding visitor to the Salton Sea. Three-year gull, formerly considered a subspecies of Western Gull. Adult is like Western but has yellow legs and feet; note also massive yellow bill with red spot; very dark gray wings with black-tipped primaries; yellow eye. Second-winter bird is like adult but tail is entirely black, bill two-toned. In first-winter plumage, shown in flight on page 161, head and body are mostly white, back dark gray, wings brown, eye dark, bill mostly dark, legs pinkish. Juvenile resembles first-winter Western Gull but white belly contrasts sharply with streaked breast; upperparts are more boldly patterned; rump whiter.

Western Gull *Larus occidentalis*

L 25" (64 cm) W 58" (147 cm) Variable, four-year gull. Adults north of Monterey have paler backs and darker eyes than southern birds. All adults have white head, dark gray back, pink legs, very large bill. In winter, head is moderately streaked with brown in northern birds, faintly streaked in southern. Third-winter plumage resembles second-winter Yellow-footed Gull but tail is mostly white. Second-winter bird has a dark gray back, yellow eye, two-toned bill, very dark wings. First-winter bird is one of the darkest young gulls; bill is black; in flight (page 161), distinguished from young Herring Gull by contrast of dark back with paler rump. Note also the sootier underparts and head, heavier bill. Juvenile is like first-winter but darker. Western Gulls hybridize extensively with Glaucous-winged Gulls in the northwest; hybrids are seen all along the west coast in winter; two ages are shown here. These are easily confused with Thayer's Gull (page 152); note large bill, pattern of wing tips. Western Gulls are rare inland.

Glaucous-winged Gull *Larus glaucescens*

L 26" (66 cm) W 58" (147 cm) Variable, four-year gull. Adult has white head, moderately streaked with brown in winter. Body is white, mantle pale gray; primaries are the same color as remainder of wing above, paler below. Eye dark; bill large, yellow with red spot; legs pink. Third-winter bird is like adult but has some buff on body, bill is smudged black; some have a partial tail band. In second-winter plumage, back is gray, rest of body and wings are pale buff to white with little mottling; tail evenly gray; bill mostly dark. First-winter bird (shown in flight on page 161) is uniformly pale gray-brown to whitish with little mottling or contrast; primaries are the same color as the mantle, and not translucent. Young Glaucous Gull (page 152) has sharply two-toned bill, translucent primaries. Young Thayer's Gull (page 152) is smaller, with smaller bill, more speckled body plumage, and contrastingly darker primaries. Glaucous-winged Gull hybridizes extensively with Western Gull; with Herring Gull in south-central Alaska; with Glaucous Gull farther north. Hybrids are extremely variable. Glaucous-winged Gull is rare inland.

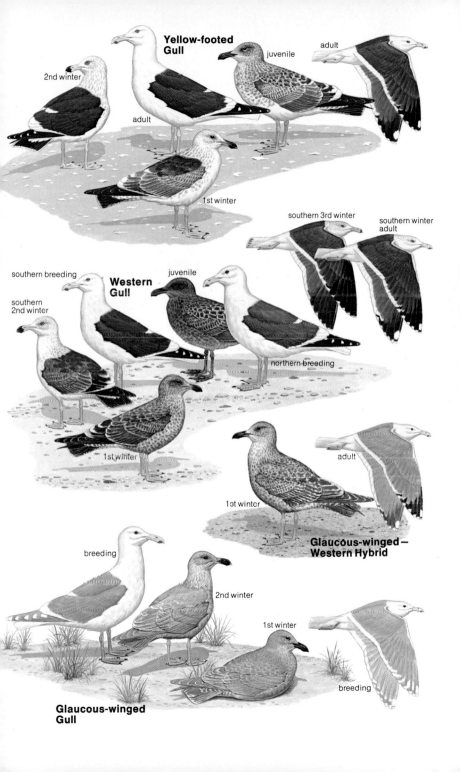

Yellow-footed Gull

2nd winter

adult

juvenile

adult

1st winter

southern 3rd winter

southern winter adult

southern breeding

Western Gull

juvenile

southern 2nd winter

northern breeding

1st winter

adult

1st winter

Glaucous-winged – Western Hybrid

breeding

2nd winter

1st winter

Glaucous-winged Gull

breeding

Black-legged Kittiwake *Rissa tridactyla*

L 17" (43 cm) W 36" (91 cm) Highly pelagic two-year gull. Adults have a white head, nape smudged with gray in winter; dark eye; unmarked yellow bill; white body; gray mantle, darkest on back and inner wings; inner primaries pale; wing tips inky black. Legs black. First-winter bird has dark half-collar; black bill, usually pale at base; black spot behind eye; dark tail band; and in flight (page 160), shows a dark W across the wings. Distinguished from young Bonaparte's Gull (page 146) by half-collar, paler secondaries, slightly forked tail, larger size; from young Sabine's Gull by half-collar, dark carpal bar. A very few young birds have pinkish legs. Nests in large cliff colonies; winters at sea. Seen uncommonly from shore on the west coast, commonly in some years; rarely on the east coast.

Red-legged Kittiwake *Rissa brevirostris*

L 15" (38 cm) W 33" (84 cm) Highly pelagic two-year gull. Adult distinguished from Black-legged Kittiwake by coral red legs; shorter, thicker bill; darker mantle; wings are not paler on inner primaries as in Blackleg; broader white trailing edge on wings; dusky underwings. In first-winter plumage, wing pattern resembles Sabine's Gull (page 160), but Red-legged Kittiwake is the only gull to have an all-white tail in first winter; similar to young Blackleg but lacks W pattern on wings. Breeds in cliff colonies, sometimes close to Black-legged Kittiwakes. Very rare away from breeding grounds, even in winter. Extremely rare south to Oregon.

Sabine's Gull *Xema sabini* *L 13¹/₂" (34 cm) W 33" (84 cm)*

Two-year gull with striking black, gray, and white wing pattern in all ages. Breeding adult has dark gray hood with thin black ring at bottom; black bill with yellow tip; forked tail. First-summer bird is like adult but hood is incomplete; may have spots on tail. In juvenile plumage (see also page 160), wing pattern is like adult but muted; crown and nape are soft gray-brown; bill shows little or no yellow; tail has dark band. Sabine's Gull winters at sea in the Southern Hemisphere; almost all adults migrate out of North America before acquiring white head and dark nape of winter plumage. Juveniles depart before acquiring first-winter plumage. Common migrant off west coast, uncommon along shore; very rare migrant, mostly juveniles, on east coast and in interior.

Ivory Gull *Pagophila eburnea* *L 17" (43 cm) W 37" (94 cm)*

Two-year arctic gull, ghostly pale. Adults in all plumages are strikingly white with a yellow-tipped bill, black eyes, black legs. First-winter birds have a variable amount of speckling on the body, heaviest around the face; always show tail band and spots on tips of primaries. A short-necked, stocky gull with long wings. Winters primarily in arctic seas; very rare vagrant south along the Atlantic coast to Massachusetts and inland to the Great Lakes.

Black-legged Kittiwake

breeding

winter adult

1st winter

Red-legged Kittiwake

breeding

breeding

1st summer

breeding

1st winter

Sabine's Gull

breeding

1st summer

juvenile

Ivory Gull

adult

adult

1st winter

Gulls in Flight

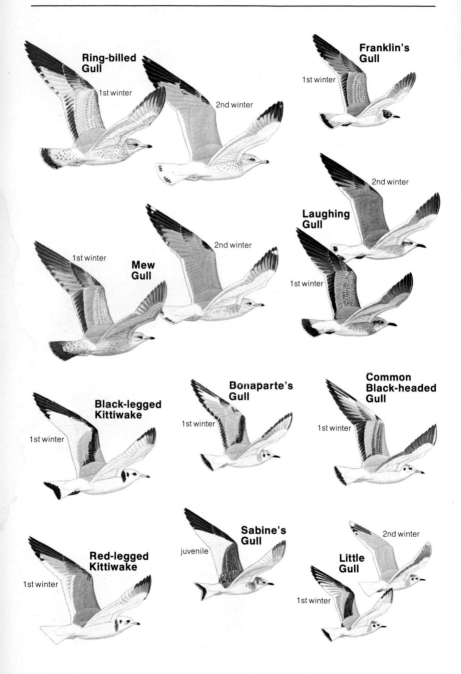

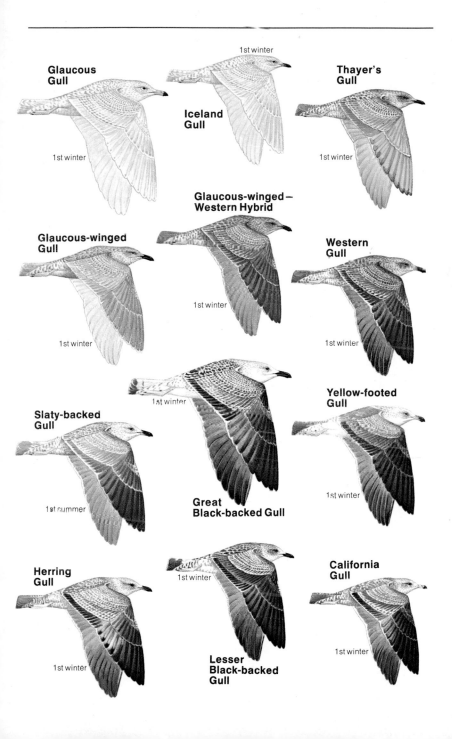

Glaucous Gull
1st winter

Iceland Gull
1st winter

Thayer's Gull
1st winter

Glaucous-winged—Western Hybrid

Glaucous-winged Gull
1st winter

1st winter

Western Gull
1st winter

Slaty-backed Gull
1st summer

1st winter

Yellow-footed Gull
1st winter

Great Black-backed Gull

Herring Gull
1st winter

1st winter

Lesser Black-backed Gull

California Gull
1st winter

Terns

Distinguished from gulls by pointed wings and bill and by feeding technique: terns plunge-dive into the water after prey. Most species have a forked tail.

🎵 **Common Tern** *Sterna hirundo* L 14¹/₂" (37 cm) W 30" (76 cm)
Medium gray above, with black cap and nape; paler gray below; undertail coverts white. Bill red, usually black-tipped. Slightly stockier than the Arctic Tern, with flatter crown, longer neck and bill. In flight, usually displays a dark wedge, variably shaped, near tip of upperwing. Note also that head projects farther than in Arctic Tern. Common Tern's shorter tail gives it a chunkier look. Early juvenile is brownish above, white below, with mostly dark bill. Juvenile and all winter plumages have dark bar on shoulders; forehead is white, but crown and nape blackish; compare with juvenile Forster's Tern (next page). Full adult breeding plumage is acquired by third spring. Siberian subspecies, *S.h. longipennis*, seen regularly in western Alaska, is darker overall; bill and legs black. Common and widespread, Common Terns nest in large colonies. Very rare in winter in southern Florida. Calls are similar to Arctic Tern; distinctive in Common Tern is a low, piercing, drawn-out *kee-ar-r-r-r*.

🎵 **Arctic Tern** *Sterna paradisaea* L 15¹/₂" (39 cm) W 31" (79 cm)
Medium gray above, with black cap and nape; paler gray below; undertail coverts white. Bill deep red. Slightly slimmer than the Common Tern, with rounder head, shorter neck and bill. In flight, upperwing appears uniformly gray, lacking dark wedge of Common Tern; underwing shows very narrow black line on trailing edge of primaries; all flight feathers appear translucent. Note also that head does not project as far as in Common Tern. In perched bird, Arctic Tern's long tail extends markedly farther beyond wing tips; legs are shorter. Juvenile plumage largely lacks brownish wash of juvenile Common; shoulder bar less distinct; secondaries whitish. Forehead is white, but crown and nape blackish; compare with juvenile Forster's Tern (next page). Full adult breeding plumage is acquired by third spring. Arctic Terns migrate well offshore; casual inland during migration, especially in spring. Calls include a raspy *tr-tee-ar*, higher pitched than in Common Tern.

Aleutian Tern *Sterna aleutica* L 13¹/₂" (34 cm) W 29" (74 cm)
Dark gray above and below, with white forehead, black cap, black bill, black legs. In flight, distinguished from Common and Arctic Terns by shorter tail and by white forehead and dark, white-edged bar on secondaries, most visible from below. Juvenile is buff and brown above; legs and lower mandible reddish. Aleutian Terns nest in loose colonies, sometimes with Arctic Terns. Migration routes and winter range unknown. Call is a squeaky *twee-ee-ee*, unlike any other tern.

Common Tern

breeding

1st summer

juvenile

2nd summer

longipennis
breeding

breeding

1st fall

Arctic Tern

breeding

1st summer

1st fall

breeding

juvenile

Aleutian Tern

breeding

juvenile

♪ **Roseate Tern** *Sterna dougallii* *L 15¹/₂" (39 cm) W 29" (74 cm)*
Breeding adult is pale gray above with black cap and nape;
white below with slight pinkish cast visible in good light. Paler
overall than Common and Arctic Terns (preceding page) and
Forster's Tern; lacks dark trailing edge on underside of outer
wing. Bill mostly black with variable amount of red at base.
Wings shorter than in Common and Arctic Terns; flies with
rapid wingbeats. Deeply forked all-white tail extends well beyond wings in standing bird. Legs and feet bright red-orange.
Juvenile's brownish cap extends over forehead; mantle looks
coarsely scaled, lower back barred with black; bill and legs
black. First-summer bird has white forehead. Full adult plumage is attained by second winter. Uncommon and highly maritime, Roseate Terns usually come ashore only to nest. Very
rare inland during migration; casual migrant on Gulf coast.
Call is a soft *chi-wee;* alarm signal a drawn out *zra-ap,* like rip-
ping cloth.

♪ **Forster's Tern** *Sterna forsteri* *L 14¹/₂" (37 cm) W 31" (79 cm)*
Breeding adult is pale gray above, with black cap and nape;
snow white below. Distinguished from Roseate Tern by mostly
orange bill, orange legs and feet, and by much slower wing
stroke. Legs and bill longer than in Common and Arctic Terns
(preceding page). Long, deeply forked gray tail has white outer
edges. In flight, displays pale upperwing area formed by silvery primaries. In winter plumage, Forster's is sometimes mistaken for Common Tern, which normally winters outside
U. S.; note lack of dark shoulder bars; most have dark eye
patches not joined at nape as in Common Tern; a few have
dark streaks on nape. Juvenile and first-winter bird have
shorter tails than adults. Juvenile has ginger brown cap, dark
eye patch; shoulder bar is faint or absent. Forster's Terns nest
in widely scattered colonies in fresh or saltwater marshes.
Calls include a hoarse *kyarr,* lower pitched and shorter than in
Common Tern.

Gull-billed Tern *Sterna nilotica* *L 14" (36 cm) W 34" (86 cm)*
Breeding adult is pale gray above, white below, with black
crown and nape, stout black bill, black legs and feet. Stockier
and paler than Common Tern (preceding page); wings broader; tail shorter and only moderately forked. Winter birds have
white crown with fine, dark streaks. Juvenile has pale edgings
on upperparts, bill is brownish. Fairly common but local, the
Gull-billed Tern nests in salt marshes and on beaches; often
seen hunting for insects in fields and marshes. Rare inland.
In western U. S., nests only at Salton Sea. Adult call is a raspy, sharp *kay-wack;* call of immature is a faint, high-pitched
peep peep.

164

Roseate Tern

juvenile

breeding

juvenile

1st summer

breeding

breeding

Forster's Tern

1st winter

juvenile

winter

winter

Gull-billed Tern

juvenile

breeding

winter

Least Tern *Sterna antillarum* *L 9" (23 cm) W 20" (51 cm)*
Smallest North American tern. Breeding adult is gray above, with black cap and nape, white forehead, orange-yellow bill with dark tip; underparts are white; legs orange-yellow. In flight, black wedge on outer primaries is conspicuous; note also the short, deeply forked tail. Juvenile is pinkish-buff above, with brownish U-shaped markings; crown is dusky; wings show dark shoulder bar. By first fall, upperparts are gray, crown whiter, but dark shoulder bar is retained. First-summer birds are more like adults but have dark bill and legs, shoulder bar, black line through eye, dusky primaries. Fairly common and local on east and Gulf coasts; less common and declining inland and in west. Nests in colonies on beaches, sandbars. Winters from Central America south. Calls include high-pitched *kip* notes and a harsh *chir-ee-eep*. Flight is rapid and buoyant.

Black Tern *Chlidonias niger* *L 9³/₄" (25 cm) W 24" (61 cm)*
Breeding adult is mostly black, with dark gray back, wings, and tail, white undertail coverts. In flight, shows uniformly pale gray underwing and fairly short tail, slightly forked. Juvenile and winter birds are white below, with dark gray mantle and tail; dark ear patch extends from dark crown; flying birds show dark bar on side of breast. First-summer birds can be almost all-white below or patchy black-and-white; full breeding plumage is acquired in second spring. Adults also appear patchy black-and-white as they molt into winter plumage in late summer. These birds in particular can be confused with White-winged Tern. Bill black in all plumages. Black Terns are common inland, nesting on lakeshores and in marshes; common in coastal areas during migration. Calls include a metallic *kik* and a slurred *k-seek*.

White-winged Tern *Chlidonias leucopterus*
L 9¹/₂" (24 cm) W 23" (58 cm) Eurasian species, casual vagrant to east coast, very rare inland and on western Aleutians. Bill and tail shorter than in Black Tern; tail less deeply notched. In breeding plumage, white tail, whitish upperwing coverts, and black wing linings are distinctive; upperwing shows black outer primaries. Molting birds are patchy black-and-white but whitish tail and rump are distinctive. Winter adult has white wing linings; lacks dark bar on sides of breast. Juvenile's brown back contrasts with grayish wing coverts and whitish rump. Juveniles and winter adults have crown speckled with black rather than solid black; dark ear patch not usually connected to crown. Formerly called White-winged Black Tern.

Least Tern

breeding

juvenile

breeding

1st summer

Black Tern

breeding

winter

1st summer

breeding

juvenile

breeding

White-winged Tern

juvenile

winter

molting adult

Sandwich Tern *Sterna sandvicensis*
L 15" (38 cm) W 34" (86 cm)   Long, slender, black bill, tipped with
yellow. Breeding adult is pale gray above with black crown,
short black crest. In flight, shows long, slender wings with
some dark in the outer primaries. White tail is deeply forked,
comparatively short. Legs and feet black. Adult in winter
plumage, seen as early as July, has a white forehead, streaked
crown, grayer tail. Juvenile's bill often lacks yellow tip; by late
summer, juvenile loses the dark V-shaped markings and spots
on back and scapulars. Tail is less deeply forked than in adult.
Sandwich Terns nest on coastal beaches and islands. Calls include abrupt *gwit gwit* and *skee-rick* notes, similar to calls of
Elegant Tern. Very rare spring visitor to southern California.

Elegant Tern *Sterna elegans* *L 17" (43 cm) W 34" (86 cm)*
Bill longer, thinner than in Royal Tern; color ranges from
reddish-orange to yellow in some juveniles. Elegant Tern is
slightly smaller and slimmer overall than Royal. In flight, note
that undersides of primaries are mostly pale; compare with
Caspian Tern. Breeding adult Elegant Tern is pale gray above
with black crown and nape, black crest; white below, often
with pinkish tinge. Winter adult and juvenile have white forehead; black on crown extends forward around eye and over top
of crown; compare with Royal Tern. Juvenile has large spots
on upperparts. Elegant Terns disperse northward after breeding season as far as northern California. Sharp *kee-rick* call is
similar to Sandwich Tern.

♪ Royal Tern *Sterna maxima* *L 20" (51 cm) W 41" (104 cm)*
Orange-red bill, thinner than in Caspian Tern. In flight, shows
underside of primaries mostly pale; tail is more deeply forked.
Adult Royal Tern shows white crown most of year; black cap is
acquired for brief breeding season. In nonbreeding plumage
and juvenile, note that black on nape does not usually extend
to encompass eye; compare with Elegant Tern. Royal Terns
nest in dense colonies. Casual north of breeding range along
Atlantic coast in late summer; uncommon winter visitor to
coast of southern California. Calls include a bleating *kee-rer*
and a plover-like whistled *tourreee*.

♪ Caspian Tern *Sterna caspia* *L 21" (53 cm) W 50" (127 cm)*
Large, stocky tern; stout orange to coral red bill, much thicker
than in Royal Tern. In flight, shows darker underside of primaries than Royal; tail is less deeply forked. Adult acquires black
cap in breeding season; in nonbreeding plumage and immature, crown is dusky or streaked; never shows white forehead
of Royal Tern. Caspian Terns nest in small colonies along
coasts and inland lakes, rivers, marshes. Adult's calls include
low, harsh *kowk* and *ca-arr*. Immature has a distinctive call, a
high-pitched, whistled *whee-you*.

Sandwich Tern

juvenile

breeding

juvenile

winter

Elegant Tern

winter

breeding

juvenile

Royal Tern

breeding

juvenile

juvenile

winter

Caspian Tern

winter

immature

breeding

Bridled Tern *Sterna anaethetus* L 15" (38 cm) W 30" (76 cm)
Common on nesting grounds in the Bahamas and West Indies; regular in summer in the Gulf of Mexico, well offshore, and in the Gulf Stream to North Carolina. Tropical storms may drive them as far north as New England. Brownish-gray above with black cap, white collar. Slimmer than Sooty Tern; wings more pointed; underwings and tail edges more extensively white. A close look shows that the Bridled Tern's white forehead patch extends behind the eye; the Sooty's stops at the eye. Juvenile resembles adult but with pale mottling above.

Sooty Tern *Sterna fuscata* L 16" (41 cm) W 32" (81 cm)
Large breeding colony located on the Dry Tortugas, Florida; also nests on islands off Texas and Louisiana. This large tern spends nearly all its time in the air over tropical seas. Severe storms can carry it many miles inland and as far north as coastal New England and the Maritime Provinces. Striking plumage pattern: blackish above, white below; white forehead. Black bill and legs. Tail is deeply forked and edged with white. Juvenile is sooty-brown overall, with whitish stippling on back; pale lower belly and undertail coverts; pale wing linings. Sooties do not dive; they feed on small fish and squid plucked from the water's surface. Nesting colonies are noisy day and night; typical call is a high, nasal *wacky-wack*.

Black Noddy *Anous minutus* L 13¹/₂" (34 cm) W 30" (76 cm)
Tropical species, extremely rare in North America; a few are seen among Brown Noddies on the Dry Tortugas. Smaller than Brown Noddy, with shorter legs, slightly blacker plumage, whiter cap; bill is longer, finer. Most sightings are of immatures, which have less extensive white on crown.

Brown Noddy *Anous stolidus* L 15¹/₂" (39 cm) W 32" (81 cm)
Nests in colonies on the Dry Tortugas, Florida. Sometimes seen along Gulf coast to Texas after storms; hurricanes may drive them as far as North Carolina. Overall dark gray-brown color is broken only by a whitish-gray cap; in immature this is only a small whitish line on the forehead. Unlike other terns, noddies have a long, wedge-shaped tail with only a small notch at tip. Feeding over open ocean, they snatch prey from the surface. Usually silent; Brown Noddy's rippling, crowlike *karrk* is heard mostly around the breeding colonies.

Black Skimmer *Rynchops niger* L 18" (46 cm) W 44" (112 cm)
No other birds but the skimmers have a lower mandible longer than the upper. There is no mistaking the Black Skimmer, a long-winged coastal bird, as it furrows the shallows with its red, black-tipped bill, nodding to seize small fish with a sudden snap. At rest, its black back and crown, white face and underparts, red legs, and bill shape are distinctive. Juvenile is mottled dingy brown above. A few pairs nest in California around San Diego and the Salton Sea. Winter adults are browner above than breeding adults, and show white collar.

Bridled Tern
adult

juvenile

Sooty Tern
juvenile

adult

Black Noddy
adult

immature

Brown Noddy
adult

Black Skimmer
juvenile

breeding

winter

Auks and Puffins (Family Alcidae)

These black-and-white "penguins of the north" have set-back legs that give them an upright stance on land. In flight, they zigzag on rapid wingbeats.

Razorbill Alca torda L 17″ (43 cm)

A chunky bird, big-headed and thick-necked; black above, white below. Pointed tail, heavy head, and massive, arching bill distinguish Razorbill from murres in all plumages. Swimming birds often hold tail cocked up. A white band crosses the bill, another runs from bill to eye. Immature lacks white line from eye; bill is smaller but still distinctively shaped. Nests on rocky cliffs. Winters in large numbers on the Grand Banks off Newfoundland. A few winter well offshore as far south as Maryland, coming closer to shore in stormy weather.

Common Murre Uria aalge L 17¹/₂″ (45 cm)

Large and long-necked, with a long, slender, pointed bill. Upperparts dark sooty-brown; underparts white. Some Atlantic birds have a "bridle"—a white eye ring and spur. In winter plumage, dark line extends from eye across white cheek. Juvenile has a shorter bill; more extensively mottled throat and browner upperparts generally distinguish it from Thick-billed Murre. Molting birds are more difficult to identify. Abundant off west coast, common off east. Nests in colonies on rocky cliffs; winters at sea.

Thick-billed Murre Uria lomvia L 18″ (46 cm)

Stocky, with a dark, thick, fairly short bill, uniformly curved from thick base to blunt tip. Upperparts of adult are blacker than Common Murre; white of underparts rises to a sharp point at the throat. In Pacific birds, bill is slightly longer and more slender than in Atlantic birds. On both coasts, most birds show a white line on cutting edge of upper mandible. In immature and winter plumage, face is more extensively dark than Common Murre. First-summer bird is browner above than adult and may retain much of winter plumage. Molting birds are harder to identify. Nests in colonies on rocky cliffs. Abundant on breeding grounds; winters at sea. On east coast, much more common south of Canada than Common Murre.

Dovekie Alle alle L 8¹/₄″ (21 cm)

A plump little seabird with short neck, stubby bill; in flight, whirs on rapid wingbeats. Breeding adult is black above, white below; black upper breast contrasts sharply with pure white underparts. In winter plumage, throat, chin, and lower face are white, with white curving around behind eye. Abundant on their breeding grounds in the far north, Dovekies winter chiefly in the North Atlantic; casual farther south. In some years, found at scattered inland locations after fall storms.

Razorbill

winter

breeding

breeding

immature

Common Murre

bridled

breeding

juvenile

winter

breeding

Thick-billed Murre

Atlantic breeding

Atlantic breeding

Pacific winter

breeding

winter

Dovekie

breeding

Black Guillemot *Cepphus grylle* *L 13" (33 cm)*

Long, black bill; fairly long, slender neck; swims with head held high. Breeding adult black overall, with large white patch on upperwing. Winter adult white; upperparts heavily mottled with black except on nape; wing patch appears less distinct. Juvenile is sooty above; sides gray-mottled; wing patch mottled. Fairly common in the east; usually seen close to shore in breeding season. Uncommon breeder in Alaska, where it overlaps with Pigeon Guillemot. In all plumages, gleaming white axillaries and wing linings distinguish Black from Pigeon Guillemot.

Pigeon Guillemot *Cepphus columba* *L 13¹/₂" (34 cm)*

Long, black bill; fairly long, slender neck; swims with head held high. Breeding adult black overall, with large white upperwing patch marked by black triangle. Winter adult white with black-mottled upperparts; wing patch appears less distinct. Juvenile is dusky above; crown and nape darker; wing patch obscured by black edgings; breast and sides gray-mottled. Compare especially with juvenile Marbled Murrelet. First-winter Pigeon Guillemot resembles winter adult but is darker overall. Fairly common; usually seen close to shore in breeding season. Range overlaps Black Guillemot in western Alaska. In all seasons, dark or dusky axillaries and wing linings distinguish Pigeon from Black Guillemot.

Marbled Murrelet *Brachyramphus marmoratus*

L 9³/₄" (25 cm) Black bill, longer than bill of Kittlitz's Murrelet. Tail entirely dark. Breeding adult dark above, heavily mottled below. In winter plumage, white on scapulars distinguishes Marbled from other murrelets except Kittlitz's, which has a white face, shorter bill, and nearly complete breast band. Juvenile resembles winter adult but is dusky-mottled below; by first winter, underparts are mostly white. Fairly common throughout breeding range; rare in southern California. Seen in coastal waters; nests inland, sometimes in trees. Highly vocal; calls, sharp *kir-kir* and lower *keee*. Murrelets have more pointed wings and faster flight than auklets.

Kittlitz's Murrelet *Brachyramphus brevirostris*

L 9¹/₂" (24 cm) Black bill, shorter than bill of Marbled Murrelet. Outer tail feathers white. Breeding adult's dark upperparts heavily patterned with buff, white, gray, tawny. Throat, breast, and flanks are mottled; belly white. Winter plumage is grayer above than winter Marbled Murrelet; note also extensive white on face, making eye conspicuous; broad white collar, nearly complete breast band, white edges on secondaries. Juvenile distinguished by shorter bill, paler face, pale outer tail feathers. Fairly common but local; found in coastal waters.

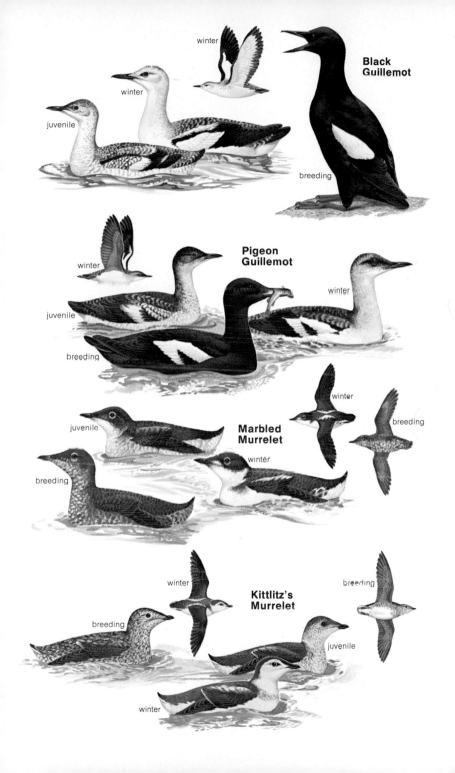

Black Guillemot

winter

winter

juvenile

breeding

Pigeon Guillemot

winter

juvenile

breeding

winter

Marbled Murrelet

juvenile

winter

breeding

winter

breeding

Kittlitz's Murrelet

winter

breeding

juvenile

breeding

winter

Xantus' Murrelet *Synthliboramphus hypoleucus*

L 9³/₄" (25 cm) Slate black above, white below. Southern California form, *S.h. scrippsi,* has a partial white eye ring. The form that breeds on islands off western Baja California, *hypoleucus,* has an extensive white facial pattern; seen rarely off southern and central California coast in fall. Both forms are distinguished from Craveri's Murrelet by lack of partial dark collar; slightly shorter, stouter bill; and snow white wing linings, visible when birds rise to flap wings or run along surface before taking off. Usually seen a few miles offshore; nests in colonies on rocky sea islands, ledges, and sometimes amid dense vegetation. Uncommon to fairly common; regular postbreeding wanderer as far north as Washington. Call, a shrill whistle or series of whistles, can be heard year round.

Craveri's Murrelet *Synthliboramphus craveri*

L 10" (25 cm) Slate black above, white below. Distinguished from Xantus' Murrelet by dusky-gray wing linings; dark partial collar extending onto breast; slightly slimmer, longer bill. In good light, upperparts have a brownish tinge. Usually seen a few miles offshore. Breeds on rocky islands in the Gulf of California and off western Baja California; numbers vary from year to year. Regular postbreeding wanderer to coast of southern and central California. Call is a shrill whistle or series of whistles, heard year round.

Ancient Murrelet *Synthliboramphus antiquus*

L 10" (25 cm) Black crown and nape contrast with gray back. White streaks on head and nape of breeding adult give it a distinctively "ancient" look. Note also black chin and throat, yellowish bill. Winter adult's black bib is smaller and flecked with white; streaks on head are much less prominent. Immature lacks white streaking on head; throat is mostly white; distinguished from juvenile Marbled Murrelet (preceding page) by heavier, paler bill and by contrast between head and back. In flight, the Ancient Murrelet holds its head higher than other murrelets; dark stripe on body at base of wing contrasts with white underparts, white wing linings. Uncommon to common; breeds primarily on the Aleutians and other islands off western Alaska; winters occasionally as far south as Baja California. Call, heard year round, is a low, piping whistle.

Cassin's Auklet *Ptychoramphus aleuticus* *L 9" (23 cm)*

Small, plump, dark gray bird; wings more rounded than in murrelets; bill short and stout, with pale spot at base of lower mandible; pale eyes. Upperparts are dark gray, shading to paler gray below, with whitish belly. Prominent white crescents above and below eye. Juvenile is paler overall; throat whitish. Common; nests in colonies on isolated cliffs and headlands. Highly pelagic, generally seen farther from shore than murrelets. Call, heard only on breeding grounds, is a weak croaking. Rare in winter in south coastal Alaska.

**Xantus'
Murrelet**

hypoleucus

scrippsi

**Craveri's
Murrelet**

**Ancient
Murrelet**

immature

winter

breeding

**Cassin's
Auklet**

Parakeet Auklet *Cyclorrhynchus psittacula* L 10" (25 cm)

In breeding plumage, acquired by late January, broad upturned bill is orange-red; white plume extends back from eye; dark slate upperparts and throat contrast with white underparts; sides are mottled gray. In winter plumage, bill becomes duskier; underparts, including throat, are entirely white. Compare especially with larger Rhinoceros Auklet (next page). Immature resembles winter adult. Comparatively long-necked and small-headed. Like other auklets, wings are rounded, wingbeats fluttery in comparison to those of murrelets. Fairly common on nesting grounds; nests in scattered pairs on rocky shores, sea cliffs. Found in pairs or small flocks in winter, generally on open ocean. Winters casually as far south as California. Silent except on breeding grounds, when call is a musical trill, rising in pitch.

Crested Auklet *Aethia cristatella* L 10¹/₂" (27 cm)

Sooty-black overall; prominent quail-like crest curves forward from forehead; narrow white plume trails from behind bright yellow eye. Breeding adult's bill is enlarged by bright orange plates. In winter plumage, bill is smaller and browner; crest and plume reduced. Immature lacks crest and plume; bill much smaller. Common and gregarious; often seen flying in large flocks that may include Parakeet and Least Auklets. Nests in crevices of sea cliffs, rocky shores. Winters throughout breeding range and east to Kodiak Island. Silent except on nesting grounds, where it gives honking and grunting calls.

Whiskered Auklet *Aethia pygmaea* L 7³/₄" (20 cm)

Dark overall; three white plumes splay from each side of face; thin, quail-like crest curls forward over bill. In breeding plumage, stubby bill is orange-red with white tip. In winter, bill is dusky, plumes and crest less conspicuous. Immature is paler below; crest absent. A fairly common auklet; nests on rocky shores and cliffs of central Aleutians and islands off the Siberian coast. Feeds primarily in tidal rips.

Least Auklet *Aethia pusilla* L 6¹/₄" (16 cm)

Small, chubby, and short-necked; dark above, with white-tipped scapulars and primaries; forehead and lores streaked with white bristly feathers. Stubby, knobbed bill is dark red, with pale tip. In breeding plumage, acquired by January, a streak of white plumes extends back from behind eye; underparts are variable, heavily mottled with gray or nearly all-white. In winter plumage, underparts are entirely white. Immature resembles winter adult. Abundant and gregarious, Least Auklets are found in immense flocks. Nest on boulder-strewn beaches and islands. Winter throughout the Aleutians; often seen far from shore. Chattering calls are heard only on the nesting grounds.

Parakeet Auklet
breeding
breeding
winter

Crested Auklet
breeding
immature
winter
breeding

Whiskered Auklet
breeding
breeding
immature
winter

Least Auklet
breeding
winter
winter
immature

Rhinoceros Auklet *Cerorhinca monocerata* L 15" (38 cm)
A large, heavy-billed auklet with large head and short, thick neck. Blackish-brown above; paler on sides, neck, and throat. In flight, whitish on belly blends into dark breast; compare with extensively white underparts of similar Parakeet Auklet (preceding page). In breeding plumage, acquired by February, Rhinoceros Auklet has prominent white plumes and a pale yellow "horn" at base of orange bill. Winter adult lacks horn; plumes are less distinct, bill paler. Immatures lack horn and plumes; bill is dusky, eyes darker. Compare with much smaller Cassin's Auklet (page 176). Rhinoceros Auklets are common along most of the west coast in fall and winter; often seen in large numbers close inshore.

Atlantic Puffin *Fratercula arctica* L 12¹⁄₂" (32 cm)
Breeding adult distinguished by massive, brightly colored, grooved bill; white face and underparts contrast with dark upperparts. Winter adult has smaller, duller bill; face is dusky. In juvenile and first-winter birds, face is even duskier, bill much paler and smaller. Full adult bill takes five years to develop. The only east coast puffin. In flight, distinguished from murres and Razorbill by red-orange legs, rounded wings, grayish wing linings, absence of white trailing edge. Locally common in breeding season; winters at sea. Casual south to Maryland in winter. Formerly called Common Puffin.

Horned Puffin *Fratercula corniculata* L 15" (38 cm)
A stocky North Pacific species with thick neck, large head, massive bill; underparts are white in all plumages. Breeding adult's face is white, bill brightly colored. Dark, fleshy "horn" extending up from eye is visible only at close range. Winter adult's bill is smaller, duller; face is gray. Bill of juvenile and first-winter birds smaller and duskier than adult; full adult bill takes several years to develop. In flight, bright orange legs are conspicuous; wings are rounded; wing linings grayish; wings lack white trailing edge. Locally common; winters at sea and around breeding areas. Irregular straggler along the west coast to southern California.

Tufted Puffin *Fratercula cirrhata* L 15" (38 cm)
Stocky, with thick neck, large head, massive bill. Underparts are dark in adults. Breeding adult's face is white, bill brightly colored; pale yellow head tufts droop over back of neck. Winter adult has smaller, duller bill; face is dusky, tufts shorter or absent. Juvenile has smaller, dusky bill; dark eye; white or dark underparts. First-winter bird looks like juvenile until spring molt. Full adult bill takes several years to develop. Red-orange feet are conspicuous in flight; wings are rounded; wing linings grayish; wings lack white trailing edge. Fairly common in northern breeding range; less common in California. Winters far out at sea.

immature

winter

Rhinoceros Auklet

breeding

Atlantic Puffin

breeding

winter

juvenile

Horned Puffin

juvenile

winter

breeding

juvenile

Tufted Puffin

juvenile

winter

breeding

American Vultures (Family Cathartidae)

Small, unfeathered head and hooked bill aid these scavengers in consuming carrion. Weak talons are ill suited for grasping live prey. Vultures do not build nests, but lay their eggs in a sheltered spot: cliff ledge or cave, hollow log, abandoned building. Flocks often roost together at night.

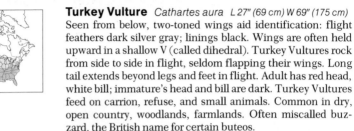

Turkey Vulture *Cathartes aura* L 27" (69 cm) W 69" (175 cm)
Seen from below, two-toned wings aid identification: flight feathers dark silver gray; linings black. Wings are often held upward in a shallow V (called dihedral). Turkey Vultures rock from side to side in flight, seldom flapping their wings. Long tail extends beyond legs and feet in flight. Adult has red head, white bill; immature's head and bill are dark. Turkey Vultures feed on carrion, refuse, and small animals. Common in dry, open country, woodlands, farmlands. Often miscalled buzzard, the British name for certain buteos.

Black Vulture *Coragyps atratus* L 25" (64 cm) W 57" (145 cm)
Wings short, broad; in flight, shows large white patches at base of primaries. Tail is short; feet usually extend to edge of tail or beyond. Flight heavy, with rapid flapping and short glides, usually with wings flat. Gregarious and aggressive. Less efficient at spotting carrion, Black Vultures may flock to a Turkey Vulture's find and claim it. Occasionally prey on unprotected young birds and small mammals. Common in open country and around human settlements, where they scavenge in garbage dumps and at fishing wharves. Range is apparently expanding in the northeast.

California Condor *Gymnogyps californianus*
L 47" (119 cm) W 108" (274 cm)   Rare and declining; found in arid foothills and mountains of southern and central California. Huge size is distinctive. Adult has white wing linings, orange head; immature's wing linings are mottled, head dusky. Condors soar on flat wings, circling for altitude, then giving one deep wingbeat to soar off at great speed in search of large carrion—deer, cattle, sheep. Condors spend much of the day in roosts, preening, sunning, bathing in shallow streams. Present population numbers probably fewer than 20. Intensive conservation programs continue.

Turkey Vulture

adult

immature

Black Vulture

California Condor

immature

adult

adult

adult

Kites, Hawks, Eagles (Family Accipitridae)

A large, worldwide family of diurnal birds of prey, equipped with large, hooked bills and strong talons. Males are usually smaller than the females.

Golden Eagle *Aquila chrysaetos*

L 30-40″ (76-102 cm) W 80-88″ (203-224 cm) Brown, with golden wash over back of head and neck; dark bill; tail faintly banded. Immatures, seen in flight from below, show well-defined white patches at base of primaries, white tail with distinct dark terminal band. Compare with first-year Bald Eagle's proportionately larger head, longer tail, blotchier underwing pattern. Golden Eagle often soars with wings slightly uplifted. Inhabits mountainous or hilly terrain, hunting over open country for small mammals, snakes, birds; also eats carrion. Nests on cliffs or in trees. Rare in the east; fairly common in the west.

White-tailed Eagle *Haliaeetus albicilla*

L 26-35″ (66-89 cm) W 72-94″ (183-239 cm) Ranges over most of northern Eurasia and Greenland in diminishing numbers. Rare visitor to outer Aleutians, where it may nest. Note short, wedge-shaped white tail. Plumage mottled; head may be very pale and appear white at a distance. Immature's head is pale, tail dark with white mottling, somewhat longer than adult's tail and less wedge-shaped.

Steller's Sea-Eagle *Haliaeetus pelagicus*

L 27-37″ (69-94 cm) W 80-95″ (203-241 cm) Nests in northeastern Asia; very rare visitor to Aleutians, Pribilofs, and Kodiak Island. White shoulders show as white leading edge of wings in flight. Immense bill; white, wedge-shaped tail; white thighs. Immatures lack white shoulder patches; end of tail is dark.

Bald Eagle *Haliaeetus leucocephalus*

L 31-37″ (79-94 cm) W 70-90″ (178-229 cm) Adults readily identified by white head and tail, huge yellow bill. First-year birds are mostly dark, may be confused with immature Golden Eagle; compare blotchy white on underwing and tail with Golden Eagle's more sharply defined pattern; note also Bald Eagle's proportionately larger head and bill, longer tail. Neck is shorter and tail longer than White-tailed Eagle; Steller's Sea-Eagle has longer, wedge-shaped tail. Flat-winged soar distinguishes young Bald Eagle from Turkey Vulture. Bald Eagles require four or five years to reach full adult plumage. Common in Alaska, rare in the east, Bald Eagles are seen most often on seacoasts or near rivers and lakes. Feed mainly on fish. Nest in tall trees. Seriously diminished in number due to shooting, pesticides, and human encroachment; intense recovery programs appear to be stabilizing populations in the east.

Golden Eagle
immature
adult
adult

White-tailed Eagle
immature
adult

Steller's Sea-Eagle
immature
adult

Bald Eagle
1st year
2nd year
1st year
adult
adult

Mississippi Kite *Ictinia mississippiensis*

L 14¹/₂" (37 cm) W 35" (89 cm) Long, pointed wings; long tail. Dark gray above, paler below, with pale gray head. White secondaries show in flight as white wing patch. Dark primaries sometimes show chestnut at the base. Black tail readily distinguishes Mississippi from Black-shouldered Kite. Compare also with male Northern Harrier (next page). Juvenile is heavily streaked and spotted, with pale bands on tail. First-summer bird (page 206) resembles adult but wings and tail are like juvenile. At all ages, may be confused with Peregrine Falcon (page 204), but flight is more leisurely and buoyant. Gliding, banking, wheeling in the wind, Mississippis are active and graceful as they pursue flying insects. Also drop to the ground, feetfirst, upon insects, mice, lizards, frogs. Gregarious, often nesting in loose colonies. Found in open woodlands and swamps, semiarid rangelands. Regular straggler far north and west of usual range. Winters to South America.

American Swallow-tailed Kite *Elanoides forficatus*

L 23" (58 cm) W 48" (122 cm) Seen in flight, deeply forked tail and sharply defined pattern of black and white are like no other large bird except the highly pelagic young Magnificent Frigatebird (page 38). Perched, the Swallowtail's coloring more closely resembles Black-shouldered and Mississippi Kites; again, look for long, forked tail. Young birds are similar to adults, but are streaked on head and breast. Agile and graceful in flight, Swallowtails snatch flying insects, also drop down feetfirst upon snakes, lizards, young birds; do not hover. Often eat prey in flight; also drink in flight, skimming the water like swallows. Found in open woods, bottomlands, wetlands. Nest in the tops of tall trees. Somewhat social; several may hunt in the same territory. Population has declined in recent years; range is diminishing. Strays are seen in spring and summer as far north as Ontario and Nova Scotia and as far west as Arizona. Most winter in South America.

Black-shouldered Kite *Elanus caeruleus*

L 16" (41 cm) W 42" (107 cm) Long, pointed wings; long tail. White underparts and mostly white tail distinguish adults from the similar Mississippi Kite. Compare also with male Northern Harrier (next page). Juvenile has pale gray tail; underparts and head are lightly streaked with rufous. In all ages, black shoulders show in flight as black leading edge of inner wings from above, small black patches from below. Flight is graceful, buoyant; often hovers while hunting, unlike any other North American kite. Eats mainly rodents, insects. Populations have fluctuated strongly, are now on the increase, with range expanding rapidly. Fairly common in brushy grasslands, farmlands. Formerly known as White-tailed Kite.

juvenile

♂

♀

Mississippi Kite

American Swallow-tailed Kite

juvenile

adult

Black-shouldered Kite

Snail Kite *Rostrhamus sociabilis*

L 17" (43 cm) W 46" (117 cm) Male is slate black, with white up-pertail and undertail coverts, white tail with broad, dark band and paler terminal band; legs orange-red; eyes and facial skin reddish. Female is dark brown, with white on forehead and throat. Immatures resemble adult female but have boldly streaked head and underparts, paler legs. Hunting flight is slow, with considerable flapping of wings, and with head down as the kite searches for apple snails, its chief and perhaps only food. Seizing a snail, the bird flies to a regular perch to eat it. A tropical species, the Snail Kite is resident in southern Florida but very rare and local. Formerly called Everglade Kite.

Hook-billed Kite *Chondrohierax uncinatus*

L 16" (41 cm) W 33" (84 cm) Tropical species, uncommon over most of its range. Seen very rarely in southern Texas. Plumage varies considerably. Look for large, heavy bill with long hook; banded tail. Males are generally gray overall, with barred un-derparts. Females are brown, with a reddish collar and red-dish, barred underparts. Immatures have whitish underparts flecked with dark brown. Black-phase adults are all-black ex-cept for single white or grayish tail band and whitish tail tip; immatures are mostly brownish-black, with two or three gray tail bands. In flight, all Hook-billed Kites show broad, rounded wings and long tail. Chiefly a bird of forests and swamps. Eats insects, small amphibians, but prefers snails of various kinds. A pile of broken snail shells beneath a tree may indicate a perch or nest site above.

Northern Harrier *Circus cyaneus*

L 17-23" (43-58 cm) W 38-48" (97-122 cm) White rump and owl-like facial disk distinctive in all ages and both sexes. Body slim; wings long and narrow with somewhat rounded tips. Adult male is grayish above, mostly white below, with black wing tips. Female is brown above, whitish below with heavy brown streaking on breast and flanks, lighter streaking and spotting on belly. Immatures resemble adult female but are washed with cinnamon below and on wing linings. Harriers generally perch low and fly close to the ground, wings upraised, as they search for mice, rats, frogs, and other prey. Fairly common in wetlands and open fields. Seldom soar high except during mi-gration and in exuberant, acrobatic courtship display. Males migrate later in fall, earlier in spring, than females and imma-tures. Formerly called Marsh Hawk.

**Snail
Kite**

immature

black phase

black phase
immature

molting immature

**Hook-billed
Kite**

immature

immature

**Northern
Harrier**

Accipiters

Low-flying woodland hawks with short, rounded wings and long tails for speed and agility. Females are larger than males. Three species occur in North America.

Sharp-shinned Hawk *Accipiter striatus*
L 10-14" (25-36 cm) W 20-28" (51-71 cm) Distinguished from Cooper's Hawk by shorter, squared tail, often appearing notched when folded, and smaller head and neck. Adult lacks strong contrast between crown and back. Immature is whitish below with bold, blurry, reddish streaking on breast and belly; narrow white tip on tail; head less tawny than in Cooper's or Northern Goshawk. In flight (see also page 207), note smaller head and proportionately short tail and long wings. Fairly common over much of its range; found in mixed woodlands. Migrates mostly along ridges and coastlines, often in larger flocks than Cooper's or Goshawk.

Cooper's Hawk *Accipiter cooperii*
L 14-20" (36-51 cm) W 29-37" (74-94 cm) Distinguished from Sharp-shinned Hawk by longer, rounded tail, larger head, and, in adult, stronger contrast between back and crown. Immature has whitish or buffy underparts with fine streaks on breast; streaking is reduced or absent on belly; white undertail coverts; white tip on tail broader than on Sharpshin or Northern Goshawk. Tail proportionately longer, wings shorter than Goshawk. In flight (see also page 207), note large head, and proportionately long tail and short wings. Uncommon and may be declining. Inhabits broken woodlands or streamside groves, especially deciduous. Preys largely on songbirds, some small mammals. Sometimes perches on telephone poles, unlike Sharpshins. Migrates mostly along ridges and coastlines, usually singly or in groups of two or three.

Northern Goshawk *Accipiter gentilis*
L 21-26" (53-66 cm) W 40-46" (102-117 cm) Conspicuous eyebrow, flaring behind eye, separates dark crown from blue-gray back. Underparts are white with dense gray barring; appear gray at a distance. Adult has conspicuous fluffy white undertail coverts, more extensive than in Sharpshin and Cooper's. Immature is brown above, buffy below, with dense, blurry streaking, heaviest on flanks. In all ages, tail has wavy bands and a thin white tip; in immature, dark bands are bordered with white. In flight (see also page 207), note proportionately short tail, long wings. Sometimes confused with Gyrfalcon (page 204). Fierce and bold even for an accipiter, the Goshawk inhabits deep, conifer-dominated mixed woodlands; preys chiefly on ground-dwelling birds and ducks, also on other birds, and mammals as large as hares. Uncommon; winters irregularly south of mapped range in east. Migrates mostly along ridges and coastlines; southward irruptions occur in some winters.

Sharp-shinned Hawk

immature

immature ♀

♂

Cooper's Hawk

immature

immature ♀

♂

immature

immature ♀

♂

Northern Goshawk

Buteos

High-soaring hawks, most with broad, banded tails and rounded wings. Buteos are among the easiest daytime birds of prey to spot, especially in migration.

♪ Red-shouldered Hawk *Buteo lineatus*

L 19" (48 cm) W 40" (102 cm) A long-winged, long-tailed buteo. In flight, shows pale crescent at base of primaries (see also page 207). Reddish shoulders and white barring on dark wings visible from above; from below, note reddish wing linings and underparts. Tail has narrow white bands. Florida subspecies is smaller and paler. Western forms are much darker red below; red shoulders less conspicuous. Immature is whitish or buffy below, with variable dark streaks. Fairly common, Redshouldered Hawks inhabit moist, mixed woodlands; often seen near streams. Prey on snakes, frogs, mice, crayfish, sometimes young birds. Call is an evenly spaced series of clear, high *kee-ah* or *kah* notes.

♪ Broad-winged Hawk *Buteo platypterus*

L 16" (41 cm) W 34" (86 cm) White underwings have dark borders; tail has broad, equal-width black and white bands. Wings broad but more pointed than Red-shouldered Hawk's; wing linings buffy or white; tail shorter, broader. Immatures variable; typical immature has black whisker streak, dark-bordered underwings, indistinct brown and white bands on tail; very similar to immature Redshoulder but paler below and lacks crescent-shaped pale patch on wing. Rare dark phase (page 207) breeds in western Canada. A woodland species, the Broadwing perches low waiting for prey: mice, frogs, insects, or snakes. Call is a thin, shrill, monotone whistle: *pee-teee*. Migrates along ridges, river valleys, and shorelines, usually in very large flocks. Very rare migrant in west. A few winter in extreme southern Florida and coastal southern California.

Gray Hawk *Buteo nitidus* *L 17" (43 cm) W 35" (89 cm)*

Tropical species; very local nester in southeastern Arizona. Casual in New Mexico, rare in Rio Grande Valley. Gray upperparts, gray-barred underparts and wing linings, rounded wing tips, and broad bands on a longer tail distinguish it from Broadwinged Hawk (see also page 207). Immature very like immature Broadwing, but has white eyebrow, pale rump; dark trailing edge on wings is smaller or absent. Inhabits deciduous growth along streams with nearby open land. Fast-flying, solitary; swoops from perch in foliage on lizards, snakes, frogs.

adult

immature

eastern

adult

eastern

immature

Red-shouldered Hawk

Florida

western

adult

immature

Broad-winged Hawk

immature

adult

immature

adult

immature

adult

Gray Hawk

adult

immature

♂ **Red-tailed Hawk** *Buteo jamaicensis*

L 22" (56 cm) W 50" (127 cm) Our most common buteo; wings broad and fairly rounded; plumage extremely variable. Most adult Redtails, especially in the east, show a belly band of dark streaks on whitish underparts; dark bar on leading edge of underwing, contrasting with paler wing linings; reddish uppertail; paler red undertail; and variable pale mottling on scapulars, contrasting with dark mantle. The Great Plains form, "Krider's Hawk," has paler upperparts, whitish tail with pale reddish wash; lacks very white underwing of similar Ferruginous Hawk (next page). Some southwestern Redtails lack belly band and mottling on scapulars; have uniformly light underparts. Dark phase of western form has dark wing linings and underparts, obscuring the shoulder bar and belly band; tail is dark reddish above. In "Harlan's Hawk," formerly considered a separate species, the dark phase has dusky-white tail, diffuse blackish terminal band, and reddish wash; shows some white streaking on its dark breast; may lack scapular mottling. "Harlan's Hawk" breeds in Alaska and Canada, winters primarily in central U. S. Immatures of all forms have gray-brown tails with many blackish bands; otherwise heavily brown-streaked and spotted below. Habitat variable: woods with nearby open land; also plains, prairie groves, desert. Preys on rodents. Distinctive call, a harsh, descending *keeeeer*.

Swainson's Hawk *Buteo swainsoni*

L 21" (53 cm) W 52" (132 cm) Distinguished from other buteos by long, narrow, pointed wings. In light phase, whitish or buffy-white wing linings contrast with darkly barred brown flight feathers. Dark bib; underparts otherwise whitish to pale buff. Lacks Redtail's pale mottling on scapulars; bill smaller than Redtail's. Dark-phase bird is dark brown; lacks sharp contrast between wing linings and flight feathers. Intermediate colorations between light and dark phases include a reddish plumage. Light-phase and intermediate immatures have dark whisker streak and conspicuous whitish eyebrows that meet on the forehead; underparts boldly streaked, with streaks running together to make brown patches on the sides of the breast. Less contrast between wing linings and flight feathers than adult birds. Swainson's Hawk soars over open plains, prairie, and desert with uptilted wings in teetering, vulture-like flight. Perches on posts, banks, or stones and pounces on prey, largely insects. Very rare fall visitor to eastern U. S. from New Jersey south, usually in flocks of Broad-winged Hawks. Winters in South America. Rare but regular in southern Florida in winter; very rare in southern Texas in winter.

Red-tailed Hawk

immature

"Harlan's Hawk"

adult

"Krider's Hawk"

light phase

dark phase

light phase
immature

Swainson's Hawk

dark phase

light phase

light phase

intermediate

Rough-legged Hawk *Buteo lagopus*

L 22" (56 cm) W 56" (142 cm) Long white tail with dark band or bands identifies this hawk in all plumages. Adult male has multibanded tail with a broad blackish subterminal band. Adult female's tail is brown toward tip with a thin black subterminal band. Immatures show a single broad brown tail band. Wings are long, fairly narrow. Seen in flight from above, white at base of tail is conspicuous; note small white patches at base of primaries on upperwings. From below, look for dark wrist patches, legs feathered to the toes. In the common light phase, pale head contrasts with darker back and dark belly band, especially in females and immatures. Dark phase is uncommon. A hawk of open country, the Roughleg often hovers while hunting. Perches low or on the ground. During breeding season gives a soft, plaintive courting whistle. Alarm call is a loud screech or squeal. Roughlegs migrate in loose flocks but are otherwise generally seen singly or in pairs.

Ferruginous Hawk *Buteo regalis*

L 23" (58 cm) W 53" (135 cm) Rust back and shoulders; paler head; white tail washed with pale rust. Wings are long, broad. On upperwing surface, large white patches make a bold flash. Seen from below, flight feathers lack barring; rusty leggings form a conspicuous V against whitish underparts. Dark phase is uncommon; absence of dark tail bands distinguishes it from similar dark-phase Rough-legged Hawk. Immature Ferruginous Hawk almost or entirely lacks red leggings; resembles Great Plains form of Red-tailed Hawk (preceding page), but has larger white wing patches, lacks dark bar on leading edge of underwing. The Ferruginous Hawk inhabits dry, open country. Often hovers when hunting. Perches in trees, on poles, or on the ground. In breeding season, gives harsh, gull-like alarm calls, *kree-a, ke-a-ah,* or *kaah.* Fairly common, but may be declining over much of range. Rare wanderer east to Wisconsin, Illinois, Arkansas, Louisiana in migration; rare migrant in Minnesota, may also breed there.

White-tailed Hawk *Buteo albicaudatus*

L 23" (58 cm) W 50" (127 cm) Wings fairly long and pointed; at rest, wing tips project to or beyond end of tail. Short tail is white with single black band. Rusty shoulders highly visible against dark gray upperparts. Underparts and wing linings vary from snow white to lightly barred. White-tailed Hawk requires two years to acquire full adult plumage. First-year birds are brown above, heavily streaked below; shoulder feathering edged with rust; tail faintly barred. Best identified by wing and tail shape. Whitetail's call is a repeated series of high-pitched, musical *kil-la* or *ke* notes. Fairly common in southernmost Texas, in open coastal grasslands and semiarid inland brush country. Hunts chiefly in flight, dropping down upon prey.

Rough-legged Hawk

♀

♂

dark phase ♂

immature

Ferruginous Hawk

immature

adult

White-tailed Hawk

adult

1st year

adult

1st year

Common Black-Hawk *Buteogallus anthracinus*

L 21" (53 cm) W 50" (127 cm) Wings broad and rounded; tail short, broad. Adult uniformly blackish, but tail has broad white band and narrow white tip. Legs and cere (fleshy area at base of bill) bright yellow. Whitish patch at base of primaries is smaller and less distinct than on Black Vulture (page 182). Distinguished from Zone-tailed Hawk by broader wings; broader tail with different pattern; more extensive yellow under eye. Immature generally buffy on underparts and wing linings; best identified by shape. Distinctive call, a harsh, high-pitched *ka-a-a-ah*. Rare, local, and declining; found along rivers and streams. Hunts from low perch, preying primarily on crustaceans, frogs, fish, and reptiles. Casual in summer north to Utah; very rare in winter in southeastern Texas.

Harris' Hawk *Parabuteo unicinctus*

L 21" (53 cm) W 46" (117 cm) Chocolate brown above and below, with conspicuous chestnut shoulder patches, leggings, and wing linings; white at base and tip of long tail. Immature similar above but streaked below; chestnut shoulders are less distinct than in adult. Inhabits semiarid woodland, brushland. Nests in mesquite, yucca, and saguaro. Declining in southern Texas and southern Arizona. May straggle north and west of range, but birds sighted there may have escaped from falconers.

Zone-tailed Hawk *Buteo albonotatus*

L 20" (51 cm) W 51" (130 cm) Slate black or dark gray overall, with barred flight feathers. Legs and cere bright yellow. Has slimmer wings than Common Black-Hawk, and longer tail with several whitish bands. Soars teetering on uptilted wings like Turkey Vulture, which it resembles. Look for Zone-tailed Hawk's banded tail, yellow cere; head is larger than Turkey Vulture and feathered. Immature has narrowly barred grayish tail, some white flecking on breast. Uncommon; found in mesa and mountain country, often near watercourses; drops from low glide on rodents, lizards, fish, frogs. Call is an insistent squealing whistle.

Short-tailed Hawk *Buteo brachyurus*

L 15¹/₂" (39 cm) W 35" (89 cm) A small, chunky hawk, resident but uncommon in Florida south of the Panhandle; in winter, found south of Lake Okeechobee. Two color phases. Adults are black above, but underparts and wing linings are either all-black or all-white; tail dark-banded. Immatures are either buff below with some dark streaks or dark with some buff mottling. Found in mixed woodland-grassland.

Common Black-Hawk

adult

immature

Harris' Hawk

adult

immature

adult

Turkey Vulture for comparison

immaturo

adult

Zone-tailed Hawk

adult

Short-tailed Hawk

light phase

light phase

dark phase

Osprey *Pandion haliaetus*

L 22-25" (56-64 cm) W 58-72" (147-183 cm) Dark brown above, white below, with white head, prominent dark eye stripe. Males are usually all-white below; females have a prominent necklace of dark streaking. Immature is edged with pale buff above; underparts slightly buffy. In flight, the Osprey's long, narrow wings are bent back at the wrist, like a gull's; dark wrist patches are conspicuous. Wings are slightly arched in soaring. Ospreys nest near fresh or salt water; eat fish almost exclusively. Hovering over water, they dive toward prey, then plunge feetfirst to snatch it. Bulky nests are built in trees, on sheds, poles, docks; also on platforms specially constructed for Ospreys. Conservation programs and elimination of DDT in recent years have halted decline of species. Now fairly common in coastal range. Uncommon and local inland; seen chiefly during migration. Calls include a loud, whistled *kyew kyew kyew kyew kyew*.

Falcons and Caracara (Family Falconidae)

These powerful hunters are distinguished from hawks by their long wings, bent back at the wrist and, except in the Crested Caracara, narrow and pointed. Females are larger than the males.

Aplomado Falcon *Falco femoralis*

L 15-16¹⁄₂" (38-42 cm) W 40-48" (102-122 cm) Once fairly common in open grasslands and deserts from southern Texas to southern Arizona; now uncommon and local from southern Mexico south, very rare in southwestern U.S. In flight, long, pointed, and rather narrow wings and long, banded tail resemble immature Mississippi Kite (page 186). Note slate gray crown, conspicuously marked head; dark patches on sides contrast with whitish or cinnamon breast and cinnamon belly. Immature is cinnamon below, with streaked breast.

Crested Caracara *Polyborus plancus*

L 23" (58 cm) W 50" (127 cm) Large head, long neck, long legs. Blackish-brown overall, with white throat and neck, red bare facial skin. Immature is edged and spotted with buff above, streaked below. Inhabits open brushlands; often seen on the ground in company with vultures. Feeds on carrion; also hunts small animals. In flight, shows white patches at ends of rounded wings. Call is a harsh cackle, for which the bird is named. Uncommon and perhaps declining in U. S. range.

Osprey

♀

immature ♀

immature ♀

Aplomado Falcon

♂

adult

immature

Crested Caracara

Eurasian Kestrel *Falco tinnunculus*

L 13¹/₂" (34 cm) W 29" (74 cm) Very rare vagrant in Alaska and on the east coast. Resembles American Kestrel, but note larger size and single, not double, dark facial stripe. Male has russet wings, gray tail; male American Kestrel's wings are gray, tail russet. Found in open country, farms, and towns. Hovers as it hunts for rodents, large insects, lizards.

American Kestrel *Falco sparverius*

L 10¹/₂" (27 cm) W 23" (58 cm) Smallest and most common of our falcons. Identified by russet back and tail, double black stripes on white face. Note male's blue-gray wings; reddish tail and back readily distinguish it from Merlin and from much larger Peregrine Falcon (next page; see also page 206). Immatures resemble adults but have more streaking on underparts. Found both in open country and in cities, kestrels feed on insects, small reptiles and mammals, hovering over prey before plunging. Also feed on small birds, chiefly in winter. Call is a shrill, loud *killy killy killy*. Formerly called Sparrow Hawk.

Merlin *Falco columbarius* *L 12" (31 cm) W 25" (64 cm)*

Male is gray-blue above; female dark brown. Both are heavily streaked below. Merlins lack the strong facial pattern and russet upperparts of kestrels. Plumage varies geographically from the very dark form, *F.c. suckleyi,* of the Pacific northwest to the pale *richardsonii* of central Canada and the Midwest. The widespread *columbarius* is intermediate in plumage. In flight (page 206), strongly barred tail distinguishes Merlin from the much larger Peregrine and Prairie Falcons. Nests in open woods or wooded prairies; otherwise found in a variety of habitats. Preys on birds, caught in flight, usually by a sudden burst of speed rather than by diving. Also eats large insects, small rodents. Uncommon; very local in southern portion of range. Most often sighted during migration. Formerly called Pigeon Hawk.

Eurasian
Kestrel
♀

immature ♂
♂

American
Kestrel

♂

suckleyi
♀
♂

columbarius
♀

Merlin

♀

♂

richardsonii

Prairie Falcon *Falco mexicanus*
L 15¹/₂-19¹/₂″ (39-50 cm) W 35-43″ (89-109 cm) Pale brown above; creamy-white and heavily spotted below. Crown is streaked; facial markings narrower, paler than those of similar immature Peregrine Falcon. Compare also with female Merlin (preceding page). In flight, all ages show distinctive dark axillaries and wing coverts. Immature is buffy below. Prairie Falcons inhabit dry, open country, prairies, occasionally woodlands. Prey chiefly on birds, pursuing them in flight with spectacular speed; also dive upon rodents, lizards, large insects. Uncommon to fairly common. Small numbers winter throughout the breeding range.

Peregrine Falcon *Falco peregrinus*
L 16-20″ (41-51 cm) W 36-44″ (91-112 cm) Crown and nape black; black wedge extends below eye, forming a distinctive helmet, absent in smaller Merlin (preceding page) and similar Prairie Falcon. Plumage varies from pale in the subspecies *F.p. tundrius* of the north to very dark in *pealei* on the northwest coast and Aleutians. Intermediate *anatum* subspecies of the west once ranged the continent. Immature Peregrine is dark brownish above, forehead pale; underparts heavily streaked. In flight, in all forms and ages, absence of contrasting axillaries and wing coverts distinguishes Peregrine from Prairie Falcon. Peregrines inhabit open country near cliffs, often near seabird colonies; occasionally seen in cities. Prey chiefly on birds. Rare and local in the west. Eastern populations declined seriously in recent decades, due largely to pesticides. Peregrines are now being reintroduced in many parts of their former range, but most eastern sightings, usually along the coast, are of migrating *tundrius* birds. Uncommon in winter in U.S.

Gyrfalcon *Falco rusticolus*
L 20-25″ (51-64 cm) W 50-64″ (127-163 cm) Heavily built; wings broad-based and pointed. Tends to fly low, flushing prey which it then pursues with speed and power. Plumages vary from white, found mostly in the far northeast, to dark, mostly in the western range. Tail may be barred or unbarred. Dark phase and variable gray phase resemble Peregrine Falcon but lack dark helmet. The Gyrfalcon inhabits open tundra near rocky outcrops and cliffs. In winter, generally seen in coastal areas. Preys chiefly on large birds. Uncommon throughout its range; winters irregularly south to dashed line on map.

Prairie Falcon

pealei

immature adult

Peregrine Falcon

anatum

adult

tundrius

immature

adult

immature

Gyrfalcon

gray phase dark phase

white phase

Female Hawks in Flight

Black-shouldered Kite

Mississippi Kite

1st summer

Hook-billed Kite

Snail Kite

American Kestrel

Peregrine Falcon

anatum

Merlin

columbarius

Gyrfalcon

gray phase

Prairie Falcon

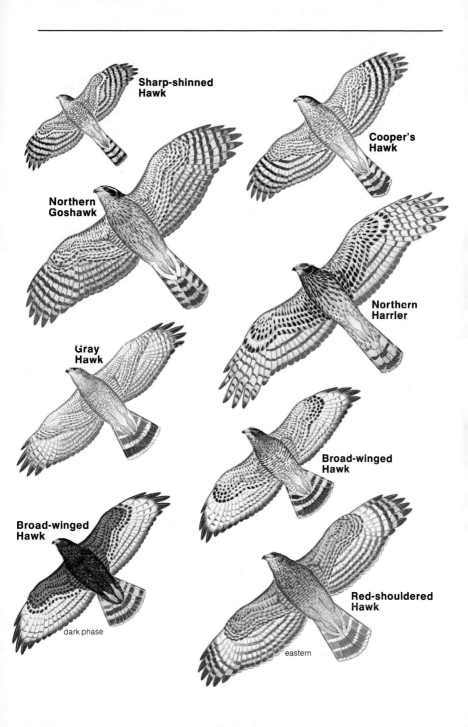

Sharp-shinned
Hawk

Cooper's
Hawk

Northern
Goshawk

Northern
Harrier

Gray
Hawk

Broad-winged
Hawk

Broad-winged
Hawk

dark phase

Red-shouldered
Hawk

eastern

Female Hawks in Flight

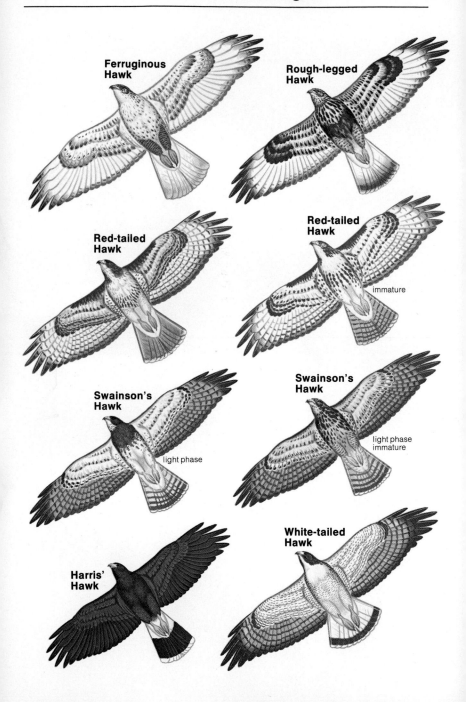

Ferruginous Hawk

Rough-legged Hawk

Red-tailed Hawk

Red-tailed Hawk

immature

Swainson's Hawk

light phase

Swainson's Hawk

light phase immature

Harris' Hawk

White-tailed Hawk

Grouse, Ptarmigan (Family Phasianidae)

Ground-dwelling game birds with short, strong bills, feathered nostrils, and short, rounded wings. Flight is brief but strong. Males perform elaborate courtship displays. Some species use the same strutting grounds, known as leks, year after year.

♪ **Ruffed Grouse** *Bonasa umbellus* L 17″ (43 cm)
Black ruffs on sides of neck give this bird its name. Note also multibanded tail with a wide, dark band near tip; dark band is incomplete in the female. The two color phases, red and gray, are most apparent in tail color. Ruffed Grouse are fairly common in mixed woodlands. Flushed birds burst into flight with a roar of wings. In spring, the male attracts females to his territory by raising ruffs and crest, fanning his tail, and beating his wings to make a hollow, accelerating drumming noise.

♪ **Spruce Grouse** *Dendragapus canadensis* L 16″ (41 cm)
Male has dark throat and breast, edged in white; red eye combs. Over most of range, both sexes have black tail with chestnut tip. Birds of the northern Rockies and Cascades, "Franklin's Grouse," have white spots on uppertail coverts; male's tail is all-dark. In all forms of Spruce Grouse, females have two color phases, red and gray; generally resemble female Blue Grouse but are smaller and have black barring and white spots below. Juveniles resemble red-phase female. Spruce Grouse inhabit open coniferous forests with dense undergrowth. Frequently seen along roadsides or perched in trees. Female's high-pitched call is thought to be territorial. In courtship display, male spreads his tail, erects red combs above eyes, and rapidly beats his wings. Some males give a series of deep hoots, lower pitched than those of the Blue Grouse. In territorial flight display, male flutters upward; "Franklin's Grouse" ends this performance by beating his wings together, making a clapping sound.

♪ **Blue Grouse** *Dendragapus obscurus* L 20″ (51 cm)
Male's sooty-gray plumage sets off yellow-orange comb above eye. On each side of neck, white-based feathers cover an inflatable bare patch, the neck sac, purple in Rocky Mountain birds, yellow in coastal birds. Females are mottled brown above, with plain gray belly. Both sexes have dark tail with gray band, except populations in the northern Rockies, which show no band. Blue Grouse spend the summer in deciduous forests, moving to higher altitude fir forests in winter. Call is a series of hoots, higher pitched than those of the Spruce Grouse. Courting males stand in a high spot and inflate their neck sacs to amplify their hooting. Male courtship display also involves fluttering above the ground or making short circular flights, then strutting in front of the female with tail fanned, body tipped forward, head drawn in, wings dragging the ground.

gray phase ♂

red phase ♂

Ruffed Grouse

red phase ♀

red phase ♀

gray phase ♀

Spruce Grouse

"Franklin's Grouse"

♂

♂

Blue Grouse

northern Rockies ♂

coastal ♂

southern Rockies ♀

Ptarmigans

Hardy northern birds with feathered legs and feet. Plumage is molted three times a year, matching seasonal changes in habitat. Birds are dark and mottled in summer, more finely mottled in early fall, and white in winter. Red eye combs can be inflated or concealed in courtship and aggression displays.

White-tailed Ptarmigan *Lagopus leucurus*

L 12¹/₂" (32 cm) Distinguished in all seasons by white tail. Winter plumage is all-white except for dark bill and eye, red eye comb. In summer, body is mottled blackish or brown with white belly, wings, and tail. Spring and fall molts give a patchy white appearance. Locally common on rocky alpine slopes, high meadows. Calls include a henlike clucking and soft, low hoots. Small numbers have been introduced in the central High Sierra with apparent success.

Rock Ptarmigan *Lagopus mutus* L 14" (36 cm)

Mottled summer plumage is dark brown or grayish-brown, male generally lacks the reddish tones of male Willow Ptarmigan. In all-white winter plumage, male has a black line from bill through eye, lacking in male Willow Ptarmigan. In both sexes, bill is slightly smaller than in Willow Ptarmigan. Females are otherwise hard to distinguish from Willows. Plumage is patchy white during spring and fall molts. Both species have white wings and black tail year round. The Rock Ptarmigan is common on high, rocky slopes, tundra; in breeding season, generally prefers higher and more barren habitat than does the Willow Ptarmigan. Small numbers regularly winter south of resident range. Calls include low growls and croaks and noisy cackles.

Willow Ptarmigan *Lagopus lagopus* L 15" (38 cm)

Mottled summer plumage of male is generally redder than in Rock Ptarmigan. All-white winter plumage lacks the black eye line found in male Rock Ptarmigan. Bill is slightly larger in Willow Ptarmigan. Female is otherwise hard to distinguish from Rock Ptarmigan. Both species retain white wings and black tail year round. Plumage is patchy white during spring and fall molts. Willow Ptarmigan is common on tundra, especially in thickets of willow and alder. In breeding season, generally prefers wetter, brushier habitat than Rock Ptarmigan. Calls include low growls and croaks, noisy cackles. In courtship and territorial displays, male utters a raucous *go-back go-back go-backa go-backa go-backa*.

White-tailed Ptarmigan

winter

summer ♀

molting fall ♂

summer ♂

Rock Ptarmigan

winter ♀

summer ♀

summer ♂

winter ♂

fall ♂

summer ♀

Willow Ptarmigan

molting spring ♂

winter

summer ♂

summer ♂

Greater Prairie-Chicken *Tympanuchus cupido*

L 17" (43 cm) Heavily barred with dark brown, cinnamon, and pale buff above and below. Short rounded tail is all-dark in male, barred in female. Male has fleshy yellow-orange eye combs. Both sexes have elongated dark neck feathers, longer in males and erected during courtship to show inflated golden neck sacs. Courting males make a deep *oo-loo-woo* sound like blowing across the top of an empty bottle, known as a "booming" display. Uncommon, local, and seriously declining. Found in areas of natural tallgrass prairie interspersed with cropland. A small dark form, the endangered "Attwater's Prairie-Chicken," is found in small numbers in southeast Texas. Greater Prairie-Chicken was once considered to be a single species with Lesser Prairie-Chicken.

Lesser Prairie-Chicken *Tympanuchus pallidicinctus*

L 16" (41cm) Resembles Greater Prairie-Chicken, but slightly smaller, paler, less heavily barred below. Male has yellow eye combs, blackish tail; female's tail barred. Courting male displays dull orange-red neck sacs and erects dark neck tufts. Rare, local, and declining in sagebrush and shortgrass prairie country. Male's courtship "booming" is similar to Greater Prairie-Chicken, but notes are higher pitched.

Sharp-tailed Grouse *Tympanuchus phasianellus*

L 17" (43 cm) Very similar to prairie-chickens, but underparts are scaled and spotted, not barred; tail is mostly white and pointed, not dark and rounded. Yellowish eye combs are less prominent. Compare with female Ring-necked Pheasant (page 222). Birds are darkest in Alaska and northern Canada, palest in the Plains. Male has longer tail than female; purplish neck sacs are inflated during courtship display. His courting notes include cackling and a single, low *coo-oo,* accompanied by rattling of quills. Sharp-tailed Grouse inhabits grasslands, sagebrush, woodland edges, and river canyons. Where ranges overlap, occasionally hybridizes with Greater Prairie-Chicken and Blue Grouse (page 210).

Sage Grouse *Centrocercus urophasianus* L 28" (71 cm)

Blackish belly, long pointed tail feathers, and very large size are distinctive. Male is larger than female and has yellow eye combs, black throat and bib, and large white ruff on breast. In flight, dark belly and absence of white outer tail feathers distinguish this bird from Sharp-tailed Grouse. Courting male raises and fans tail, and rapidly inflates and deflates air sacs, emitting a loud, bubbling popping. Common and widespread throughout western sagebrush of foothills and plains.

Greater Prairie-Chicken
♀
♂

Lesser Prairie-Chicken
♀
♂

Sharp-tailed Grouse

Sage Grouse
♀
♂
♀

Northern Bobwhite *Colinus virginianus* L 9³/₄" (25 cm)
Mottled reddish-brown quail with short gray tail. Flanks are
striped with reddish-brown. Throat and eye stripe are white in
male, buffy in female. Juvenile is smaller and duller; compare
with Japanese Quail. Common in brushlands and open woodlands, the Northern Bobwhite feeds and roosts in coveys except during nesting season. Male's spring call is a rising,
whistled *bob-white;* whistled *hoy* call is heard year round. The
Bobwhite population in the northwest was introduced. At
northern edge of range, numbers are greatly reduced after
harsh winters. The "Masked Bobwhite," an endangered subspecies, has been reintroduced from Mexico to its former
range in southern Arizona. Male has striking black throat and
bright cinnamon underparts.

Japanese Quail *Coturnix japonica* L 7¹/₂" (19 cm)
Rarely seen in the wild; attempts to establish this Asian gamebird in North America have met with little success, although
this species is often raised on hunting preserves. Smaller than
the Northern Bobwhite; appears almost tailless. Mottled
brown above, buffy below, with pale eye stripes. Female is
heavily streaked on breast. A secretive quail, more often heard
than seen. Calls include a low *chuck-churrr.* Formerly considered a subspecies of Coturnix Quail.

♪ **Montezuma Quail** *Cyrtonyx montezumae* L 8³/₄" (22 cm)
Plump, short-tailed quail. Male has distinctive facial pattern
and rounded pale brown crest on back of head. Back and wings
mottled black, brown, and tan; breast dark chestnut; sides and
flanks dark gray with white spots. Female is mottled pinkish-
brown below with less distinct head markings. Juvenile is
smaller, paler, with dark spotting on underparts. Fairly common but local in open juniper- or pine-oak woodlands of semiarid slopes and mountains. Tends to freeze rather than run or
fly from intruders. Call is a loud, quavering, descending whinny. Formerly called Harlequin Quail.

♪ **Scaled Quail** *Callipepla squamata* L 10" (25 cm)
Grayish quail with conspicuous white-tipped crest. Bluish-
gray breast and mantle feathers have dark edges, creating a
shingled or scaly effect. Female's crest is buffy and smaller.
Males in southernmost Texas tend to show a dark chestnut
patch on belly. Juvenile resembles adult but is more mottled
above, with less conspicuous scaling. Fairly common; found
on barren mesas and plateaus, semidesert scrublands. In fall,
forms large coveys. During breeding season, both sexes give a
location call when separated, a low, nasal *chip-churr,* accented
on the second syllable.

Northern Bobwhite

♂

♀

"Masked Bobwhite"

juvenile

Japanese Quail

♀

♂

Montezuma Quail

♀

♂

juvenile

Scaled Quail

♂

♂

juvenile

Gambel's Quail *Callipepla gambelii* L 11" (28 cm)

Grayish above, with prominent teardrop-shaped plume. Unscaled underparts and chestnut sides streaked with white distinguish Gambel's from California Quail. Male has dark forehead, black throat and patch on belly. Smaller juvenile is tan and gray with pale mottling and streaking. Shows less scaling and streaking than darker California juvenile; nape and throat are grayer. Common in desert scrublands and thickets, usually near permanent water source. Gregarious; in fall and winter, assembles in coveys of as many as 40 birds. Calls include varied grunts, cackles, chuckles, and a plaintive *qua-el;* loud, querulous *chi-ca-go-go* call similar to California Quail but usually has four notes rather than three. Sometimes hybridizes with Scaled Quail (preceding page) and California Quail in areas where range and habitat overlap. Introduced population in Idaho may become permanently established.

California Quail *Callipepla californica* L 10" (25 cm)

Gray and brown above, with prominent teardrop-shaped plume. Scaled underparts and brown sides streaked with white distinguish California from Gambel's Quail. Body color varies from grayish over most of range to brown in coastal mountains of California; extremes are shown here in females. Male has pale forehead, black throat, and chestnut patch on belly. Juvenile is smaller; resembles Gambel's juvenile, but is darker and shows traces of scaling on underparts. Common in open woodlands, brushy foothills, stream valleys, suburbs, usually near permanent water source. Gregarious; in fall and winter, assembles in coveys of up to 200 birds. Calls include varied grunts, cackles, and chuckles; loud, emphatic *chi-ca-go* call similar to Gambel's Quail but usually has three notes rather than four. Most populations in northeastern portion of range and in Utah are probably introduced.

Mountain Quail *Oreortyx pictus* L 11" (28 cm)

Gray and brown above, with two long, thin head plumes, sometimes appearing as one; gray breast; chestnut sides boldly barred with white; chestnut throat outlined in white. Sexes alike, but female has shorter head plumes. Amount of brown and gray in upperparts varies in different forms of this species. Smaller juvenile has grayer underparts and longer head plumes than Gambel's or California Quail juveniles. Locally common in brushy ravines, mountain slopes, at altitudes up to 10,000 feet. Non-migratory but descends to lower altitudes in winter. Gregarious, forming coveys of as many as 20 birds in fall and winter. The mating call, a clear, descending *quee-ark,* can be heard up to a mile away. An enthusiastic imitation of this call may lure this somewhat secretive species into view.

Gambel's Quail

juvenile

Scaled-Gambel's Hybrid

gray form ♀

brown form ♀

California Quail

brown form juvenile

Mountain Quail

juvenile

brown form ♂

gray form ♀

Chukar *Alectoris chukar* L 14" (36 cm)

Asian species, introduced in North America as a gamebird. Brownish-gray above; flanks boldly barred black and white; buffy face and throat outlined in black; breast gray; belly buff; outer tail feathers chestnut. Bill and legs are red. Lacks white eyebrow of similar Red-legged Partridge. Sexes are similar, but males are slightly larger and have small leg spurs. Juvenile is smaller and mottled; lacks bold black markings of adults. Chukars have become established in rocky, arid, mountainous areas of the west; game farm birds are released for hunting in the east. In fall and winter, Chukars feed in coveys of 5 to 40 birds. Calls include a series of rapid *chuck chuck chuck* notes and a shrill *whitoo* alarm note.

Black Francolin *Francolinus francolinus* L 14" (36 cm)

Asian species, successfully established in Louisiana and parts of south Florida. Male's glossy black plumage is heavily marked with white and buff; white cheek patch; chestnut collar. Female is mottled brown overall, with paler chestnut patch on nape. A secretive bird, partial to dense vegetation, grassy fields, and croplands. Song of male is a loud, rhythmic *chik-cheek-cheek-keraykek*.

Red-legged Partridge *Alectoris rufa* L 14" (36 cm)

A European species, widely introduced to North America but has not yet become established. Browner above than similar Chukar, with conspicuous white eyebrow, whitish chin and throat, black bib with gray speckles; flanks are gray, barred with black, white, and chestnut. Legs and bill red. A bird of mountainous regions and open, arid lands in the west; feeds chiefly on seeds and leaves, and on roots and tubers it digs from the ground with its bill. Call is a harsh, staccato *chuck-chuck-chuck-chukuk*.

Gray Partridge *Perdix perdix* L 12¹⁄₂" (32 cm)

Widely and successfully introduced from Europe. Grayish-brown bird with rusty face and throat, paler in female. Male has large brown patch on belly. Flanks are barred with reddish-brown; outer tail feathers rusty. Inhabits open farmlands, grassy fields. In fall, forms coveys of 12 to 15 birds. Calls include a hoarse *kee-ah*.

Himalayan Snowcock *Tetraogallus himalayensis*

L 28" (71 cm) Large Asian bird, apparently successfully established only in the Ruby Mountains of northeastern Nevada. Gray-brown overall, with tan streaking above. Whitish face and throat are outlined with chestnut stripes; undertail coverts white. Inhabits mountainous terrain, flying downslope early in the day and feeding on tubers and plants as it walks slowly back uphill. Clucks and cackles constantly as it feeds.

Chukar

♀

juvenile

Black
Francolin

♀

♂

Red-legged
Partridge

♂

♀

Gray
Partridge

♂

Himalayan
Snowcock

♂

Ring-necked Pheasant *Phasianus colchicus*

♂ L 33″ (84 cm) ♀ L 21″ (53 cm) Introduced from Asia, this large, flashy game bird has a long, pointed tail and short, rounded wings. Male is iridescent bronze overall, mottled with brown, black, and green; head varies from dark, glossy green to purplish, with fleshy red eye patches and iridescent ear tufts. Often shows a broad white neck ring. Legs spurred, unfeathered. Female is buffy overall, much smaller and duller than male. Ring-necked Pheasants are locally common throughout North America's grain belt; elsewhere local populations are not firmly established. Found in open country, farmlands, brushy areas, woodland edges; roosts in trees. When flushed, rises almost vertically with a loud whirring of wings. Male's territorial call is a loud, penetrating *kok-cack*. Both sexes give hoarse, croaking alarm notes. White-winged forms (not shown) have been established in some parts of the west. The Green Pheasant, a Japanese form once considered a separate species, has been introduced in tidewater Virginia and southern Delaware.

Wild Turkey *Meleagris gallopavo*

♂ L 46″ (117 cm) ♀ L 37″ (94 cm) Largest game bird native to North America; slightly smaller, more slender than domesticated bird. Male has dark, iridescent body, flight feathers barred with white, red wattles, blackish breast tuft, spurred legs; bare-skinned head is blue and pink. Tail, uppertail coverts, and lower rump feathers are tipped with chestnut on eastern birds, buffy-white on western birds. Female and immature smaller, duller than male, often lack breast tuft. Birds of the open forest, Wild Turkeys forage mostly on the ground for seeds, nuts, acorns, insects. At night they roost in trees. In spring a male's gobbling call may be heard a mile away. Stocked in much of former range; may become more widely established.

Chachalacas (Family Cracidae)

Tropical-forest birds with short, rounded wings and long tails. Generally secretive but highly vocal. One species of this family is found in North America.

Plain Chachalaca *Ortalis vetula* L 22″ (56 cm)

Gray to brownish-olive above, with small head, slight crest; long, lustrous, dark green tail tipped with white. Patch of bare skin on throat, usually grayish, is pinkish-red in breeding male. Inhabits tall chaparral thickets along the Rio Grande; feeds in trees, chiefly on leaves and buds. Introduced to Georgia's Sapelo Island. Male's voice is a deep, ringing *cha-cha-lac;* female's voice higher pitched. The sound of a flock in full chorus is memorable.

Ring-necked Pheasant
♂
♀
♀
♂ ♀
"Green Pheasant"

♂
eastern
♀
Wild Turkey

♂
Plain Chachalaca
western ♂

Pigeons and Doves (Family Columbidae)

Familiar traits of the city pigeon—plump body and small, bobbing head—hold true for our other pigeons and doves. Usually the larger species are called pigeons, the smaller ones doves. All are strong, fast fliers. Immatures have pale-tipped feathers, lack the neck markings of adults. Pigeons and doves feed chiefly on grain, other seeds, and fruit.

Band-tailed Pigeon *Columba fasciata* L 14¹/₂″ (37 cm)
Purplish head and breast; dark-tipped yellow bill, yellow legs; broad gray tail band. Adult has narrow white band on nape. Flocks in flight resemble Rock Doves but are uniform, not varied, in plumage and lack contrasting white rump or black band at end of tail. Locally common in low-altitude coniferous forests in the northwest, oak or oak-conifer woodlands in the southwest; also increasingly in suburban gardens, parks. Eats berries, nuts, and acorns. Call is a low *coo-cooo*. Rare in Alaska; absent from Central Valley of California. Casual in winter north to central Arizona and New Mexico.

Red-billed Pigeon *Columba flavirostris* L 14¹/₂″ (37 cm)
Rare visitor to the lower Rio Grande Valley; the only all-dark Texas pigeon with a red bill. Distinctive call heard in early spring and summer, a long, high-pitched *cooooo* followed by three loud *up-cup-a-coo*'s. Perches in tall trees above a brushy understory; forages for seeds, nuts, figs. Seldom comes to the ground except to drink.

White-crowned Pigeon *Columba leucocephala*
L 13¹/₂″ (34 cm) A large, square-tailed pigeon of the Florida Everglades and Keys. Crown patch varies from shining white in adult males to grayish-white in most females and grayish-brown in immatures. Otherwise this species looks all-black; the iridescent collar is visible only in good light. Flocks commute from nest colonies in coastal mangroves to feed inland on fruit. Most winter on Caribbean islands. Calls: loud, deep *coo-cura-cooo* or *coo-croo*.

Rock Dove *Columba livia* L 12¹/₂″ (32 cm)
The highly variable city pigeon; multicolored forms were developed over centuries of near-domestication. Birds most closely resembling their wild ancestors have head and neck darker than back, black bars on inner wing, white rump, black band at end of tail. Introduced from Europe by early settlers, now widespread and common, particularly in urban settings. Nests and roosts chiefly on high window ledges, bridges, barns. Feeds during the day in parks and fields. Call is a soft *coo-cuk-cuk-cuk-cooo*.

**Band-tailed
Pigeon**

**Red-billed
Pigeon**

**White-crowned
Pigeon**

♂

♀

**Rock
Dove**

color variations

Mourning Dove *Zenaida macroura* *L 12" (31 cm)*
Trim-bodied with long tail tapering to a point. Black spots on upperwing; pinkish wash on underparts. In flight, shows white tips on outer tail feathers. Juvenile has heavy spotting and scaled effect on wings. Call is a mournful *oowoo-woo-woo-woo*. Our most abundant and widespread dove; inhabits farmyards, grassy meadows, cultivated fields, frequents backyard feeders, suburbs, towns, and cities. Wings produce a fluttering whistle as the bird takes flight. May breed as far north as southeastern Alaska.

Zenaida Dove *Zenaida aurita* *L 10" (25 cm)*
West Indian species, very rare visitor to the Florida Keys, where it formerly bred, and to the southernmost Florida mainland. Distinguished from Mourning Dove by white on trailing edge of secondaries and by shorter, rounded, gray-tipped tail. Lacks white wing patches and white tail tips of White-winged Dove. Feeds on open ground close to water, usually near mangroves. Call similar to the Mourning Dove's but briefer and faster.

White-winged Dove *Zenaida asiatica* *L 11¹/₂" (29 cm)*
Large white wing patches and shorter, rounded tail distinguish this species from Mourning Dove. Compare also with Zenaida Dove. Feeds on grain, wild seeds, and cactus fruits and blossoms. Nests singly or in large colonies in dense mesquite, mature citrus groves, riparian woodlands, and saguaro-paloverde deserts. Drawn-out, cooing call, *who-cooks-for-you*, has many variations.

Ringed Turtle-Dove *Streptopelia risoria* *L 11" (28 cm)*
Old World species, popular as a cage bird. Small populations established, but not expanding, around Los Angeles, Miami, Tampa, Houston, and Mobile. Occasional strays may be seen throughout U.S. Some birds lack the narrow black collar; a few are pure white. Call is a soft, rolling *coo-curroo*.

Spotted Dove *Streptopelia chinensis* *L 12" (31 cm)*
An Asian species introduced in Los Angeles in early 1900s; now well established in southern California parks and gardens, forest edges, farmlands. Named for spotted collar, distinct in adults, obscured in young birds. Wings and long, white-tipped tail are more rounded than in Mourning Dove; wings are unmarked. Call, a harsh *oo-hoo-oo-hurrrrp*.

juvenile

Mourning Dove

Zenaida Dove

White-winged Dove

Ringed Turtle-Dove

Spotted Dove

Common Ground-Dove *Columbina passerina*

L 6¹/₂" (17 cm) A stocky dove with scaled effect on head and breast; short tail, often raised. Bright chestnut primaries and wing linings visible in flight. Male has a slate gray crown, pinkish-gray underparts. Female is grayer, more uniformly colored. Call: a soft, ascending *wah-up*. Forages on open ground in the east and brushy rangeland in the west. Sometimes breeds north of its usual Gulf coast range; casual as far north as New York and Oregon in fall and winter.

Ruddy Ground-Dove *Columbina talpacoti* *L 6³/₄" (17 cm)*

Widespread in Latin America; a rare visitor to south Texas. Lacks scaling of similar Common Ground-Dove. Male has gray crown and rich chestnut upperparts. Female, less ruddy, has a chestnut wash on wings and uppertail coverts. Both show black on underwing coverts and sides of tail.

Inca Dove *Columbina inca* *L 8¹/₄" (21 cm)*

Plumage conspicuously scalloped, especially on the belly. In flight, shows chestnut on wings like Common Ground-Dove, but note the Inca Dove's longer, white-edged tail. Found in cactus and mesquite country, usually near human habitations, often in parks and gardens. Wanders north to Kansas and Oklahoma. Call, a double *cooo-coo*.

White-tipped Dove *Leptotila verreauxi* *L 11¹/₂" (29 cm)*

This large, plump dove has a whitish forehead and throat and dark back. In flight, white tips show plainly on fanned tail. Gleans the ground along the Rio Grande Valley, keeping close to woodlands with dense understory. May perch high in trees. Low-pitched call is like the sound produced by blowing across the top of a bottle. Formerly called White-fronted Dove.

Ruddy Quail-Dove *Geotrygon montana* *L 9³/₄" (25 cm)*

A chunky tropical dove; casual on the Florida Keys. Male's rich rufous upperparts and prominent buffy line under the eye are distinctive. Females are brown above and have a plainer facial pattern. In both sexes, underparts are cinnamon buff. Quail-doves are so named because they resemble quails and have a similar terrestrial life-style.

Key West Quail-Dove *Geotrygon chrysia* *L 12" (31 cm)*

West Indian species, now rare over most of its range; casual visitor on the Keys and south Florida. Larger and proportionately longer tailed than Ruddy Quail-Dove, with a white line under the eye. Upperparts, primaries, and tail are chestnut, glossed with purple and green. Male is highly iridescent above; female is duller. In both sexes, underparts are whitish.

Common Ground-Dove ♂ ♀ ♂

Ruddy Ground-Dove ♀ ♂ ♂

Inca Dove

White-tipped Dove

Ruddy Quail-Dove ♂ ♀

Key West Quail-Dove ♂

Parrots (Family Psittacidae)

Colorful, noisy birds with hooked beaks. Popular as cage birds. Escapes of many different species can be seen in the wild. Most of those shown here have established wild breeding populations.

Rose-ringed Parakeet *Psittacula krameri* L 16" (41 cm)
Small breeding populations of this Asian and African species established around Miami and Los Angeles by escaped cage birds. Note long, narrow tail. Adult male is bright green with reddish bill, black chin, pink collar, and blue wash on nape. Yellow wing linings conspicuous in flight. Adult female has shorter tail; lacks pink collar and black chin. Immature resembles female, but has pink bill; male requires three years to attain full adult plumage. Call is a repeated screeching *kee-ak*. Usually feeds around gardens and orchards.

Budgerigar *Melopsittacus undulatus* L 7" (18 cm)
Commonly called "parakeet," this popular cage bird can be seen in the wild throughout most of continent. Breeding populations seem to be established near Miami and along southwestern Florida coast. Plumage highly variable. In the most common variety in the wild, upperparts are yellow, heavily barred with black; rump and underparts are green, iris white. White wing stripe conspicuous in flight. Male has blue cere, gray-blue legs. Female's cere is brown, legs pinkish. Immature is duller, with barred forehead, dark iris; black throat spots less distinct or absent. Budgies give a warbling call in flight or a muffled screech. Generally found in suburban neighborhoods. Native to Australia.

Canary-winged Parakeet *Brotogeris versicolorus*
L 8³/₄" (22 cm) South American species, established as a fairly common breeder along southeast Florida coast, less common around Los Angeles. Adult is dull green overall with blue-green outer primaries. Remaining flight feathers are mostly white with yellow tinge. In flight, these white wing patches appear translucent. Immature shows less white, more yellow, on wing. Canary-winged Parakeet's noisy call is a rapid series of shrill metallic notes. Inhabits residential areas.

Monk Parakeet *Myiopsitta monachus* L 11¹/₂" (29 cm)
Escaped cage birds of this South American species have established breeding populations in Florida. Local escapes can be seen almost anywhere, but most birds are sighted in Atlantic coast states. Adult is green above with grayish face and throat. Breast is brown-gray with whitish barring; note diffuse yellowish band across belly. Immatures show a green tinge on forehead. In flight, Monk Parakeet appears dark below except for paler face and throat. Call is a loud, staccato shriek. Often feeds in gardens, orchards, or cultivated fields. Builds large, bulky stick nest in tree or atop telephone pole.

Rose-ringed
Parakeet

Budgerigar

Canary-winged
Parakeet

Monk
Parakeet

Red-crowned Parrot *Amazona viridigenalis*
L 12½" (32 cm) Rare fall and winter visitor to southern Texas
from Mexico. Escaped cage birds have established breeding
populations in southeastern Florida and suburban Los Angeles. Adult male has red crown, forehead, lores; blue-violet eyebrow; red wing patch. Female and immature show less red on
head. Call is a harsh, screaming *kree-o krak krak krak.*

Yellow-headed Parrot *Amazona oratrix* *L 14" (36 cm)*
A Mexican species, popular as a cage bird. Breeds in suburban
areas of southeastern Florida and around Los Angeles. Adult's
green plumage sets off yellow head and thighs, red shoulder,
red wing patch. Immature shows less yellow on head. Yellow-
headed Parrots give a variety of raucous calls: a loud *kurrawk,*
whistles, and metallic shrieks.

Thick-billed Parrot *Rhynchopsitta pachyrhyncha*
L 15" (38 cm) Resident but increasingly rare in highland forests
of Mexico. May be very rare fall and winter vagrant to southeastern Arizona, but no reliable sightings since 1930s. Adult is
green overall with red forehead, black bill, and red eyebrow;
compare with Red-crowned Parrot. Bright yellow underwing
patch shows in flight. Immatures lack red eyebrow; bill is light
buff. Thickbills are known for loud screeching.

Trogons (Family Trogonidae)

These beautifully colored
tropical birds have long,
squared-off tails, small feet,
and short, broad bills.
Unlike parrots, trogons
usually are solitary and quiet.

Elegant Trogon *Trogon elegans* *L 12½" (32 cm)*
Male is bronze green above, bright red below, with white
breast band. At close range, look for copper highlights on uppertail. Female is brown above, with white, teardrop-shaped
ear spot on gray-brown head. Juvenile resembles female, but
wing coverts are spotted with pale buff, underparts barred. In
comparison to Eared Trogon, note Elegant's yellow bill, white
breast band, and delicately barred undertail. Call is a monoto-
nous croaking *co-ah.* Prefers dry, wooded terrain. Vagrants are
seen in southwestern New Mexico and southern Texas. Formerly called Coppery-tailed Trogon.

Eared Trogon *Euptilotus neoxenus* *L 14" (36 cm)*
Rare and irregular fall and winter visitor from Mexico to pine
forests in the mountains of southeastern Arizona. Larger than
Elegant Trogon. Male is varying shades of iridescent green
above, bright red below. Ear tufts not easily seen in the field.
Female's bill, head, and breast are gray. In comparison to Elegant Trogon, note Eared Trogon's black bill, green wing coverts, lack of white breast band and barring on undertail. Call,
a loud upslurred squeal ending in a *chuck* note.

Red-crowned Parrot

Yellow-headed Parrot

immature

Thick-billed Parrot

Elegant Trogon

♂

♀

♂

♀

Eared Trogon

♂

♀

Cuckoos and Anis (Family Cuculidae)

A large family, widespread in the Old World. Only a few species are seen in North America. Most are slender and long-tailed; two toes point forward, two back.

Common Cuckoo *Cuculus canorus* L 13" *(33 cm)*
Old World species, casual spring and summer visitor to central and western Aleutians and Pribilofs. Closely resembles Oriental Cuckoo. Adult male and adult gray-phase female are gray above, paler below, with whitish belly narrowly barred with gray. Barring is slightly narrower and underparts paler than in Oriental Cuckoo. Hepatic-phase female is rusty-brown above, heavily barred with black on back and tail; rump unmarked or lightly spotted. In flight, this species and the Oriental Cuckoo resemble a small falcon. Male's song is the familiar *cuc-coo* for which the family is named.

Oriental Cuckoo *Cuculus saturatus* L 13" *(33 cm)*
Eurasian species, very rare summer visitor to western Aleutians and Pribilofs. Closely resembles Common Cuckoo. Adult male and adult gray-phase female are gray above, paler below, with whitish belly barred in dark gray. Barring is slightly broader and underparts are buffier than in Common Cuckoo. Hepatic-phase female is rusty-brown above, heavily barred with black on back, rump, and tail. The Oriental Cuckoo has a four-note call: *du-du-du-du*.

Smooth-billed Ani *Crotophaga ani* L 14¹/₂" *(37 cm)*
Huge bill has a ridged upper mandible that rises above the crown and arches downward at base. Compare with Groove-billed Ani's smaller bill. Bill shape distinguishes anis from grackles (page 424). Black overall with iridescent bronze overtones. Long tail is often dipped and wagged. Found in farmlands, scrublands; often seen feeding on insects stirred up by grazing cattle. Gregarious; several pairs usually share a nest and take turns incubating the eggs. Casual north to New Jersey and along Gulf coast. Call, a whining, rising *quee-lick*.

Groove-billed Ani *Crotophaga sulcirostris* L 13¹/₂" *(34 cm)*
Bill smaller than in Smooth-billed Ani, does not extend above crown. Black overall with iridescent purple and green overtones; long tail, often dipped and wagged. Bill shape distinguishes this species from grackles (page 424). Grooves in bill are visible only at very close range; absent in some adults and young birds. Common in farmlands along Rio Grande Valley; often seen feeding on insects stirred up by grazing cattle. Casual north to Minnesota and west to California. Gregarious; several pairs usually share a nest and take turns incubating the eggs. Call is a liquid *tee-ho*, accented on the first syllable.

**Common
Cuckoo**

hepatic phase ♀

**Oriental
Cuckoo**

hepatic phase ♀

**Groove-billed
Ani**

**Smooth-billed
Ani**

♪ **Mangrove Cuckoo** *Coccyzus minor* *L 12" (31 cm)*
Black mask and buffy underparts distinguish this species from other cuckoos. Upperparts grayish-brown; lacks rufous primaries of Yellow-billed Cuckoo. Black tail feathers are broadly tipped with white. In Florida subspecies, *C.m. maynardi,* paler throat and breast contrast with buffy flanks and belly. Underparts are entirely buffy in *continentalis,* a very rare vagrant along the Gulf coast from Mexico to northwest Florida. In all juveniles, mask is paler, tail pattern muted. Found chiefly in mangrove swamps. Like other cuckoos, perches quietly near center of tree. Call is a slow, guttural *gaw gaw gaw.*

♪ **Yellow-billed Cuckoo** *Coccyzus americanus*
L 12" (31 cm) Grayish-brown above, white below; rufous primaries; lower mandible yellow. Undertail patterned in bold black and white. In juvenile plumage, held well into fall, tail has a much paler pattern; may be confused with Black-billed Cuckoo. Common in open woods, orchards, and streamside willow and alder groves. Song sounds hollow and wooden, a rapid staccato *kuk-kuk-kuk* that usually slows and descends to a *kakakowlp-kowlp* ending. Once numerous but now a very rare breeder in California and southern Oregon. Rare vagrant to the Maritime Provinces during fall migration.

♪ **Black-billed Cuckoo** *Coccyzus erythropthalmus*
L 12" (31 cm) Grayish-brown above, whitish below. Bill is usually all-dark; may show yellow at base of lower mandible. Note also reddish eye ring. Undertail patterned in gray with white tipping; compare with juvenile Yellow-billed Cuckoo. Juvenile Black-billed has a buffy eye ring; undertail is whiter; pale underparts may have buffy tinge; may show a little rusty-brown on outer wing. Adult lacks the rufous primaries of Yellow billed Cuckoo. Common; found in woodlands and along streams. Song usually consists of three- or four-note phrases, *cu-cu-cu* or *cu-cu-cu-cu,* repeated several times. Very rare breeder in north Texas, west Tennessee, and west Idaho.

Greater Roadrunner *Geococcyx californianus*
L 23" (58 cm) Unmistakable; a large ground-dwelling cuckoo streaked with brown and white. Speeds across the desert on long, strong legs. Note long, heavy bill, conspicuous bushy crest, and long, white-edged tail. Short, rounded wings show a white crescent on primaries. Common in scrub desert and mesquite groves; less common in chaparral. Eats insects, lizards, snakes, rodents, and small birds. Song is a dovelike cooing, descending in pitch.

Mangrove Cuckoo

maynardi

continentalis

Yellow-billed Cuckoo

juvenile

Black-billed Cuckoo

juvenile

Greater Roadrunner

Owls

These distinctive birds of prey are divided by structural differences into two families, the Barn Owls (Tytonidae) and the Typical Owls (Strigidae). All have immobile eyes in large heads. Fluffy plumage makes their flight nearly soundless. Many species hunt at night and roost during the day. To find an owl, search the ground for regurgitated pellets of fur and bone below a nest or roost. Listen for flocks of small songbirds noisily mobbing a roosting owl.

Common Barn-Owl *Tyto alba* L 16" (41 cm)
A pale owl with dark eyes in a heart-shaped face. Upperparts are rusty-brown; underparts vary from white to cinnamon. Compare with Snowy Owl (next page), which is all-white, has a round head, yellow eyes. The Barn Owl roosts and nests in dark cavities in city and farm buildings, cliffs, trees. In winter, look for it in dense conifers. Common in the west; uncommon in the east. Typical call is a raspy, hissing screech.

Short-eared Owl *Asio flammeus* L 15" (38 cm)
Tawny; boldly streaked on breast; belly paler, more lightly streaked. Ear tufts are barely visible. In flight, long wings show buffy patch above, black wrist mark below; these markings are usually more prominent than in Long-eared Owl. A bird of open country, marshes, tundra, weedy fields; nests on the ground. Hunts chiefly at dawn and dusk. Flight is wavering, with floppy wingbeats. During the day it roosts on the ground or on open, low perches: short poles, muskrat houses, duck blinds. Fairly common. Somewhat gregarious in winter; groups may gather where prey is abundant. Typical call heard in nesting season is a raspy, high barking.

♪ Long-eared Owl *Asio otus* L 15" (38 cm)
A slender owl with long, close-set ear tufts. Boldly streaked and barred on breast and belly. Wings generally have a less prominent buffy patch and smaller black wrist mark than Short-eared Owl; facial disk is rusty. Lives in thick woods, nesting in trees; hunts only at night. By day it roosts in a tree, close to the trunk, motionless until approached closely. Fairly common. Gregarious in winter; flocks roost in dense evergreens. Call is one or more long *hooo*'s.

♪ Great Horned Owl *Bubo virginianus* L 22" (56 cm)
Size, bulky shape, and white throat separate this owl from the smaller Long-eared Owl; ear tufts distinguish it from other large species. Common; habitats vary from forest to city. Nests in trees, caves, or on the ground. Chiefly nocturnal. Takes prey as large as skunks, grouse. Call is a series of three to eight loud, deep hoots, the second and third hoots often short and rapid. A pale form inhabits forests at tundra's edge in central Canada; compare with Snowy Owl (next page).

Common
Barn-Owl

Short-eared
Owl

Long-eared
Owl

pale form

Great
Horned
Owl

♪ Barred Owl *Strix varia* L 21" (53 cm)

A chunky owl with dark eyes, dark barring on upper breast, dark streaking below. Common in dense coniferous or mixed woods of river bottoms and swamps; also in upland woods, particularly during winter. Chiefly nocturnal; daytime roost is well hidden. Easily flushed; does not generally tolerate close approach. Distinctive call, a rhythmic series of loud hoots, often transcribed as *who-cooks-for-you, who-cooks-for-you-all*. Northwestern portion of range is expanding rapidly; may soon overlap range of similar Spotted Owl. May be very rare breeder on southern coast of Alaska.

♪ Great Gray Owl *Strix nebulosa* L 27" (69 cm)

Heavily ringed facial disks make the yellow eyes look small. Lacks ear tufts. Inhabits boreal forests and wooded bogs in the far north, dense coniferous forests and meadows in the mountains farther south. Hunts over forest clearings and nearby open country, chiefly by night but also at dawn and dusk; hunts by day during summer in northern part of range. Call is a series of deep, resonant *whoo*'s. Uncommon except in the northernmost part of its range; rare and irregular winter visitor to limit of dashed line on map.

♪ Spotted Owl *Strix occidentalis* L 17½" (45 cm)

Large and dark-eyed, with white spotting on head, back, and underparts, rather than the barring and streaking of the similar Barred Owl. Inhabits thickly wooded canyons, humid forests. Strictly nocturnal. Call is a series of three or four hesitant, doglike barks and cries. Uncommon; decreasing in number due to habitat destruction.

Snowy Owl *Nyctea scandiaca* L 23" (58 cm)

A large white owl, with rounded head, yellow eyes. Dark bars and spots are heaviest on young birds; old males may be pure white. An owl of open tundra; nests on the ground; preys chiefly on lemmings, hunting by day during the arctic summer, as well as at night. Retreats from northernmost part of range in winter; at least a few are seen annually to limit indicated by dashed line on map. In years when lemming population plummets, Snowys may wander in winter as far south as Alabama. These irruptives, usually heavily barred younger birds, are highly visible, perched conspicuously on the ground or on low stumps, fence posts, and buildings.

Barred
Owl

Great Gray
Owl

Spotted
Owl

Snowy
Owl

immature

♪ Eastern Screech-Owl *Otus asio* *L 8¹/₂" (22 cm)*

A small owl with yellow eyes, prominent ear tufts, and usually a pale bill. Red phase predominates in the south, gray in the north and in southernmost Texas. A very pale gray form, *O.a. maxwelliae*, is found in northwestern part of range. Eastern Screech-Owls are common in a wide variety of habitats: woodlots, forests, swamps, orchards, parks, suburban gardens. Strictly nocturnal; best located and identified by voice and at night. Two typical calls: a series of quavering whistles, descending in pitch; and a long single trill, all on one pitch. The second call is usually sung in duets by male and female. Formerly classified with Western Screech-Owl as a single species; range separation is not yet fully known.

♪ Western Screech-Owl *Otus kennicottii* *L 8¹/₂" (22 cm)*

A small owl with yellow eyes, prominent ear tufts, and usually a dark bill. Generally gray overall; some birds in the humid coastal northwest are brownish. Strictly nocturnal; best located and identified by voice and at night. Two common calls: a series of short whistles accelerating in tempo; and a short trill followed immediately by a longer trill. Second call is sung in duets by male and female. Common in open woodlands, streamside groves, desert, suburban areas, parks. Where range overlaps that of Whiskered Screech-Owl, the Western Screech-Owl is generally found at lower elevations. Formerly classified with Eastern Screech-Owl as a single species; range separation is not yet fully known.

♪ Whiskered Screech-Owl *Otus trichopsis* *L 7¹/₄" (18 cm)*

Small size, yellow eyes, prominent ear tufts. Closely resembles gray Western Screech-Owl; identification must be based on voice. Two common calls: a series of short whistles on one pitch and at a fairly even tempo; and a series of very irregular hoots, like Morse code. The second call is usually sung in duets by male and female. Strictly nocturnal. Inhabits dense oak and oak-conifer woodlands, primarily at elevations from 4,000 to 6,000 feet. Where range overlaps that of Western Screech-Owl, the Whiskered is usually found at higher elevations.

Eastern Screech-Owl

red phase

gray phase

gray phase juvenile

maxwelliae

northwest coast

Western Screech-Owl

Whiskered Screech-Owl

♪ Flammulated Owl *Otus flammeolus* L 6³/₄" (17 cm)

Dark eyes; small ear tufts, often indistinct; variegated red and gray plumage. Birds in the northern part of the range are generally grayer; southern birds redder. Common in oak and pine woodlands, especially ponderosa. Sometimes nests in loose colonies. Strictly nocturnal; daytime roost is well hidden. Best located at night by its call, a long series of single or sometimes paired hollow hoots. Highly migratory. Very rare vagrant east to Louisiana and Florida.

♪ Elf Owl *Microthene whitneyi* L 5³/₄" (15 cm)

Our smallest owl. Yellow eyes; very short tail. Lacks ear tufts. Common in desert lowlands and in canyons, especially in oaks and sycamores; fairly common in foothills. Rare and declining in Texas; formerly more widespread in California. Strictly nocturnal; roosts and nests in cavities in saguaros and trees. Most easily spotted at dawn or dusk. Call is an irregular series of high *churp*s and chattering notes. Not seen in U. S. in winter.

♪ Ferruginous Pygmy-Owl *Glaucidium brasilianum*

L 6³/₄" (17 cm) Long tail, reddish with dark or dusky bars. Upperparts gray-brown; crown faintly streaked. Eyes yellow; black nape spots look like eyes on the back of the head. White underparts streaked with reddish-brown. Inhabits saguaro deserts and low, open woodlands in Arizona; Rio Grande Valley woodlands in Texas. Found at lower elevations than Northern Pygmy-Owl. Chiefly diurnal; most active at dawn and dusk. Roosts in crevices and cavities. Most common call is a rapid, repeated *took*. Unlike other North American owls, pygmy-owls fly with quick, unmuffled wingbeats.

♪ Northern Pygmy-Owl *Glaucidium gnoma* L 6³/₄" (17 cm)

Long tail, dark brown with pale bars. Upperparts are either rusty-brown or gray-brown; crown spotted; underparts white with dark streaks. Eyes yellow; black nape spots look like eyes on the back of the head. Inhabits dense woodlands in foothills and mountains. Found at higher elevations than Ferruginous Pygmy-Owl. Chiefly diurnal; most active at dawn and dusk. Unlike other North American owls, pygmy-owls fly with quick, unmuffled wingbeats. Nests in cavities. Call is a mellow, repeated *hoo* or *hoo hoo*. An aggressive predator, sometimes catching birds larger than itself, this owl is a favorite target for songbirds. Birders may locate the owl by watching for mobbing songbirds and, conversely, attract songbirds by imitating the owl's call.

red phase

Flammulated Owl

gray phase

Ferruginous Pygmy-Owl

Elf Owl

Northern Pygmy-Owl

gray phase

red phase

♪ **Northern Saw-whet Owl** *Aegolius acadicus* L 8" (20 cm)
Reddish-brown above; white below with reddish streaks; bill
dark; facial disks reddish, without dark border. Juvenile
strongly reddish above, tawny-rust below. The Saw-whet inhabits dense coniferous or mixed forests, wooded swamps,
tamarack bogs. Its call, heard primarily in breeding season, is a
monotonously repeated single-note whistle; also gives a raspy
call like the sound of a saw being sharpened. Strictly nocturnal; roosts during daylight in or near nest hole in breeding season. In winter, preferred roost is in dense evergreens. Large
concentrations of regurgitated pellets and heavy white "wash"
build up below favored winter roosts. Saw-whets are hard to locate but, once found, can be closely approached. Difficulty in
locating this species obscures information about numbers and
distribution. Very rarely reported over most of winter range.

Northern Hawk-Owl *Surnia ulula* L 16" (41 cm)
Long tail, falcon-like profile, and black-bordered facial disks
identify this owl of the northern forests. Underparts are barred
in brown. Flight is low and swift; sometimes hunts during daylight as well as at night. It is most often seen, however, perched
high in a spruce tree. Usually can be closely approached. Call
is a rapid, sharp *ki-ki-ki-ki*. Basically non-migratory but retreats slightly in winter from northernmost part of range. Vagrants are only rarely seen south of mapped range.

♪ **Boreal Owl** *Aegolius funereus* L 10" (25 cm)
White underparts streaked with chocolate brown. Whitish facial disk has a distinct black border; bill is pale. Darker above
than similar Northern Saw-whet Owl. Juvenile is chocolate
brown below. The Boreal Owl inhabits dense northern forests
and muskeg. Irruptive, usually in small numbers; otherwise
seldom seen south of mapped range, but this may be due to difficulty of locating it. Recently discovered breeding at isolated
locations at high elevations in the Rockies. Strictly nocturnal;
roosts during daylight in dense cover. Its call, heard only in
breeding season, is a short series of rapid, hollow *hoo* notes.

Burrowing Owl *Athene cunicularia* L 9¹/₂" (24 cm)
Long legs distinguish this ground dweller from all other small
owls. Adult is boldly spotted and barred. Juvenile is buffy below. An owl of open country; often seen in prairie dog towns;
also at home on golf courses, road cuts, airports. Nests in single pairs or, more commonly, in small colonies. Nocturnal;
perches during daylight at entrance to burrow nest or on low
post. Typical call is a soft *coo-coooo*. Disturbed in its nest, the
Burrowing Owl often gives an alarm call that effectively imitates the sound of a rattlesnake.

**Northern
Saw-whet
Owl**

juvenile

**Northern
Hawk-Owl**

**Boreal
Owl**

juvenile

Burrowing Owl

juvenile

Nightjars (Family Caprimulgidae)

Wide mouth helps these night-hunters snare flying insects. In daylight they roost on the ground or lengthwise along low branches, camouflaged by their muted, intricate plumage. Most species are best located and identified by their distinctive calls.

♪ Chuck-will's-widow *Caprimulgus carolinensis*
L 12" (31 cm) Our largest nightjar. Mottled buff-brown overall; wings rounded; tail long, rounded. Loud whistling song sounds like *chuck-will's-widow;* also utters a low growling flight call as it hunts. Larger and redder than Whip-poor-will; buff-brown throat and whitish necklace contrast with dark breast. Male's tail has less white than in male Whip-poor-will; tips of outer feathers are buff. Female's tail lacks white. Common in oak-pine woodlands, live oak groves. A few birds stray north of normal range and breed in coniferous woods.

♪ Whip-poor-will *Caprimulgus vociferus* *L 9³/₄" (25 cm)*
Mottled gray-brown overall; wings rounded; tail long, rounded. Song is a loud *whip-poor-will,* mellow in eastern birds, with accent on first and last syllables; rough and burry in southwestern birds, with strongest accent on last syllable. Whip-poor-will is smaller and grayer than Chuck-will's-widow; dark throat contrasts with white or buffy necklace and pale underparts. Male's tail shows much more white than in male Chuck-will's-widow. Female's tail has contrasting pale tip on dark outer feathers. Fairly common in open coniferous and mixed woodlands in the east, mountain woodlands in the southwest. Breeds locally in southern California.

♪ Buff-collared Nightjar *Caprimulgus ridgwayi*
L 8³/₄" (22 cm) Rare, irregular and local in desert canyons of southwestern New Mexico, southeastern Arizona, where it usually roosts on the ground by day. Gray-brown plumage resembles Whip-poor-will's, but note buff collar across nape. Song is an accelerating series of *cuk* notes ending with *cuka-cheea*. Also known as Ridgway's Whip-poor-will.

♪ Common Poorwill *Phalaenoptilus nuttallii* *L 7³/₄" (20 cm)*
Our smallest nightjar, distinguished from nighthawks (next page) by short, rounded tail and short, rounded wings lacking white markings. Outer tail feathers tipped with white, more boldly in males than in females. Song is a whistled *poor-will,* with a final *ip* note audible at close range. Upperparts mottled brownish-gray. Broad white band crosses dark throat and breast. Fairly common in sagebrush and on coastal chaparral slopes; often seen on roadsides. Known to hibernate in cold weather; may winter north into normal breeding range.

Chuck-will's-widow

♂

♀

Whip-poor-will

♀

♂

♂

♀

Buff-collared
Nightjar

♂

Common
Poorwill

♂

♂ **Common Pauraque** *Nyctidromus albicollis* L 11" (28 cm)

In flight, long, rounded tail and short, rounded wings distinguish Pauraque from nighthawks. Broad white bands on wings distinguish it from other nightjars (preceding page). White tail patches conspicuous on male, smaller and often buffy on female. In close view, note chestnut ear patch. Common in woodland clearings and scrub of Rio Grande Valley; winters in streamside thickets. Active chiefly at night. Flies close to the ground; often lands on roads and roadsides. Distinctive song, one or more low *pur* notes followed by a higher, descending *wheeer*.

♂ **Common Nighthawk** *Chordeiles minor* L 9¹/₂" (24 cm)

Wings long, pointed; tail slightly forked. Bold white wing bar is farther from wing tip than in Lesser Nighthawk. Nasal *peent* call distinguishes Common from both Lesser and Antillean Nighthawks. Subspecies vary in overall color from dark brown in eastern birds to pale gray in the northern Great Plains form, *C.m. sennetti;* color variations are subtle in adults, distinct in juveniles. Pale spotting on wing coverts contrasts with darker back. Throat white in male, buffy in female; underparts whitish, with bold dusky bars. Female may be slightly buffy below. Juvenile lacks white tail band, shows little or no white on throat. Found in open woodlands, suburbs, towns, the Common Nighthawk is active in daylight and at night. Roosts on the ground and on branches, posts, roofs; flies higher than Lesser Nighthawk. As male swoops to ground in courtship display, wings make a hollow booming sound. Common over most of range.

♂ **Antillean Nighthawk** *Chordeiles gundlachii*

L 9¹/₂" (24 cm) Regular spring migrant on Dry Tortugas from West Indies; occasionally seen on Florida Keys and southeast Florida mainland. Wings long, pointed; tail slightly forked. Female lacks white tail band. Call, a variable katydid-like *pity-pit-pit,* best distinguishes Antillean from Common Nighthawk. Note also the buffier underparts. Formerly considered a subspecies of Common Nighthawk.

♂ **Lesser Nighthawk** *Chordeiles acutipennis* L 9" (23 cm)

Resembles Common Nighthawk but wings are shorter, more rounded, with shorter outermost primary; pale wing bar closer to tip. Male has white tail band. Female lacks tail band; wing bar smaller, buffy. Juvenile's wing bar much smaller; often indistinct in juvenile female. In all plumages, upperparts are uniformly mottled. Throat usually white; may be buffy in females. Underparts buffy, with faint barring. Fairly common; found primarily in dry, open country, scrubland, desert. Active chiefly at night. Flies low, with a more fluttery wingbeat than Common Nighthawk. Often seen over ponds or perched on roadsides. Distinctive call, a rapid, tremulous trill. Casual in winter in southern California and on Texas coast, in spring and fall on Louisiana coast.

Common Pauraque

Common Nighthawk

sennetti
juvenile

Antillean Nighthawk

Lesser Nighthawk

Swifts (Family Apodidae)

These fast-flying birds spend most of the day aloft, feeding on insects in midair.

Long, pointed wings bend closer to the body than those of the similar swallows.

Chimney Swift *Chaetura pelagica* L 5¹/₄" (13 cm)
Small, cigar-shaped body with very short, squared-off tail. The only swift over most of its range, but may occasionally be seen with Vaux's Swift. The Chimney Swift is usually darker below; wings longer than Vaux's; has louder, chattering call, greater tendency to soar, and distinctive rocking display: with wings upraised, bird rocks from side to side. Nests in chimneys, barns, hollow trees. Rare but regular in southern California. Winters mainly in northeastern Peru.

Black Swift *Cypseloides niger* L 7¹/₄" (18 cm)
Blackish above and below; tail slightly forked, often fanned in flight. Distinguished from male Purple Martin (page 296) by wing shape. Uncommon; best seen at dawn and dusk near nesting colonies on protected cliffs, often beneath waterfalls. Winters mainly in Central America; seldom seen in migration.

Vaux's Swift *Chaetura vauxi* L 4³/₄" (12 cm)
Small, cigar-shaped body with short, stubby tail. Occasionally seen with similar Chimney Swift, Vaux's is usually paler below and on rump but may become darkened by soot. Vaux's is less inclined to soar than Chimney Swift. Call is softer, higher pitched, more insectlike. Fairly common; found in woodlands near lakes and rivers. Nests in hollow trees, seldom in chimneys. In winter, very rare in southern California and Texas, casual on Gulf coast from Louisiana to Florida.

Fork-tailed Swift *Apus pacificus* L 7¹/₄" (18 cm)
Asian species, casual fall and summer vagrant on western Aleutians and Pribilofs. A large swift with deeply forked tail; white rump conspicuous in flight from above. Formerly called White-rumped Swift.

White-collared Swift *Streptoprocne zonaris*
L 8¹/₂" (22 cm) Tropical species with a few records from scattered locations in the United States. A large, black swift; note white collar, slightly forked tail. Soars with wings bent down.

White-throated Swift *Aeronautes saxatalis*
L 6¹/₂" (17 cm) Black and white above and below, with long, notched tail. Distinguished from Violet-green Swallow (page 296) by longer, narrower wings, bicolored pattern below. In poor light, sometimes mistaken for Black Swift; look for White-throated's smaller size, more rapid wingbeats. Common in mountains, rocky canyons, cliffs. Nests in cliff crevices.

rocking display

Black Swift

Chimney Swift

Vaux's Swift

Fork-tailed Swift

White-collared Swift

White-throated Swift

Hummingbirds (Family Trochilidae)

Tiny, colorful birds that hover at flowers to sip nectar with needlelike bills. Often identified by twittery calls or chattering "chase notes" given when driving intruders away. Wings also make distinctive whistles. Males have iridescent throat feathers, called a gorget.

Green Violet-ear *Colibri thalassinus* *L 4³/₄" (12 cm)*
Tropical species, rare in southern and central Texas. Green overall; bill slightly downcurved. Male has blue-violet patches on face and breast. Female slightly duller; violet chest patch smaller or absent. Song is a repeated *tsip-tsup*.

Cuban Emerald *Chlorostilbon ricordii* *L 4¹/₂" (11 cm)*
West Indian species, very rare in south Florida in fall and winter. Note pinkish lower mandible, deeply forked tail. Male is green overall with white undertail coverts. Female is grayish below. Call is a metallic *tchiw-tchiw*.

Buff-bellied Hummingbird *Amazilia yucatanensis*
L 4¹/₄" (11 cm) Mexican species, fairly common in Rio Grande delta, especially around Brownsville, Texas. Casual in winter to Louisiana coast. Bronze green above, with chestnut tail. Bill pinkish-red with black tip. Throat and breast metallic green; belly buffy. Calls are shrill and squeaky.

Berylline Hummingbird *Amazilia beryllina* *L 4¹/₄" (11 cm)*
Casual summer visitor from Mexico to mountains of southeastern Arizona; occasionally breeds there. Green above and below, with chestnut wings, rump, and tail. Base of lower mandible red. Male's lower belly is chestnut, female's grayish.

Bahama Woodstar *Calliphlox evelynae* *L 3³/₄" (10 cm)*
Rare stray from Bahamas to southeastern Florida; sightings so far have been of adult females or immatures. Dull bronze green above, cinnamon below, with white breast. Male has a metallic purple-red gorget. Female is paler below; tail more rounded, outer feathers rufous at base, tipped with pale cinnamon. Immatures resemble adult females, but young male gradually acquires purple on throat. Call is a staccato *tit tit tit*.

Lucifer Hummingbird *Calothorax lucifer* *L 3¹/₂" (9 cm)*
Bronze green above; bill downcurved. Male is purple on throat and sides of neck; lacks purple crown of male Costa's Hummingbird (page 258); tail is deeply forked. In female, note pale streak behind eye; tail is more rounded; outer tail feathers reddish at base, tipped with white; underparts are rich buff. Young male begins to show purple spotting on throat by late summer. Uncommon in Chisos Mountains of Texas; casual in southeastern Arizona in summer. Calls are shrill, squeaky *chip* notes.

Green
Violet-ear

Cuban
Emerald

Berylline
Hummingbird

Buff-bellied
Hummingbird

immature ♂

Bahama
Woodstar

♀

immature ♂

Lucifer
Hummingbird

♪ Broad-billed Hummingbird *Cynanthus latirostris*

L 4" (10 cm) Adult male is dark green above and below, with white undertail coverts, a glittering blue gorget, and mostly red bill. Broad, forked tail is blackish-blue. Adult female is duller above, gray below; often shows a narrow white eye stripe; tail is square-tipped. Juveniles resemble female. By late summer, juvenile male begins to show blue and green flecks on throat, green on sides; dark, forked tail helps distinguish it from White-eared Hummingbird. Common in desert canyons, low mountain woodlands. Chattering *je-dit* call is similar to Ruby-crowned Kinglet. Male's display call is a whining *zing*. Rare in southern California during fall and winter.

♪ White-eared Hummingbird *Hylocharis leucotis*

L 3³⁄₄" (10 cm) Rare summer visitor from Mexico to southeastern Arizona mountains. Bill shorter than in Broad-billed Hummingbird; broad white stripe borders black ear patch; tail square. Adult male has dark purple crown and chin, emerald green gorget; display call is a repeated, silvery *tink tink tink*. Chattering calls are loud and metallic.

Violet-crowned Hummingbird *Amazilia violiceps*

L 4¹⁄₂" (11 cm) Crown violet; underparts entirely white; upperparts bronze green; tail greenish. Long bill is mostly red. Uncommon in U. S. range. Favors streamside locations in low mesquite-sycamore or higher oak-sycamore canyons. Call is a loud chattering similar to Broad-billed Hummingbird. Male's song is a series of sibilant *ts* notes.

Blue-throated Hummingbird *Lampornis clemenciae*

L 5" (13 cm) Adult male's throat is blue, female's gray. Broad white eye stripe and faint white whisker stripe border dark ear patch. Tail has broad white tips on outer feathers; compare with female Magnificent Hummingbird. Uncommon; found in mountain canyons, especially near streams. Casual north of mapped range. Male's call is a loud, repeated *seep*.

Magnificent Hummingbird *Eugenes fulgens*

L 5¹⁄₄" (13 cm) Adult male is green above, with purple crown; metallic green throat; breast and upper belly black and green; lower belly dull brown. Tail is dark green and deeply notched. Female is duller, lacks purple crown; squarish tail has small grayish-white tips on outer feathers; compare female Blue-throated Hummingbird. Fairly common in high mountain meadows, canyons. Casual north of mapped range. Distinctive call is a sharp *chip*. Formerly called Rivoli's Hummingbird.

Plain-capped Starthroat *Heliomaster constantii*

L 5" (13 cm) Casual stray in summer and fall from Mexico to arid foothills and deserts of southeastern Arizona. Broad white whisker stripe and white tufts on flanks are conspicuous. Throat shows variable amount of red; note also very long bill, white patch on rump.

Broad-billed Hummingbird

♀

immature ♂

♂

♂

White-eared Hummingbird

♀

♂

Blue-throated Hummingbird

♀

♂

Violet-crowned Hummingbird

♀

Magnificent Hummingbird

♂

Plain-capped Hummingbird

Ruby-throated Hummingbird *Archilochus colubris*

L 3³/₄" (10 cm) The only hummingbird seen over most of the east. Metallic green above. Adult male's brilliant red throat appears black in poor light; underparts are whitish; sides and flanks dusky-green; tail forked. Female's throat is whitish; underparts grayish-white, with buffy wash on sides; tail is similar to female Black-chinned Hummingbird. Juveniles and immatures resemble adult female but some, and perhaps some adult females, have a golden cast on upperparts, unlike Black-chinned Hummingbird. Immature male may begin to show red gorget by early fall. As with all hummingbirds, adult males migrate much earlier than females and immatures. Ruby-throats are common in gardens and woodland edges. Very rare north to Alaska. Similar hummingbirds seen in the southeast in winter are likely to be Black-chinned Hummingbirds, but females and immatures of these two species are almost indistinguishable. Rubythroat generally has a greener crown, shorter bill. Calls are almost identical.

♂ Black-chinned Hummingbird *Archilochus alexandri*

L 3³/₄" (10 cm) Metallic green above. In good light, male shows violet band at lower border of black throat. Underparts are whitish, sides and flanks green. Female's throat can be all-white or show faint dusky or greenish streaks. Immatures resemble adult female; immature male can begin to show violet on lower throat in early fall. Common in low mountains, lowlands, and along coasts. Call is a soft *tchew;* chase note combines high squeals and *tchew* notes. A few Blackchins winter in the southeast; may be mistaken for Ruby-throated Hummingbirds. Females and immatures of these species are almost indistinguishable; see Rubythroat description for details.

Costa's Hummingbird *Calypte costae* *L 3¹/₂" (9 cm)*

Male has deep violet crown and gorget extending far down sides of neck. Female is generally grayer above, whiter below, than female Black-chinned Hummingbird; note also tail differences. Best distinguished by voice. Call is a high, metallic *tink,* often given in a series. Male's call is a loud *zing.* Fairly common in desert washes, dry chaparral.

♂ Anna's Hummingbird *Calypte anna* *L 4" (10 cm)*

Male's head and throat are deep rose red, the color extending a short distance onto sides of neck. Female's throat usually shows red flecks, often forming a patch of color. In both sexes, underparts are grayish, washed with a varying amount of green. Bill is proportionately short. Immatures resemble female; immature male usually shows some red on crown. Juveniles lack red on throat; may be confused with smaller female Black-chinned and Costa's Hummingbirds. Abundant in coastal lowlands; in winter, also found in mountains and deserts. Common call note, a sharp *chick,* is sometimes given in a rapid series. Male's song is a jumble of high squeaks and raspy notes.

juvenile ♂

**Ruby-throated
Hummingbird**

♀

immature ♂

♂

♂

immature ♂

♀

**Black-chinned
Hummingbird**

immature ♂

♂

♀

**Costa's
Hummingbird**

immature ♂

♀

juvenile

**Anna's
Hummingbird**

Black-chinned ♀

Costa's ♀

Anna's ♀

♂

Calliope Hummingbird *Stellula calliope* L 3¹/₄" *(8 cm)*
Smallest North American bird. Male golden green above, white below, with greenish flanks. Purple-red feathers on throat form streaks or V-shaped gorget. Female is green above; underparts tinged with pale cinnamon, especially on flanks; throat spotted or lightly streaked. Very short, mostly green tail distinguishes female Calliope from female Allen's and Rufous Hummingbirds. Juveniles resemble adult female. Immature male shows some red feathers on throat by late summer. Common along streams in high meadows, canyons. Often holds tail cocked up while feeding. Relatively silent; male's courtship call is a high *see-ree*.

♪ Broad-tailed Hummingbird *Selasphorus platycercus*
L 4" *(10 cm)* Except during late-summer molt, male's wing-beats produce a loud, trilling whistle. Both sexes are metallic green above. Male has rose red throat; white underparts with green sides. Female has speckled throat, pale cinnamon wash on flanks; broad green tail shows red mostly on outer feathers. Common in the Rockies and Great Basin mountains. Calls include a sharp *chip*.

Rufous Hummingbird *Selasphorus rufus* L 3³/₄" *(10 cm)*
Tail mainly reddish; pattern similar to Allen's Hummingbird. Adult male identified by reddish-brown back, sometimes with speckles or patches of green; crown is green; gorget is iridescent orange-red. Female and immatures inseparable in the field from Allen's Hummingbird. Female distinguished from female Calliope and Broad-tailed by redder tail and by contrast of reddish sides, flanks, and undertail coverts with white breast and belly. Juveniles resemble adult female; immature male may show reddish-brown back before acquiring orange-red gorget. Common in forests, woodland edges, thickets; breeds in lowlands and mountains. Migrates chiefly along mountain ridges in fall, lowlands in spring. Casual in fall in the east, rare in spring. Wing whistle and calls are similar to Allen's Hummingbird. Male in courtship display flies in an oval pattern, swooping down, then flying more slowly upward.

♪ Allen's Hummingbird *Selasphorus sasin* L 3³/₄" *(10 cm)*
Tail mainly reddish; pattern similar to Rufous Hummingbird. Adult male identified by all-green back and crown; gorget is iridescent orange-red. Adult female inseparable in the field from female Rufous; distinguished from female Calliope and Broad-tailed by redder tail and contrast of reddish sides, flanks, and undertail coverts with white breast and belly. Allen's Hummingbird is common in brush and woodlands. Migrates earlier in fall and spring than Rufous Hummingbird. Male's wingbeats produce a high, thin, trilling whistle. Calls include a sibilant *chup;* chase note, *zeee-chuppity-chup*. Wing whistle and calls similar to Rufous Hummingbird. In display flight, male drops from a great height, swoops back and forth in a half circle several times, then flies back up to start again.

Calliope Hummingbird

♂

♀

Broad-tailed Hummingbird

♂

♀

Rufous Hummingbird

immature ♂

♂

♀

green-flecked ♂

Allen's Hummingbird

♂

Calliope ♀

Allen's ♀

Rufous ♀

Broad-tailed ♀

Kingfishers (Family Alcedinidae)

Stocky, short-legged body; large head, with oversize bill and, in two species, a ragged crest. Look for kingfishers near woodland streams and ponds and in coastal areas. They hover over water or watch from low perches, then plunge headfirst to catch a fish. Heavy bill and stubby feet also serve for digging long nest burrows in stream banks.

Belted Kingfisher *Ceryle alcyon L 13" (33 cm)*
The only kingfisher seen in most of North America. Both male and female have slate blue breast band. Female has rust belly band and flanks, may be confused with female Ringed Kingfisher where ranges overlap; note white belly and undertail coverts. Juvenile resembles adult but has rust spotting in breast band. Common along rivers and brooks, ponds and lakes, estuaries; perches conspicuously. Solitary except in nesting season. Call is a loud, dry rattle.

Ringed Kingfisher *Ceryle torquata L 16" (41 cm)*
Similar to but larger than Belted Kingfisher; generally frequents larger rivers and ponds, perches on higher branches. Male is entirely rust below. Female has slate blue breast, narrow white band, rust belly and undertail coverts. Juveniles resemble adult female, but juvenile male's breast is largely rust. Resident in lower Rio Grande Valley; occasionally wanders northward to central Texas in fall and winter. Call is a harsh rattle, lower pitched and slower than in Belted Kingfisher. In flight, gives a slow, measured series of *chack* notes.

Green Kingfisher *Chloroceryle americana L 8³/₄" (22 cm)*
Smallest of our kingfishers; crest inconspicuous. Green above, with white collar; white below, with dark green spotting. Male has rust breast band; female has a band of green spots. Juvenile resembles adult female. Fairly common resident of lower Rio Grande Valley; less common on Edwards Plateau. A few wander along the Texas coast in fall and winter; rare straggler in southern Arizona in winter. Call is a faint but sharp *tick tick*. Often perches on low, inconspicuous branches.

Belted Kingfisher

Ringed Kingfisher

Green Kingfisher

Woodpeckers (Family Picidae)

Strong claws, short legs, and stiff tail enable woodpeckers to climb tree trunks. Sharp bill is used to chisel out insect food and nest holes, and to drum a territorial signal to rivals.

Golden-fronted Woodpecker *Melanerpes aurifrons*
L 9³/₄" (25 cm) Black-and-white barred back, white rump, black tail; golden orange nape, paler in females; yellow feathering above bill. Male has a small red cap. Yellow tinge on belly not easily seen. Juvenile has streaked breast, brownish crown. In flight, all plumages show white wing patches, white rump, black tail. Similar Red-bellied and Gila Woodpeckers have barred tails. The Golden-fronted Woodpecker is fairly common in dry woodlands, pecan groves, mesquite brushlands. Call, a rolling *churr-churr* or cackling *kek-kek*, is slightly louder and raspier than Red-bellied Woodpecker.

Red-bellied Woodpecker *Melanerpes carolinus*
L 9¹/₄" (24 cm) Black-and-white barred back; white uppertail coverts; central tail feathers barred. Crown and nape red in males; females have red nape only. Reddish tinge on belly. Juvenile has streaked breast, dark gray crown. In all plumages, white wing patches and white uppertail coverts flash in flight. Similar Golden-fronted Woodpecker has black tail. Red-bellied Woodpeckers are common in open woodlands, suburban backyards. May be extending breeding range northward. Withdraws in winter from higher elevations and northern edge of range. Call, a rolling *churr* or *chiv-chiv*, is slightly softer than that of the Golden-fronted Woodpecker.

Gila Woodpecker *Melanerpes uropygialis* *L 9¹/₄" (24 cm)*
Black-and-white barred back and rump; central tail feathers barred. Male has a small red cap. Female and juvenile lack head markings. In all plumages, white wing patches and barred tail visible in flight. A familiar and conspicuous inhabitant of towns, scrub desert, cactus country. Bores nest holes in giant saguaros as well as in cottonwood trees and mesquite. Calls, a rolling *churr* or loud, sharp *yip*.

Northern Flicker *Colaptes auratus* *L 12¹/₂" (32 cm)*
Brown barred back; spotted underparts, with black crescent bib. White rump conspicuous in flight; lacks white wing patches. Females lack red or black whisker stripe. The three forms were once considered separate species: Yellow-shafted Flicker east of the Rockies; Red-shafted west of the Rockies; Gilded Flicker in the southwest. Intergrades of these three forms are regularly seen in the midwest and southwest. Large, active, and noisy, Flickers are common in open woodlands and suburban areas; often feed on the ground. Calls include a rapid *wik-wik-wik-wik* and *wick-er, wick-er, wick-er,* and a single, loud *klee-yer*.

**Golden-fronted
Woodpecker**

♂

♀

♀

♂

**Red-bellied
Woodpecker**

♂

**Gila
Woodpecker**

♂

♀

"Yellow-shafted" ♂

"Red-shafted" ♂

**Northern
Flicker**

"Gilded" ♂

"Red-shafted" ♂

"Gilded" ♂

"Yellow-shafted" ♂

Red-headed Woodpecker

Melanerpes erythrocephalus L 9¹/₄" (24 cm) Entire head, neck, and throat are bright red in adults, contrasting with blue-black back and snowy-white underparts. Juvenile is brownish; acquires red head during gradual winter molt. Look for distinctive white inner wing patches and white rump, highly visible in all ages in both perched and flying birds. Call, a loud *queark* similar to Red-bellied Woodpecker, but harsher and sharper. Inhabits open woods, farmlands, bottomlands, parks, backyards. Forages on tree trunks and on the ground for insects, berries, acorns; occasionally seen fly-catching. Bores nest holes in dead trees, fence posts, telephone poles, but uses any handy cavity to store acorns for winter. Red-headed Woodpeckers have become rare in the northeast, due in part to habitat loss and competition with Starlings for nest holes. Somewhat more numerous in the rest of their range; a rare permanent resident in Utah's Uinta Basin.

Acorn Woodpecker   *Melanerpes formicivorus*

L 9" (23 cm) Black chin, yellowish throat, white cheeks and forehead, red cap. Female has smaller bill than male, less red on crown. In flight, white rump and small white patches on outer wings are conspicuous. Common in oak woods or pine forests where oak trees are abundant. Sociable, generally found in small, noisy groups. Distinctive call, a raucous *ja-cob ja-cob*. Eats chiefly acorns and other nuts in winter, insects in summer. In the fall, this woodpecker is sometimes seen drilling small holes in tree trunks and pounding an acorn into each hole for a winter food supply. Often reuses the same hole-riddled trees year after year.

White-headed Woodpecker   *Picoides albolarvatus*

L 9¹/₄" (24 cm) Head and throat white. Male has a small red patch on back of head. Body is black above and below except for white wing patches, conspicuous in flight. Call is a sharp *chick-chick*. Found in open coniferous forests at altitudes of about 4,000 feet and above; casual at lower altitudes in winter. Feeds primarily on seeds from the cones of ponderosa and sugar pine. Also pries away loose bark in search of insects and larvae. Fairly common over most of range; rare and local in the north.

Lewis' Woodpecker   *Melanerpes lewis   L 10³/₄" (27 cm)*

Greenish-black head and back, with gray collar and breast; dark red face, pinkish belly. In flight, its darkness, large size, and slow, steady wingbeats give it a crow-like appearance. Juvenile lacks collar and red face; underparts may be only faintly pink. Common in open woodlands of interior foothills and valleys; less common on coast. Sometimes forms large flocks in winter. Irregular winter wanderer in some years south of range. Main food is insects, mostly caught in the air; also eats fruit, acorns, other nuts. Stores acorns, which it first shells, in tree bark crevices.

Red-headed Woodpecker

juvenile

Acorn Woodpecker

♀

♂

White-headed Woodpecker

♂

♀

juvenile

Lewis' Woodpecker

Sapsuckers

These woodpeckers drill evenly spaced rows of holes in trees, then visit these "wells" for sap and the insects attracted to it.

All three species have a white rump, white wing patches, and at least some yellow on the belly. Calls include plaintive mews.

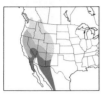

Williamson's Sapsucker *Sphyrapicus thyroideus*

L 9" (23 cm) Male has black back, white rump, large white wing patch; black head with narrow white stripes, bright red chin and throat. Breast is black, belly yellow, flanks barred with black and white. Female's head is brown; back, wings, and sides barred with dark brown and white; rump white; lacks white wing patch and red chin; belly has small yellow patch; breast has large dark patch. Juveniles resemble adults but are duller; attain adult plumage by first winter. Fairly common in dry, piney forests of the western mountains; moves south or to lower elevations in winter.

Red-breasted Sapsucker *Sphyrapicus ruber*

L 8¹/₂" (22 cm) Red head, nape, and breast; large white wing patch; white rump. Back is black, lightly spotted with yellow in northern subspecies, *S.r. ruber;* more heavily marked with white in southern *daggetti.* Belly is yellow in *ruber,* head darker red; *daggetti* has paler belly, paler head with longer white whisker stripe. Briefly held juvenile plumage is brownish, showing little or no red. Common in coniferous or mixed forests in coastal ranges, usually at lower elevations than the Williamson's Sapsucker. Small numbers of *ruber* move southward in winter. Red-breasted Sapsucker was formerly considered a subspecies of Yellow-bellied Sapsucker.

Yellow-bellied Sapsucker *Sphyrapicus varius*

L 8¹/₂" (22 cm) Red forecrown; black-and-white head; black back, with whitish or buffy mottling and barring; white rump; large white wing patch. Chin and throat red in males; females of the eastern and northern subspecies, *S.v. varius,* have white chin and throat; in the western *nuchalis,* female has white chin and varying amount of red on throat. Both sexes of *nuchalis* have red patch on back of crown. Juveniles of both subspecies are brownish. Juvenile *nuchalis* resembles adult by first fall; *varius* retains juvenile plumage until first spring. The two subspecies very rarely interbreed in narrow range of overlap in Alberta; *varius* hybridizes rarely with Red-breasted Sapsucker, *nuchalis* more often. Common in deciduous forests. Highly migratory. *S.v. varius* is casual in the west during winter, but *nuchalis* has not been seen in the east.

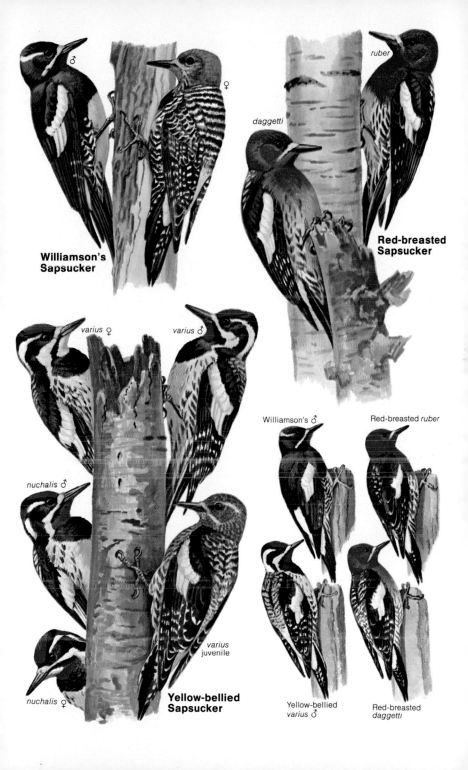

Williamson's Sapsucker

♂
♀

Red-breasted Sapsucker

ruber

daggetti

varius ♀   varius ♂

nuchalis ♂

nuchalis ♀

varius
juvenile

Yellow-bellied Sapsucker

Williamson's ♂   Red-breasted ruber

Yellow-bellied
varius ♂

Red-breasted
daggetti

♪ Downy Woodpecker *Picoides pubescens* *L 6¾″ (17 cm)*

White back generally identifies both this woodpecker and similar Hairy Woodpecker. Downy is smaller, with a much smaller bill; outer tail feathers generally have faint bars or spots. Birds in the Pacific northwest have pale gray-brown back and underparts. Rocky Mountain birds show less spotting on wings. Females may be confused with female Three-toed Woodpecker; note Downy's conspicuous eyebrow and lack of barring on sides. Calls include a soft *pik* note and a high whinny. Common; often seen at backyard feeders, in parklands and orchards, as well as in forests.

♪ Hairy Woodpecker *Picoides villosus* *L 9¼″ (24 cm)*

White back generally identifies both this woodpecker and similar Downy Woodpecker. Hairy Woodpecker is larger, with much larger bill; outer tail feathers are entirely white. Birds in the Pacific northwest have pale gray-brown back and underparts. Rocky Mountain birds have less spotting on wings. Females easily confused with female Three-toed Woodpecker, but note Hairy's conspicuous eyebrow and lack of barring on sides. Juvenile Hairy Woodpeckers, particularly in Maritime Provinces, have some barring on back and flanks, but sides are not barred. Forehead is spotted with white; crown streaked with red or orange in young males. Hairy's calls include a loud, sharp *peek* and a slurred whinny. Inhabits dense mature forests; may move to open woods in winter. Rare at southeastern edge of range.

Three-toed Woodpecker *Picoides tridactylus*

L 8¾″ (22 cm) Black-and-white barring down center of back distinguishes Three-toed Woodpecker from similar Black-backed. Both have heavily barred sides. Male's yellow cap is more extensive in Three-toed. Barring on back varies from heavy and dense in eastern form, *P.t. bacatus*, to lighter in northwestern *fasciatus*. In Rocky Mountain subspecies, *dorsalis*, back may be mostly white rather than barred. Females resemble female Hairy or Downy Woodpecker; look for heavily barred sides. Call is a single *pik*. Three-toed is found in coniferous forests, especially in burned-over areas. Less common than Black-backed in the east.

Black-backed Woodpecker *Picoides arcticus*

L 9½″ (24 cm) Solid black back, heavily barred sides. Male has distinct yellow cap. Similar Three-toed Woodpecker has barred back. The Black-backed Woodpecker inhabits coniferous forests; often found in burned-over areas. Forages on dead conifers, flaking away large patches of loose bark rather than drilling into it, in search of larvae and insects. Call note is a single, sharp *kik*. Uncommon. In winter, withdraws from highest altitudes in northernmost part of range; may visit wooded valleys.

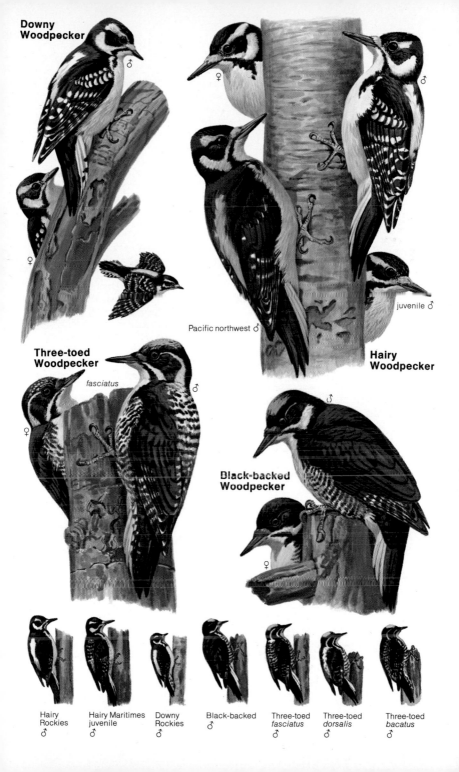

Downy Woodpecker

♂

♀

Hairy Woodpecker

♀

♂

juvenile ♂

Pacific northwest ♂

Three-toed Woodpecker

fasciatus

♀

♂

Black-backed Woodpecker

♂

♀

Hairy
Rockies
♂

Hairy Maritimes
juvenile
♂

Downy
Rockies
♂

Black-backed
♂

Three-toed
fasciatus
♂

Three-toed
dorsalis
♂

Three-toed
bacatus
♂

♪ Ladder-backed Woodpecker *Picoides scalaris*

L 7¹/₄" (18 cm) Spotted sides, black-and-white facial markings, and voice separate this species from the Golden-fronted and Gila Woodpeckers (page 264). In California, may be confused with Nuttall's Woodpecker. Ladderback shows less black on face; white barring on back more pronounced and extends to nape. White outer tail feathers are evenly barred rather than spotted. Call, a crisp *pick,* different from Nuttall's *pweek;* also gives a descending whinny. Where their ranges overlap, these two species may hybridize. Ladder-backed Woodpecker is common in dry brushlands, mesquite and cactus country; often seen in towns and rural areas. Feeds on beetle larvae from small trees; also eats cactus fruits, forages on the ground for insects.

Red-cockaded Woodpecker *Picoides borealis*

L 8¹/₂" (22 cm) Black-and-white barred back, black cap, and large white cheek patch identify this woodpecker more readily than the barely visible red tufts on the male's head. Similar Hairy and Downy Woodpeckers (page 270) have solid white or gray-brown backs. Voices differ, too: Red-cockaded's raspy *sripp* note or high-pitched *tsick* more nasal than in Hairy or Downy. This species inhabits pine or pine-oak woodlands; prefers longleaf, slash, or yellow pines. Bores nest hole only in a large living pine afflicted with heartwood disease, then drills small holes around the nest opening. Pine pitch oozing down the trunk from these holes may repel predators; also makes the tree a distinctive signpost. Populations have decreased with the loss of highly specialized habitat.

♪ Nuttall's Woodpecker *Picoides nuttallii*   *L 7¹/₂" (19 cm)*

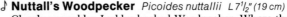

Closely resembles Ladder-backed Woodpecker. Where their ranges overlap, the two species may hybridize. Nuttall's shows more black on face; white bars on back are narrower, with solid black just below the nape. White outer tail feathers are sparsely spotted rather than barred. Call, a single or repeated sharp *pweek,* different from the Ladderback's *pick;* also gives a high-pitched whinny. Nuttall's prefers less arid habitat than the Ladderback; usually seen on chaparral slopes, wooded canyons, streamside trees. Forages on tree trunks, generally probing crevices and chipping away loose bark rather than drilling.

Strickland's Woodpecker *Picoides stricklandi*

L 7¹/₂" (19 cm) Solid brown back distinguishes this species from all other woodpeckers. Female lacks red patch on back of head. Compare with female sapsuckers (page 268), especially Williamson's, and with the Northern Flicker (page 264). Fairly common resident in the foothills and mountains of Arizona and New Mexico. Generally found in oak or pine-oak forests or canyons. Formerly called Arizona Woodpecker or Brown-backed Woodpecker.

Ladder-backed Woodpecker

Red-cockaded Woodpecker

Nuttall's Woodpecker

Strickland's Woodpecker

Ladder-backed
♂

Nuttall's
♂

Strickland's
♂

Red-cockaded
♂

Ivory-billed Woodpecker *Campephilus principalis*

L 19¹/₂" (50 cm)   May be extinct in North America; a few may still survive in pine forests of eastern Cuba. Unconfirmed sightings in recent years in Georgia, Florida, Louisiana, and Texas may actually have been the smaller Pileated Woodpecker; last confirmed sightings were in the 1950s. Note especially the Ivorybill's black chin and ivory bill and the extensive white wing patches visible in perched birds. Females have black rather than red crests. Compare also the black-and-white wing patterns of Ivorybills and Pileated Woodpeckers in flight. Distinctive call note is a high-pitched, nasal *yank* similar to White-breasted Nuthatch but louder. Our largest woodpecker, the Ivorybill requires large tracts of old-growth river forest; dead and dying trees supply nesting sites and food, the larvae of wood-boring beetles. Loss of habitat has brought the species to the brink of extinction.

Pileated Woodpecker *Dryocopus pileatus*

L 16¹/₂" (42 cm)   Perched bird is almost entirely black on back and wings, lacking the Ivorybill's large white wing patches. White chin and dark bill also distinguish Pileated Woodpecker, along with smaller size. Compare also the wing patterns of the two species in flight. Pileated is the largest woodpecker commonly seen. Female's red cap is less extensive than in male. Juvenile plumage, held briefly, resembles adult but is paler overall. Call is a loud, rising and falling *wuck-a-wuck-a-wuck-a,* similar to Flicker. Generally uncommon and localized throughout much of its range; prefers dense, mature forest; but also seems to be adapting to human encroachment, becoming more common and more tolerant of disturbed habitats, especially in the east. In woodlots and parklands as well as deep woods, listen for its slow, resounding hammering; look for the long rectangular or oval holes it excavates. Carpenter ants in fallen trees and stumps are its major food.

Ivory-billed Woodpecker

Pileated Woodpecker

Tyrant Flycatchers (Family Tyrannidae)

From its perch on a branch, a typical flycatcher darts out and snaps up an insect. Drab colors predominate in this family. Most species have bristly "whiskers"; broad-based, flat bill; large head; and erect posture. Some species in dull summer plumage may be distinguishable only by voice.

Eastern Kingbird *Tyrannus tyrannus* *L 8¹/₂" (22 cm)*
Black head, back slate gray; tail has broad white terminal band. Underparts white with pale gray wash across breast. Orange-red crown patch is seldom visible. Juvenile is brownish-gray above, darker on breast. A large, upright-perching bird, common and conspicuous in woodland clearings, farms, orchards, often near water. Call is a series of harsh *dzeet* notes and twitterings.

Gray Kingbird *Tyrannus dominicensis* *L 9" (23 cm)*
Pale gray above, with blackish mask. Red crown patch seldom visible. Bill long and thick. Underparts mostly white, with pale yellowish wash on belly and undertail coverts. Distinguished from Eastern Kingbird by forked tail with no white terminal band. Juvenile plumage, held well into fall, is browner above. Gray Kingbirds are common on the Florida Keys, local in mangroves on mainland. Song is a buzzy *pe-cheer-ry*, accented on second syllable. Casual wanderer north along Atlantic coast to Massachusetts, along Gulf coast to southeastern Texas.

Loggerhead Kingbird *Tyrannus caudifasciatus*
L 9" (23 cm) West Indian species, rare visitor to southernmost Florida. Grayish-olive above, darker on entire head; yellow crown patch seldom visible; bill long and thick; all wing coverts have distinct whitish edges; tail is tipped with buffy-white. Underparts mostly white, with pale yellowish wash on belly and undertail coverts. Lack of blackish mask distinguishes Loggerhead from Gray Kingbird; bill is much larger than in Eastern Kingbird. Call is a rolling, chattering *teeerrp.*

Thick-billed Kingbird *Tyrannus crassirostris*
L 9¹/₂" (24 cm) Large kingbird with very large bill. Adult is dusky brown above, with blackish mask and a seldom-seen yellow crown patch; whitish underparts washed with pale gray on breast, pale yellow on belly and undertail coverts. Yellow is brighter and more extensive in fresh fall adult and in first-fall birds, which have buffy edgings on wing coverts. Immature resembles Tropical Kingbird (next page), but has heavier bill and dark cap without ear patch. Thick-billed Kingbirds are common in the Guadalupe Canyon, uncommon elsewhere in southeastern Arizona. Casual during fall and winter in western Arizona and southern California. Perches high in sycamores of streamside lowlands. Call is a loud, high-pitched *weeerr.*

juvenile

**Eastern
Kingbird**

**Gray
Kingbird**

**Loggerhead
Kingbird**

fall

summer

**Thick-billed
Kingbird**

Western Kingbird *Tyrannus verticalis* L 8³/₄″ (22 cm)

Black tail, with white edges on outer feathers in fresh plumage. Bill much shorter than in Tropical and Couch's Kingbirds. Upperparts ashy-gray, paler than in Cassin's Kingbird, tinged with olive on back. Throat and breast pale grayish; belly bright lemon yellow. Male's red crown patch is usually concealed. Juvenile has slightly more olive on back, buffy edges on wing coverts, brownish tinge on breast, duller yellow belly. Common in dry, open country; perches on fences, telephone lines. Regular straggler in late fall and early winter along east coast from the Maritime Provinces south. Call is a sharp *whit*.

♪ Cassin's Kingbird *Tyrannus vociferans* L 9″ (23 cm)

Dark brown tail; narrow buffy tips and lack of white edges on outer tail feathers help distinguish this species from Western Kingbird. Bill is much shorter than in Tropical and Couch's Kingbirds. Upperparts darker gray than in Western, washed with olive on back. White chin contrasts with dark gray head and breast. Belly dull yellow. Male's red crown patch is usually concealed. Juvenile is duller, slightly browner above, often with bold buffy edges on wing coverts. Fairly common in varied habitats; generally prefers denser foliage than does Western Kingbird. Most common call, given year round, is a short, loud *chi-bew*, accented on second syllable.

♪ Tropical Kingbird *Tyrannus melancholicus* L 9¹/₄″ (24 cm)

Almost identical to Couch's Kingbird. Bill is thinner; back slightly grayer, less green. Distinctive call is a very rapid, twittering *pip-pip-pip-pip*. Distinguished from Western and Cassin's Kingbirds by larger bill, darker ear patch, and slightly notched tail. Juvenile is duller overall, with buffy edges on wing coverts. Uncommon and local in southeastern Arizona; found in lowlands near water; often nests in cottonwoods. Rare but regular during fall and winter along the west coast to Washington.

♪ Couch's Kingbird *Tyrannus couchii* L 9¹/₄″ (24 cm)

Almost identical to Tropical Kingbird. Bill is thicker; back slightly greener, less gray. Distinctive calls, a shrill, rolling *breeeer;* and a more common *kip kip kip*. Distinguished from Western and Cassin's Kingbirds by larger bill, darker ear patch, slightly notched tail. Juvenile is duller overall, with buffy edges on wing coverts. Fairly common in Rio Grande Delta in summer; rare in winter. Found in groves and shrubs, generally close to water. Rare vagrant along Gulf coast. Formerly classified as a subspecies of Tropical Kingbird.

Western
Kingbird

Cassin's
Kingbird

Tropical
Kingbird

Couch's
Kingbird

Western

Cassin's

Couch's

Tropical

Scissor-tailed Flycatcher *Tyrannus forficatus*

L 13" (33 cm) Adult has extremely long outer tail feathers, white with black tips; tail is often spread in flight. Male's tail is longer than female's. Upperparts are pearl gray, underparts whitish, with salmon pink sides, flanks, and undertail coverts. Salmon pink wing linings and reddish axillaries show in flight. Juvenile and immature are paler overall with shorter tail; distinguished in flight from Western Kingbird (preceding page) by buffy-pink wing linings, salmon axillaries, and black-tipped white outer tail feathers. Distinguished from immature Fork-tailed Flycatcher by lack of contrast between head and back. Common and conspicuous throughout most of breeding range; found in semi-open country. Winters primarily from central Mexico to Panama, but small numbers remain in southernmost Florida and the Keys. Casual winter visitor in southeastern Louisiana. Casual wanderer north of range from British Columbia to Maine. Calls include a harsh *kek* and a repeated *ka-leep*.

Fork-tailed Flycatcher *Tyrannus savana* *L 14¹/₂" (37 cm)*

Tropical species, rare summer and fall vagrant along Atlantic coast, in interior to upper Midwest and Texas. Extremely long black tail flutters in flight. Back is gray; head and wings black. In flight, white underparts and white wing linings distinguish Fork-tailed from Scissor-tailed Flycatcher. Many sightings are of immatures, which resemble adult but have a shorter tail. Distinguished from immature Scissor-tailed Flycatcher by contrast between head and back.

Sulphur-bellied Flycatcher *Myiodynastes luteiventris*

L 8¹/₂" (22 cm) Our only flycatcher streaked above and below. Pale yellow underparts, boldly streaked with black; dark ear patch. Upperparts streaked black and brown, often with an olive tinge; rump and tail rusty-red. Fairly common in deciduous or mixed woodlands of mountain canyons, generally at elevations between 5,000 and 6,000 feet. Inconspicuous; frequently perches high in the canopy. Loud call sounds like the squeaking of a rubber duck, *kip-kip-kip squellya-squellya*. Song is a soft *tre-le-re-re*.

Great Kiskadee *Pitangus sulphuratus* *L 9³/₄" (25 cm)*

Distinctive striped black-and-white head; yellow crown patch is often concealed. Underparts bright lemon yellow; upperparts brown, with reddish-brown wings and tail. Fairly common in south Texas; found chiefly in wet woodlands or near watercourses. In addition to fly-catching, dives for fish like a kingfisher, but does not totally submerge. Calls include a loud, slow, deliberate *kis-ka-dee* and an incessant chattering. Rare vagrant in southeastern Arizona and north along Gulf coast of Texas. Formerly known as Kiskadee Flycatcher.

juvenile

juvenile

♂

Scissor-tailed Flycatcher

♂

Sulphur-bellied Flycatcher

Fork-tailed Flycatcher

Great Kiskadee

Great Crested Flycatcher *Myiarchus crinitus*

L 8³/₄" (22 cm) Dark olive above, with bushy crest; large bill, upper mandible dark, lower buffy-orange at base. Gray throat and breast contrast with lemon yellow belly and undertail coverts. Seen from below or in flight, dusky tail feathers show extensively reddish inner webs. Common in open deciduous forests, orchards; feeds high in the canopy. Distinctive call, a loud whistled *wheep*. Also gives a rolling *prrrr-eet*. Casual in west during fall migration.

Brown-crested Flycatcher *Myiarchus tyrannulus*

L 8³/₄" (22 cm) Brownish-olive above, with bushy brown crest; large, dark bill is longer, thicker, and broader than bill of Ash-throated Flycatcher. Throat and breast pale gray; belly and undertail coverts lemon yellow. Seen from below or in flight, dusky tail feathers show reddish inner webs, less extensive than in Great Crested or Ash-throated Flycatchers. Fairly common but local in saguaro desert, river groves, lower altitudes of mountain woodlands. Song is a clear musical whistle, a rolling *whit-will-do*. Call, a sharp *whit*. Formerly called Weid's Crested Flycatcher.

Ash-throated Flycatcher *Myiarchus cinerascens*

L 8¹/₂" (22 cm) Grayish-brown above, with bushy crest; dark bill, shorter and thinner than bill of Brown-crested Flycatcher. Throat and breast pale gray, belly and undertail coverts pale yellow; underparts generally paler than in Brown-crested. Seen from below or in flight, dusky tail shows more extensive reddish inner margins; all tail feathers are tipped with brown. In all *Myiarchus* flycatchers, briefly held juvenile plumage shows mostly reddish tail. Ash-throated Flycatcher is common in a wide variety of habitats, including deserts, chaparral, woodlands. Casual fall and winter visitor to east. Calls include *ka-brick* or *ka-wheer,* accented on second syllable, and a rough *prrrt*. Song is a gurgly *tea-for-two*.

Dusky-capped Flycatcher *Myiarchus tuberculifer*

L 7¹/₄" (18 cm) Brownish-olive above, with darker bushy crest; all-dark bill, proportionately large. Wing bars are dull reddish-buff, in contrast to other flycatchers on this page. Throat and breast gray, darker on sides of breast; belly and undertail coverts lemon yellow, usually brighter than in Ash-throated Flycatcher. Dark tail shows only slight reddish edgings around each feather. Fairly common in sycamores and live oaks of mountain canyons, dense streamside woodlands. Call is a mournful, descending *peeur;* also gives a rolling whistled *pree-pree-prrreeit*. Casual in west Texas during migration. Casual visitor in southern and central California, Nevada, Colorado. Formerly called Olivaceous Flycatcher.

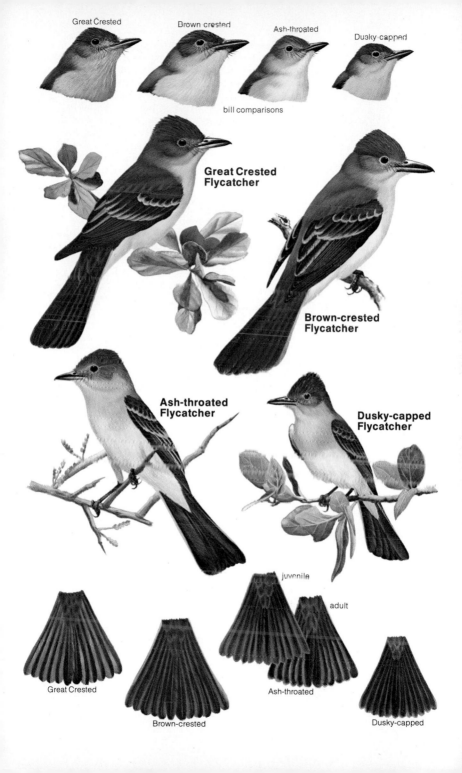

Great Crested

Brown crested

Ash-throated

Dusky-capped

bill comparisons

Great Crested Flycatcher

Brown-crested Flycatcher

Ash-throated Flycatcher

Dusky-capped Flycatcher

juvenile

adult

Great Crested

Brown-crested

Ash-throated

Dusky-capped

Greater Pewee *Contopus pertinax* *L 8″ (20 cm)*

A large flycatcher; sometimes shows slender, pointed crest. Upper mandible is dark, lower entirely orange. Wing bars indistinct. In worn summer plumage, upperparts are grayish-olive; pale throat and yellowish-white belly and undertail coverts contrast only slightly with gray breast. Fresh fall birds are slightly greener above, yellower below, but underparts always show less contrast than in Olive-sided Flycatcher; note also longer tail. Fairly common in mountain pine-oak woodlands. Casual during winter in southern Arizona, southern California. Distinctive song, a whistled *ho-say ma-re-ah*. Call is a repeated *pip*. Formerly called Coues' Flycatcher.

Olive-sided Flycatcher *Contopus borealis* *L 7¹/₂″ (19 cm)*

Large flycatcher with proportionately short tail. Deep brownish-olive above; white tufts on sides of rump distinctive but not often visible. Throat, center of breast, and belly are dull white or pale yellow. Sides and flanks are brownish-olive and streaked; streaking may extend across breast. Bill is mostly black; center of lower mandible dull yellow. Juvenile is browner above, yellower below, with browner sides. Fairly common in coniferous forests, bogs. Distinctive song, a clear *quick-three-beers*, the second note higher. Typical call is a repeated *pip*.

♪ Eastern Wood-Pewee *Contopus virens* *L 6¹/₄″ (16 cm)*

Generally indistinguishable from Western Wood-Pewee except by range and voice. Distinctive song is a clear, slow, plaintive *pee-a-wee*, the second note lower, mixed with an occasional downslurred *pee-yer*. Calls include a loud *chip* and clear, whistled, rising *pweee* notes. Plumage variable; generally dark grayish-olive above; throat dull white; breast and sides dark gray; belly, flanks, and undertail coverts whitish or pale yellow. Distinct wing bars, whitish in adult, buffy in juvenile and fall immature. Bill of adult has black upper mandible, dull orange lower mandible with black tip. Juvenile and immature may have all-dark bill. Eastern Wood-Pewees are common and widespread in a variety of woodland habitats, from mature deciduous forests to urban shade trees.

♪ Western Wood-Pewee *Contopus sordidulus*

L 6¹/₄″ (16 cm) Generally indistinguishable from Eastern Wood-Pewee except by range and voice. Calls include a harsh, slightly descending *peeer* and clear whistles that resemble *pee-yer* of Eastern Wood-Pewee. At dawn and dusk, sings three-note *tswee-tee-teet* phrases mixed with the *peeer* note. Also gives a sharp *chip* call. Plumage variable. Bill may be all-dark or have yellow-orange on lower mandible. Common in open deciduous and mixed woodlands. Range of each species in area of overlap is uncertain; not known to interbreed.

Greater Pewee

Olive-sided Flycatcher

fall

summer

immature

Eastern Wood-Pewee

juvenile

Western Wood-Pewee

Eastern Phoebe *Sayornis phoebe* L 7" (18 cm)

Brownish-gray above, darkest on head, wings, tail. Underparts mostly white with pale olive wash on sides and breast; fresh fall birds are washed with yellow below. Molts before migration. Distinguished from pewees (preceding page) by all-black bill, lack of distinct wing bars, and habit of pumping and spreading its tail while perched. Lacks eye rings of *Empidonax* flycatchers. Juvenile plumage, held only briefly, is browner above, with two buff wing bars, cinnamon rump. Common in woodlands, farmlands, suburbs, often nesting in eaves, rafters, and under bridges. Distinctive song a harsh, emphatic *fee-be,* accented on first syllable. Typical call note is an emphatic *chip.* Rare fall migrant and winter visitor in southwest and on west coast.

Black Phoebe *Sayornis nigricans* L 6³/₄" (17 cm)

Black head, upperparts, breast; white belly and undertail coverts. Juvenile plumage, held briefly, is browner, with two cinnamon wing bars, cinnamon rump. Common in woodlands, parks, suburbs; prefers to nest near water. Frequently pumps and spreads its tail while perched. Four-syllable song, a rising *pee-wee* followed by a descending *pee-wee.* Calls include a loud *tseee* and a sharper *tsip.*

Say's Phoebe *Sayornis saya* L 7¹/₂" (19 cm)

Grayish-brown above, darkest on head, wings, and tail; breast and throat are pale grayish-brown; belly and undertail coverts tawny. Juvenile plumage, held briefly, is browner above; shows two cinnamon wing bars. Fairly common in dry, open areas, canyons, cliffs; perches on bushes, boulders, fences. Frequently pumps and spreads its tail while perched. Song is a fast *pit-tse-ar,* often given in fluttering flight. Typical call is a thin, plaintive *pee-ee,* slightly downslurred. Highly migratory; casual vagrant in fall and winter on the east coast from Quebec and Nova Scotia south to Florida.

Vermilion Flycatcher *Pyrocephalus rubinus* L 6" (15 cm)

Adult male striking red and brown. Adult female grayish-brown above, with blackish tail; throat and breast white, with dusky streaking; belly and undertail coverts are peach; note also whitish eyebrow and forehead. Juvenile resembles adult female but is spotted rather than streaked below; belly white, often with yellowish tinge. Fall immature birds more closely resemble the respective adults. Fairly common and approachable; found in streamside shrubs, bottomlands, small wooded ponds. Male in breeding season sings during fluttery display flight a soft, tinkling *pit-a-see pit-a-see;* also sings while perched. Typical call is a sharp *tsik.* Pumps and spreads its tail while perched. Casual winter visitor to coastal southern California and the Gulf coast.

Eastern Phoebe

summer

fall

Black Phoebe

juvenile

Say's Phoebe

immature ♀

♀

Vermilion Flycatcher

immature ♂

♂

juvenile

Empidonax Flycatchers

The bane of bird watchers, flycatchers of the genus *Empidonax* are extremely difficult to identify. All are drab, with pale eye rings and wing bars. As spring turns to summer, plumages grow duller from wear. Some species molt before their fall migration, acquiring bright fresh plumage in late summer. Identification depends upon voice, habitat, behavior, and subtle differences in size, bill shape, and tail length.

♪ **Gray Flycatcher** *Empidonax wrightii* L 6" *(15 cm)*
Gray above, with a slight olive tinge in fresh fall plumage; whitish below, belly washed with pale yellow in fall. Head is proportionately small and rounded; white eye ring inconspicuous on pale gray face. Long bill; lower mandible pinkish-orange at base, darker at tip. Long tail, with thin, whitish outer edge. Perched bird drops its tail slowly downward, like a phoebe. Juvenile is brownish-gray above, with pale buffy wing bars; underparts tinged brownish-buff. Fairly common in dry habitat of Great Basin, especially in yellow pine or pinyon-juniper mixed with sagebrush, rabbitbrush. Song is a vigorous *chi-wip* or *chi-bit* followed by a liquid *whilp* and trailing off in a gurgle. Call, a loud *wit.*

♪ **Dusky Flycatcher** *Empidonax oberholseri* L 5³/₄" *(15 cm)*
Grayish-olive above; yellowish below, with whitish throat, pale olive wash on upper breast. Pale lores; conspicuous white eye ring. Bill mostly dark, orange at base of lower mandible. Bill and tail slightly longer than Hammond's Flycatcher; outer tail feathers have whitish edges. Perched bird flicks tail upward. Juvenile has grayer head, buffy wing bars, buffy tinge on breast and flanks. Worn late-summer birds are variably gray and drab. Molt occurs after fall migration; fresh fall birds are quite yellow below. Common in tall shrubs, open woodlands. Calls include a *wit* note softer than Gray Flycatcher; mournful *deehic* call is heard on breeding grounds. Song has three or four phrases: a clear *sillit;* a lower *tsurrp;* another high *sillit,* often omitted; and a clear, high *seet.*

♪ **Hammond's Flycatcher** *Empidonax hammondii*
L 5¹/₂" *(14 cm)* A small Empid, fairly large-headed and short-tailed. White eye ring. Grayish head contrasts with grayish-olive back; throat grayish-white; gray or olive wash on breast and sides; belly tinged with pale yellow. Molt occurs before migration; fall birds are brighter olive above and yellower below. Short, slightly notched tail edged with gray. Tail is flicked upward often and energetically; wings are often flicked simultaneously, usually unlike Dusky Flycatcher. Bill is slightly shorter, thinner, darker than Dusky's. Common in coniferous forests at high elevations. Migrates fairly late in fall, early in spring. Call note is a sharp *peek.* Song resembles Dusky's but is hoarser, more emphatic.

Gray Flycatcher

fall

summer

Dusky Flycatcher

summer

winter

Hammond's Flycatcher

summer

fall

♪ **Least Flycatcher** *Empidonax minimus* *L 5¹/₄" (13 cm)*
Smallest Empid in the east. Proportionately large-headed.
Gray above, sometimes with olive tinge; bold white eye ring;
two white wing bars. Throat whitish; breast washed with gray;
belly and undertail coverts pale yellow or tinged with yellow.
Underparts are usually paler overall than Hammond's Flycatcher (preceding page). Bill short, triangular, with lower
mandible mostly pale. Adults molt to fresh plumage after fall
migration. Juvenile is browner above, wing bars buffy. Common in the east, rare migrant through most of west. Inhabits
open deciduous woods, orchards, parks. Song is a dry *che-bek,*
accented on second syllable. Call note, a sharp *whit.*

♪ **Acadian Flycatcher** *Empidonax virescens* *L 5³/₄" (15 cm)*
Olive above, with yellow eye ring, two buffy or whitish wing
bars; very long primaries. Bill proportionately long and broad-
based, with yellowish lower mandible. Underparts vary; most
birds show pale grayish throat, pale olive wash across upper
breast, white lower breast, and yellow belly and undertail coverts. Worn late-summer birds show almost no yellow below.
Molts before migration; fresh fall birds have bright buffy wing
bars. Juvenile's brownish-olive upperparts are edged with
buff; wing bars buffy; underparts whitish with olive wash on
breast. Common; found in the deep shade of mature woodlands, swamps. The only Empid in the southeastern lowlands
during the summer; range is expanding in the northeast. Call
note is an emphatic *weece.* Song, an explosive *wick-up.* On
breeding grounds, also gives a Flicker-like *ti ti ti ti ti.*

♂ **Willow Flycatcher** *Empidonax traillii* *L 5³/₄" (15 cm)*
Lacks conspicuous eye ring. Upperparts brownish-olive; eastern birds slightly grayer above. Whitish throat contrasts with
pale olive breast; belly pale yellow. Distinguished from pewees
(page 284) by habit of flicking tail upward and by smaller bill,
shorter wings. Molts after fall migration. Common in mountain meadows, along streams; dry, brushy upland pastures, especially in hawthorn; orchards. Habitat generally drier than
that of Alder Flycatcher. Call is a liquid *wit.* Distinctive song, a
sneezy *fitz-bew;* often sings during spring migration. On
breeding grounds, also gives a rising *breeet.* Formerly classified with Alder Flycatcher as one species, Traill's Flycatcher.

♪ **Alder Flycatcher** *Empidonax alnorum* *L 5³/₄" (15 cm)*
Generally indistinguishable from Willow Flycatcher, but note
conspicuous eye ring, slightly greener upperparts, slightly
shorter bill. Best identified by range, habitat, and song. Common in bogs, ponds, birch and alder thickets. Where ranges
overlap, Alder Flycatcher is found in denser, wetter habitat.
Call is a loud, piping *peep.* Distinctive song, a falling, buzzy
fee-beeo. On breeding grounds, also utters a hoarse *wheer.*

Least Flycatcher

juvenile

adult

adult

Acadian Flycatcher

juvenile

Willow Flycatcher

Alder Flycatcher

♪ **Yellow-bellied Flycatcher** *Empidonax flaviventris*
L 5½" (14 cm) Proportionately short-tailed and big-headed. Brownish-olive above, yellowish below. Broad yellow eye ring. Lower mandible entirely pale orange. Tail is grayish-brown; wings blackish, with whitish or yellow wing bars. Underparts show a broad olive "vest," more extensive than in Acadian Flycatcher; lacks pale area between olive vest and yellow belly. Also, throat is yellow, rather than whitish; bill smaller. Molts after migration; worn late-summer birds are grayer above. Common in bogs, swamps, damp coniferous woods. Song is a leisurely liquid *che-lek;* also a plaintive rising *per-wee.* Distinctive call, a loud, sneezy *chew.*

♪ **Western Flycatcher** *Empidonax difficilis* L 5½" (14 cm)
Brownish-green above, yellow below, with a broad brownish-olive "vest." Broad yellowish or whitish eye ring, often broader behind eye. Lower mandible entirely bright orange. Tail longer than Yellow-bellied Flycatcher's; wings browner and wing bars less conspicuous. Molts after migration; worn late-summer birds are paler below. Juveniles are browner above, with buffy wing bars; whiter below, almost entirely white in some coastal birds. Subspecies vary in size, brightness of plumage, and voice. Coastal birds sing a series of single, up-slurred *suwheet* notes, often interspersed with *pik* notes. Song of interior birds is two-noted, a loud *whee-seet,* the second note higher. A common species, the Western Flycatcher breeds in moist open woodlands, boreal forests, shady canyons.

Buff-breasted Flycatcher *Empidonax fulvifrons*
L 5" (13 cm) Smallest *Empidonax* flycatcher. Brownish above; breast cinnamon buff, paler on worn late-summer birds. White eye ring; pale wing bars; small bill, with lower mandible entirely pale orange. Buff-breasteds molt before migration. Rare and local; nest in small colonies in dry coniferous or mixed woodlands of canyon floors. Call note is a soft *pwit.* Typical song, a quick *chicky-whew* or *chee-lick.*

♪ **Northern Beardless-Tyrannulet**
Camptostoma imberbe L 4½" (11 cm) Grayish-olive above and on breast; dull white or pale yellow below. Indistinct whitish eyebrow; small, slightly curved bill. Crown is darker than nape in many birds; often raised slightly in a bushy crest. Distinguished from Ruby-crowned Kinglet (page 322) by buffy wing bars and lack of bold eye ring. Fairly common but local; often found near streams in sycamore, mesquite, and cottonwood groves. Difficult to spot; best located by voice. Song on breeding grounds is a descending series of loud, clear *peer* notes. Call, a loud, whistled *pee-yerp.*

Acadian Flycatcher for comparison

Yellow-bellied Flycatcher

Western Flycatcher

juvenile

Buff-breasted Flycatcher

Northern Beardless-Tyrannulet

Rose-throated Becard *Pachyramphus aglaiae*

L 7¼" (18 cm) Rosy throat and pale or dusky underparts distinctive in male. In female, note dark crown, brown back. A stocky, large-headed, short-tailed bird; bushy crest sometimes raised. Winter immature male shows partially pink throat; full adult plumage is acquired after second summer. Quiet and inconspicuous, Becards are found in wooded canyons and bottomlands. Foot-long nest is generally suspended from limb of cottonwood or sycamore. Uncommon and local in southeastern Arizona; rare visitor along Rio Grande in Texas. Distinctive call is a thin, mournful, descending *seeoo*, sometimes preceded by chatter.

Larks (Family Alaudidae)

Ground dwellers of open fields, Larks are slender-billed seed and insect eaters. They seldom alight on trees or bushes. On the ground, they walk rather than hop.

Eurasian Skylark *Alauda arvensis* *L 7¼" (18 cm)*
Subspecies *A.a. arvensis,* introduced to Vancouver Island in the early 1900s, is resident there and on San Juan Islands on open slopes and fields. Plain brown bird with slender bill; slight crest is raised when bird is agitated. Upperparts heavily streaked; buffy-white underparts streaked on breast and throat. Dark eye prominent. The highly migratory Asian subspecies, *pekinensis,* seen rarely in western Alaska and along the Pacific coast, is darker, more heavily streaked above. All juveniles have a scaly brown mantle. In flight, Skylarks show a conspicuous white trailing edge on inner wing, white-edged tail. Song is a continuous outpouring of trills and warblings, delivered in high, hovering or circling song flight. Call, a liquid *chirrup* with buzzy overtones.

Horned Lark *Eremophila alpestris* *L 7¼" (18 cm)*
Head pattern distinctive in all subspecies: black "horns," white or yellowish face and throat with broad black stripe under eye; black bib. Female duller overall, horns less prominent. Conspicuous in flight is the dark tail with white outer feathers, brown central feathers. In winter plumage, black areas on head and breast are partially obscured by pale edgings. Brief juvenile plumage is dark above with white, wedge-shaped speckling. Subspecies vary widely in overall colors; extremes are shown here: pale *E.a. enthymia;* dark *alpestris;* yellowish *sierrae;* streaked *insularis;* and reddish *rubea.* Widespread and common, Horned Larks prefer dirt fields, gravel ridges, shores. Calls include a high-pitched *tsee-ee* or *tsee-titi.* Song is a weak twittering, delivered from the ground or in flight.

Rose-throated Becard

♂

1st fall ♂

♀

Eurasian Skylark

pekinensis

arvensis

Horned Lark

enthymia ♂

alpestris ♂

♀

sierrae ♂

juvenile

insularis ♂

rubea ♂

Swallows (Family Hirundinidae)

Slender bodies with long, pointed wings resemble swifts, but wrist angle is sharper and farther from the body; flight is more fluid. Adept aerialists, swallows dart to catch flying insects. Flocks perch in long rows on rooftops and wires.

Tree Swallow *Tachycineta bicolor* L 5³/₄″ (15 cm)

Dark, glossy blue-green above, white below. White cheek patch does not extend above eye as in Violet-green Swallow. Lacks white at edges of rump. Female is duller overall. Juvenile is gray-brown above, white below, with diffuse gray breast band. First-fall birds are like juvenile but show varying amount of adult color on crown and back; may be confused with Bank Swallow (next page); resemble adult by winter. Tree Swallows are common in any wooded habitat near water, especially where dead trees are abundant, providing nest holes. Also nests in fence posts, barn eaves, nest boxes. Generally migrates north earlier in the spring, lingers farther north in winter than other swallows. Flocks in migration may number in the thousands.

Violet-green Swallow *Tachycineta thalassina*

L 5¹/₄″ (13 cm) White on cheek extends above eye; white flank patches extend onto sides of rump. Compare with similar Tree Swallow. May also be confused with White-throated Swift (page 252). Female is duller above than male. Juvenile is gray-brown above; white areas other than rump patch may be mottled or grayish. Common in open woodlands, suburbs, and in coastal areas from central California north. A late-spring migrant; nests in hollow trees or rock crevices, often forming loose colonies.

Bahama Swallow *Tachycineta cyaneoviridis*

L 5³/₄″ (15 cm) Breeds in northern Bahamas; casual visitor to the Florida Keys, especially Big Pine Key, and mainland. Commonly found in pine trees. Deeply forked tail separates this species from the similar Tree Swallow.

Purple Martin *Progne subis* L 8″ (20 cm)

Male is all dark, glossy purplish-blue. Female and juvenile are pale gray below. First-spring males have some purple feathering below. In flight, male especially resembles European Starling (page 346); look for forked tail, longer wings, and typical swallow flight, short glides alternating with rapid flapping. Purple Martins are locally common where suitable nest sites are available. In the east and midwest, multiple-unit Martin houses encourage communal nesting; in the west, pairs more commonly nest in old woodpecker holes. Western population may be decreasing because of Starling competition. Very early spring migrant in south; winters in South America.

Tree
Swallow

♂

♀

1st fall

Violet-green
Swallow

♂

♂

Bahama
Swallow

Purple
Martin

♂

1st spring
♂

♀

Bank Swallow *Riparia riparia* L 5¹/₄" (13 cm)

Brownish-gray breast band, often extending in a line down center of breast. Throat is white; note also white line on rear border of ear patch. Gray-brown upperparts contrast with darker wings; compare with darker tones and longer wings of Northern Rough-winged Swallow. Compare also with Tree Swallow (preceding page). Locally common throughout most of range. Nests in large colonies, excavating nest burrows in steep riverbank cliffs, gravel pits, and highway cuts. Winters in South America; migrates in large flocks. Wingbeats are shallow and rapid.

Northern Rough-winged Swallow

Stelgidopteryx serripennis L 5¹/₂" (14 cm) Pale brown above, whitish below, with gray-brown wash on chin, throat, and upper breast. Lacks Bank Swallow's well defined breast band; wings are longer, wingbeats deeper and slower. Nests in crevices in steep riverbanks or other cliffs and in culverts and under bridges; does not form colonies. Migrates in small flocks.

Cliff Swallow *Hirundo pyrrhonota* L 5¹/₂" (14 cm)

Squarish tail and buffy rump distinguish this swallow from all others except Cave Swallow. Most Cliff Swallows have blackish throat, pale forehead. Southwestern form has cinnamon forehead like Cave Swallow, but throat is dark. All juveniles are much duller and grayer than adults; throat is paler. Locally common around farms, rural settlements, in open country on cliffs. Range expanding southward in the east. Nests in colonies, building gourd-shaped mud nests. This is the famed swallow of California's San Juan Capistrano Mission.

Cave Swallow *Hirundo fulva* L 5¹/₂" (14 cm)

Squarish tail; buffy rump. Distinguished from most Cliff Swallows by buffy throat, cinnamon forehead; compare especially with southwestern form of Cliff Swallow, which has a blackish throat. A Central American and Caribbean species, the Cave Swallow is apparently expanding its range in the U.S. Nests in colonies in limestone caves, sinkholes, culverts, and under bridges, sometimes with Barn and Cliff Swallows. Casual spring migrant in extreme southern Florida.

Barn Swallow *Hirundo rustica* L 6³/₄" (17 cm)

Cinnamon underparts and long, deeply forked tail mark this common species. Throat is reddish-brown. Juvenile paler below; tail shorter but noticeably forked. Generally nests on or inside farm buildings, under bridges, and inside culverts, in pairs or small colonies. Range expanding in southeast. Asian forms seen regularly in western Alaska have whitish underparts and a dark breast band below tawny throat.

Bank Swallow

Northern Rough-winged Swallow

Cliff Swallow

juvenile

southwestern

Cave Swallow

Barn Swallow

juvenile

Harsh voice and aggressive manner draw attention to these large, often gregarious birds. Crows and ravens are somber in hue, jays and magpies more colorful. In most species, bristles cover nostrils. Powerful all-purpose bill efficiently handles a varied diet.

♪ **Scrub Jay** *Aphelocoma coerulescens* L 11¹/₂″ (29 cm)
Blue head without crest; blue wings; long blue tail; whitish throat bordered by streaked blue-gray breast band. Back is bluish-gray. Birds of the interior are duller overall, with less contrast above, less conspicuous breast band. Juvenile is grayish above, with blue on wings and tail. Isolated Florida subspecies has whitish forehead. Common inhabitant of scrub oak, chaparral, pinyon-juniper stands, and residential areas. Winter visitors, usually the paler interior birds, are sometimes seen in desert areas. Flight is distinctively undulating. Varied calls include a raspy, repeated *shreeep*.

♪ **Gray-breasted Jay** *Aphelocoma ultramarina*
L 11¹/₂″ (29 cm) Blue above, with slight grayish cast on back; lacks crest. Distinguished from Scrub Jay by absence of white throat, white eyebrow, and conspicuous breast band. Texas birds are generally darker above. Arizona juvenile has pale bill. Common in oak canyons of the southwestern mountains, where it greatly outnumbers Scrub Jay. Calls include a harsh, ringing *week*, given singly or in a series. Often nests in small, loose colonies; all birds share in the work of feeding nestlings. Flight is more direct than that of Scrub Jay. Formerly called Mexican Jay.

Pinyon Jay *Gymnorhinus cyanocephalus* L 10¹/₂″ (27 cm)
Blue overall; blue throat streaked with white; lacks crest; bill long, spiky; tail short. Immature is paler, grayer overall. Generally seen in large flocks, often numbering in the hundreds; nests in loose colonies. Flight is direct, with rapid wingbeats, unlike Scrub Jay's undulating flight. Typical flight call is a high, piercing *mew*, audible over long distances. Common in pinyon-juniper woodlands of interior mountains and high plateaus; in southern California, prefers yellow pine woodlands.

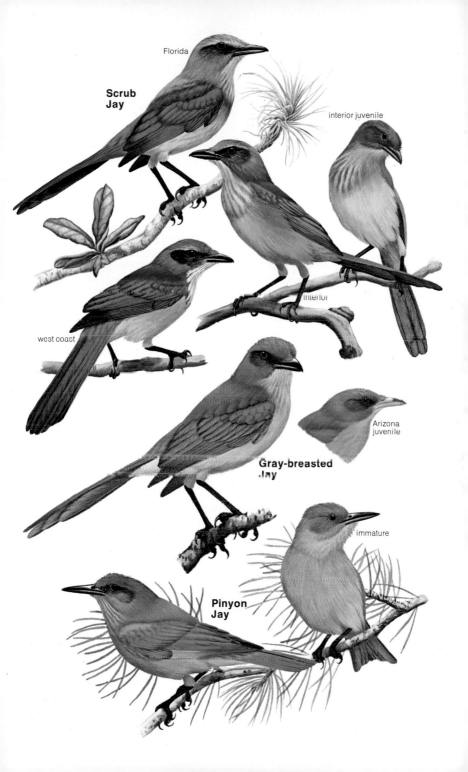

Florida

Scrub Jay

interior juvenile

west coast

interior

Arizona juvenile

Gray-breasted Jay

immature

Pinyon Jay

Blue Jay *Cyanocitta cristata* L 11" (28 cm)
Crested jay with black barring and white patches on blue wings and tail, black necklace on whitish underparts. Most common call of its varied repertoire is the familiar piercing *jay jay jay;* another resembles a squeaky pump handle. Common inhabitant of suburban gardens, parks, woodlands. Generally very active and noisy. Range is expanding steadily to northwest; casual fall and winter visitor to Oregon and California. In the eastern Rockies, hybridizes with Steller's Jay.

Steller's Jay *Cyanocitta stelleri* L 11¹/₂" (29 cm)
Black crest, throat, and upper breast. Subspecies vary slightly in overall coloring. Northwest coast form, *C.s. stelleri,* has blue-tipped feathers over eye; Rocky Mountain form, *macrolopha,* shows white flecking. One subspecies (not shown), resident only on the Queen Charlotte Islands off British Columbia, is almost entirely black above. Juvenile is duller than adult, with grayish underparts. Where ranges overlap in the eastern Rockies, Steller's Jay sometimes hybridizes with Blue Jay; replaces Blue Jay in coastal forests and mountains farther west. Typical call is a harsh *shaack* or series of *shaack* notes. Common in pine-oak woodlands and coniferous forests. Often scavenges at campsites. Casual winter visitor to lower elevations of Great Basin, Central Valley, and southwestern deserts.

Gray Jay *Perisoreus canadensis* L 11¹/₂" (29 cm)
A fluffy, long-tailed jay with small bill, no crest. The representative subspecies shown here have distinctive head patterns: *P.c. canadensis,* common in northern boreal forests, has a white collar and forehead, with brownish crown and nape; *capitalis,* common in the southern Rockies, has a paler crown, head appears mostly white; *obscurus,* resident along the northwest coast from Alaska to California, has a larger, darker cap extending to the crown, with underparts paler than in other forms. Juveniles of all forms are sooty-gray overall, with faint white whisker stripe. Common in coniferous forests, Gray Jays are familiar campsite visitors, boldly snatching food scraps from around campfires or even from inside tents. Call notes include a whistled *wheeoo* and a low *chuck*. Formerly called Canada Jay.

Clark's Nutcracker *Nucifraga columbiana* L 12" (31 cm)
Gray body with black wings and black central tail feathers. White wing patches and white outer tail feathers are conspicuous in flight. Wingbeats are deep, slow, crowlike. Locally common in high coniferous forests at timberline; sometimes wanders to lower elevations in fall and winter. About every ten or fifteen years, Nutcrackers irrupt into desert and lowland areas of the west. Often seen at campsites or picnic grounds where it boldly steals or begs for food scraps. Calls include a very nasal, grating, drawn-out *kra-a-a.*

Blue Jay

Steller's Jay

stelleri

macrolopha

Gray Jay

juvenile

canadensis

capitalis

obscurus

Clark's Nutcracker

Brown Jay *Cyanocorax morio* L 16¹/₂" (42 cm)

Tropical species; range extends to southern tip of Texas. Resident but rare in woodlands and mesquite along the Rio Grande. Very large jay with long, broad tail. Overall dark, sooty brown except for pale belly. Adult usually has black bill; juvenile bill is yellow. In transition to adult plumage, many Brown Jays have blotchy yellow and black bills. A noisy species; its harsh scream is similar to the call of a Red-shouldered Hawk. Another call sounds like a hiccup.

Green Jay *Cyanocorax yncas* L 10¹/₂" (27 cm)

Tropical species; range extends to southern tip of Texas. Resident and locally common in brushy areas and streamside growth of the lower Rio Grande Valley. Colorful plumage blends with dappled sun and shade in woodland habitat of this tropical jay. In winter it may visit ranches and towns, where it regularly comes to feeders. Lively and noisy; gives a variety of calls, including a low, throaty rattle. Somewhat inquisitive; often comes to investigate human intruders.

Black-billed Magpie *Pica pica* L 19" (48 cm)

Readily identified as a magpie by black-and-white markings and unusually long tail with iridescent green highlights. White wing patches flash in flight. Black bill distinguishes this species from look-alike Yellow-billed Magpie. Ranges almost overlap, and Blackbills occasionally stray south of normal range in winter. Common inhabitant of open woodlands and thickets in rangelands and foothills, especially along watercourses. Typical calls include a whining *mag* and a series of loud, harsh *chuck* notes. Birds occasionally seen throughout the east may be escaped cage birds.

Yellow-billed Magpie *Pica nuttalli* L 16¹/₂" (42 cm)

Nearly identical to Black-billed Magpie, but rarely occurs in the Blackbill's normal range. Distinguished by its yellow bill and by a yellow patch of bare skin, variable in size, around the eye. Calls are similar to Blackbill; both species roost and feed in flocks, usually nest in loose colonies. Common resident of rangelands and foothills of northern and central Sacramento Valley. Not prone to wandering, but casual north almost to Oregon. Prefers oak groves or streamside stands of trees. Also found in cultivated fields and residential areas.

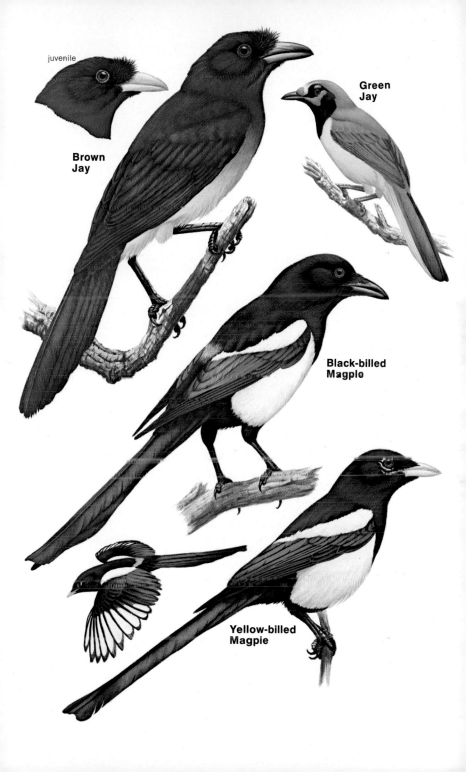

juvenile

Brown Jay

Green Jay

Black-billed Magplo

Yellow-billed Magpie

♪ **Mexican Crow** *Corvus imparatus* L 14¹/₂" (37 cm)
Unknown in U. S. until late 1960s, now winters along Rio Grande in open rangeland or brushland. Can be seen in large numbers at the Brownsville, Texas, municipal dump. Resembles American Crow, but is smaller and glossier, and ranges do not overlap. Distinctive call note, a low, guttural croak.

♪ **American Crow** *Corvus brachyrhynchos* L 17¹/₂" (45 cm)
Our largest crow. Long, heavy bill is noticeably smaller than in ravens. Fan-shaped tail distinguishes all crows from ravens in flight. Adult readily identified by familiar *caw* call. Juvenile's higher pitched, nasal *cah* begging call resembles call of similar Fish Crow. The American Crow is common throughout most of its range in a wide variety of habitats, including southwestern deserts in winter. Usually seen in flocks except during the nesting season.

Northwestern Crow *Corvus caurinus* L 16" (41 cm)
(Not pictured.) This species inhabits northwestern coastal areas and islands, where it is a common scavenger along the shore. Closely resembles American Crow. Very difficult to distinguish in the field. Northwestern Crow is slightly smaller; call is hoarser, lower. Best clue is range. Considered by many authorities to be a subspecies of American Crow.

♪ **Fish Crow** *Corvus ossifragus* L 15¹/₂" (39 cm)
Closely resembles American Crow. Best identified by voice, a high, nasal, single- or double-note *cah*. Note, however, that juvenile American Crow's begging call is similar. Fish Crow favors tidewater marshes and low valleys along eastern river systems; less frequent inland, except along rivers. Sometimes seen in flocks with American Crows.

♪ **Chihuahuan Raven** *Corvus cryptoleucus* L 19¹/₂" (50 cm)
Long, heavy bill. Long, wedge-shaped tail distinguishes both raven species from crows in flight. Most common call, a low, drawn-out croak, usually slightly higher pitched than call of Common Raven. Neck feathers are white at the base, but this distinguishing field mark is hard to see and to compare with the Common Raven's grayish-based neck feathers. The Chihuahuan Raven is common in desert areas; less likely to be found in mountainous terrain than the Common Raven. Formerly called White-necked Raven.

♪ **Common Raven** *Corvus corax* L 24" (61 cm)
Large bird with long, heavy bill and long, wedge-shaped tail. Most common call is a low, drawn-out croak. Larger than Chihuahuan Raven; call is usually slightly lower pitched. At close range, note Common Raven's thicker, shaggier throat feathers. The Common Raven is found in a variety of habitats but particularly in mountains and rugged coastal areas, cliffs, canyons, deserts. Numerous in western portion of range; uncommon and local, but spreading, in Appalachians.

Mexican Crow

American Crow

Fish Crow

Chihuahuan Raven

Common Raven

Wrentit (Family Muscicapidae)

Smaller and livelier than most other members of the thrush family (page 320), the Wrentit more closely resembles its namesakes, the wrens and titmice.

Wrentit *Chamaea fasciata* L 6¹/₂″ (17 cm)
A perky little brown bird with a long, rounded tail, usually cocked. Plumage varies from reddish-brown in northern populations to grayish in southern birds. Note also distinct cream-colored eye and lightly streaked buffy breast. Common in chaparral and coniferous brushland, Wrentits are often heard before they are seen. Male's loud song, sung year round, begins with a series of accelerating staccato notes and runs into a descending trill: *pit-pit-pit-tr-r-r-r*. Female's song lacks trill.

Titmice and Chickadees (Family Paridae)

Small, hardy birds with short bills, short wings, and drab plumage. Active and agile, they often hang upside down from twigs to feed, and flock together when not nesting.

Tufted Titmouse *Parus bicolor* L 6¹/₂″ (17 cm)
Prominent gray crest and blackish forehead identify this bird over most of its range. In southern Texas, adult birds have whitish foreheads and blackish crests; were formerly considered a separate species, the Black-crested Titmouse. In south-central Texas, zone of overlap between black-crested and gray-crested forms, birds show varied brown foreheads, dark gray crests. Common inhabitant of deciduous woodlands, mesquite, parklands, and suburban areas; a familiar visitor to feeders. Typical song is a loud whistled *peter peter peter*.

Plain Titmouse *Parus inornatus* L 5³/₄″ (15 cm)
Western titmouse with small gray crest. Plumage varies from gray-brown in coastal birds to very drab gray in interior populations. Common and conspicuous resident of deciduous or mixed woodlands; favors oak, juniper, pinyon, pine. Typical call, a harsh *tsick-a-dee-dee*, resembles that of chickadees; song, heard chiefly in spring, is a whistled *weety weety weety*.

Bridled Titmouse *Parus wollweberi* L 5¹/₄″ (13 cm)
Black-and-white facial pattern distinctive. Unlike other titmice, Bridled Titmouse has a small black bib. Crest distinguishes it from similar Mountain Chickadee (next page). Back and wings are gray; underparts whitish. Most common call is a rapid, high-pitched variation of *chick-a-dee-dee*. Less active and conspicuous than other family members. Common resident of woodland stands of oak, juniper, and sycamore in the mountains of southern Arizona and New Mexico.

northern

southern

Wrentit

Tufted Titmouse

"Black-crested Titmouse"

coastal

interior

Plain Titmouse

Bridled Titmouse

♪ Black-capped Chickadee *Parus atricapillus*

L 5¹/₄" (13 cm) Black cap and bib and white cheeks readily identify this chickadee over most of its widespread range. Usual
range barely overlaps that of look-alike Carolina Chickadee;
periodic fall and winter irruptions temporarily push Blackcap's
range farther south. Note that Blackcap's secondaries are
broadly edged in white; lower edge of black bib is a bit more
ragged. These differences are obscured in worn late-summer
birds. Best distinction is voice. Blackcap's call is a lower, slower version of *chick-a-dee-dee-dee* than Carolina's call; typical
song, a clear, whistled *fee-bee* or *fee-bee-ee,* the first note higher
in pitch. Where ranges overlap, the two species may hybridize.
In the Appalachians, Blackcap generally inhabits higher elevations. Common in open woodlands, clearings, suburban areas. Usually forages in thickets, low branches of trees.

♪ Carolina Chickadee *Parus carolinensis L 4³/₄" (12 cm)*

Black cap and bib and white cheeks readily identify this small
bird over most of its range. At northern edge, its range in some
winters is invaded by the look-alike Black-capped Chickadee.
Note that Carolina lacks broad white edgings on secondaries;
lower edge of black bib is usually neater. Best distinction is
voice. Carolina's call is a higher, faster version of *chick-a-dee-
dee-dee* than Blackcap's call; typical song is a four-note whistle, *fee-bee fee-bay.* Where ranges overlap, the two species may
hybridize. In the Appalachians, Black-capped Chickadee generally inhabits higher elevations; the Carolina prefers valleys,
foothills. Common in open deciduous forests, woodland clearings and edges, suburban areas. Feeds in trees and thickets;
rarely descends to ground.

Mexican Chickadee *Parus sclateri L 5" (13 cm)*

Only breeding chickadee in its range. Extensive black bib is
distinctive, along with dark gray flanks and relatively short tail.
Lacks white eyebrow of neighboring Mountain Chickadee.
Song is a warbled whistle; call note, a husky buzz. A Mexican
species, common resident in pine, spruce-fir forests; found in
U. S. only in Chiricahua Mountains of southeastern Arizona
and Animas Mountains of southwestern New Mexico.

Mountain Chickadee *Parus gambeli L 5¹/₄" (13 cm)*

White eyebrow and pale gray sides distinguish this species
from other chickadees; lack of crest separates it from the
similar Bridled Titmouse (preceding page). Rocky Mountain
forms are tinged with buff on back, sides, and flanks, and have
broader white eyebrows. Call is a hoarse *chick-adee-adee-adee;*
typical song, a three- or four-note descending whistle, *fee-bee-
bay* or *fee-bee fee-bee.* Common in high-altitude coniferous forests in nesting season; may also occur at lower elevations.
Winters at lower altitudes in streamside groves and in open
mixed woodlands.

fall

**Black-capped
Chickadee**

summer

**Carolina
Chickadee**

**Mexican
Chickadee**

**Mountain
Chickadee**

Rockies

♪ Chestnut-backed Chickadee *Parus rufescens*

L 4³/₄" (12 cm) Sooty-brown cap, white cheeks, black bib; back chestnut. Over most of its range, this species has bright chestnut sides and flanks; birds on central California coast show almost no chestnut tones below. Common in coniferous forests; also found in deciduous woodlands. Call is a hoarse, rapid *tseek-a-dee-dee*. Generally feeds high in the trees.

♪ Siberian Tit *Parus cinctus* *L 5¹/₂" (14 cm)*

Gray-brown above, whitish below, with white cheek patch, black bib, buffy sides and flanks. Distinguished from Boreal Chickadee by larger cheek patch, longer tail, paler flanks, and pale edges on wing coverts; also by call, a series of peevish *dee deer* notes. Rare; found in willows and spruces bordering tundra. Formerly called Gray-headed Chickadee.

♪ Boreal Chickadee *Parus hudsonicus* *L 5¹/₂" (14 cm)*

Gray-brown above, whitish below, with white cheeks, black bib, brown sides and flanks. Distinguished from Siberian Tit by smaller cheek patch, shorter tail, uniformly gray wing coverts, darker flanks; also by call, a slow, nasal *tseek-a-day-day*. Fairly common in coniferous forests. In some winters, small numbers wander hundreds of miles south of normal range.

Verdins (Family Remizidae)

Small, spritely birds with finely pointed bills. They inhabit arid scrub country, where they feed in brush, chickadee-style, and build spherical nests.

Verdin *Auriparus flaviceps* *L 4¹/₂" (11 cm)*

Adult's dull gray plumage sets off chestnut shoulder patches, yellow head and throat. Juvenile is brown-gray overall; shorter tail helps distinguish it from Bushtit. Common in mesquite and other dense thorny shrubs of the southwestern desert. Song is a plaintive three-note whistle, the second note higher. Calls include a series of rapid *chip* notes.

Bushtit (Family Aegithalidae)

Longer tail distinguishes these tiny birds from other chickadee-like species. Usually feeds in large, busy, twittering flocks. Nest is an elaborate hanging structure.

Bushtit *Psaltriparus minimus* *L 4¹/₂" (11 cm)*

Gray above, paler below; fresh fall male may have pale pink flanks. Coastal birds have brown crown; interior birds show brown ear patch. Juvenile male and occasional adult males in the southwest have black mask, were formerly considered a separate species, the Black-eared Bushtit. Common in open oak and pinyon-juniper woodlands, chaparral.

coastal
central
California

**Chestnut-backed
Chickadee**

**Siberian
Tit**

**Boreal
Chickadee**

"Black-eared Bushtit"
juvenile ♂

interior ♂

juvenile

Verdin

interior ♀

Bushtit

coastal ♂

Creepers (Family Certhiidae)

Little tree-climbers whose curved bills dig insects and larvae from bark. Stiff tail feathers serve as props.

Brown Creeper *Certhia americana* L 5¹/₄″ (13 cm)
Camouflaged by streaked brown plumage, Creepers spiral upward from base to branches of a tree, then fly to a lower place on another tree. Call note is a soft, sibilant *see;* song, a high-pitched, variable *see see see titi see.* Fairly common but hard to spot. Nests in coniferous, mixed, or swampy forests. In winter, found in any woodland. Generally solitary, but sometimes seen in winter flocks of titmice and nuthatches.

Nuthatches (Family Sittidae)

These short-tailed acrobats climb up, down, and around tree trunks and branches, foraging for insects and larvae. Winter flocks roam with chickadees, kinglets.

♪ White-breasted Nuthatch *Sitta carolinensis*
L 5³/₄″ (15 cm) Black cap tops all-white face and breast; extent of black above and rust below is variable. Female duller, grayer overall. Rocky Mountain and Great Basin birds have longer bills. Found in leafy trees in the east, oaks and conifers in the west. Typical song, a rapid series of nasal whistles on one pitch. Call, a low-pitched, nasal *yank.* Many retreat in winter from northernmost range and highest altitudes.

♪ Red-breasted Nuthatch *Sitta canadensis* L 4¹/₂″ (11 cm)
Black cap, white eyebrow, bold, black eye line, rust underparts; female and juveniles have duller head, paler underparts. Resident in northern and subalpine conifers; gleans small branches, outer twigs. High-pitched, nasal call sounds like a toy tin horn. Irruptive migrant; numbers and winter range vary yearly depending on the conifer seed crop.

♪ Pygmy Nuthatch *Sitta pygmaea* L 4¹/₄″ (11 cm)
Gray-brown cap; creamy-buff underparts. Pale nape spot visible at close range. Dark eye line bordering cap, most distinct in interior populations. Range closely parallels ponderosa forest, except for birds in California bishop pines. Roams in loose flocks. Typical notes, a high, rapid *peep peep* and a piping *wee-bee.* Western counterpart of Brown-headed Nuthatch.

♪ Brown-headed Nuthatch *Sitta pusilla* L 4¹/₂″ (11 cm)
Brown cap; dull buff underparts. Pale nape spot visible at close range. Narrow dark eye line borders cap. Fairly common; range closely parallels that of the loblolly pine. Call is a repeated double note like the squeak of a rubber duck. Feeding flocks also give twittering, chirping, and talky *bit bit bit* calls. Southeastern counterpart of Pygmy Nuthatch.

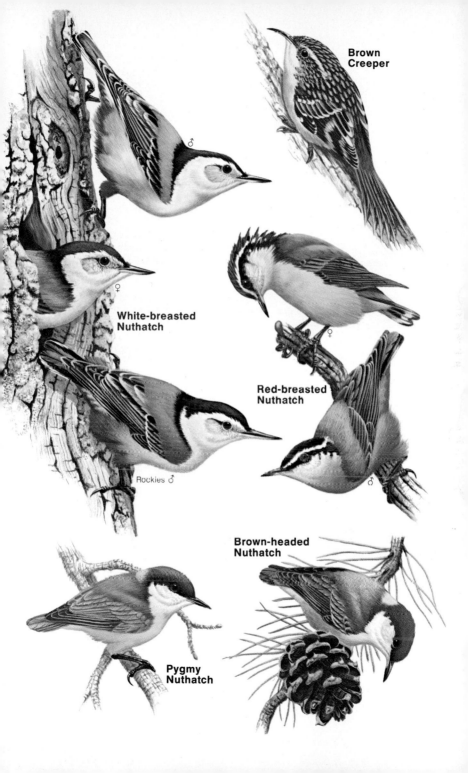

Brown Creeper

White-breasted Nuthatch

♂

♀

Rockies ♂

Red-breasted Nuthatch

♀

♂

Brown-headed Nuthatch

Pygmy Nuthatch

Wrens (Family Troglodytidae)

Common throughout most of North America, wrens are chunky birds with slender, slightly curved bills and uptilted tails. Loud song and aggressive territorial defense belie their small size. Highly inquisitive, wrens can often be lured into view by squeaky noises.

House Wren *Troglodytes aedon* L 4³/₄" (12 cm)
Plain wren; lacks prominent field marks. Brown above with faint eyebrow; wings and tail finely barred. Distinguished from Winter Wren by longer tail and less prominent barring on belly. Juvenile shows a bright rufous rump and darker buff on lower parts. Eastern birds are browner above, buffy below; western birds grayer above, paler below. Southern Arizona form, "Brown-throated Wren," has buffier throat and breast and a more conspicuous eyebrow. Common in brush and shrubs, orchards and farmyards, urban gardens, parks. Exuberant song, a cascade of bubbling whistled notes.

Winter Wren *Troglodytes troglodytes* L 4" (10 cm)
Stubby tail; dark barring on belly. Eastern form has traces of mottling on breast; in western birds, breast is more uniformly buffy-brown. On western Alaska islands, including Aleutians and Pribilofs, birds are larger than continental birds. Uncommon and secretive, nests in dense brush, especially along stream banks, in moist coniferous woods; in winter may be found in any type of woodland. Very rare in south Florida. Song, a rapid series of melodious high trills, much higher than House Wren; call, an explosive *chimp-chimp*.

♪ Carolina Wren *Thryothorus ludovicianus* L 5¹/₂" (14 cm)
Deep rusty-brown above, warm buff below; white throat and prominent white eye stripe. Common in the concealing underbrush of moist woodlands and swamps, wooded suburban areas. Vivacious, melodious song, a loud, clear *teakettle teakettle teakettle* or *cheery cheery cheery*. Sings any time of day or year. Nonmigratory, but after mild winters resident populations extend north of mapped range. After harsh winters, range limits retract.

Bewick's Wren *Thryomanes bewickii* L 5¹/₄" (13 cm)
Long, sideways-flitting tail, edged with white spots; long white eyebrow. Eastern birds are reddish-brown above; western birds much grayer. Found in brushland, hedgerows, stream edges, open woods. More common in the west than the House Wren. Declining east of the Rockies, especially in areas east of the Mississippi. Song variable, a high, thin buzz and warble. Like other wrens, sings with head held high, tail tucked down and under.

"Brown-throated Wren"

western
juvenile

**House
Wren**

eastern

western

**Winter
Wren**

Aleutians

eastern

western

**Carolina
Wren**

western

**Bewick's
Wren**

eastern

♪ **Marsh Wren** *Cistothorus palustris* L 5" (13 cm)
Plain brown crown; bold white eye line; black triangle on upper back, streaked with white; underparts largely whitish. Fairly common but local; found in reedy marshes, cattail swamps, either freshwater or brackish. Large, football-shaped nest with side entrance is built a foot or more above water, anchored to reeds. Secretive, but may climb a cattail to investigate intruders. Sings day and night in breeding season, a series of loud, rapid, reedy notes and liquid rattles. Alarm call is a sharp *tsuk,* often doubled. Formerly known as the Long-billed Marsh Wren.

♪ **Sedge Wren** *Cistothorus platensis* L 4¹/₂" (11 cm)
Crown and back streaked; eyebrow whitish, indistinct; underparts largely buff. Nests in wet, grassy meadows or shallow sedge marshes; globular nest is similar to that of Marsh Wren. Winters in brackish coastal marshes. Uncommon, local, and shy; more often heard than seen. Song is a weak staccato trill or chatter; call note, a rich *chip,* often doubled. Disturbed, this wren may fly up and flutter away, quickly dropping back into cover. Formerly called Short-billed Marsh Wren.

♪ **Canyon Wren** *Catherpes mexicanus* L 5³/₄" (15 cm)
An inconspicuous brown wren with white throat and breast, chestnut belly. Flattened crown and long bill aid in extracting insects from deep crevices. Common in steep, shady canyons and cliffs, near water; may also build its cup nest in stone buildings, chimneys. Loud silvery song, a decelerating, descending series of liquid *tee*'s and *tew*'s. Typical call is a sharp *jeet.* Nonmigratory; may withdraw in winter from northernmost range, highest altitudes. Note separate population in the Black Hills of South Dakota and Wyoming.

Rock Wren *Salpinctes obsoletus* L 6" (15 cm)
Dull gray-brown above with contrasting cinnamon rump and buffy tail tips, broad blackish tail band. Breast finely streaked. Fairly common in arid and semiarid habitats, sunny talus slopes, scrublands, dry washes. Frequently bobs its head, especially when alarmed. Song is a variable mixture of buzzes and trills; call note, a buzzy *tick-ear.* Unique clue to its presence, a patch of pebbles or rock chips leading to a rock-sheltered nest.

Cactus Wren *Campylorhynchus brunneicapillus*
L 8¹/₂" (22 cm) Streaked back, heavily barred wings and tail, and broad white eyebrow distinguish this large wren from the similar Sage Thrasher (page 336). Breast is densely spotted; crown solid brown. Common in cactus country and arid hillsides and valleys. Song a low-pitched, harsh, rapid *cha cha cha cha cha,* a familiar voice of the desert, heard any time of year or day. Bulky nests, tucked deep into the protective spines of cholla cactus or thorny bushes, are built for roosting as well as nesting.

Marsh Wren

Sedge Wren

Canyon Wren

Rock Wren

Cactus Wren

Thrushes (Family Muscicapidae)

Eloquent songsters of woodlands and open marshes, thrushes include many familiar species. With narrow notched bills they feed on insects and fruit.

Dusky Warbler *Phylloscopus fuscatus* L 5¹/₂" (14 cm)
Asian species, very rare stray on western Alaska islands; one recorded on Farallon Islands off California. Dusky-brown upperparts distinguish this species from Arctic Warbler; underparts dull whitish to buff. Unlike Arctic, it has a slightly rounded tail, no wing bar; bill shorter, thinner. Call, a harsh *tsack* similar to Arctic Warbler. Frequently flicks wings.

Gray-spotted Flycatcher *Muscicapa griseisticta*
L 5³/₄" (15 cm) Small Asian flycatcher, very rare late-spring migrant on the western Aleutians. Gray-brown above, white below; breast streaked with gray-brown; faint white bar on wing. White eye ring and lores; thin white line over bill. Tail is short and notched. Perches upright.

Arctic Warbler *Phylloscopus borealis* L 5" (13 cm)
Yellowish-white eyebrow, often curves upward behind eye. Square tail, olive upperparts, and pale wing bar all unlike Dusky Warbler. Bill thicker, less downcurved than Orange-crowned Warbler (page 356); lacks streaking on sides or flanks. Wing bar may wear off by late summer. In the Alaskan form, *P.b. kennicotti,* underparts on immature and fall adult are yellower than on breeding adult. Extremes are shown here. Song, given from conspicuous perch, is a loud, toneless repetition of reedy and buzzy notes. Calls include a harsh *tsack* resembling that of Dusky Warbler. Fairly common in western Alaska; nests on grassy tundra or in willow thickets. Siberian form, *borealis,* is a casual migrant on western Aleutians; note the much larger bill.

Middendorff's Grasshopper-Warbler
Locustella ochotensis L 6" (15 cm) Asian species, casual fall migrant on westernmost Aleutians. Big, chunky warbler with whitish-tipped, wedge-shaped tail. Bill hefty and slightly downcurved. Fall bird is yellowish-brown below, with a faintly streaked breast. In breeding plumage, underparts are mostly whitish, lack streaking.

Red-breasted Flycatcher *Ficedula parva* L 5" (13 cm)
(Not pictured.) Eurasian species, rare on the western Aleutians. Breeding male has a reddish-brown throat, bordered by a gray breast band; female's throat and breast are buffy-white. On all Red-breasteds, tail is black, with a large white oval on each side of base.

320

Dusky Warbler

Gray-spotted Flycatcher

kennicotti fall

kennicotti breeding

borealis

Arctic Warbler

Middendorff's Grasshopper-Warbler

breeding

fall

Golden-crowned Kinglet *Regulus satrapa* *L 4" (10 cm)*
Tiny and plump. Orange crown patch of male is bordered in yellow and black; female's crown is yellow with black borders. Upperparts grayish-olive; underparts whitish; two white wing bars. Broad white eyebrow, striped crown, and paler underparts distinguish Golden-crowned from Ruby-crowned Kinglet. Common in coniferous woodlands. Call is a series of very high, thin *tsee* notes. Song, pitched almost inaudibly high, is a series of *tsee* notes accelerating into a trill.

Ruby-crowned Kinglet *Regulus calendula* *L 4¹⁄₄" (11 cm)*
Tiny and plump. Grayish-olive above, with two white wing bars. Male's red crown patch seldom visible. Dusky underparts and lack of striped crown distinguish this species from Golden-crowned Kinglet. Compare also with Hutton's Vireo (page 350). Common in woodlands, thickets, brush. An active, nervous bird; flicks wings rapidly when calling. Calls include a scolding *je-dit je-dit*. Song begins with several high, thin *tsee* notes, followed by descending *tew* notes and concluding with a rich warbling of three-note phrases.

♪ Blue-gray Gnatcatcher *Polioptila caerulea*
L 4¹⁄₂" (11 cm) Male is blue-gray above, female grayer; long tail is black above with white outer feathers; mostly white below. Underparts grayish-white. Female distinguished from female Black-capped Gnatcatcher by call, longer tail, and more distinct eye ring. Call is a thin, querulous *pwee*. Song, a series of melodious but wheezy warbles. Active and conspicuous; common in woodlands, thickets, chaparral.

Black-capped Gnatcatcher *Polioptila nigriceps*
L 4¹⁄₄" (11 cm) Mexican species, casual in spring and summer in southeastern Arizona; very rare breeder there. Distinguished from Black-tailed Gnatcatcher by mostly white undertail, white outer tail feathers, and longer bill. Breeding male's black cap is distinctive from Blue-gray Gnatcatcher; female and winter male best identified by tail pattern and voice. Distinctive call is a whining, descending *mew*, similar to coastal form of Black-tailed Gnatcatcher.

♪ Black-tailed Gnatcatcher *Polioptila melanura*
L 4¹⁄₂" (11 cm) Blue-gray above, grayish-white below; slightly darker above, much darker below in coastal California form. Tail is mostly black above and below. Male's black cap is absent in winter plumage but sides of crown often show black. Bill is shorter than in the Black-capped Gnatcatcher; white eye ring more distinct. Interior forms inhabit desert washes, arid brushlands; calls include a rapid series of *jee* notes on one pitch and a raspy *cheeer*, similar to a House Wren's call. Coastal form is found on sagebrush mesas and dry coastal slopes; distinctive call is a rising and falling series of three kittenlike *mew* notes.

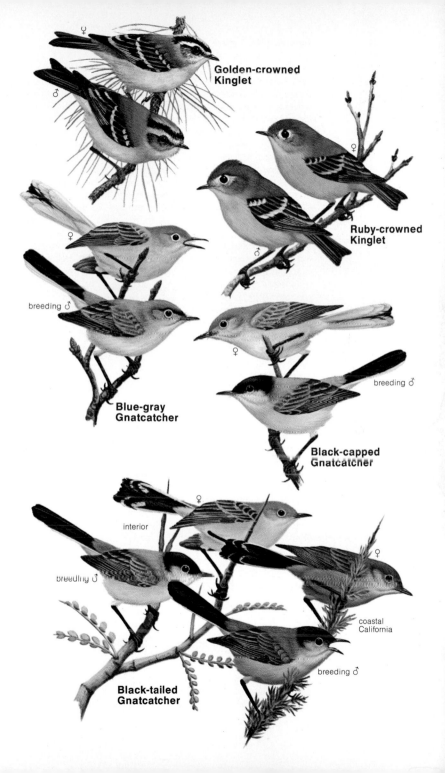

Golden-crowned
Kinglet

Ruby-crowned
Kinglet

breeding ♂

Blue-gray
Gnatcatcher

breeding ♂

Black-capped
Gnatcatcher

interior

breeding ♂

coastal
California

breeding ♂

Black-tailed
Gnatcatcher

Eastern Bluebird *Sialia sialis* *L 7" (18 cm)*
Chestnut throat, breast, sides of neck, sides and flanks; contrasting white belly, white undertail coverts. Male is uniformly deep blue above; female duller. The subspecies resident in the mountains of southeastern Arizona is paler overall. Compare with male Lazuli Bunting (page 384). All forms distinguished from Western Bluebird by chestnut on throat and sides of neck and by white, not grayish, belly and undertail. Found in open woodlands, farmlands, orchards. Nests in holes in trees and posts; also uses nest boxes. Call note is a musical, rising *chur-lee*, extended in song to *chur chur-lee chur-lee*. Serious decline in recent decades was due largely to competition with Starling and House Sparrow for nesting sites. Provision of specially designed boxes by concerned bird watchers has resulted in a promising comeback.

Western Bluebird *Sialia mexicana* *L 7" (18 cm)*
Male's upperparts and throat are deep purple-blue; breast, sides, and flanks chestnut; belly and undertail coverts grayish. Most birds show some chestnut on shoulders and upper back. Female duller, brownish-gray above; breast and flanks tinged with chestnut, throat pale gray. Common in open woodlands, farmlands, orchards; in desert areas during winter, found in mesquite-mistletoe groves. Nests in holes in trees, posts; also in boxes. Call note, a mellow *few*, extended in brief song to *few few fawee*.

Mountain Bluebird *Sialia currucoides* *L 7¹/₄" (18 cm)*
Male is sky blue above, paler below, with whitish-blue belly and undertail coverts. Female is brownish-gray overall, with white belly and undertail coverts; white edgings on coverts give folded wing a scalloped look. In fresh fall plumage, female's throat and breast are tinged with red-orange, but grayish-brown flanks distinguish her from female Eastern Bluebird. Note also the longer, thinner bill and longer wings of Mountain Bluebird. Inhabits open rangelands, meadows, generally at elevations above 5,000 feet; in winter, primarily found in open lowlands, desert. Often hovers above prey, chiefly insects, before dropping to catch them; also catches insects in flight. Nests in tree cavities; occasionally in buildings. Call note, a thin *few;* song, a low, warbled *tru-lee*. Highly migratory; casual in the east during migration and winter.

Townsend's Solitaire *Myadestes townsendi*
L 8¹/₂" (22 cm) Large and slender; gray overall, with bold white eye ring. Buff wing patches and white outer tail feathers are most conspicuous in flight. Fairly common in coniferous forests on high mountain slopes; in winter, also in wooded valleys, canyons, wherever juniper berries are available. Nests on the ground. Often seen on a high perch, from which it sometimes fly-catches. Call note, a high-pitched *eek;* song, a loud, complex, melodious warbling. Highly migratory; casual in winter as far east as Newfoundland and New York.

Eastern
Bluebird

juvenile

♂

southwestern ♂

Western
Bluebird

♀

♂

♀

♂

Mountain
Bluebird

juvenile

Townsend's
Solitaire

♪ **Wood Thrush** *Hylocichla mustelina* *L 7³⁄₄" (20 cm)*
Reddish-brown above, brightest on crown and nape; rump and tail brownish-olive. Bold white eye ring conspicuous on streaked face. Whitish below, with large dark spots on throat, breast, and sides. A large, plump bird, common in swamps and moist deciduous or mixed woods. Loud, liquid song of three- to five-note phrases, most notes differing in pitch, each phrase usually ending with a complex trill. Calls include a rapid *pit pit pit*. Range expanding in the northeast.

♪ **Veery** *Catharus fuscescens* *L 7" (18 cm)*
Reddish-brown above, white below, with gray flanks, grayish face, indistinct grayish eye ring. Upperparts are darker, breast has more spotting, in western *C.f. salicicolus* than in eastern *fuscescens*. Gray flanks distinguish *salicicolus* from the *C.u. ustulatus* form of Swainson's Thrush. Common but shy; found in dense, moist woodlands, streamside thickets. Migrates chiefly east of dashed line on map. Southeastern portion of range expanding. Song is a rolling series of descending *veer* notes; typical call, a low, whistled *phew*.

♪ **Swainson's Thrush** *Catharus ustulatus* *L 7" (18 cm)*
In general, uniformly brownish above, with buffy lores and bold buffy eye ring. Bright buffy breast with dark spots, brownish-gray sides and flanks. Pacific coast forms, such as *C.u. ustulatus,* are reddish-brown above and less distinctly spotted below; closely resemble *C.f. salicicolus* form of Veery, but note buffy-brown sides and flanks. Fairly common but shy; found in moist woodlands, swamps, thickets. Song is an ascending spiral of varied whistles; common call, an abrupt *whit*.

♪ **Gray-cheeked Thrush** *Catharus minimus* *L 7¹⁄₄" (18 cm)*
Gray-brown above, with indistinct eye ring. Underparts white, with bold dark spots on breast. Flanks brownish-gray. Breast usually less buffy than Swainson's; sometimes shows a pale yellow tinge instead. New England mountain form, *C.m. bicknelli,* is a warmer brown above; resembles *C.u. swainsoni* form of Swainson's Thrush, but lacks distinctly buffy lores and bold eye ring. Fairly common but very shy; found in coniferous or mixed woodlands. Migrates chiefly east of dashed line on map. Thin, nasal song is somewhat like Veery's, but often rises sharply at end; call, a downslurred *wee-ah*.

♪ **Hermit Thrush** *Catharus guttatus* *L 6³⁄₄" (17 cm)*
Upperparts vary from brown-olive to gray-brown; tail always reddish; whitish eye ring always conspicuous. Breast buffy or whitish. Widespread eastern forms, such as *C.g. faxoni,* have buff-brown flanks. The larger, paler western mountain forms, such as *auduboni,* and the smaller Pacific coast forms, such as *guttatus,* have grayish flanks. Fairly common but shy; found in coniferous or mixed woodlands, thickets. Song is a clear, serene series of flutelike notes, the similar phrases repeated at different pitches. Calls include a low *chuck*.

Wood Thrush

Veery

salicicolus

fuscescens

Swainson's Thrush

ustulatus

swainsoni

bicknelli

minimus

Gray-cheeked Thrush

auduboni

guttatus

faxoni

Hermit Thrush

Varied Thrush *Ixoreus naevius* *L 9¹/₂" (24 cm)*

Male has grayish-blue nape and back, orange eyebrow and wing bars; underparts orange with black breast band. Female distinguished from American Robin (next page) by smaller size, orange eyebrow and wing bars, dusky breast band, absence of black-and-white throat markings. Juvenile resembles female but has white belly, scalier looking throat and breast. Common in dense, moist woodlands, especially coniferous forests. Generally feeds in trees but also sometimes forages on ground for earthworms, insects, berries. Call is a soft *took;* song, a slow series of variously pitched notes, all rapidly trilled. Winter wanderers are seen regularly as far east as New England and south to Virginia, chiefly at feeders.

Eye-browed Thrush *Turdus obscurus* *L 8¹/₂" (22 cm)*

Asian species, regular spring migrant in the Aleutians, rare in fall. Brownish-olive above, with distinct white eyebrow. Belly is white, sides pale buffy-orange. Male has dark gray face, nape, throat, and breast; female's throat is white and streaked. Call is a thin *zip-zip*.

Dusky Thrush *Turdus naumanni* *L 9¹/₂" (24 cm)*

Asian species, casual spring migrant in westernmost Aleutians, rare in western Alaska and on St. Lawrence Island. White eyebrow conspicuous on blackish head. Upperparts strongly patterned; rump rust-colored; wings extensively rust. Below, white edgings give a scaly look to dark breast and sides. Note also distinctive white crescent across breast. Call is a raspy *shack shack* similar to Fieldfare.

Fieldfare *Turdus pilaris* *L 10" (25 cm)*

Breeds from Greenland to Siberia; winters to Mediterranean and China. Rare vagrant in Alaska, casual in eastern Canada, northeastern U.S. A large bird; gray head and rump contrast with brown upper back, blackish tail. Below, arrowhead-shaped spots pattern the breast and sides. White wing linings flash in flight. Song is a noisy twittering; distinctive call note, a raspy, repeated *shack shack*.

Varied
Thrush

juvenile

♀

♂

Eye-browed
Thrush

♀

♂

Dusky
Thrush

Fieldfare

♪ **American Robin** *Turdus migratorius* L 10" (25 cm)
Gray-brown above, with darker head and tail; bill yellow; underparts brick red; lower belly white. Most western birds are paler and duller overall than eastern and northwestern forms. In most eastern birds (shown here), tail has conspicuous white corners. Juvenile's underparts are tinged with cinnamon, heavily spotted with brown. Compare with spotted thrushes (page 326). Common and widespread, the Robin brightens both forest and suburb with its loud, liquid song, a variable *cheerily cheer-up cheerio*. Varied calls include a rapid *tut tut tut*. Often seen on lawns, head cocked as it searches for earthworms; also eats insects, berries. Nests in shrubs and trees and on sheltered windowsills, eaves. In winter, found in moist woodlands, swamps, suburbs, parks. Numbers vary greatly from winter to winter in the southwest and in California.

Rufous-backed Robin *Turdus rufopalliatus* L 9¹/₄" (24 cm)
Mexican species, casual visitor in winter to southern Arizona, rare from southern and southwest Texas to southern California. Distinguished from American Robin by bright reddish-brown back and wing coverts, gray head, and more extensively streaked throat. Somewhat secretive; found in treetops and dense shrubbery.

Clay-colored Robin *Turdus grayi* L 9" (23 cm)
Mexican species, casual visitor and very rare breeder in southernmost Texas. Brownish-olive above; tawny-buff below; pale buffy throat is lightly streaked with olive. Lacks white around eye conspicuous in American Robin. Very shy; forages in dense thickets, streamside brush, woodlands. Calls include a nasal *meeoo;* song resembles American Robin's but is slower, clearer, much less varied.

Aztec Thrush *Ridgwayia pinicola* L 9¹/₄" (24 cm)
Mexican species, rare visitor to southeastern Arizona, southern Texas. Male is sooty-brown above, with white patches on wings and uppertail coverts; tail broadly tipped with white; breast is dark; belly and undertail coverts white. Female is paler. Juvenile is heavily streaked above with creamy-white; underparts whitish, heavily streaked with brown.

American Robin

juvenile

♀

♂

Rufous-backed Robin

Clay-colored Robin

juvenile

♂

♀

Aztec Thrush

Northern Wheatear *Oenanthe oenanthe* *L 5¾" (15 cm)*
Tail is distinctive in both sexes, all ages: white rump, white tail with dark central feathers and dark terminal band. Eastern birds are cinnamon buff below; western birds are whitish with a tinge of buff. Males in fall and winter resemble females. Compare immature to Siberian Accentor. Wheatears are active, perky little birds, bobbing their tails and flitting from rock to rock in search of seeds and insects. Prefer open, stony habitats. Nests are built in rocky crevices or other cavities. Fairly common on breeding grounds; casual along Atlantic coast during migration; rare on Pacific coast, very rare inland.

Bluethroat *Luscinia svecica* *L 5¾" (15 cm)*
Colorful throat pattern distinguishes breeding male from all other birds. Both sexes and all ages have rusty patches at base of tail. A small population of Bluethroats summers in northern Alaska, nesting on the tundra in thickets near water. Generally furtive and shy, staying hidden in brush. In courtship, however, males sing from high perches. Their loud, melodious song often begins with a crisp, metallic *ting ting ting*. Bluethroats winter in Asia and Africa.

Siberian Rubythroat *Luscinia calliope* *L 5¾" (15 cm)*
Asian bird, casual spring and fall migrant in western Alaska, particularly on the Aleutians. Adult male's bright red throat is unmistakable. Female and immature have white throats, sometimes tinged with red; compare with Bluethroat, which has rusty tail patches and paler underparts.

Accentors (Family Prunellidae)

Eurasian birds, found mostly in mountainous country. Sparrowlike, but with thin bills. All are ground feeders. Song is a high, jingling warble. One species visits North America.

Siberian Accentor *Prunella montanella* *L 5½" (14 cm)*
Casual fall visitor in western and northern Alaska. Somewhat resembles female and immature Northern Wheatear, but eyebrow and underparts are a uniform bright tawny-buff, with a diffuse dark breast band and a patch of gray on sides of neck. Also note the dark crown and streaked upperparts. The two whitish wing bars are only faintly visible.

Northern Wheatear

western ♀

eastern breeding ♂

eastern immature

western breeding ♂

juvenile

eastern immature

Bluethroat

breeding ♂

immature ♀

♀

Siberian Rubythroat

♀

♂

immature

Siberian Accentor

Shrikes (Family Laniidae)

These masked hunters scan the countryside from lookout perches, then swoop down on insects, rodents, snakes, small birds. Lacking talons, "butcher-birds" impale their prey on thorns or barbed wire or wedge it into a tree fork to eat it or store it for later.

Loggerhead Shrike *Lanius ludovicianus L 9″ (23 cm)*
Slightly smaller and darker than Northern Shrike. Head and back bluish-gray; underparts white, very faintly barred. Broad black mask extends above eye and thinly across top of bill. All-dark bill, shorter than in Northern Shrike, with smaller hook. Rump varies from gray to whitish. Does not pump tail when perched. Juvenile paler and barred overall, with brownish-gray upperparts; acquires adult plumage by first fall. Loggerheads hunt in open or brushy areas, diving from a low perch, then rising swiftly to the next lookout. In flight, wings are darker, white wing patches smaller, than in Northern Mockingbird. Song is a medley of low warbles and harsh, squeaky notes; calls include a harsh *shack-shack*. Fairly common over much of range; rare and declining in northeast. A few may winter in northern part of range.

Northern Shrike *Lanius excubitor L 10″ (25 cm)*
Slightly larger than Loggerhead Shrike, with paler head and back, lightly barred underparts; rump whitish. Mask less extensive than in Loggerhead Shrike. Bill longer, with a more distinct hook; base of lower mandible pale. Juvenile is brownish, more heavily barred below than adult. Immature is grayer; retains barring on underparts until first spring. Fairly common; often perches high in tall trees, pumping tail upward in characteristic motion. Song and calls are similar to Loggerhead. Southern range limit and numbers on wintering grounds vary unpredictably from year to year.

Mimic Thrushes (Family Mimidae)

Notable singers, unequaled in North America for the rich variety and volume of their song. Some mimic the songs of other species. All have rather drab plumage and long tails. They feed on insects, seeds, berries.

Gray Catbird *Dumetella carolinensis L 8¹/₂″ (22 cm)*
Plain dark gray with a black cap and a long, black tail, often cocked; undertail coverts chestnut. Generally stays hidden in low, dense thickets in deciduous woodlands and in residential areas. Song is a variable mixture of melodious, nasal, and squeaky notes; some individuals are good mimics. Most readily identified by its call, a downslurred, catlike *mew*.

Northern Mockingbird
for comparison

**Loggerhead
Shrike**

juvenile

**Northern
Shrike**

immature

juvenile

**Gray
Catbird**

Northern Mockingbird *Mimus polyglottos* *L 10" (25 cm)*
Dull gray above; paler below. White outer tail feathers and white wing patches flash conspicuously in flight and in territorial and courtship displays. Readily distinguished from shrikes (preceding page) by slimmer bill and lack of mask. Mockingbirds inhabit rural thickets and woodland edges but are more often seen in towns and suburbs. Song is a mixture of original and imitative phrases, each repeated several times. Imitates other birds' songs, squeaky gates, pianos, barking dogs, etc. Spring song, sung only by males, may continue for hours, day or night. Both sexes sing in fall, claiming feeding territories. Aggressive territorial defense; may attack any intruder. Range has been expanding northward in recent years.

Bahama Mockingbird *Mimus gundlachii* *L 11" (28 cm)*
Caribbean species, casual on Dry Tortugas and southern Florida Keys. Larger and browner than Northern Mockingbird, with streaking on neck and flanks; tail tipped white. Lacks white patches on wings. Song is richly varied but not known to include imitations.

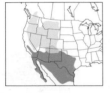

Sage Thrasher *Oreoscoptes montanus* *L 8¹/₂" (22 cm)*
Pale eye, white wing bars, and white-cornered tail distinguish this small thrasher. Juvenile has streaked head and back, may be confused with Cactus Wren (page 318). Song is a long, continuous series of warbled phrases; does not imitate other birds. Call notes include a sharp *chuck* and a high *churr*. Found in sagebrush plains; sings from the tops of bushes. Casual vagrant to eastern U.S.

Brown Thrasher *Toxostoma rufum* *L 11¹/₂" (29 cm)*
Reddish-brown above, heavily streaked below. Distinguished from Long-billed Thrasher by shorter bill, redder head, and yellow eye. Immature's eye may be gray or brown. Compare also with Wood Thrush (page 326). Common in hedgerows, brush, woodland edges, often close to human habitation. Sings, from a high, open perch, a long series of varied phrases, each phrase usually given only two or three times. Seldom imitates other birds. Rare visitor in fall and winter as far west as California; casual in spring.

Long-billed Thrasher *Toxostoma longirostre*
L 11¹/₂" (29 cm) Closely resembles Brown Thrasher but has gray head and neck, orange eye, and longer, more curved bill. Song is very much like Brown Thrasher's. Inhabits dense bottomland thickets, woodland edges, chaparral, searching the ground for insects. In spring and early summer, sings from a high, open perch.

juvenile

Northern Mockingbird

juvenile

Sage Thrasher

Bahama Mockingbird

Brown Thrasher

Long-billed Thrasher

♪ **Curve-billed Thrasher** *Toxostoma curvirostre*
L 11" (28 cm) Breast mottled; bill all-dark, longer and more strongly curved than in Bendire's Thrasher. Breast spots are indistinct in the widespread form, *T.c. palmeri*. Curvebills from southeastern Arizona to Texas, such as *curvirostre*, are heavily mottled below and have pale wing bars and conspicuous white edges on tail. All immatures and early-winter adults have darker spotting. Distinctive call, a sharp *whit-wheet*, sometimes three-noted. Song is elaborate, melodic, includes low trills and warbles. Common; found in streamside brush, canyons, semiarid brushlands.

♂ **Bendire's Thrasher** *Toxostoma bendirei L 9³⁄₄" (25 cm)*
Breast mottled; bill shorter and less curved than in Curve-billed Thrasher; base of lower mandible pale. Distinctive arrowhead-shaped spots on breast are not present in worn late-summer plumage. Fairly common; found in open farmlands, grasslands, brushy desert. Song is a sustained, melodic warbling, each phrase repeated one to three times. Low *chuck* call is seldom heard.

♂ **Crissal Thrasher** *Toxostoma dorsale L 11¹⁄₂" (29 cm)*
Large and slender, with a distinctive chestnut undertail patch and a dark whisker streak. Eye light brown or yellowish. Very secretive, hiding in underbrush. Song varied and musical, cadence more leisurely than in Curve-billed Thrasher. Calls include a repeated *chideery* and a whistled *toit-toit*. Found mainly in dense mesquite and willows along streams and washes; also in low-desert chaparral.

Le Conte's Thrasher *Toxostoma lecontei L 11" (28 cm)*
Palest of the thrashers, with sandy gray plumage, darker tail; undertail coverts tawny. Bill and eye are dark. Prefers arid, sparsely vegetated habitats. Runs with surprising speed, tail straight up, across open desert or along sandy washes. Song, heard chiefly at dawn and dusk, is loud, melodious, and sometimes repetitious. Calls include a whistled *tew-eep* and a sharp, ascending *quit*. Uncommon over most of range; very rare in the San Joaquin Valley.

♪ **California Thrasher** *Toxostoma redivivum L 12" (31 cm)*
Plump and dark, distinguished by pale eyebrow, dark eye, dark cheeks. Pale throat contrasts with dark breast; belly and undertail coverts tawny-buff. Most common call, a low, flat *chuck*. Song loud and sustained, with some clear but mostly guttural phrases, often repeated once or twice. Imitates other species and sounds. Common in chaparral-covered foothills and brushy parkland where there is open ground under low, thick-woven branches.

curvirostre

palmeri

**Bendire's
Thrasher**

**Curve-billed
Thrasher**

**Crissal
Thrasher**

**Le Conte's
Thrasher**

**California
Thrasher**

Pipits and Wagtails (Family Motacillidae)

Sparrow-size ground dwellers with slender bills. Most species pump their tails up and down as they walk in open fields in search of insects and seeds.

♪ Water Pipit *Anthus spinoletta* L 6½" (17 cm)

Brownish-gray above; faintly streaked, except on hindneck and rump. Breeding birds have grayer tinge above, less streaking below. Underparts usually uniformly rich buff in fresh fall plumage, often becoming whitish in late winter; moderately streaked below. Eyebrow matches color of underparts. Bill mostly dark; legs dark. Tail has white outer feathers. An Asian subspecies, *A.s. japonicus,* seen rarely in western Alaska, is more boldly streaked below; legs pinkish. Common and widespread, the Water Pipit nests on tundra in the north, high mountains farther south. Winter flocks are found in fields, beaches. Call, given in flight, is a sharp *pip-pit* or *jee-eet.* Song is a rapid series of *chee* or *cheedle* notes.

♪ Sprague's Pipit *Anthus spragueii* L 6½" (17 cm)

Dark eye prominent in pale buff face. Pale edges on rounded back feathers give a scaly look; rump is streaked. Underparts whitish, with buffy wash and short, indistinct streaking on breast. Legs pinkish. Outer tail feathers are more extensively white than in Water Pipit. Uncommon, secretive, and somewhat solitary. Does not pump tail. Nests in grassy fields. Call is a loud, squeaky *squeet,* usually given two or more times. Song, given incessantly in high flight, is a descending series of musical *tzee* and *tzee-a* notes.

Olive Tree-Pipit *Anthus hodgsoni* L 6½" (17 cm)

Asian species, rare migrant on St. Lawrence Island and Aleutians. Grayish back, faintly streaked. Eyebrow orange-buff in front of eye, white behind eye. White stripe extends down below grayish ear patch. Throat and breast a rich buff, with large spots on breast. Belly pure white. Bill is mostly dark; legs pinkish. Call is a buzzy *tsee.*

Pechora Pipit *Anthus gustavi* L 6" (15 cm)

Asian species, casual in western Alaska. Resembles immature Red-throated Pipit, but note more prominent mantle stripes, buff outer tail feathers, and pale yellow wash on breast contrasting with white belly. Call, a hard *pwit* or *pit.*

Red-throated Pipit *Anthus cervinus* L 6¼" (16 cm)

Reddish head and breast distinctive in breeding male; less extensive in breeding female and fall birds. Immatures and some breeding females show no red; compare with Pechora Pipit. Fairly common on northwestern Alaska breeding grounds; regular migrant along Pacific coast. Call, given in flight, is a piercing high *see* or *see-eep.*

340

Water Pipit

breeding

winter

japonicus winter

Sprague's Pipit

Olive Tree-Pipit

Pechora Pipit

breeding ♀

Red-throated Pipit

breeding ♂

immature

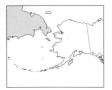

White Wagtail *Motacilla alba* L 7¹/₄" (18 cm)
Breeding adult has black nape and central tail feathers, gray back; face and underparts white, with black eye line, black throat and bib, and usually a black chin. In flight, shows mostly dark wings. Juveniles and immatures are indistinguishable from Black-backed Wagtail. Uncommon to rare on Alaska breeding grounds. Bobs its head as it walks; frequently wags its tail. Calls include a two-note *tschizzik*.

Black-backed Wagtail *Motacilla lugens* L 7¹/₄" (18 cm)
Siberian species, regular migrant on western Aleutians, rare on Bering Sea islands; vagrant on west coast. Similar to White Wagtail in all plumages. Breeding adult has blacker back; usually shows white chin. Adult in flight shows mostly white wings. Winter adult has a black, crescent-shaped breast band; resembles winter White Wagtail except for wing pattern. Juveniles of the two species are brownish above, with two faint wing bars. Immature is like winter adult but retains juvenile flight feathers. Calls are similar to White Wagtail. Formerly classified as a subspecies of White Wagtail.

Yellow Wagtail *Motacilla flava* L 6¹/₂" (17 cm)
Grayish-olive above, yellow below, with a tail shorter than other wagtails. In breeding plumage, the Alaska form, *M.f. tschutschensis* has a speckled breast band. Asian birds, *simillima,* seen regularly on Aleutians and Pribilofs, are greener above, yellower below. Females are duller overall. Winter adults and immatures vary from whitish to bright yellow below. Juveniles look like immatures but breast band tends to be blacker. Common to uncommon on Alaska breeding grounds; casual fall migrant in California. Call is a loud *tsweep*.

Gray Wagtail *Motacilla cinerea* L 7³/₄" (20 cm)
Eurasian species, casual spring migrant in western Alaska; very rare in fall. Gray above, yellow below, with one white wing bar. Breeding male has black throat. Females and winter birds have whitish throat, paler underparts. In flight, yellowish rump and white wing stripe distinguish Gray from Yellow Wagtail. Distinctive call is a metallic *chink-chink*.

Dippers (Family Cinclidae)

Stocky, robust birds that lead an aquatic life, wading and even swimming in mountain streams to feed.

American Dipper *Cinclus mexicanus* L 7¹/₂" (19 cm)
Adult is sooty-gray overall, with dark bill; tail and wings are short. Juvenile has paler, mottled underparts, pale bill. Fairly common but solitary, Dippers are found along clear, rushing mountain streams, as high as timberline. Generally nonmigratory, but may descend to lower elevations in winter. Loud, bubbling, wrenlike song is heard year round.

342

White Wagtail

breeding

breeding ♂

breeding ♀

winter ♂

immature

Black-backed Wagtail

tschutschensis breeding ♀

immature

Yellow Wagtail

tschutschensis breeding ♂

juvenile

simillima breeding ♂

Gray Wagtail

♀

breeding ♂

juvenile

American Dipper

Waxwings (Family Bombycillidae)

Red, waxy tips on secondary wing feathers are often indistinct and sometimes absent altogether. All waxwings have sleek crests, silky plumage, and yellow-tipped tails. Where berries are ripening, waxwings come to feast in amiable, noisy flocks. Gorged birds may loll on branches or lawns, barely able to fly.

Bohemian Waxwing *Bombycilla garrulus* L 8¹/₄″ (21 cm)
Larger and grayer than Cedar Waxwing; underparts gray; undertail coverts cinnamon. White and yellow spots on wings. In flight, whitish wing patch is conspicuous. Juvenile browner above, streaked below, with pale throat. Nests in open coniferous or mixed woodlands. Winter range varies widely and unpredictably; large flocks visit scattered locations, feeding on berries, small fruits. Also eat insects, flower petals, sap. Irregular winter wanderer to the northeast, usually in small numbers. In any season, individuals are sometimes seen in flocks of Cedar Waxwings. Distinctive call, a buzzy twittering, lower and harsher than call of Cedar Waxwing.

Cedar Waxwing *Bombycilla cedrorum* L 7¹/₄″ (18 cm)
Smaller and browner than Bohemian Waxwing; belly pale yellow; undertail coverts white. Lacks yellow spots on wings. Juvenile's streaked plumage is held into autumn, may be seen in migration. Nests in open habitats where berries are available: cedar, mountain ash, mulberry, pyracantha. Also feeds on insects, flower petals, sap. Highly gregarious in winter; flocks may number in the thousands. Call is a soft, high-pitched, trilled whistle.

Silky Flycatchers (Family Ptilogonatidae)

This New World tropical family of slender, crested birds is closely related to the waxwings. Family's common name describes their soft, sleek plumage and agility in catching insects on the wing.

Phainopepla *Phainopepla nitens* L 7³/₄″ (20 cm)
Male is shiny black; white wing patch conspicuous in flight. In both sexes, note distinct crest, long tail, red eyes. Juvenile resembles adult female; both have gray wing patches. Phainopeplas nest in early spring in mesquite brushlands, feeding chiefly on insects, mistletoe berries. In late spring they move into cooler, wetter habitat and raise a second brood. Distinctive call note is a single, low-pitched, whistled *wurp?* Song is a brief warble, seldom heard. Rare postbreeding wanderer north and east of range.

Bohemian Waxwing

juvenile

juvenile

Cedar Waxwing

♂

♀

Phainopepla

Bulbuls (Family Pycnonotidae)

Dull colors camouflage these forest-dwelling birds of Asia and Africa. Noisy, active behavior makes some conspicuous. One species now inhabits North America.

Red-whiskered Bulbul *Pycnonotus jocosus* L 7″ (18 cm)
Asian species, popular as a cage bird. Some birds escaped from captivity in 1960 in Miami, Florida, and are now established as a small population. Found in small flocks in suburbs and parklands of south Miami. Red ear patch and red undertail coverts are distinctive. Crest not apparent in flight. Juvenile lacks ear patch; undertail coverts are paler.

Starlings (Family Sturnidae)

Chunky, dark, glossy birds, generally gregarious and bold. Three species of this large, widespread Old World family are now resident in North America.

Crested Myna *Acridotheres cristatellus* L 9¾″ (25 cm)
Asian species, introduced in Vancouver, British Columbia, in the 1890s. Fairly common in Vancouver, casual in surrounding area, but apparently not spreading. Identified by bushy crest on forehead, yellow bill and legs, white wing patch.

Hill Myna *Gracula religiosa* L 10½″ (27 cm)
Asian species, excellent mimic, popular as a cage bird. A small population of escaped or released birds is resident in the area of Homestead, Florida. Glossy black body; bill red to orange; yellow wattles, yellow legs, white wing patch.

European Starling *Sturnus vulgaris* L 8½″ (22 cm)
Adult in breeding plumage is iridescent black with a yellow bill. In fresh fall plumage, feathers are tipped with white and buff, giving an overall speckled appearance; bill becomes brownish. Black spring plumage appears as the feather tips wear off. Distinguished in flight from other black birds by short, square tail, stocky body, and short, pointed wings, broad at the base. Juvenile is gray-brown above, paler below, with brown bill. Introduced in New York a hundred years ago, the Starling quickly spread across the continent; now abundant in a variety of habitats. Bold and aggressive, often competes successfully with native species for nest holes. Varied call notes include squeaks, warbles, chirps, and twittering; also imitates the songs of other species. Usually seen in large flocks, sometimes in company with grackles, blackbirds.

Red-whiskered Bulbul

Crested Myna

juvenile

Hill Myna

Common Grackle
for comparison

Brown-headed
Cowbird
for comparison

European Starling

fall

winter

breeding

juvenile

Vireos (Family Vireonidae)

Short and sturdy bills slightly hooked at the tip characterize these small songbirds. Some have eye rings linked by loral stripes to form "spectacles;" these vireos always have wing bars. Other species have eyebrow stripes and no wing bars. Vireos are generally chunkier and less active than warblers. Intricate cup nest is suspended from the fork of a branch.

♪ **Black-capped Vireo** *Vireo atricapillus* L 4¹/₂" (11 cm)
Olive above, white below, with yellowish flanks, yellowish wing bars. Male's glossy black cap contrasts with white spectacles. Female's dark gray head and smaller size distinguish her from Solitary Vireo (next page). Immature birds are browner above, buffy below. Fairly common but somewhat hard to find, the Black-capped Vireo stays hidden in oak scrub, thickets. An active feeder, sometimes even hanging upside down to search for insects. Best located by song, a persistent string of hurried, twittering, varied two- or three-note phrases.

♪ **White-eyed Vireo** *Vireo griseus* L 5" (13 cm)
Grayish-olive above; white below, with pale yellow sides and flanks; two whitish wing bars; yellow spectacles. Distinctive white eye visible at close range. Juvenile is duller, with gray or brown eyes. Populations on the Florida Keys are grayer above, with less yellow below; bill larger. Common in dense, moist thickets and tangles. Typical song is a loud, scolding, variable five- to seven-note phrase beginning and usually ending with a sharp *chick*.

Yellow-throated Vireo *Vireo flavifrons* L 5¹/₂" (14 cm)
Bright yellow spectacles, throat, and breast; white belly; two white wing bars. Upperparts olive, with contrasting gray rump. Compare with the Pine Warbler's greenish-yellow rump, streaked sides, thinner bill, and less distinct spectacles. The Yellow-throated Vireo is fairly common in most of its breeding range. Rare in winter along entire Gulf coast and in northern Florida; most birds winter from eastern Mexico south. Song is a slow repetition of harsh two- or three-note phrases separated by long pauses: *de-ar-ie come-here;* often concludes with a rising *three-eight*.

Thick-billed Vireo *Vireo crassirostris* L 5¹/₂" (14 cm)
Caribbean species, very rare visitor to Florida Keys and Dry Tortugas. Gray head with yellow spectacles; two yellowish-white wing bars; underparts entirely yellow.

**Black-capped
Vireo**

♀

♂

immature

**White-eyed
Vireo**

Florida Keys

**Yellow-throated
Vireo**

**Thick-billed
Vireo**

Pine Warbler
for comparison

♪ Bell's Vireo *Vireo bellii* L 4³⁄₄″ (12 cm)

Dull grayish-olive above, whitish below, with yellow sides, indistinct white spectacles, two faint white wing bars, the lower bar more prominent. Subspecies vary from drab gray in west coast and southwest birds to brighter olive in interior birds; extremes are shown here. An active, nervous vireo; feeds in dense brush, occasionally in treetops. Song is a series of fast, harsh, scolding notes. Generally common in moist woodlands, bottomlands, mesquite. Seriously declining in southern California, due largely to brood parasitism by cowbirds. Range is expanding slightly in the northeast.

♪ Hutton's Vireo *Vireo huttoni* L 5″ (13 cm)

Grayish-olive above, with large white spot on lores, white eye ring broken by dark spot above eye. Two broad white wing bars. Underparts buffy-olive, with whitish belly. Subspecies vary from the grayer birds of the southwest to the greener forms of the west coast. Distinguished from female Ruby-crowned Kinglet by larger size, thicker bill, white lore spot, and broken eye ring; also by voice: Hutton's Vireo sings a repeated rising or descending *ch-weet ch-weet;* calls include a low *chit*. Found in moist woodlands, especially in live oaks.

♪ Gray Vireo *Vireo vicinior* L 5¹⁄₂″ (14 cm)

Gray above, white below; white eye ring; dull white lores; wings brownish, with two faint wing bars, the lower bar more prominent; long tail. Fairly common in dry, brushy mesas, foothills; found in chaparral, mesquite, and pinyon-juniper stands. Flits restlessly through the undergrowth, flicking its tail as it forages. Song is a varied musical *chu-wee chu-weet,* faster and sweeter than song of western Solitary Vireo.

♪ Solitary Vireo *Vireo solitarius* L 5¹⁄₂″ (14 cm)

Bold white spectacles; two bold white or yellowish wing bars. In eastern birds, bluish-gray head contrasts with greenish back; underparts are white with greenish-yellow flanks. West coast form is duller, paler overall. Rocky Mountain birds are dark gray above, with at most only a tinge of yellow on flanks; compare with Gray Vireo. The Solitary Vireo is common throughout its range in mixed woodlands. Feeds slowly, deliberately, generally staying fairly high in shrubs and trees. Song is a series of rich, variable two- to six-note phrases: *chu-wee cheerio*. Song of western forms is burrier, lower, less melodious than eastern forms or similar song of Red-eyed Vireo (next page). Eastern Solitary's song is higher and sweeter than Red-eyed Vireo.

Ruby-crowned Kinglet
for comparison

interior

Bell's Vireo

west coast

west coast

Hutton's Vireo

southwest

Gray Vireo

Rockies

west coast

Solitary Vireo

eastern

🎵 **Red-eyed Vireo** *Vireo olivaceus* *L 6" (15 cm)*
Blue-gray crown; white eyebrow bordered above and below with black. Dark olive back, darker wings and tail; white underparts. Lacks wing bar. Ruby red eye visible at close range. First-fall bird has brown iris. Immatures and some fall adults have pale yellow wash on flanks and undertail coverts. Distinctive subspecies of southeast Texas, *V.o. flavoviridis,* is greener above, bright yellow on sides, flanks, and undertail coverts; black lines bordering eyebrow are less distinct; formerly considered a separate species, Yellow-green Vireo. The Red-eyed Vireo is abundant in eastern woodlands; rare migrant west of black line on map. Persistent song, sung all day long, a series of deliberate, short, variable phrases. Calls include a short scolding *mew*.

Black-whiskered Vireo *Vireo altiloquus* *L 6¹/₄" (16 cm)*
Black whisker stripe and larger bill distinguish this species from Red-eyed Vireo. Blue-gray crown; white eyebrow bordered above and below with black. Dark olive back; whitish underparts with yellowish wash on sides and flanks. Dark red eye visible at close range. Common in summer in the mangrove swamps of Florida Keys and along Florida coasts. Casual along rest of Gulf coast and in Florida interior. Song consists of deliberate one- to four-note phrases, somewhat hoarser and more emphatic than song of Red-eyed Vireo.

🎵 **Warbling Vireo** *Vireo gilvus* *L 5¹/₂" (14 cm)*
Gray upperparts, washed with olive in western birds; underparts white. Dusky eye line; white eyebrow, without dark upper border; brown eye. Lacks wing bars. Smaller and paler than Red-eyed Vireo; whiter below than Philadelphia Vireo; crown does not contrast strongly with back. Distinguished from Tennessee Warbler by larger size, thicker bill. Western first-fall birds are slightly greener above than eastern immatures, and have extensively yellow sides, yellow flanks and undertail coverts. Warbling Vireos are common across most of North America in summer; found in open deciduous woods. Song is a long melodious warbling. Male often sings from the nest.

🎵 **Philadelphia Vireo** *Vireo philadelphicus* *L 5¹/₄" (13 cm)*
Breeding adult variably yellow below, with whitish belly. Gray-green above, with contrasting gray cap, dull grayish-olive wing bar, dull white eyebrow, dark eye line. First-fall bird and most fall adults are entirely yellow below, palest on belly. Yellow throat and breast distinguish Philadelphia from Warbling Vireo. Similar Tennessee Warbler has thinner bill, whiter underparts. Philadelphia Vireo is uncommon throughout its range; found in open woodlands, burned-over areas, streamside willows and alders. Song resembles that of Red-eyed Vireo but is generally slower, thinner, and higher pitched.

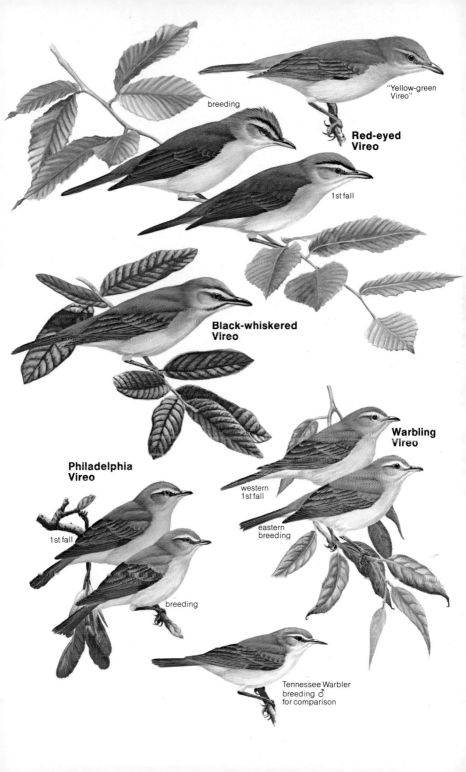

breeding

"Yellow-green Vireo"

Red-eyed Vireo

1st fall

Black-whiskered Vireo

Warbling Vireo

western 1st fall

eastern breeding

Philadelphia Vireo

1st fall

breeding

Tennessee Warbler breeding ♂ for comparison

Warblers, Sparrows (Family Emberizidae)

A large family related by genetic characteristics but outwardly diverse. Includes such distinct groups as the sparrows, orioles, and wood warblers.

Prothonotary Warbler *Protonotaria citrea*

L 5¹/₂″ (14 cm) Large, plump, and short-tailed. Male's head and underparts golden yellow, fading to white undertail coverts; wings blue-gray, without wing bars; blue-gray tail has large white patches. Female duller, head less golden. Both sexes have large, prominent dark eyes. Fairly common. The only eastern warbler that nests in tree cavities or other crannies; usually selects a low site along streams or surrounded by sluggish or stagnant water. Casual or rare vagrant across entire continent during migration, especially in fall. Song is a series of loud, ringing *zweet* notes.

Blue-winged Warbler *Vermivora pinus* L 4³/₄″ (12 cm)

Male has bright yellow crown and underparts, white or yellowish-white undertail coverts, black eye line, blue-gray wings with two white wing bars. Female duller overall. In both sexes, bill is long and slender; bold white spots at end of tail are visible from below. Locally common; inhabits brushy meadows, second-growth woodlands. Song is a wheezy *beee-bzzz*. Range is expanding at northeastern and western edges. Hybridizes with Golden-winged Warbler where ranges overlap. Hybrids are of two main types, the more frequent "Brewster's Warbler" and the rare "Lawrence's." Several variations are shown here.

Golden-winged Warbler *Vermivora chrysoptera*

I 4³/₄″ (12 cm) Male has black throat, black ear patch bordered in white; yellow crown and wing patch. Female similar but duller. In both sexes, conspicuous white spots on end of tail are visible from below; underparts are grayish-white; bill long and slender. Fairly common in overgrown pastures, briery woodland borders. Song is a soft *bee-bz-bz-bz*, longer than similar song of Blue-winged Warbler. Hybrids of these two species (see above) sing the song of either or both parents or variations all their own.

Prothonotary Warbler

♀

♂

Blue-winged Warbler

♀

♂

"Brewster's Warbler"

♂

♀

Golden-winged Warbler

♀

♂

Blue-winged — Golden-winged Hybrids

"Lawrence's Warbler"

♀

♂

♂

Tennessee Warbler *Vermivora peregrina* *L 4³/₄" (12 cm)*

Plump, short-tailed, with long, straight bill. Adult male in spring is green above with gray crown, bold white eyebrow; white below. Female is tinged with yellow or olive overall, especially during winter. Adult male in fall resembles spring adult female but shows more yellow below. Juvenile also yellowish below; may be confused with young Orange-crowneds, but Tennessee has fainter wing bars and white undertail coverts. Spring male may be confused with Warbling and Red-eyed Vireos (page 352); note especially Tennessee Warbler's slimmer bill, greener back. Song is a series of descending *tseet* notes, often ending in a higher pitched trill. Fairly common. Found in deciduous and mixed woodlands in summer, mixed open woodlands and brushy areas during migration. Generally feeds high in trees. Winters primarily from central Mexico to Venezuela; casual winter vagrant to coastal California. Most migration is east of the Rockies.

Orange-crowned Warbler *Vermivora celata*

L 5" (13 cm) Olive above, paler below. Yellow undertail coverts and faint, blurred streaks on sides of breast distinguish this species from similar Tennessee Warbler. Note also that Orange-crowned's bill is thinner and slightly downcurved; tail is longer. Plumage varies from the brighter, yellower birds of western U. S., such as *V.c. lutescens,* to the grayer *celata* which breeds across Alaska and Canada and winters primarily in southeastern U. S. Tawny-orange crown, absent in some females and immatures, is seldom discernible in the field. Immatures can be particularly drab. Young birds are similar to juvenile Tennessees but show yellow undertail coverts and bolder wing bars. Fairly common in the west; rarer in the east. Inhabits open, brushy woodlands, forest edges, thickets; generally feeds in low branches. Song consists of a high-pitched trill followed by a slow, lower trill; call note, a sharp *chip*.

♪ Bachman's Warbler *Vermivora bachmanii* *L 4³/₄" (12 cm)*

Our rarest warbler; on the verge of extinction. Most of the rare sightings are in South Carolina's I'On Swamp. Bill is very thin, long, somewhat downcurved; undertail coverts white in both sexes. Male has yellow forehead, chin, and shoulders; black crown and bib. In some males, probably younger adults, there is less black on crown and throat, less yellow on shoulders, and more white on lower belly. Female generally drabber, crown gray, throat and breast gray or yellow. Inhabits swamps, low-lying woodlands. Distinctive song, typically a rapid series of buzzes on one pitch; sounds like Northern Parula. Bachman's Warbler is often confused with Hooded Warbler (page 372). Bachman's once bred in wet woodlands throughout southeastern U. S. but was probably never numerous. Winters in Cuba and Isle of Pines.

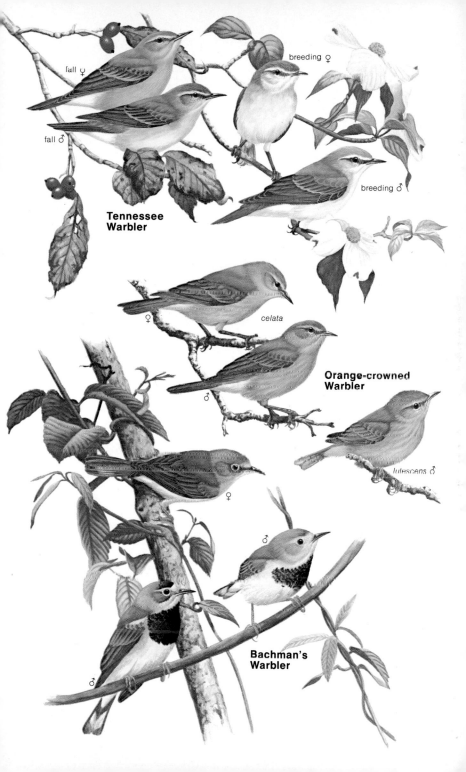

fall ♀

fall ♂

breeding ♀

breeding ♂

**Tennessee
Warbler**

celata

♀

♂

**Orange-crowned
Warbler**

lutescens ♂

♀

♂

♂

**Bachman's
Warbler**

Nashville Warbler *Vermivora ruficapilla* L 4³/₄" (12 cm)
Bold white eye ring, gray head, olive upperparts. Throat and underparts yellow; white area between yellow belly and yellow undertail is most conspicuous in western birds. Male's small reddish crown patch is seldom discernible in the field. Female is slightly duller than male. Fall immature is even duller; head may be brownish-gray or grayish-olive. Common; found in second-growth woodlands, spruce bogs; nests on the ground. Typical song is a series of high-pitched *see-weet* notes followed by a lower short trill.

Virginia's Warbler *Vermivora virginiae* L 4³/₄" (12 cm)
Bold white eye ring; plain gray head and back, greenish-yellow rump. Underparts whitish with yellow patch on breast, yellow undertail coverts. Male's small reddish crown patch is seldom discernible in the field. Female is duller overall. Fall immature is brownish-gray above, with little or no yellow on breast. Common in brushlands and pinyon-juniper woods, usually at altitudes between 6,000 and 9,000 feet; nests on the ground. Song is a rapid, accelerating series of thin notes, often ending with several lower notes.

Colima Warbler *Vermivora crissalis* L 5³/₄" (15 cm)
Mexican species; range extends to the Chisos Mountains of Big Bend National Park, Texas. Larger and browner than Virginia's Warbler; sides brown. Song is a rapid, high trill ending with one or two lower notes.

Lucy's Warbler *Vermivora luciae* L 4¹/₄" (11 cm)
Gray above, whitish below. Male's reddish crown patch and rump are distinctive. Female and immatures duller, reddish areas paler. Immature female may lack red on crown. Fairly common in mesquite and cottonwoods along watercourses. Nests in tree cavities. Lively song, a short trill followed by several lower, whistled notes: *weeta weeta weeta che che che*.

Northern Parula *Parula americana* L 4¹/₂" (11 cm)
A tiny, short-tailed warbler, gray-blue above with yellowish-green upper back, two bold white wing bars. White eye ring broken by black eye line. Throat and breast bright yellow, belly white. In male, reddish and black bands cross breast. In female, bands are fainter or absent. Common in coniferous or mixed woods, especially near water. Rare vagrant throughout the west during migration. Song is a rising buzzy trill ending with an abrupt lower *zip*.

Tropical Parula *Parula pitiayumi* L 4¹/₂" (11 cm)
Resident but rare in the Rio Grande Valley of Texas. Black mask and lack of white eye ring distinguish Tropical from Northern Parula. Male has only one breast band, generally indistinct. Song similar to that of Northern Parula. Formerly called Olive-backed Warbler.

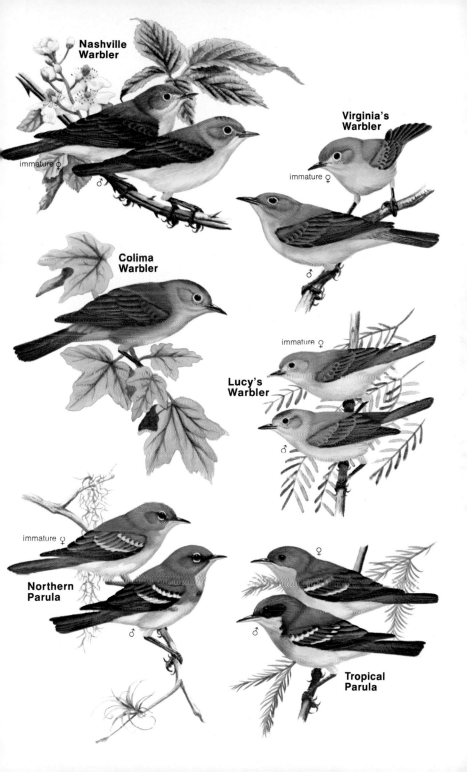

Nashville Warbler

immature ♀

♂

Virginia's Warbler

immature ♀

♂

Colima Warbler

Lucy's Warbler

immature ♀

♂

Northern Parula

immature ♀

♂

Tropical Parula

♀

♂

Black-and-white Warbler *Mniotilta varia* L 5¹/₄" *(13 cm)*
The only warbler that regularly creeps along branches and up and down tree trunks like a nuthatch. Boldly striped on head and most of body. Male's throat and cheeks are black in breeding plumage; in winter, throat is white, sometimes with black spots. Female has gray cheeks, white throat. Immatures have buffy sides and undertail coverts. In all birds, undertail coverts are streaked. Compare with Blackpoll Warbler (page 368). Common in mixed woodlands. Song is a slow series of high, thin *wee-see* notes, the second note lower.

Black-throated Blue Warbler *Dendroica caerulescens* L 5¹/₄" *(13 cm)* Male's black throat, cheeks, and sides separate blue upperparts, white underparts. Bold white patch at base of primaries. Appalachian males are darker above. Female's pale eyebrow is distinct on dark face; upperparts brownish-olive; underparts buffy. White wing patch smaller than in male. This species inhabits deciduous forests; usually seen in lower or mid-level branches. Typical song, a slow series of four or five raspy notes, the last note higher: *I am so la-zee*. Call is a single *chup* or *tup*. Casual fall migrant in California; otherwise rare throughout the west. A few birds winter in the Gulf states; most migrate to the Caribbean.

Cerulean Warbler *Dendroica cerulea* L 4³/₄" *(12 cm)*
Short-tailed warbler. Adult male is blue above, with dark streaks, two wide white wing bars; white below, with black breast band, black streaking on sides. Female has greenish mantle, blue-green crown, yellowish eyebrow, throat, and breast. Fall immatures resemble female but young male shows more blue above, young female is browner. Fairly common but local; found in swamps, bottomlands, mixed woodlands near water; stays high in the trees. Song is a short, fast, accelerating series of buzzy notes on one pitch, often ending in a higher, buzzy trill. Fall migration begins as early as July; return in mid-April. Range is expanding in northeast and south.

Blackburnian Warbler *Dendroica fusca* L 5" *(13 cm)*
Fiery orange throat conspicuous in adult males; note also broad white wing patch. Female and immatures have paler throat, two white wing bars. Orange or yellow crown stripe and white in outer tail feathers are distinct in all males, less so in all females. Fairly common in coniferous or mixed forests of northern breeding range, pine-oak woodlands in the Appalachians. Generally stays high in the upper branches. Variable song of thin, high notes; commonly a short series of *seet-say* notes followed by a very high trill. Vagrants are occasionally seen in coastal California during fall migration; rare elsewhere west of the Mississippi.

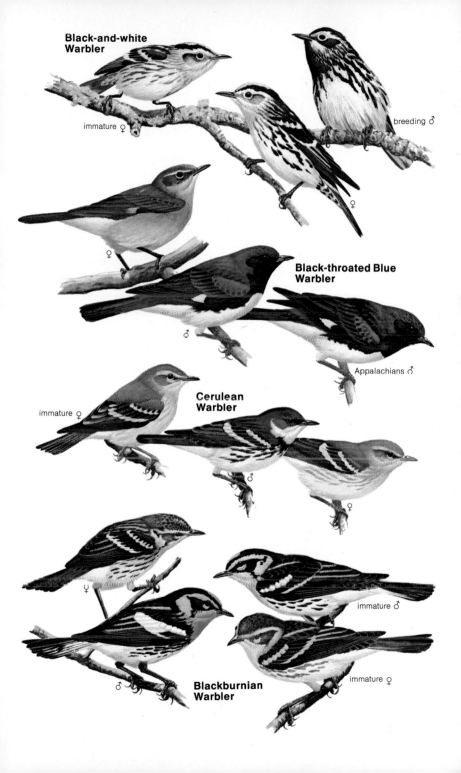

Black-and-white Warbler

immature ♀

breeding ♂

♀

♀

Black-throated Blue Warbler

♂

Appalachians ♂

Cerulean Warbler

immature ♀

♂

♀

♀

immature ♂

♂

Blackburnian Warbler

immature ♀

Chestnut-sided Warbler *Dendroica pensylvanica*
L 5″ (13 cm) Adults in spring have bright yellow crown, black
eye line, black whisker stripe; chestnut on sides. Note also
boldly streaked back; two pale yellow wing bars. Fall adults
and immatures are lime green above, with white eye ring; underparts whitish. Immature generally lacks streaking on back,
usually lacks chestnut sides; wing bars are bright yellow. Fairly common in second-growth deciduous woodlands. A small
population breeds along the Front Range in Colorado. Casual
migrant on west coast. Song is a whistled *please please pleased
to meetcha.*

Cape May Warbler *Dendroica tigrina* *L 5″ (13 cm)*
All plumages have yellow on face, the color extending to sides
of neck. Note also short tail; yellow rump; thin bill, slightly
downcurved. Breeding male's chestnut ear patch and tiger-
striped underparts distinctive; wing patch white. Female
drabber, grayer, with two narrow white wing bars. Fall adults
and immatures are even grayer; immature male's chestnut ear
patch less distinct. Immature female can have gray face and
only a tinge of yellow below and on rump. Fairly common in
black spruce forests. Song is a high, thin *seet seet seet seet.*
Call, a very high, thin *sip.* Winters in West Indies; casual
migrant on west coast. A few birds may winter in southernmost Florida.

Magnolia Warbler *Dendroica magnolia* *L 5″ (13 cm)*
Male is blackish above, with white wing patch, yellow rump;
broad white tail patches. White eyebrow conspicuous. Underparts yellow, streaked on breast and sides; undertail coverts
white. Female duller; has two wing bars. Fall adults and immatures are drabber, with grayish-olive upperparts; white eyebrow fainter; faint gray band across breast. Compare with
immature Prairie Warbler (page 366). Fairly common in moist
coniferous forests. Winters in southern Mexico, Central
America and West Indies. Casual in southern Florida in winter. Casual on west coast during migration. Song is a musical
weety-weety-weeteo.

Yellow-rumped Warbler *Dendroica coronata*
L 5¹/₂″ (14 cm) Yellow rump, yellow patch on side, yellow crown
patch, white tail patches. In northern and eastern birds ("Myrtle Warbler"), note white eyebrow, white throat and sides of
neck, contrasting cheek patch. Western birds ("Audubon's
Warbler") have yellow throat. "Audubon's" that breed in the
mountains of southeast Arizona are blacker above and below.
All females and fall males are duller than breeding males but
show same basic pattern. Abundant; nests in coniferous or
mixed woodlands. Variable song, a slow, trilling warble, usually rising or falling at the end. "Myrtles" are uncommon in winter in the west; "Audubon's" are rare in the east.

Chestnut-sided Warbler

breeding ♀

fall

breeding ♂

Magnolia Warbler

breeding ♀

breeding ♂

breeding ♀

breeding ♂

Cape May Warbler

fall ♀

immature ♀

fall ♂

fall ♂

breeding ♀

southwestern
breeding ♂

breeding ♂

fall ♀

fall ♀

breeding ♂

Yellow-rumped Warbler

"Audubon's
Warbler"

"Myrtle
Warbler"

Black-throated Gray Warbler *Dendroica nigrescens*
L 5″ (13 cm) Adult plumage is basically the same year round: black-and-white head; gray back streaked with black; white underparts, sides streaked with black; small yellow spot between eye and bill. Lacks central crown stripe of Black-and-white Warbler (page 360). Male has black throat and bib; female's throat is white with black streaks. Immature is brownish-gray above, streaking indistinct. Inhabits dry, open woodlands, brushlands, chaparral. Song, a buzzy *weezy weezy weezy weezy-weet*, accented on last note. Rare spring and fall vagrant on Gulf coast east to Alabama; very rare on east coast.

Townsend's Warbler *Dendroica townsendi* *L 5″ (13 cm)*
Dark crown, dark ear patch bordered in yellow. Olive above, streaked with black; yellow breast, white belly, yellowish black-streaked sides. Adult male's throat and upper breast are black; female and immatures have streaked lower throat. Immature female is duller overall, lacks streaking on back. Fairly common; nests in coniferous forests. Song is similar to Black-throated Gray Warbler. Townsend's-Hermit Warbler hybrids are occasionally seen; usually have yellowish, streaked underparts of Townsend's Warbler, yellow head of Hermit Warbler.

Hermit Warbler *Dendroica occidentalis* *L 5¹/₂″ (14 cm)*
Yellow head, with dusky or black markings extending from nape onto crown. Male has black chin and throat; in female and immatures, chin is yellowish, throat dusky or dark. Fall immature female is more olive above. Fairly common in Pacific coast mountain forests; nests in tall conifers. During migration, also seen in lowlands. Song, *seezle seezle seezle seezle zeet-zeet*. Sometimes hybridizes with Townsend's Warbler.

Black-throated Green Warbler *Dendroica virens*
L 5″ (13 cm) Olive above. Yellow face with greenish ear patch. Underparts white, tinged with yellow on undertail coverts and often on breast. Male has black throat and upper breast and black-streaked sides. Female and immatures show much less black below; immature female generally has black streaking only on sides. Fairly common in coniferous or mixed forests in summer. Generally stays high in the trees. Typical song, a dreamy, lisping *zee zee zee zo zee*.

Golden-cheeked Warbler *Dendroica chrysoparia*
L 5¹/₂″ (14 cm) Dark eye line, lack of clearly outlined ear patch, and lack of yellow on underparts distinguish this species from similar Black-throated Green Warbler. Male black above, with black crown, black bib, black-streaked sides. Female and immature male duller, upperparts olive with dark streaks; chin yellowish or white; sides of throat streaked. Immature female shows less black on underparts. Uncommon. Nests on Edwards Plateau in central Texas; winters in Mexico. Song, *bzzzz layzee dayzee*, ends on a high note.

Black-throated Gray Warbler ♀ ♂

Townsend's Warbler ♀ ♂

Townsend's-Hermit Hybrid ♂

Hermit Warbler ♀ ♂

Black-throated Green Warbler ♀ ♂

Golden-cheeked Warbler ♀ ♂

immature ♀♀

Golden-cheeked

Black-throated Green

Townsend's

Hermit

Yellow-throated Warbler *Dendroica dominica*

L 5¹/₂" (14 cm) Plain gray back and large white patch on each side of neck distinguish Yellow-throated from Grace's Warbler. Throat and upper breast bright yellow; rest of underparts white, with black streaks on sides; bold white eyebrow sometimes tinged with yellow. In the east, some birds show dark yellow lores, instead of white. Male has black crown and face; in female, black on crown is less extensive. Fairly common in live oak and pine woodlands, cypress, sycamores. Usually forages high in the trees, creeping methodically along the branches. Song is a descending series of clear, down-slurred whistles ending with a sharp accent. Casual in west during migration.

Grace's Warbler *Dendroica graciae* L 5" (13 cm)

Black-streaked gray back and absence of white neck patches distinguish Grace's from Yellow-throated Warbler. Throat and upper breast bright yellow; rest of underparts white, with black streaks on sides; yellow eyebrow, becomes white behind eye. Female slightly duller and browner above. Grace's Warbler inhabits coniferous or mixed forests of southwestern mountains, especially yellow pines. Song consists of rapid downslurred whistles, often followed by more rapid whistles rising in pitch. Usually forages high in the trees, creeping along branches or darting out to catch flying insects. Rare vagrant to southern California during migration, chiefly in fall.

Kirtland's Warbler *Dendroica kirtlandii* L 5³/₄" (15 cm)

Blue-gray above, strongly black-streaked on back; yellow below, streaked on sides; white eye ring, broken by dark lores and eye line; two whitish wing bars, thin and indistinct. Adult female slightly duller; immature female is even duller and brownish above. Song is loud and lively, a variable series of low, sharp notes followed by slurred whistles. The Kirtland's Warbler is an endangered species; present population estimated at fewer than 500. Known to nest only in a protected area in north-central Michigan, where controlled plantings and fires produce the required habitat, thickets of young jack pines. Heat from the fires opens pine cones and frees the seeds. Kirtland's Warblers are rarely seen in migration; only known wintering grounds are in the Bahamas.

Prairie Warbler *Dendroica discolor* L 4³/₄" (12 cm)

Olive above, with faint chestnut streaks on back; bright yellow eyebrow, yellow patch below eye; bright yellow below, streaked with black on sides of neck and body. Two pale yellow wing bars. Female and immature male are duller. Immature female very drab, grayish-olive above; absence of gray breast band distinguishes her from similar fall female Magnolia Warbler (page 362). Common in open woodlands, scrublands, overgrown fields, mangrove swamps. Generally forages in lower branches and brush, twitching its tail. Distinctive song, rising, buzzy *zee* notes.

Yellow-throated Warbler

yellow-lored ♂

white-lored ♂

♀

Grace's Warbler

♂

immature ♀

Kirtland's Warbler

♀

♂

♀

Prairie Warbler

♂

immature ♀

Bay-breasted Warbler *Dendroica castanea*

L 5¹/₂" (14 cm) Breeding male has chestnut crown, throat, and sides; black face; creamy patch at each side of neck; two white wing bars. Female is paler; throat buffier; chestnut on crown and sides less distinct. Fall adults and immatures resemble Blackpoll Warbler and immature Pine Warbler. In Bay-breasted Warbler, upperparts are brighter green, especially on crown and nape; underparts show little or no streaking, flanks usually buffy; legs entirely dark; undertail coverts are buffy or whitish. Fairly common; nests in open coniferous forests. Migrates earlier in fall than Blackpoll; most migration is east of dashed line on map. Regular vagrant in the west. Song consists of high-pitched double notes.

Blackpoll Warbler *Dendroica striata* *L 5¹/₂" (14 cm)*

Solid black cap, white cheeks, and white underparts identify breeding male; back and sides boldly streaked with black. Compare with Black-and-White Warbler (page 360). Breeding female is duller overall, slightly greenish above; crown is streaked. Fall adults and immatures resemble Bay-breasted Warbler and immature Pine Warbler. In Blackpoll, upperparts are duller; underparts mostly pale greenish-yellow, with dusky streaking on sides; legs are pale on front and back, dark on sides; undertail coverts are usually white. Common; nests in coniferous forests. Migrates later in fall than Bay-breasted Warbler. Most migration is east of dashed line on map, overland in spring, along and off coast in fall. Song is a series of high-pitched *tseet* notes.

Pine Warbler *Dendroica pinus* *L 5¹/₂" (14 cm)*

Relatively large-billed. Male is greenish-olive above, without streaking; throat and breast are yellow, with dark streaks on sides of breast; belly white; undertail coverts white. Female is usually duller. Immature male is brownish-olive on upperparts, pale yellow on underparts, with brownish flanks. In immature female, underparts are largely white, with pale brownish-gray flanks; pale throat and sides of neck set off dark cheek patch. Common in open pine forests and groves in summer, mixed woodlands during migration and winter. Song is a twittering but musical trill.

Palm Warbler *Dendroica palmarum* *L 5¹/₂" (14 cm)*

Breeding adults have rufous cap, yellow eyebrow. Eastern birds are yellow below, with streaks on breast and sides. Western birds are mostly grayish below, browner above. Fall adults and immatures are drab; underparts grayish except for yellow undertail coverts; eyebrow is white. Fairly common. A ground-dwelling warbler; nests in brush at edge of spruce bogs. During migration and winter, found in woodland borders, open brushy areas, marshes. Constantly wags its tail as it forages. Most migration is east of dashed line on map, but seen regularly on west coast in fall and winter. Song is a rapid trill of low whistles and buzzy notes.

Bay-breasted Warbler

fall ♂

breeding ♀

immature ♀

breeding ♂

Blackpoll Warbler

fall adult ♂

breeding ♀

immature

breeding ♂

Pine Warbler

♀

immature ♀

♂

immature ♂

eastern breeding

Palm Warbler

western fall

western breeding

Yellow Warbler *Dendroica petechia* L 5" (13 cm)

Yellow overall; reddish streaks below, distinct in male, faint or absent in female. Back, wings, and tail yellowish-olive, with yellow wing bars and tail spots. Immature male resembles adult female; immature female is much duller, almost gray in some subspecies. In all ages, dark eye is prominent in uniformly yellow face. A plump, short-tailed warbler, common in wet habitats, especially in willows; open woodlands, orchards. Song is a clear, variable *sweet sweet sweet I'm so sweet*.

♪ Mourning Warbler *Oporornis philadelphia* L 5¹⁄₄" (13 cm)

Lack of bold white eye ring distinguishes adult male from Connecticut and MacGillivray's Warblers. Adult female and immatures may show a thin, incomplete eye ring very hard to distinguish from the bold white crescents above and below eye of MacGillivray's. Immatures, especially females, generally have more yellow in throat than MacGillivray's. Field identification is often extremely difficult. Mourning Warbler's call is a flat, hollow *chip;* song has two parts: a series of slurred two-note phrases, usually followed by two or more phrases on a lower pitch. Fairly common; found in dense undergrowth, thickets, moist woods. Mourning Warblers hop; Connecticuts walk. Spring migration generally follows the Appalachians and the Mississippi River.

MacGillivray's Warbler *Oporornis tolmiei* L 5¹⁄₄" (13 cm)

Bold white crescents above and below eye distinguish all plumages from male Mourning and all Connecticut Warblers. MacGillivray's broad eye crescents may be very hard to distinguish from thin, incomplete eye ring on female and immature Mourning Warblers. Immature MacGillivray's Warblers generally have grayer throat than immature Mournings. Field identification is often extremely difficult. Call is a sharp, thin *tsik;* song has two parts: a buzzy trill ending in a downslur. Fairly common; found in dense undergrowth. MacGillivray's Warblers hop; Connecticuts walk. Casual migrant east to Mississippi.

♪ Connecticut Warbler *Oporornis agilis* L 5³⁄₄" (15 cm)

Bold white eye ring conspicuous on male's gray hood, female's browner hood. Underparts dull yellowish, upperparts brownish-olive. Immature drabber overall, with brownish, incomplete hood. A large, stocky warbler; long undertail coverts give it a short-tailed appearance. Uncommon; found in spruce bogs, moist woodlands. Generally feeds on the ground or on low limbs. Walks rather than hops. Loud, accelerating song repeats a short series of explosive *beech-er* or *whip-ity* notes. Spring migration chiefly west of the Appalachians.

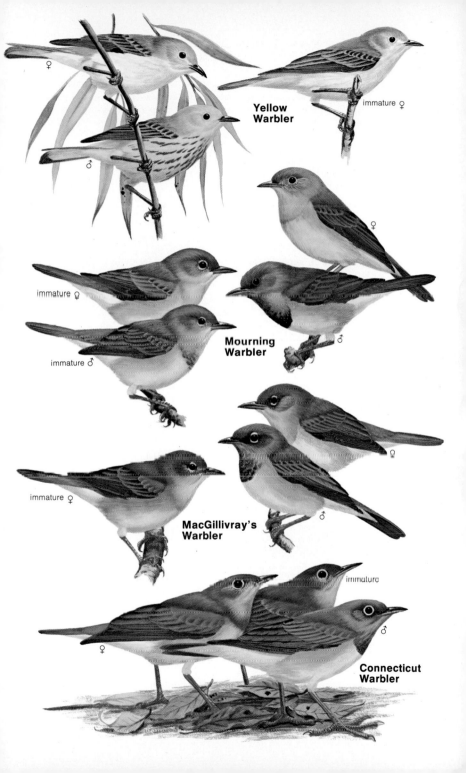

Yellow Warbler

♀

♂

immature ♀

♀

immature ♀

immature ♂

Mourning Warbler

♂

immature ♀

♀

♂

MacGillivray's Warbler

immature

♀

♂

Connecticut Warbler

♪ **Kentucky Warbler** *Oporornis formosus* L 5¹/₄" (13 cm)
Bold yellow spectacles separate black crown from black on
face and sides of neck; underparts are entirely yellow, upperparts bright olive. Black areas are duller on female, very drab
on immature. A short-tailed, long-legged warbler, common in
rich, moist woodlands; nests and feeds on the ground in dense
undergrowth. Song is a series of rolling musical notes, *churry
churry churry,* much like the song of the Carolina Wren; call is
a low *chuck.* Winters from central Mexico to Venezuela; rare
vagrant in California.

Canada Warbler *Wilsonia canadensis* L 5¹/₄" (13 cm)
Black necklace on bright yellow breast identifies adult male
year round; note also bold yellow spectacles. In female and immature, eye ring is paler, necklace dusky and indistinct. Male
is blue-gray above, adult and young females are duller. Common in dense woodlands and brush. Usually forages in undergrowth or low branches, but also seen fly-catching. Song
begins with one or more short, sharp *chip*'s and continues as a
rich and highly variable warble. Winters in South America.
Casual migrant in California and southwest; occasionally seen
in other western states.

Wilson's Warbler *Wilsonia pusilla* L 4³/₄" (12 cm)
Olive above; yellow below. Tail is all-dark above and below.
Male has yellowish face, small black cap. In female and immature, cap is dusky or olive, forehead yellowish. Lack of white in
tail helps distinguish female from female Hooded Warbler.
Color of underparts varies geographically from bright yellow in
the west to greenish-yellow in the east. Song is a series of short,
descending, abruptly slurred notes; call, a sharp *chip.* A fairly
common warbler, much more numerous in the west than in
the east; stays close to the ground in dense, moist woodlands
and bogs, willow thickets, streamside tangles.

Hooded Warbler *Wilsonia citrina* L 5¹/₄" (13 cm)
Extensive black hood identifies adult and immature male. Females show blackish or olive crown and sides of neck; sometimes have black spots on breast. Note in both sexes that tail is
white below; seen from above, white outer tail feathers are
conspicuous as the bird flicks open its tail. Fairly common in
swamps, moist woodlands; generally stays hidden in dense
undergrowth and low branches. Sings loud, musical, whistled
variations of *ta-wit ta-wit ta-wit tee-yo.* Calls include a flat,
metallic *chink.* Casual migrant in California and southwest;
occasionally seen in other western states.

Kentucky
Warbler

♂

♀

Canada
Warbler

♀

♂

Wilson's
Warbler

♀

♂

Hooded
Warbler

♀

♂

♀

Worm-eating Warbler *Helmitheros vermivorus*
L 5¹/₄″ (13 cm) Bold, dark stripes on buffy-orange head; upperparts brownish-olive; underparts mostly buffy-orange; long, spike-like bill. Found chiefly in dense undergrowth on wooded slopes. Song is a series of rapid, sharp, dry *chip* notes, like Chipping Sparrow's song. Casual fall migrant in California and the southwest.

Swainson's Warbler *Limnothlypis swainsonii*
L 5¹/₂″ (14 cm) Pale eyebrow, conspicuous between brown crown and dark eye line. Upperparts brown-olive; underparts grayish. Bill long, spike-like. Uncommon and secretive, more often heard than seen. Song is a series of thin, slurred whistles like song of Louisiana Waterthrush; often ends with a rising *tee-oh*. Forages in undergrowth in swamps, canebrakes; also rare and local in mountain rhododendron thickets.

Ovenbird *Seiurus aurocapillus L 6″ (15 cm)*
Russet crown bordered by dark stripes; bold white eye ring; brownish upperparts; white underparts, with bold streaks of dark spots; pinkish legs. Russet crown is less distinct in fall plumage. A plump warbler, common in mature forests. Generally seen on the ground; walks, rather than hops. Typical song is a loud, rising *teacher teacher teacher*. Casual in winter along Gulf and Atlantic coasts to North Carolina. Note small breeding population along the Front Range in Colorado.

♪ Louisiana Waterthrush *Seiurus motacilla L 6″ (15 cm)*
Distinguished from Northern Waterthrush by contrast between white underparts and buffy flanks; bicolored eyebrow, pale buff in front of eye, white and much broader behind eye; larger bill; bubblegum pink legs. Uncommon; found along mountain brooks and streams in dense woodlands, less often near ponds and in swamps. A ground dweller; walks, rather than hops, bobbing its tail constantly but slowly. Call note, a sharp *chink,* is like that of Northern Waterthrush, but song is different: shrill, slurred notes followed by a brief twittering.

♪ Northern Waterthrush *Seiurus noveboracensis*
L 6″ (15 cm) Distinguished from Louisiana Waterthrush by lack of contrast in color between flanks and rest of underparts; buffy eyebrow, of even width throughout or slightly narrowing behind eye; smaller bill; drabber leg color. Some birds, especially in the west, are whiter below, with whiter eyebrow. Breeds in woodland bogs, swamps, and thickets. A ground dweller; walks, rather than hops, bobbing its tail constantly and rapidly. Call note, a sharp *chink,* is similar to that of Louisiana Waterthrush, but song is different: begins with loud, emphatic notes and ends in a downslur. Rare but regular migrant on west coast.

Worm-eating Warbler

Swainson's Warbler

Ovenbird

Louisiana Waterthrush

Northern Waterthrush

Common Yellowthroat *Geothlypis trichas* *L 5" (13 cm)*

Adult male's broad black mask is bordered above by white, below by bright yellow throat and breast; belly is whitish, undertail coverts yellow. Upperparts dark olive. Female lacks black mask; face is dark olive, like crown, back, and wings, with very pale yellow eye ring. Adults vary geographically in extent of yellow below, eastern birds generally showing less than western birds. Southwestern Yellowthroats are brightest below and show the most yellow. Immatures are duller and browner overall. Young male's mask is much less distinct than adult's; white eye ring and lack of bright yellow eyebrow distinguish it from Kentucky Warbler (page 372). Abundant; stays low in grassy fields, thickets, shrubs, marshes; often holds its tail cocked like a wren. Distinctive song, a loud, rolling *wichity wichity wichity wich*.

Rufous-capped Warbler *Basileuterus rufifrons*

L 5¹/₄" (13 cm) Casual visitor from Mexico to extreme southern Texas, very rare in southeastern Arizona. Dark olive above; reddish-brown crown and sides of head, crossed by conspicuous white eyebrow. Throat and breast bright yellow; rest of underparts whitish. Long tail, often held cocked like a wren. Inhabits dense brush and woodlands of foothills or low mountains. Song begins with musical *chip* notes and accelerates into a series of dry, whistled warbles.

Yellow-breasted Chat *Icteria virens* *L 7¹/₂" (19 cm)*

Our largest warbler. Long-tailed and thick-billed. White cheek stripe borders bright yellow throat. Belly and undertail coverts are white. Lores black in males, gray in females. For a short time during breeding season, breast may become bright orange. Inhabits dense thickets and brush. Fairly common, but solitary and shy. Unmusical song, a jumble of harsh, chattering clucks, rattles, clear whistles, and squawks. Male sings from conspicuous perch or as he hovers in brief display flight, legs dangling, wings beating slowly.

Golden-crowned Warbler *Basileuterus culicivorus*

L 5" (13 cm) (Not pictured) Rare wanderer from Mexico to woodlands along the lower Rio Grande in south Texas. Resembles Orange-crowned Warbler (page 356) but crown shows a distinct buffy-orange central stripe, bordered in black. Call is a rapidly repeated *tuck*.

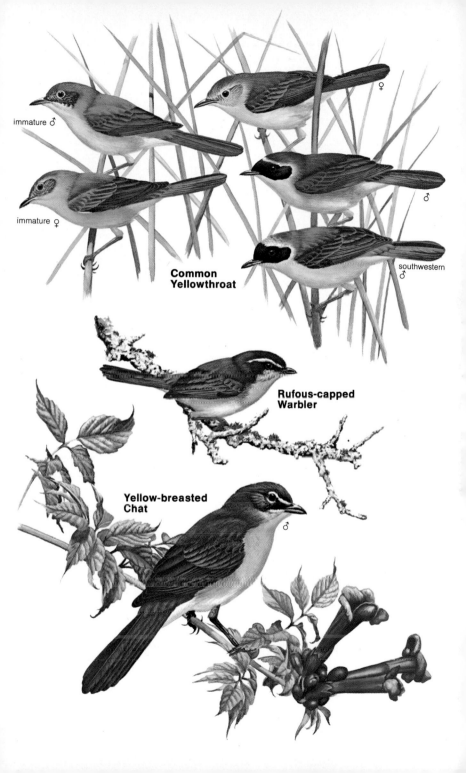

immature ♂

immature ♀

♀

♂

southwestern
♂

**Common
Yellowthroat**

**Rufous-capped
Warbler**

**Yellow-breasted
Chat**

♂

American Redstart *Setophaga ruticilla L 5¹/₄" (13 cm)*

Male glossy black, with bright orange patches on sides, wings, tail; belly and undertail coverts white. Female is gray-olive above, white below with yellow patches. Immature resembles female. By first spring, young male's patches are salmon, breast shows some black spotting; full adult male plumage is acquired by second fall. A common warbler in second-growth woodlands, small groves. Like other redstarts, actively pursues flying insects; often fans its tail and spreads its wings when perched, making the colorful patches conspicuous. Variable song, a series of high, thin notes usually followed by a wheezy, downslurred note.

Slate-throated Redstart *Myioborus miniatus*

L 6" (15 cm) Central and South American species, vagrant to southeast Arizona, southwest New Mexico. Head, throat, and back slate black, breast dark red. Tawny crown patch visible only at close range. Lacks white wing patch of similar Painted Redstart; white on outer tail feathers less extensive. Found in pine-oak canyons, forests. Typical song, a series of rapid, thin, downslurred *chee* or *tswee* notes.

Painted Redstart *Myioborus pictus L 5³/₄" (15 cm)*

Bright red breast; black head, throat, and upperparts; bold white wing patch. White outer tail feathers conspicuous as the bird fans its tail. Juvenile lacks red breast; acquires full adult plumage by end of summer. Fairly common in pine-oak canyons, pinyon-juniper forests. Song is a series of rich liquid warbles; call note, a clear, whistled *chee*.

Red-faced Warbler *Cardellina rubrifrons L 5¹/₂" (14 cm)*

Adult's red, black, and white head pattern is unique; back and tail gray, rump and underparts white. Juvenile is duller, face pinkish. A warbler of high mountains, generally found above 6,000 feet. Fairly common, especially in fir and spruce mixed with oaks. Nests on the ground. Song is a series of varied *zweet* notes, clear and ringing. Casual to southern California.

Olive Warbler *Peucedramus taeniatus L 5¹/₄" (13 cm)*

Adult male's head, throat, and nape tawny brown, marked by black ear patch. Gray back sets off two broad white wing bars, white on outer tail feathers. Female has olive crown, yellow face with dark ear patch; pale yellow throat and breast. Juvenile resembles female but is paler below. Young male's head shows some tawny color by first spring; full adult plumage is acquired by second fall. In all plumages, note long, thin bill, slightly downcurved. A Central American species; range extends into high mountains of southwestern U. S.; generally found in the open coniferous forests of elevations above 7,000 feet. Nests and forages high in the trees. Typical song is a loud *peeta peeta peeta;* call, a short, plaintive whistle.

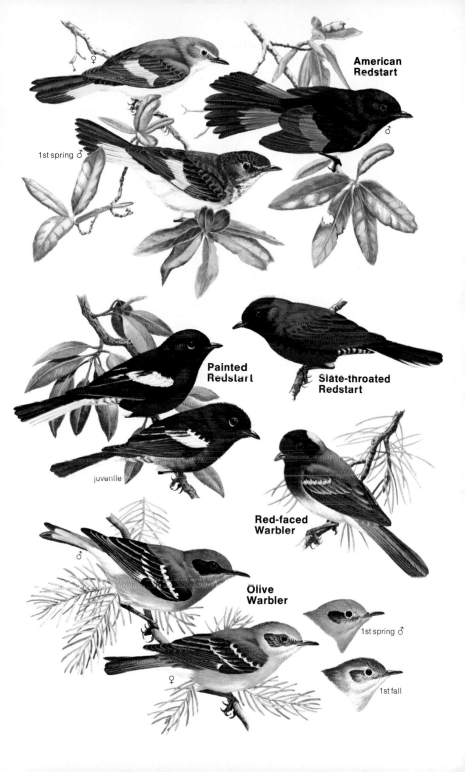

American Redstart

♀

1st spring ♂

♂

Painted Redstart

juvenile

Slate-throated Redstart

Red-faced Warbler

♂

Olive Warbler

♀

1st spring ♂

1st fall

Grosbeaks, Buntings, Sparrows

Widespread birds, at home in almost any habitat. Some, such as cardinals, are conspicuous and bold. But many sparrows stay hidden except in spring, when males sing from open perches.

Rose-breasted Grosbeak *Pheucticus ludovicianus*
L 8" (20 cm) Large finch with a massive triangular bill. Male distinctive in black head and back, rose red breast, white underparts, white wing bars, white rump. Rose red wing linings show in flight. Brown-tipped winter plumage is acquired before migration. Female's streaked plumage and yellow wing linings resemble female Black-headed Grosbeak, but underparts are more heavily and extensively streaked. Similar first-fall male is buffier above, with buffy wash across breast; red wing linings are the best distinguishing field mark. The melodious, robin-like songs of the two species are similar. Rose-breasted Grosbeak's call, a sharp *eek,* is higher pitched and squeakier than the Black-headed's call. Rose-breasteds are common in open, second-growth woodlands and dense shrubbery along water courses. Seen regularly but rarely throughout the west during migration.

Black-headed Grosbeak *Pheucticus melanocephalus*
L 8¹/₄" (21 cm) Male readily identified by cinnamon underparts, all-black head, massive bill. In flight, both sexes show yellow wing linings. Female plumage is generally buffier above and below than female Rose-breasted Grosbeak, with less streaking below; yellow wing linings distinguish her from similar first-fall male Rose-breasted. First-fall male Black-headed Grosbeak is rich buff below, with little or no streaking. The melodious, robin-like songs of the two species are similar. Black-headed Grosbeak's call, a sharp *eek,* is lower pitched and less squeaky than Rose-breasted's call. Common in open woodlands, forest edges. Casual during migration and winter to east coast. Hybridizes uncommonly with Rose-breasted Grosbeak in narrow range of overlap in the Great Plains.

Yellow Grosbeak *Pheucticus chrysopeplus* *L 9¹/₄" (24 cm)*
Mexican species, casual early-summer vagrant to southeastern Arizona, chiefly in open woodlands and river courses of foothills and mountains. Male distinguished by large size, huge bill, bright yellow plumage; black wings and tail with white patches. Female and immatures similar to male but duller; crown streaked. Compare with Evening Grosbeak (page 442).

Rose-breasted Grosbeak

breeding ♂

winter ♂

♂

1st fall ♂

1st spring ♂

♀

Black-headed Grosbeak

♀

♂

1st fall ♂

♂

♀

Yellow Grosbeak

Northern Cardinal *Cardinalis cardinalis* L 8³/₄" (22 cm)
Conspicuous crest; cone-shaped reddish bill. Male is red overall, with black face. Female is buffy-brown or buffy-olive, tinged with red on wings, crest, tail. Juvenile browner overall, bill dull brown; juvenile female lacks red tones. Bill shape helps distinguish female and juveniles from the similar Pyrrhuloxia. Abundant throughout the east, Cardinals inhabit woodland edges, swamps, streamside thickets, suburban gardens. Distinctive song, a loud, liquid whistle with many variations, including *cue cue cue* and *cheer cheer cheer* and *purty purty purty*. Both sexes sing almost year round. Nonmigratory, but this aggressive species has greatly expanded its range northward during the 20th century; apparently also expanding southwest range.

Pyrrhuloxia *Cardinalis sinuatus* L 8³/₄" (22 cm)
Thick, strongly curved bill helps distinguish this species from female and juvenile Northern Cardinal. Male Pyrrhuloxia is gray overall, with red on face, crest, wings, tail, underparts; bill orange-yellow. Female is buffy-gray with little or no red; bill dull yellow. Fairly widespread in thorny brush and mesquite thickets of dry creek beds, desert, woodland edges, ranchlands. Song is a liquid whistle, thinner and shorter than song of Northern Cardinal. Female seldom sings.

Blue Grosbeak *Guiraca caerulea* L 6³/₄" (17 cm)
Wide chestnut wing bars, large heavy bill, and larger overall size distinguish male from male Indigo Bunting (next page). Females of these two species also similar; compare bill shape, wing bars, and overall size. Juvenile resembles female; in first fall, some immatures are richer brown than female. First-spring male shows some blue above and below; acquires full adult plumage by third spring. In poor light, Blue Grosbeak resembles Brown-headed Cowbird (page 422); note bill shape and wing bars; also note Blue Grosbeak's habit of twitching and spreading its tail. Fairly common; found in low, overgrown fields, streamsides, woodland edges, brushy roadsides. Range expanding along Atlantic coast. Casual wanderer north in fall to New England and the Maritime Provinces. Somewhat secretive; listen for distinctive call, a loud, metallic *chink*. Song is a series of rich rising and falling warbles.

Blue Bunting *Cyanocompsa parellina* L 5¹/₂" (14 cm)
Mexican species, casual visitor along Gulf coast from Texas to southwest Louisiana. Smaller than Blue Grosbeak; lacks wing bars. Male is dark blue overall, paler on crown, cheeks, and rump. Darker color and thick, strongly curved bill distinguish male from male Indigo Bunting (next page). Female distinguished by bill shape, overall richer color, and lack of streaking below. Found in brushy fields and roadsides, woodland edges.

Northern Cardinal

juvenile ♂

♀

♂

Pyrrhuloxia

♀

♂

Blue Grosbeak

♂

♀

1st fall

Blue Bunting

♀

♂

1st spring ♂

Indigo Bunting *Passerina cyanea* L 5¹/₂" *(14 cm)*

Adult male deep blue overall; appears black in poor light. Smaller than similar Blue Grosbeak (preceding page); bill much smaller; lacks wing bars. In winter plumage, blue coloring is obscured by brown and buff edgings. Female is dull brown above, without obvious streaking; underparts buffy, breast faintly streaked; buffy wing bars may be indistinct. Juvenile resembles female. First-fall male shows blue tinges; becomes mostly blue by first spring. Common in woodland clearings and borders, brushy pastures. Male sings well into August, later in summer than most other singers. Song is a series of varied high-pitched phrases, usually paired. Range is expanding in west and southwest.

Lazuli Bunting *Passerina amoena* L 5¹/₂" *(14 cm)*

Adult male bright turquoise above and on throat; breast and sides cinnamon; belly white. Shows two white wing bars, the upper bar wider, more distinct; compare Bluebirds (page 324). Female is grayish-brown above, rump grayish-blue; underparts white, with buffy wash on throat and breast; wing bars buffy. Juveniles resemble female but are streaked below; immature male is mostly blue by first spring. Found in open deciduous or mixed woodlands, chaparral, especially in brushy areas near water. Song is a rapid series of varied phrases, sometimes paired; similar to Indigo Bunting's song but faster, less strident. Hybrids of these two species occur in area of range overlap.

Painted Bunting *Passerina ciris* L 5¹/₂" *(14 cm)*

Adult male's gaudy colors retained year round; slightly duller in winter. Female bright green above, paler yellow-green below. Juvenile is much drabber; look for telltale hint of green above, yellow below. Molt to first-winter plumage begins during migration. First-winter male resembles adult female but colors are brighter; by spring, may begin to show tinge of blue on head, red on breast. Locally common in low thickets, weedy tangles, streamside brush, woodland borders. Casual vagrant north on Atlantic coast to New York. Popular as a cage bird in Mexico; some sightings of adult males in the southwest may be escaped birds. Song is a rapid series of varied phrases, thinner and sweeter than song of Lazuli Bunting.

Varied Bunting *Passerina versicolor* L 5¹/₂" *(14 cm)*

Spring adult male's plumage is colorful in good light; otherwise appears black. In winter, colors are edged with brown. Female is plain gray-brown above, slightly paler below, without obvious streaking or wing bars. In close view, note that Varied Bunting's culmen is slightly curved; in Lazuli and Indigo Buntings, culmen is straighter. First-spring male Varied Bunting resembles female. Locally common in thorny thickets in washes, canyons, often near water. Song is like Painted Bunting.

Indigo Bunting

winter adult ♂

1st fall ♂

breeding ♀

1st spring ♂

breeding ♂

Lazuli Bunting

♂

1st spring ♂

♀

Painted Bunting

juvenile

♀

♂

Varied Bunting

1st spring ♂

breeding ♂

winter ♂

♀

Olive Sparrow *Arremonops rufivirgatus* L 6¹/₄" (16 cm)
Mexican species, common in southernmost Texas in dense
undergrowth, brushy areas, live oak. Dull olive above, with
brown stripe on each side of crown. Lacks reddish cap of similar Green-tailed Towhee. Song is a series of dry *chip* notes, beginning slowly and accelerating to a trill.

Green-tailed Towhee *Pipilo chlorurus* L 7¹/₄" (18 cm)
Olive above with reddish crown, distinct white throat bordered
by dark stripe and white stripe. Winter birds are duller. Juvenile has two faint olive wing bars; plumage is streaked overall;
lacks reddish crown. Clear, whistled song begins with *weet-
chur,* ends in raspy trill. Call notes include a catlike *mew.* Fairly common in dense brush, chaparral, on mountainsides and
high plateaus. Rare breeder in Guadalupe Mountains of west
Texas. Casual in winter throughout the east, chiefly at feeders.

Rufous-sided Towhee *Pipilo erythrophthalmus*
L 8¹/₂" (22 cm)   Male's black upperparts and black hood contrast
with chestnut sides, white underparts. White wing patches
and white-cornered tail conspicuous in flight. Eastern females
are brown above. In western forms, formerly known as Spotted
Towhee, both sexes are spotted with white above, have two
white wing bars. In southeastern birds, eye color varies from
red-orange to, in Florida, white. All juveniles have dark streaks
and spots but show adult wing pattern. Eastern birds' distinctive song sounds like *drink-your-tea-ee-ee-ee-ee;* call note, a
rising *tow-whee* or *chee-wink.* Songs of western forms vary;
call notes include a whining *chee-ee* and a raspy *mew.* Common throughout breeding range in dense undergrowth,
streamside thickets, forest edges, open woodlands. Like all
species on this page, forages on the ground, scratching with
both feet together.

♪ **Brown Towhee** *Pipilo fuscus* L 8¹/₂" (22 cm)
Brown or gray-brown above, paler below; buffy throat bordered with dark streaks; undertail coverts rust. Pacific coast
birds are dark, crown brown. Interior populations are paler,
with rust crown, dark spot on breast. Brown Towhees are common on brushy hillsides and wooded canyons; coastal birds are
found in chaparral, suburban gardens. Non-migratory. Song
of interior birds is a mellow chipping trill; calls include a sharp
chiup. Pacific birds' call is quite different, a metallic *chink;*
song, an accelerating series of *chink* notes.

♪ **Abert's Towhee** *Pipilo aberti* L 9¹/₂" (24 cm)
Black face; upperparts brown, underparts paler, with cinnamon undertail coverts. Song is a chipping trill; call note, a
sharp *peek.* Common within its range, but generally shy and
secretive. Inhabits desert woodlands, streamside thickets, at
lower altitudes than similar Brown Towhee. Also found in suburban yards, orchards.

Green-tailed Towhee

Olive Sparrow

immature

juvenile

western ♀

eastern ♂

western ♂

eastern ♀

eastern
juvenile

Rufous-sided Towhee

interior

interior
juvenile

Pacific coast

Abert's Towhee

Brown Towhee

♪ **Grasshopper Sparrow** *Ammodramus savannarum*
L 5" (13 cm) Buffy breast and sides, usually without obvious streaking. A chunky bird with short tail, flat head. Dark crown has a pale central stripe; note also the white eye ring and, on most adults, the yellow-orange spot in front of eye. Lacks broad buffy-orange eyebrow and blue-gray ear patch of Le Conte's Sparrow (next page). Compare also with the highly variable Savannah Sparrow, shown here and on page 392. Juvenile's breast and sides are pale buff, streaked with brown. Immatures and winter adults are buffier below but never as bright as Le Conte's Sparrow. Subspecies vary in overall color from the dark Florida form, *A.s. floridanus*, to the pale, reddish *ammolegus* of southeastern Arizona. Eastern *pratensis* is somewhat darker, brighter, and bigger billed than the widespread *perpallidus*, found over most of U. S. Fairly common in pastures, grasslands, palmetto scrub, old fields. Somewhat secretive; feeds and nests on the ground. Typical song is one or two high, thin *chip* notes followed by a brief, grasshopper-like buzz; also sings a series of varied squeaky and buzzy notes.

♪ **Baird's Sparrow** *Ammodramus bairdii* *L 5¹/₂" (14 cm)*
Head and nape rich buff with fine black streaks on nape and sides of crown, leaving a plain buff central crown stripe. Two dark stripes border each side of throat. Well-spaced dark streaks on breast form a distinct necklace; streaking extends along sides. Chestnut on scapulars and coverts adds color to the black-and-buff upperparts. Juvenile's head is paler, creamier; central crown stripe finely streaked; white edgings give a scaly appearance to the blackish upperparts; underparts are densely streaked. Uncommon, local, and declining; found in dry prairies, weedy fields. Nests and feeds on the ground. Secretive. Song consists of two or three high, thin notes, followed by a single warbled note and a low trill.

Henslow's Sparrow *Ammodramus henslowii*
L 5" (13 cm) Large flat head; large gray bill. Central crown stripe yellowish, becoming olive and streaked at back of crown, the streaks extending onto the otherwise plain olive nape. Olive head contrasts with streaked black, rust, and white upperparts. Wings are extensively chestnut. Rump and uppertail coverts bright rust and boldly streaked with black. Underparts streaked on breast and sides. Juvenile is paler, yellower, with less streaking below; compare with adult Grasshopper Sparrow. Uncommon and declining; found in wet shrubby fields, weedy meadows. In winter, found also in pine woods. Secretive, but after being flushed several times may perch in the open for a few minutes before dropping back into cover. Distinctive song, a short *se-lick,* accented on second syllable.

Grasshopper Sparrow

perpallidus

floridanus

pratensis juvenile

Savannah Sparrow for comparison

pratensis

ammolegus

Baird's Sparrow

juvenile

juvenile

Henslow's Sparrow

Le Conte's Sparrow *Ammodramus leconteii* L 5" (13 cm)

White central crown stripe, buffy forehead, and chestnut streaks on nape distinguish Le Conte's from Sharp-tailed Sparrow. Bright, broad, buffy-orange eyebrow, blue-gray ear patch, and bright buffy-orange breast and sides separate it from Grasshopper Sparrow (preceding page). Sides of breast and flanks have dark streaks. Juvenile plumage, seen only on the breeding grounds, is tinged with buff overall; crown stripe is tawny, breast heavily streaked. A bird of wet grassy fields, marsh edges. Fairly common but secretive; scurries through matted grasses like a mouse. Song is a short, insectlike buzz.

Sharp-tailed Sparrow *Ammodramus caudacutus*

L 5¹/₄" (13 cm) Gray central crown stripe and gray unstreaked nape distinguish all subspecies from Le Conte's Sparrow. Breast and sides buff, with at least some streaking; belly white. Juveniles are buffy overall, streaked below; lack gray crown stripe. Adult plumages vary in overall coloration. In east coast forms such as *A.c. caudacutus,* face shows a bright orange triangle around a dark ear patch; breast is distinctly streaked. Northeast coast *subvirgatus* is duller, grayer. Widespread inland form, *nelsoni,* has a bright buff eyebrow, a more diffuse ear patch, and diffuse streaking below; most closely resembles Le Conte's Sparrow. Common but somewhat secretive. Found in salt marshes, lakeshores, often in spartina grass. Song is a high buzzy trill ending in a lower, clearer note. Casual in winter (*nelsoni*) to California; a few birds are present every winter in coastal estuaries.

Seaside Sparrow *Ammodramus maritimus* L 6" (15 cm)

Long, spike-like bill, thick-based and thin-tipped. Tail is short, pointed. Yellow lore patch; in some birds the color extends slightly above the eye. Dark whisker stripe separates whitish throat and broad, pale stripe along cheek. Breast is white or buffy, with at least some streaking. Juveniles are duller, browner, than adults. Seaside Sparrows vary widely in overall color. Most forms, like the widespread *A.m. maritimus,* are grayish-olive above. The greener *mirabilis,* formerly called Cape Sable Sparrow, inhabits a small area in southwest Florida. Gulf Coast forms such as *fisheri* have buffier breasts. Darkest form, *nigrescens,* is blackish above, heavily streaked below; formerly called Dusky Seaside Sparrow, this subspecies is found only near Titusville, Florida, and is near extinction. In general, Seaside Sparrows are fairly common in grassy tidal marshes; rarely seen inland. Buzzy song resembles that of Red-winged Blackbird.

Le Conte's Sparrow

juvenile

nelsoni

Sharp-tailed Sparrow

caudacutus juvenile

subvirgatus

caudacutus

maritimus

fishori

nigrescens

maritimus juvenile

Seaside Sparrow

mirabilis

Vesper Sparrow *Pooecetes gramineus* L 6¹/₄″ (16 cm)
White eye ring; dark ear patch bordered in white along lower and rear edges; short, notched tail with white outer feathers. Lacks distinct eyebrow of Savannah Sparrow. Chestnut shoulder patch is distinctive but not easily seen. Birds of the east are slightly darker overall than the most widespread subspecies, shown here. Fairly common in dry, open grasslands, farmlands, forest clearings, sagebrush. Generally seen on the ground or on low perches. Song is rich and melodious, two long, slurred notes followed by two higher notes, then a series of varied, short, descending trills.

Savannah Sparrow *Passerculus sandwichensis*
L 5¹/₂″ (14 cm) Highly variable. Generally has yellow lores, often a yellowish eyebrow; pale crown stripe; dark whisker stripe. Upperparts usually streaked; tail short and notched. Sides and breast streaked, sometimes showing a central spot; belly and undertail whitish; legs and feet pink. Savannah Sparrows are common in a variety of open habitats, fresh and salt marshes, grasslands. Song begins with two or three *chip* notes, followed by two buzzy trills, the second trill lower and briefer. Call note, a thin *seep*. The numerous subspecies vary geographically in size, coloration, bill size, and extent of streaking. Dark, heavily streaked *P.s. beldingi* inhabits southern California coastal marshes. Paler, small-billed *nevadensis* is typical of western interior forms. Largest form, *rostratus,* breeds on Colorado River delta, seen in U. S. chiefly at the Salton Sea; lacks streaks on back and crown; bill very large; breast streaking indistinct. Large, pale *princeps,* formerly called Ipswich Sparrow, breeds on Sable Island, Nova Scotia, winters along east coast.

Song Sparrow *Melospiza melodia* L 6¹/₄″ (16 cm)
Highly variable. All subspecies have long, rounded tail, pumped in flight. All show broad grayish eyebrow and broad, dark stripe bordering whitish throat. Upperparts usually streaked. Underparts whitish, with streaking on sides and breast that often converges in a central spot. Legs and feet are pinkish. Juvenile is buffier overall, with finer streaking; tail faintly barred. Generally abundant, Song Sparrows inhabit brushy areas, especially dense streamside thickets. Typical song: three or four short clear notes followed by a buzzy *tow-wee,* then a trill. Distinctive call note, a nasal, hollow *chimp.* The numerous subspecies vary geographically in size, bill shape, overall coloration and streaking. *M. m. melodia* typifies eastern forms; large Aleutian forms reach an extreme in the gray-brown *maxima;* paler forms such as *saltonis* inhabit southwestern deserts; *morphna* typifies darker, redder forms of the Pacific northwest; *heermanni* is one of the dark California forms.

Vesper Sparrow

beldingi

rostratus

Savannah Sparrow

nevadensis

princeps

maxima

melodia juvenile

melodia

heermanni

Song Sparrow

morphna

saltonis

Lark Sparrow *Chondestes grammacus* L 6¹/₂" (17 cm)

Head pattern distinctive in adults; underparts are whitish marked only with dark central breast spot. Juvenile's colors are much duller; breast, sides, and crown densely streaked. In all ages, white-cornered tail is conspicuous in flight. A large, plump sparrow, fairly common west of the Mississippi on prairies, roadsides, farmlands, open woodlands, mesas; often seen in flocks, especially in winter. Song consists of two loud, clear introductory notes followed by a series of rich, melodious notes and trills and unmusical buzzes. Call note is a sharp *tsip,* often repeated as a rapid series. Formerly bred as far east as New York and Maryland; now irregular east of the Mississippi, rare or casual on east coast, mainly in fall and winter.

Black-throated Sparrow *Amphispiza bilineata*

L 5¹/₂" (14 cm) Triangular black patch on throat and breast and black lores contrast with white eyebrow, white whisker stripe, white underparts. Upperparts plain brownish-gray, without streaks or wing bars. Juvenile plumage, often held well into fall, lacks black throat, but white eyebrow is conspicuous; breast and back finely streaked; wings show two indistinct buffy bars. In all ages, note extent of white on tail, greater than in Sage Sparrow, less than in Lark Sparrow. Song is rapid, high-pitched, opening with two clear notes followed by a trill; calls are faint, tinkling notes. Fairly common in desert, especially on rocky slopes; vagrant in east in fall and winter.

Five-striped Sparrow *Amphispiza quinquestriata*

L 6" (15 cm) Mexican species, reaching its northernmost range in southeastern Arizona. Rare in breeding season, with few winter records. Throat marked with black and white stripes. Note also dark central spot at base of gray breast. Juvenile lacks streaks found on juveniles of other sparrows. Highly specialized habitat: tall, dense shrubs on rocky, semidesert hillsides, canyon slopes.

Sage Sparrow *Amphispiza belli* L 6¹/₄" (16 cm)

Gray-brown head sets off white eye ring, white lore spot or eyebrow, broad white whisker stripe. Two pale wing bars; back buffy-brown with dusky streaks. White underparts, marked with dark central breast spot, dusky streaking on sides. Juvenile is duller overall and more heavily streaked; lore spot sometimes indistinct. Birds of the California coast are much darker overall. Fairly common on alkaline flats in sagebrush and saltbush; open arid desert in winter. Coastal form found in chaparral of slopes and foothills. Often runs from intruders, tail cocked up, rather than flying. Twitches and waves its tail while singing. From a low perch, male sings a jumbled, finch-like series of rising-and-falling phrases. Twittering call consists of thin, junco-like notes.

Lark Sparrow

juvenile

Five-striped Sparrow

juvenile

Black-throated Sparrow

coastal

Sage Sparrow

juvenile

♪ **Bachman's Sparrow** *Aimophila aestivalis* L 6″ *(15 cm)*
A large sparrow with large bill, fairly flat forehead, and long, rounded, dark tail. Adults gray above, heavily streaked with chestnut or dark brown; sides of head buffy-gray; a thin dark line extends back from eye. Breast and sides buff or gray; belly whitish. Subspecies vary in overall brightness from the reddish *A.a. illinoensis* of the western part of range to the grayer and darker *aestivalis* of the south. Juvenile has a distinct eye ring; throat, breast, and sides are streaked. First-winter plumage usually retains some streaking. Inhabits dry open woods, especially pines; scrub palmetto. Secretive; best located and identified by song: one clear, whistled introductory note, followed by a variable trill or warble on a different pitch. Male sings from open perch; often heard in late summer when most other songbirds have stopped singing for the season.

♪ **Botteri's Sparrow** *Aimophila botterii* L 6″ *(15 cm)*
A large, plain sparrow with large bill, fairly flat forehead; tail long, rounded, dusky-brown, lacking white tips of similar Cassin's Sparrow. Best located and identified by song: a short, accelerating, rattly trill often preceded by two or more high sharp *tsip* or *che-lik* notes. Upperparts streaked with dull black, rust or brown, and gray; underparts unstreaked; throat and belly whitish, breast and sides grayish-buff. Subspecies *A.b. arizonae* of southeastern Arizona is redder above; *texana* of extreme southern Texas is grayer above. Juvenile's belly is buffy; breast broadly streaked, sides narrowly streaked. Secretive; inhabits grasslands dotted with mesquite, cactus, brush.

♪ **Cassin's Sparrow** *Aimophila cassinii* L 6″ *(15 cm)*
A large, drab sparrow, with large bill, fairly flat forehead. Long, rounded tail is dark gray-brown; white tips on outer feathers are most conspicuous in flight. Best located and identified by song, often given in brief, fluttery song flight: typically a soft double whistle, a trill, a low whistle, and a final higher note. Also gives a trill of *pit* notes. Gray upperparts are streaked with dull black, brown, and rust; underparts grayish-white, usually with a few short streaks on flanks. Juvenile is streaked below; paler overall than juvenile Botteri's. Secretive; inhabits arid grasslands with scattered shrubs, cactus, mesquite.

aestivalis

illinoensis

illinoensis
juvenile

**Bachman's
Sparrow**

**Botteri's
Sparrow**

arizonae

arizonae
juvenile

texana

juvenile

**Cassin's
Sparrow**

Rufous-winged Sparrow *Aimophila carpalis*
L 5³/₄" (15 cm) Pale gray head marked with two black whisker stripes on each side of face, reddish eye line; sides of crown streaked with reddish-brown. Back is gray-brown, streaked with black; two whitish wing bars. Reddish lesser wing coverts distinctive but difficult to see in the field. Underparts grayish-white, without streaking. Tail long, rounded. Juvenile's facial stripes are less distinct; wing bars buffier; bill dark; breast and sides lightly streaked. Juvenile plumage may be held as late as November. Fairly common but local; found in flat areas of tall desert grass mixed with brush, cactus. Distinctive call note, a sharp, high *seep.* Variable song, several *chip* notes followed by an accelerating trill of *chip* or *sweet* notes.

Rufous-crowned Sparrow *Aimophila ruficeps*
L 6" (15 cm) Gray head with dark reddish crown, short whitish eyebrow, white eye ring, rufous line extending back from eye, single black whisker stripe on each side of face. Gray-brown above, with reddish streaks; gray below; tail long, rounded. Lacks white wing bars of Chipping Sparrow (next page). Subspecies vary in overall color from the paler, grayer interior form to the dark, reddish Pacific coast forms and pale, reddish Arizona forms. Juvenile buffier overall, dark brown above; breast and crown streaked; may show two pale wing bars. Locally common on rocky hillsides and steep slopes of grass and brush. Distinctive call, a nasal *dear,* usually given in a series; song, a rapid, bubbling series of *chip* notes.

American Tree Sparrow *Spizella arborea* *L 6¹/₄" (16 cm)*
Gray head and nape crowned with rufous; rufous stripe behind eye; diffuse rufous whisker stripe. Gray throat and breast, with dark central spot, rufous patches at sides of breast. Back and scapulars streaked with black and rufous. Two bold white wing bars. Tail notched; outer feathers thinly edged in white. Underparts grayish-white with buffy sides. Juvenile and winter adult are buffier. In winter adult, rufous crown obscured by gray and buff edges, sometimes forming a central stripe. Juvenile is streaked above and below. Western populations are paler overall. A common species, breeds along edge of tundra, in open areas with scattered trees, brush. Winters in weedy fields, marshes. Distinguished in mixed flocks by musical *teedle-eet* call. Song usually begins with several clear *seet* notes followed by a variable rapid warble.

Field Sparrow *Spizella pusilla* *L 5³/₄" (15 cm)*
Gray face with reddish-brown crown, whitish eye ring, bright pink bill. Upperparts streaked except on gray-brown rump. Two white wing bars. Breast and sides buffy-red, belly grayish-white; legs pink. Notched brown tail, edged with gray. Juvenile is streaked below; wing bars buffy. Birds in westernmost part of range are paler and grayer overall. Fairly common in open, brushy woodlands and fields. Song is a series of clear, plaintive whistles accelerating into a brief trill.

**Rufous-winged
Sparrow**

juvenile

**Rufous-crowned
Sparrow**

coastal

interior

coastal juvenile

juvenile

breeding

winter

**American Tree
Sparrow**

western

eastern juvenile

eastern

**Field
Sparrow**

Chipping Sparrow *Spizella passerina* L 5¹/₂" (14 cm)

Breeding adult identified by bright chestnut crown, broad white eyebrow, and black line from bill through eye to ear; note also gray nape and ear patch, gray, unstreaked rump, and two white wing bars. Tail fairly long, sharply notched. In juvenile plumage, often held into October, crown is grayish-buff and heavily streaked, eyebrow buffy, ear patch brown; upperparts reddish and heavily streaked; rump may show slight streaking; underparts heavily streaked. In first winter, crown acquires some chestnut coloring, breast and sides are tinged with buff. Winter adult's crown is streaked but still shows bright chestnut color; note also brown ear patch. Widespread and common, the Chipping Sparrow is found on lawns, grassy fields, woodland edges. Song is a trill of dry *chip* notes, all on one pitch.

Clay-colored Sparrow *Spizella pallida* L 5¹/₂" (14 cm)

Brown crown with broad black streaks and a distinct buffy-gray central stripe. Broad, whitish eyebrow and whisker stripe; brown ear patch bordered with darker brown. Nape gray; back and scapulars buffy-brown, with dark streaks; rump is not streaked but color does not contrast with back as in Chipping Sparrow. Two whitish wing bars. Tail fairly long, sharply notched. Winter adult is buffier overall. Juvenile and immature birds are much buffier, making gray nape and white whisker stripe more conspicuous; in juvenile, breast and sides are streaked. Fairly common in brushy fields, groves, streamside thickets, prairies. Winters primarily from Mexico south, uncommonly in southern and western Texas. Casual during migration and winter on both coasts and in Arizona. Song is a brief series of insectlike buzzes at the same pitch or varying only slightly.

Brewer's Sparrow *Spizella breweri* L 5¹/₂" (14 cm)

Brown crown with fine black streaks; lacks central buffy-gray stripe of Clay-colored Sparrow. Prominent white eye ring. Buffy-white eyebrow and whisker stripe; ear patch pale brown with darker borders. Upperparts buffy-brown and streaked; rump buffy-brown, may be lightly streaked. Two indistinct pale wing bars. Tail fairly long, sharply notched. Juvenile is buffier overall, lightly streaked on breast and sides. Immatures and winter adults somewhat buffy below. Common; breeds in mountain meadows, sagebrush flats. Song is a series of varied bubbling notes and buzzy trills at different pitches.

Chipping Sparrow

breeding

winter

juvenile

1st winter

Clay-colored Sparrow

immature

breeding

juvenile

Brewer's Sparrow

breeding

juvenile

Black-chinned Sparrow *Spizella atrogularis*

L 5³/₄" (15 cm) Medium gray overall; back and scapulars rusty, with black streaks; bill bright pink. Male has black mask and chin; lower belly is whitish gray; tail all-dark. Female lacks black mask; black on chin is less extensive, duller, or absent. Juvenile and winter adults lack any black on face. Juvenile resembles adult female but underparts are paler and lightly streaked. Inhabits brushy arid slopes, chaparral. Plaintive, whistled song begins with slow *sweet sweet sweet* and continues in a rapid trill. Call is a high, sharp *tslip*.

Dark-eyed Junco *Junco hyemalis* *L 6¹/₄" (16 cm)*

Variable; most forms have a gray or brown head and breast sharply set off from white belly. White outer tail feathers are conspicuous in flight. Formerly separated into four species. Male of the widespread "Slate-colored" form has a dark gray hood and upperparts; female is brownish-gray. Winters mostly in eastern U. S.; very uncommon in the west. Male "Oregon Junco" of the west has blackish hood, reddish-brown back, buffy-orange sides; females generally drabber, browner. Pink-sided form of "Oregon Junco" breeding in the central Rockies has bright pinkish-cinnamon sides, blue-gray hood and black lores. "Oregon" types winter mainly in the west; casual during winter in the east. The "White-winged" form breeding in the Black Hills area is blue-gray above, usually with two white wing bars. In the "Gray-headed Junco" of the southern Rockies, pale gray hood is barely darker than underparts; back is bright rufous. In Arizona and much of New Mexico, "Gray-headed" form has an even paler throat and a large, bicolored bill, black above, bluish below. Intergrades of some forms are common. Dark-eyed Juncos breed in coniferous or mixed woodlands. In migration and winter, found in a wide variety of habitats. Song is a musical trill on one pitch. Varied calls include a sharp *dit* and, in flight, a rapid twittering.

Yellow-eyed Junco *Junco phaeonotus* *L 6¹/₄" (16 cm)*

Bright yellow eyes, set off by black lores. Pale gray above, with reddish back, reddish wing coverts and tertials; underparts paler gray. Compare especially with "Gray-headed" forms of Dark-eyed Junco. Juvenile Yellow-eyed is like reddish-backed forms of Dark-eyed Junco; eye is brown, becoming pale before changing to yellow of adult. Yellow-eyed Junco is found on coniferous and pine-oak slopes, generally above 6,000 feet. Song is a series of clear whistles and trills.

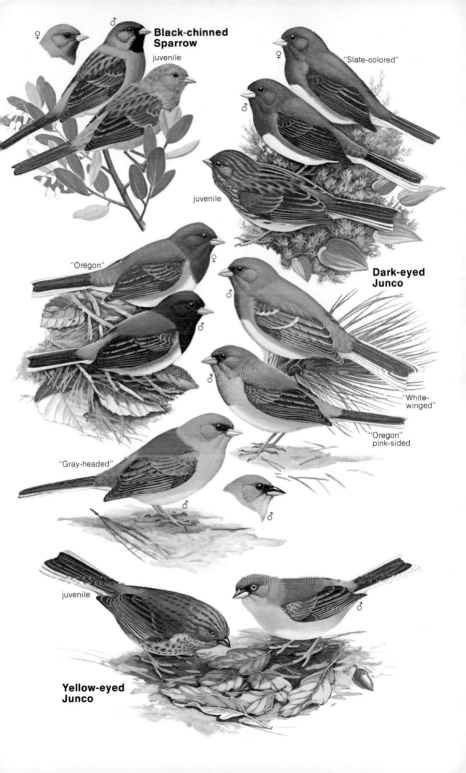

Black-chinned Sparrow

♀

♂

juvenile

juvenile

♀

"Slate-colored"

♂

Dark-eyed Junco

"Oregon"

♀

♂

♂

"White-winged"

♂

"Oregon" pink-sided

"Gray-headed"

♂

♂

juvenile

♂

Yellow-eyed Junco

Harris' Sparrow *Zonotrichia querula* *L 7¹/₂" (19 cm)*

Black crown, face, and bib; pink bill. Winter adult's crown is blackish; cheeks buffy; throat may be all-black or show white flecks, patches, or partial white band. Immature has broad buff eyebrows; white throat bordered by dark whisker stripe and dark necklace on upper breast. Fairly common; nests in stunted boreal forest; winters in open woodlands, brushlands. Casual winter visitor to rest of U. S. outside of mapped range. Song is a series of long, clear, quavering whistles, often beginning with two notes on one pitch followed by two notes on a different pitch. Calls include a loud *wink* or *seep*.

White-throated Sparrow *Zonotrichia albicollis*

L 6³/₄" (17 cm) Conspicuous white throat; mostly dark bill; dark stripes on crown; dark eye line; yellow spot between eye and bill. Broad stripe above eye may be white or tan. Upperparts rusty-brown; breast and sides gray, belly white. Juvenile's throat is grayish-white, breast and sides streaked, head stripes brown. Immature resembles adult of tan-striped phase. Common in woodland undergrowth, brush, gardens. Hunched, short-necked posture is unlike the more erect posture of White-crowned Sparrow. Song is a quavering, thin whistle, generally two single notes followed by three triple notes: *pure sweet Canada Canada Canada*. Calls include a lisping *tseet*.

White-crowned Sparrow *Zonotrichia leucophrys*

L 7" (18 cm) Black-and-white striped crown; pink or yellowish bill; chin whitish; underparts gray. Juvenile's head is brown and buff, underparts streaked. Immature Whitecrown's eye is bordered above by pale stripe; compare with immature Golden-crowned Sparrow. Forms of the High Sierra and Rockies and the Canadian tundra, such as *Z.l. leucophrys,* have black lores, large pink bill; *gambelii,* ranging from Alaska to Hudson Bay, has white lores and a smaller, yellower bill; breast and nape of *nuttalli,* a coastal form, are browner, bill and stripes on back darker, lores whitish. Common in open woodlands, brushy grasslands, roadsides, parks. Song variable; usually one or more thin whistled notes followed by a twittering trill.

Golden-crowned Sparrow *Zonotrichia atricapilla*

L 7" (18 cm) Yellow patch tops black crown; back brownish, streaked with dark brown; breast, sides and flanks grayish-brown; belly whitish. Bill dusky above, pale below. Yellow crown is less distinct on immature's brown head; throat may have small white patch. Briefly held juvenile plumage shows blackish streaks on breast and sides. Winter adults are duller overall; extent and intensity of black on crown vary. The Goldencrown is fairly common in alpine meadows, streamside thickets, boreal bogs. Winters in dense woodlands, tangles, and brush. Very rare winter visitor to the east. Song is a series of three or more raspy, whistled notes: *oh dear me.*

Harris' Sparrow

breeding

winter

winter

immature

White-throated Sparrow

juvenile

tan-striped phase

white-striped phase

juvenile

gambelii

nuttalli

leucophrys

White-crowned Sparrow

immature

Golden-crowned Sparrow

juvenile

immature

winter

breeding

Fox Sparrow *Passerella iliaca L 7" (18 cm)*
Highly variable. Most subspecies have reddish rump; reddish tail; reddish in wings; underparts heavily marked with triangular spots merging into a larger spot on central breast. Compare with Hermit Thrush (page 326); note especially bill shapes. Common; found in dense undergrowth in coniferous or mixed woodlands, chaparral. Loud, rich song, usually a few clear whistles followed by varied short buzzy trills. Reddish (fox-colored) subspecies breed across northern Canada and Alaska. The brightest, *P.i. iliaca,* breeds and winters chiefly in the east. The drabbest, *altivagans,* breeds in western Canada on eastern flank of Rockies, winters in the west. Birds of the Sierra and Rockies are grayer overall; smallest billed is the widespread *schistacea;* largest billed, *stephensi,* is resident in southern California. Dark coastal forms range from the sooty *fuliginosa* of the Pacific northwest to the paler *unalaschcensis* of southwest Alaska.

Lincoln's Sparrow *Melospiza lincolnii L 5³/₄" (15 cm)*
Buffy wash and fine streaks on breast and sides, contrasting with whitish, unstreaked belly. Gray central crown stripe, bordered by reddish-brown stripes; broad gray eyebrow; prominent buffy eye ring. Briefly held juvenile plumage is paler above and below than juvenile Swamp Sparrow. Distinguished from juvenile Song Sparrow (page 392) by slimmer bill and buffier underparts. A short-tailed sparrow, found in brushy bogs and mountain meadows; in winter prefers thickets, hedgerows, brambles. Somewhat shy but readily attracted by squeaking noises; often raises slight crest when disturbed. Two call notes: a flat *tschup,* repeated in a series as an alarm call; and a sharp, buzzy *zeee*. Lincoln's and Swamp Sparrow are the only sparrows that give this call. Rich, loud song, a rapid bubbling trill.

Swamp Sparrow *Melospiza georgiana L 5³/₄" (15 cm)*
Rufous in wings and tail contrasts with overall dark graybrown coloring. Breeding adult has reddish crown, white throat, whitish belly. Remainder of underparts gray, with diffuse, blurred streaks. Winter adult is buffier overall; crown is streaked, shows gray central stripe; sides are rich buff. Immature is even buffier than winter adult; this plumage is held through the following summer. Briefly held juvenile plumage is darker overall than juvenile Lincoln's or Song Sparrow; wings and tail redder. Fairly common but shy. Pumps tail in flight as do other *Melospiza* sparrows. Nests in dense, tall vegetation in freshwater marshes, swamps, streams; often feeds in shallow water. Winters in marshes, brushy fields, woodland edges. Typical song is a slow, musical trill, all on one pitch. Two call notes: a prolonged *zeee,* softer than call of Lincoln's Sparrow; and a metallic *chip,* like the call of an Eastern Phoebe.

unalaschcensis

**Fox
Sparrow**

fuliginosa

schistacea

stephensi

altivagans

iliaca

**Lincoln's
Sparrow**
juvenile

breeding

**Swamp
Sparrow**

winter

juvenile

immature

♪ Chestnut-collared Longspur *Calcarius ornatus*

L 6" (15 cm) White tail marked with blackish triangle. Wings short, rounded; in perched bird, wing tips barely extend to base of tail. Breeding adult male's black-and-white head, buffy face, and black underparts are distinctive; a few have chestnut on underparts. Lower belly and undertail coverts whitish. Upperparts black, buff, and brown, with chestnut collar, whitish wing bars. Breeding adult female duller and browner overall; crown streaked; underparts dull buff, with faint streaks on breast and sides. Winter adults are paler; feathers edged in buff and brown, obscuring male's black underparts. Male has small white patch on shoulder; compare with Smith's Longspur. Juvenile's pale feather edgings give upperparts a scaled look; tail pattern and bill shape distinguish juvenile from juvenile McCown's Longspur. Fall and winter birds have grayish, not pinkish, bills. Fairly common; nests in moist upland prairies. Somewhat shy; generally found in dense, tall grass, singly or in small flocks. Song, heard only on breeding grounds, is a pleasant rapid warble, given in song flight or from a low perch. Distinctive call, a two-syllable *kittle*, repeated two to five times. Also gives a soft, high-pitched rattle and a short *buzz* call. Casual during migration and winter on east coast; more common on west coast.

♪ McCown's Longspur *Calcarius mccownii* *L 6" (15 cm)*

White tail marked by dark inverted T-shape. Note also that bill is stouter and thicker based than bills of other longspurs. Wings are pointed; in perched bird, wings extend almost to tip of short tail. Breeding adult male has black crown, black whisker stripe, black crescent on breast. Underparts are otherwise whitish. Upperparts streaked with buff and brown, with gray nape, gray rump, bright chestnut wing patch. Breeding adult female has streaked crown; may lack black on breast and show less chestnut on wing. In winter adults, bill is largely pinkish; feathers are edged with buff and brown. Winter adult female is paler than female Chestnut-collared, with fewer streaks on underparts and a broader buffy eyebrow. Winter male's gray rump is conspicuous. Juvenile resembles adult female but is buffier below, with streaked breast; shows two buffy-white wing bars; pale edgings on feathers give upperparts a scaled look. Tail pattern and bill shape distinguish juvenile from juvenile Chestnut-collared Longspur. Fairly common but has declined; nests in dry shortgrass plains; in winter, also found in plowed fields, dry lake beds, often amid large flocks of Horned Larks. Look for McCown's chunkier, shorter-tailed shape, darker plumage, mostly white tail, thicker bill, and undulating flight. Song, heard only on breeding grounds, is a series of exuberant warbles and twitters, generally given in song flight. Calls include a dry rattle similar to calls of Smith's and Lapland Longspurs. Rare but regular in fall and winter on west coast, very rare on east coast.

Chestnut-collared Longspur

breeding ♂

breeding ♂

winter ♂

winter ♀

McCown's Longspur

breeding ♂

breeding ♀

winter ♀

winter ♂

juvenile

♪ **Smith's Longspur** *Calcarius pictus* L 6¹/₄" (16 cm)
Outer two feathers on each side of tail are almost entirely white. Note also that bill is thinner than in other longspurs. Breeding adult male has black-and-white head, rich buff nape and underparts. Males in all plumages have white patch on shoulder; compare with Chestnut-collared Longspur (preceding page). Breeding adult female and all winter plumages are duller; crown streaked; underparts pale buff with thin reddish-brown streaks on breast and sides; chin paler; dusky ear patch is bordered by pale buff eyebrow. Uncommon, solitary, and highly secretive, especially in winter. Nests on open tundra and damp, tussocky meadows. Winters in open, grassy areas; sometimes seen with Lapland Longspurs. Rare vagrant on east coast from Massachusetts to South Carolina. Typical call note is a dry, ticking rattle, similar to the call of Lapland and McCown's Longspurs. Song, heard only on the breeding grounds, combines ticking notes and rapid, melodious warbles, ending with a vigorous *wee-chew*.

♪ **Lapland Longspur** *Calcarius lapponicus* L 6¹/₄" (16 cm)
Outer two feathers on each side of tail are partly white, partly dark. Note also, especially in winter plumages, the reddish edges on tertials and greater coverts. Breeding adult male's head and breast are black; broad white or buffy stripe extends back from eye and down to sides of breast; nape reddish-brown. Breeding adult female and all winter plumages are duller; note dark triangle outlining buffy ear patch, dark streaks or patch on upper breast, dark streaks on side. On all winter birds, note broad buffy eyebrow. Immature female is buffy below, but belly and undertail are whiter than in Smith's Longspur; also compare head and wing patterns. Juvenile is yellowish and heavily streaked above and on breast and sides. Fairly common, Lapland Longspurs breed on arctic tundra, winter in grassy fields, grain stubble, and on shores. Often found amid flocks of Horned Larks and Snow Buntings; look for Lapland's darker overall coloring and smaller size. Song, heard only on the breeding grounds, is a rapid warbling, given chiefly in short flights. Calls include a musical *tee-lee-oo* and, in flight, a dry rattle distinctively mixed with *tew* notes.

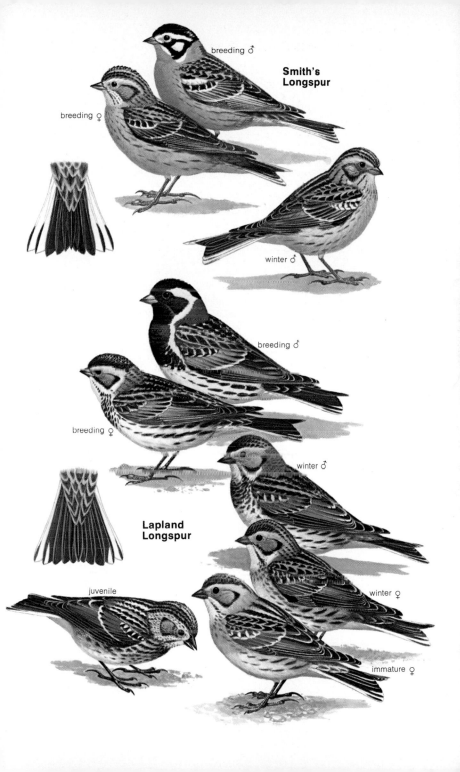

Smith's
Longspur

breeding ♂

breeding ♀

winter ♂

Lapland
Longspur

breeding ♂

breeding ♀

winter ♂

winter ♀

juvenile

immature ♀

Snow Bunting *Plectrophenax nivalis* L 6¾" (17 cm)
Rust and pale edgings of adult winter plumage wear off by
spring, producing black-and-white breeding plumage. Bill is
black in summer, orange-yellow in winter. In all seasons, note
long black-and-white wings. Males show more white overall
than females, especially in wings. Juvenile is grayish and
streaked, with buff eye ring; very similar in the field to juvenile
McKay's Bunting. First-winter plumage, acquired before migration, is darker overall than adult; rust and brown edges
wear away by spring to full adult plumage. Common and gregarious, Snow Buntings breed on tundra, rocky shores, talus
slopes. During migration and winter, found on shores and in
weedy fields, grain stubble, along roadsides, often in large
flocks that may include Lapland Longspurs and Horned
Larks. Calls include a sharp, whistled *tew*, a short buzz, and a
musical rattle or twitter. Song, heard only on the breeding
grounds, is a loud, high-pitched musical warbling.

McKay's Bunting *Plectrophenax hyperboreus*
L 6¾" (17 cm)   Adult breeding plumage mostly white, with less
black on wings and tail than on Snow Bunting. Winter plumage edged with rust or tawny-brown, but still whiter overall
than Snow Bunting. Juvenile is buffy-gray and streaked, with
gray head, prominent buff eye ring; very similar in the field to
juvenile Snow Bunting. McKay's Bunting is known to breed
only on a few islands in the Bering Sea. Rare in winter along
west coast of Alaska; casual in winter southward and on Aleutians. Calls and song similar to Snow Bunting. Some authorities consider McKay's to be a subspecies of Snow Bunting.

Rustic Bunting *Emberiza rustica* L 5¾" (15 cm)
Eurasian species; winters in China and Japan; casual spring
visitor on St. Lawrence Island; uncommon spring migrant on
western and central Aleutians, rare in fall. Breeding male's
black head is slightly crested, marked with whitish nape spot,
whitish line extending back from eye. Upperparts bright
chestnut, streaked on back with buff and blackish; outer tail
feathers white. Underparts white, with chestnut breast band,
streaks on sides. Female and fall and winter males have
brownish head pattern. Female may be confused with Little
Bunting (next page); note Rustic Bunting's larger size, heavier bill with pink lower mandible, lack of eye ring, and rusty, diffuse streaking below. Call note, a hard, sharp *jit* or *tsip*. Song,
a soft, bubbling warble.

breeding ♂

breeding ♂

winter ♀

breeding ♀

winter ♂

juvenile

Snow Bunting

winter ♀

winter ♂

breeding ♀

McKay's Bunting

breeding ♂

breeding ♂

winter ♂

Rustic Bunting

♀

breeding ♂

Common Reed-Bunting *Emberiza schoeniclus*

L 6" (15 cm) Eurasian species, rare vagrant on Aleutians in late spring. Solid chestnut lesser wing coverts distinctive in all plumages. Note also heavy bill, with strongly curved culmen. Male in breeding plumage has black head and throat, broad white whisker stripe, white nape; upperparts streaked black and rust, rump gray. Underparts white with reddish streaks along sides and flanks. Female has pale brownish rump, broad buffy-white eyebrow; dark lower border on ear patch extends forward to lower mandible; compare with female Pallas' Reed-Bunting. Fall male resembles female, but shows black on throat and a more distinct collar. Active and conspicuous, the Common Reed-Bunting often flicks and fans its tail, showing white outer tail feathers. Song is a series of squeaky notes, *tweak tweak tweak tititick*. Distinctive call, a clear, plaintive, upslurred *tseep*.

Pallas' Reed-Bunting *Emberiza pallasi* *L 5¹/₂" (14 cm)*

Asian species, very rare spring vagrant in northwest Alaska. Distinguished from Common Reed-Bunting by smaller, straighter bill, grayish lesser wing coverts. Breeding male has black and pearl gray streaks on back, two whitish wing bars. Female's buffy-brown ear patch usually has dark border only on lower rear corner. Like the Common Reed-Bunting, Pallas' often flicks and fans its tail, showing white outer feathers; note that tail is shorter than in Common Reed-Bunting. Song is a series of double notes, *tsi-tsi tsi-tsi tsi-tsi*. Distinctive call, a three-note *pee-see-oo*.

Little Bunting *Emberiza pusilla* *L 4³/₄" (12 cm)*

Eurasian species, very rare fall vagrant on Aleutians and off northwest Alaska. A small, short-legged, short-tailed bunting, with a small triangular bill, bold creamy-white eye ring, chestnut ear patch, two thin pale wing bars. Underparts whitish and heavily streaked with black in adults. Outer tail feathers are white, but this species does not usually fan its tail. In breeding plumage, shows chestnut crown stripe bordered by black stripes. Some males show chestnut on chin. Immatures and winter adults have chestnut crown, tipped and streaked with buff and black. Compare especially with female Rustic Bunting (preceding page) and female Common Reed-Bunting. Call note is a sharp *tsick*.

Gray Bunting *Emberiza variabilis* *L 6³/₄" (17 cm)*

Asian species, very rare spring vagrant on western Aleutians. A large, heavy-billed bunting; shows no white in tail. Breeding male is gray overall, prominently streaked with blackish above. Winter males are a bit browner above, paler below. Female is browner; chestnut rump is conspicuous in flight. Immature male resembles adult female above but is mostly gray below with some gray on head; immature plumage is held through first spring.

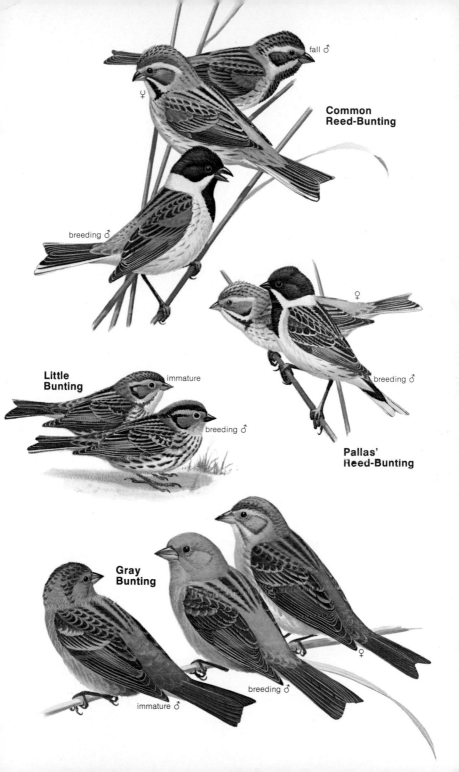

Common Reed-Bunting

♀

fall ♂

breeding ♂

Little Bunting

immature

breeding ♂

♀

breeding ♂

Pallas' Reed-Bunting

Gray Bunting

immature ♂

breeding ♂

♀

Black-faced Grassquit *Tiaris bicolor* *L 4¹/₂" (11 cm)*
West Indian species; rare stray in south Florida. Adult male mostly black below, dark olive above; head is black. Female and immatures pale gray below, gray-olive above. Song is a buzzing *tik-zeee;* call, a lisping *tst*. Might be seen amid winter flocks of Indigo Buntings.

White-collared Seedeater *Sporophila torqueola*
L 4¹/₂" (11 cm) Mexican species, casual fall and winter visitor to lower Rio Grande Valley; formerly more common and resident there. Tiny finch with thick, short bill, strongly curved; round-ed tail. Adult male is blackish and brown above, with incomplete buffy collar, often indistinct; two white wing bars; white patch at base of primaries; underparts bright buff. Female and immatures are paler below, lack cap and collar; wing bars are buffy. Bill and tail shape and buffy eye ring distinguish them from female Lazuli Bunting (page 384). Found in open grassy areas, brushlands. Song is pitched high, then low, a variable *sweet sweet sweet sweet cheer cheer cheer*. Calls include a loud, sharp *wink*.

Dickcissel *Spiza americana* *L 6¹/₄" (16 cm)*
Yellowish eyebrow, thick bill, and chestnut wing coverts identify this finch in all plumages. Breeding adult male has black bib under white chin, bright yellow breast. Breeding adult female lacks black bib, but has some yellow on breast; chestnut wing patch muted. Winter adult male has gray bib. Immatures are duller overall than adults, flanks lightly streaked; lack bib; female may show almost no yellow or chestnut. The Dickcissel breeds in open weedy meadows, grainfields, prairies. Abundant and gregarious, especially in migration, but numbers vary locally from year to year. Occurrence east of the Appalachians is spotty; population there is shrinking, although occasional breeding is reported north and south of area on map. Casual migrant and winter visitor to both coasts; more common in east; seen chiefly at feeders. Common call, often given in flight, is a distinctive electric-buzzer *bzrrrrt*. Song, a variable *dick dick dickcissel*.

Lark Bunting *Calamospiza melanocorys* *L 7" (18 cm)*
Breeding adult male is mostly black, with contrasting white patch on inner wings and under tip of tail; bill is heavy, bluish-gray. Female is streaked grayish-brown above; white below, with brown streaks, buffy sides; wing patch buffy. Immatures resemble adult female. Winter adult male looks similar, but grayer overall; retains black on chin. Over the winter, white on underparts is replaced by black; some spring males are patchy looking. In all plumages, a stocky, short-tailed bird, common in dry plains and prairies, especially in sagebrush. Distinctive call is a soft *hoo-ee*. Song, a varied series of rich whistles and trills, given from a perch or in hovering song flight. Casual in fall and winter on both coasts.

Black-faced Grassquit ♀ ♂

White-collared Seedeater ♀ ♂

breeding ♂

Dickcissel

breeding ♂

breeding ♀

early spring ♂

winter ♂

winter ♂

immature ♀

immature ♂

Lark Bunting ♀

Blackbirds and Orioles

Strong, direct flight and pointed bills mark this diverse group. Its members vary in plumage from iridescent black to yellow to brilliant orange. They frequent a wide variety of habitats.

Bobolink *Dolichonyx oryzivorus* L 7" (18 cm)
Breeding male entirely black below; hindneck is buff, fading to whitish by midsummer; scapulars and rump white. Male in spring migration shows pale edgings, remnants of midwinter molt. Breeding female is buffy overall, with dark streaks on back, rump, and sides; head is striped with dark brown. Juvenile resembles female but lacks streaking below. Fall adult and immatures resemble breeding female but are darker above, richer buff below. In all plumages, note sharply pointed tail feathers. Bobolinks nest primarily in hayfields, weedy meadows, where male's loud, bubbling *bob-o-link* song, often given in flight, is heard in spring. Flight call heard in migration is a repeated *ink*. Most birds migrate east of Great Plains; winter in South America.

♪ **Eastern Meadowlark** *Sturnella magna* L 9¹/₂" (24 cm)
Black V-shaped breast band on yellow underparts; upperparts dark, with dusky edges. In fresh fall plumage, edges are broad, obscuring black back and breast band; worn summer birds show fewer edges. Eastern Meadowlarks vary from the bright *S.m. argutula* of the southeast to the paler, grayer birds of the southwest, such as *lilianae*, which most closely resemble Western Meadowlark. Note that in *lilianae* tail shows more white than in Western Meadowlark. Eastern Meadowlarks in general are best distinguished from Westerns by voice. Eastern's song is a clear, whistled *see-you see-yeeer;* distinctive call is a buzzy *drzzt;* also gives a rattling flight call. Eastern Meadowlark is usually darker and more richly colored; dark crown stripes are more solid; cheeks gray. Eastern Meadowlarks are common; found in fields, meadows; generally prefer moister habitats than Western Meadowlark.

♪ **Western Meadowlark** *Sturnella neglecta* L 9¹/₂" (24 cm)
Black V-shaped breast band on yellow underparts; upperparts dark, with dusky edges. Plumages parallel those of Eastern Meadowlark; best distinguished by voice. Western Meadowlark's distinctive call note is a low, throaty, explosive *chuck;* also gives a rattling flight call. Song is a variable series of bubbling, flutelike notes, accelerating toward the end. Western is usually paler and grayer than Eastern; cheeks show more extensive yellow. Outer tail feathers show less white. Hybrids occur in zone of range overlap. Western Meadowlarks are common; found in fields and meadows, generally preferring drier habitat than Eastern Meadowlark. Range is expanding in the northeast.

early spring ♂

Bobolink

breeding ♂

breeding ♀

fall

juvenile

argutula fall

Eastern Meadowlark

argutula breeding

argutula juvenile

lilianae breeding

Western Meadowlark

argutula

lilianae

breeding

Yellow-headed Blackbird

Xanthocephalus xanthocephalus *L 9¹/₂" (24 cm)* Adult male's yellow head and breast, white wing patch contrast sharply with black body. Adult female is dusky-brown, lacks wing patch; color of eyebrow, lower cheek, and throat varies from yellow to buffy; belly streaked with white. Juvenile is dark brown with buffy edgings on back and wing; head mostly tawny. First-winter male resembles female but yellows are deeper, wing coverts tipped with white. Locally common throughout most of range, Yellowheads prefer freshwater marshes or reedy lakes; often seen foraging in open farmlands, grainfields. Song begins with harsh, rasping note, ends with a long, descending buzz. Call note is a hoarse *croak*. Regular fall and winter visitor to east coast. Casual in spring and fall as far north as southern Alaska.

♪ Red-winged Blackbird *Agelaius phoeniceus*

L 8³/₄" (22 cm) Glossy black male has red shoulder patches broadly tipped with buff-yellow. In perched birds, red patch can be hard to see; only yellow or whitish border shows. Females are dark brown above, heavily streaked below; sometimes show a red tinge on wing coverts or pinkish wash on chin and throat. First-year male plumage is distinguished from female Tricolored Blackbird by large reddish shoulder patch. Males of the central California form, called "Bicolored Blackbird," have pure red shoulder patches with no border; females are darker, more like spring Tricolored Blackbird. Redwing's song is a liquid, gurgling *konk-la-reee,* ending in a trill. Most common call is a *chack* note. This abundant, aggressive species is found in immense flocks in winter. Generally nests in thick vegetation of freshwater marshes, sloughs, dry fields; forages in surrounding fields, orchards, woodlands. Casual in summer as far north as northern Alaska and Mackenzie.

♪ Tricolored Blackbird *Agelaius tricolor* *L 8³/₄" (22 cm)*

Red shoulder patches broadly tipped with white identify glossy black male over most of year; tips are buffy-white in fresh fall plumage. Females show varying amounts of red on shoulder; plumage is sooty-brown and streaked overall; streaking on underparts is usually more diffuse than in female Red-winged Blackbird, but identification is extremely difficult. Tricolored Blackbird gives a variety of calls much like Redwing calls; harsh, braying *on-ke-kaaangh* song lacks Redwing's liquid tones. Commonly found in large flocks foraging in wet meadows, rice fields, rangelands; nests in large colonies in marshes.

Yellow-headed Blackbird

juvenile

♀

♂

1st winter ♂

1st year ♂

immature ♀

♀

Red-winged Blackbird

♀

"Bicolored Blackbird"

♂

fall ♀

♂

spring ♀

Tricolored Blackbird

♂

Rusty Blackbird   *Euphagus carolinus*   L 9" (23 cm)

All adults have yellow eyes. Fall adult and immature plumages are broadly tipped with rust; tertials edged with rust. Female in fall shows broad, buffy eyebrow, buffy underparts. Fall male is darker overall; eyebrow usually less distinct. The rusty feather tips wear off by spring, producing the black breeding plumage. Male has a faint greenish gloss overall; female is grayer. Juveniles resemble winter adults. Fairly common; prefers wet woodlands, bogs, swamps. Nests in shrubs or conifers near water. In fall and winter, forms large flocks with grackles and other blackbirds. Common call is a harsh *tschak;* song, a high, squeaky *koo-a-lee*. Casual in fall and winter west of mapped range; rare in southern Florida.

Brewer's Blackbird   *Euphagus cyanocephalus*

L 9" (23 cm)   Male has yellow eyes; female's are brown. Male is black year round, with purplish gloss on head and neck, greenish gloss on body and wings. A few fall males show some rusty feather edgings, but never as rusty as in Rusty Blackbird and never on tertials. Female and juveniles are gray-brown. Common in a variety of habitats; forages in large flocks with other blackbirds. Nests in farm fields, prairies, trees, brush. Typical call is a harsh *check;* song, a wheezy *que-ee* or *k-seee*. Scattered populations breed throughout the central Great Plains. Rare but regular winter visitor in the northeast.

Brown-headed Cowbird   *Molothrus ater*   L 7½" (19 cm)

Small blackbird with stubby bill. Male's brown head contrasts with metallic green-black body. Female is gray-brown above, paler below. Juvenile is paler than adult female and more heavily streaked below. Pale feather edgings give a scaled look to its back. As young males molt to adult plumage in late summer, they show a patchy pattern of buff, brown, and iridescent black. Increasingly common, Brown-headed Cowbirds are found in open woodlands, farmlands, suburbs, city parks; often forage in mixed flocks. Eggs are laid in the nests of other species. Male's song is a squeaky gurgling. Calls include a harsh rattle and squeaky whistles. Western birds are distinctly smaller than eastern birds.

Bronzed Cowbird   *Molothrus aeneus*   L 8¾" (22 cm)

Red eyes distinctive at close range. Adult male is black overall, with bronze gloss; wings and tail blue-black. Thick ruff on nape and back give male a hunchbacked look. Adult female of the Texas form, *M.a. aeneus*, is duller and blacker than male; juveniles are dark brown. In southwestern form, *milleri*, female and juveniles are much grayer than adult male. Locally common in open country, farmlands, brushy areas; forages in large flocks. Typical call is a harsh, guttural *chuck*. Song is a wheezier, shorter version of Brown-headed Cowbird's gurgling song. Formerly known as Red-eyed Cowbird.

Rusty Blackbird

fall ♀

fall ♂

breeding ♀

breeding ♂

fall variant ♂

Brewer's Blackbird

♀

♂

♀

molting juvenile ♂

juvenile

Brown-headed Cowbird

♂

milleri ♀

aeneus juvenile

aeneus ♀

♂

Bronzed Cowbird

Common Grackle *Quiscalus quiscula* L 12¹/₂″ (32 cm)
Long, keel-shaped tail, pale yellow eyes. Plumage appears all-black at a distance. In good light, males show glossy purplish head, neck, and breast. Birds in New England and west of the Appalachians and in Florida have bronze sheen on rest of body; east of the Appalachians they show more purple overall, mixed with brownish. Females are smaller and duller than males. Juveniles are sooty-brown, with brown eyes. Common Grackles are abundant and gregarious, roaming in mixed flocks in open fields, pastures, marshes, parks, and suburban areas. Song is a distinctive short, creaky *koguba-leek;* call note, a loud *chuck.* Casual visitor to Pacific states and Alaska, primarily in spring.

Boat-tailed Grackle *Quiscalus major*
♂ L 16¹/₂″ (42 cm) ♀ 14¹/₂″ (37 cm) A large grackle with very long, keel-shaped tail. Adult male is iridescent blue-black. Adult female is tawny-brown with darker wings and tail. Eye color varies from yellow in Atlantic coast birds to brown in Florida birds. Gulf coast birds are intermediate, with brown or dull yellow eyes. Juvenile males are black but lack iridescence; young females are brown but show a hint of spotting or streaking on breast. Juveniles resemble respective adults by mid-fall. In narrow zone of overlap between their ranges, Boat-taileds can be confused with Great-tailed Grackles. Generally, Boat-taileds are smaller and have brown eyes; crown is more rounded. Calls include a quiet *chuck* and a variety of rough squeaks, rattles, and other chatter. Most common song is a series of harsh *jeeb* notes. This common, noisy grackle seldom strays beyond coastal saltwater marshes, except in Florida where it inhabits inland lakes and streams. Range is expanding northward on Atlantic coast.

Great-tailed Grackle *Quiscalus mexicanus*
♂ L 18″ (46 cm) ♀ L 15″ (38 cm) A large grackle with very long, keel-shaped tail, golden yellow eyes. Adult male is iridescent black with purple sheen on head, back, and underparts. Adult female's upperparts are brown; underparts cinnamon buff on breast to grayish-brown on belly; shows less iridescence than male. Juveniles resemble respective adults but are even less glossy and show some streaking on underparts. Juvenile males are like adult males by mid-fall. Females west of central Arizona are smaller, males are paler below, than eastern birds. In narrow zone of range overlap, Great-tailed Grackles can be confused with Boat-tailed Grackles. Great-taileds always have yellow eyes and are usually larger, with a flatter crown. Varied calls include clear whistles and loud *clack*s. Common, especially in open flatlands with scattered groves of trees and in marshes, wetlands. Casual far north of breeding range; rapidly expanding north and west.

Common Grackle

purple ♂ bronze ♂ juvenile

juvenile ♀

Boat-tailed Grackle

juvenile ♂

♀

♂

Great-tailed Grackle

juvenile ♀

♀

♂

western ♀

Scott's Oriole *Icterus parisorum* L 9" (23 cm)

Adult male's black hood extends to back and breast; rump, wing patch, and remainder of underparts lemon yellow. Adult female is yellowish-olive and streaked above, dull greenish-yellow below; throat shows some black. First-fall birds resemble adult female; immature male shows black throat by first spring. Females and immatures average more streaking above and are grayer and larger overall than female Orchard Oriole. Common in arid and semiarid habitats. Call note is a harsh *shack;* song, a mixture of rich, whistled phrases, suggestive of Western Meadowlark. A few Scott's Orioles winter in southern California deserts.

Orchard Oriole *Icterus spurius* L 7¹/₄" (18 cm)

Adult male is chestnut above and below, with black hood. Adult female is dull olive above, with two white wing bars; greenish-yellow below. Immatures resemble adult female; immature male has black bib and, sometimes, traces of chestnut by first spring. Lack of orange tones distinguishes female and immatures from most plumages of Northern Oriole. Locally common in suburban shade trees, orchards, streamside groves. Calls include a sharp *chuck*. Song is a loud, rapid burst of varied whistled notes, downslurred at the end. Casual migrant in Arizona and coastal California.

Audubon's Oriole *Icterus graduacauda* L 9¹/₂" (24 cm)

Tropical species, resident but uncommon in southern Texas. Male distinguished from Scott's Oriole by greenish-yellow back. Female is slightly duller. Secretive; generally seen foraging on ground. Song is a series of soft, three-note warbles. Formerly called Black-headed Oriole.

Northern Oriole *Icterus galbula* L 8³/₄" (22 cm)

Formerly considered two species: "Baltimore Oriole," *I.g. galbula,* in the east; "Bullock's Oriole," now *I.g. bullockii,* in the west. Adult male "Baltimore" has black hood and upper back, bright orange rump and underparts; black tail has large orange patches on outer feathers. Adult male "Bullock's" differs by having large white wing patch, orange face with black eye line. Adult female "Bullock's" is gray-olive above; head and breast pale yellow; belly whitish. Adult female "Baltimore" is brownish-olive above, with blackish markings on head; underparts dull orange, palest on belly. Young male "Baltimore" resembles adult female but is brighter. First-fall female is duller, grayer above, lacks black markings on head. Young male "Bullock's" resembles female; shows some black on throat by first fall. The two subspecies interbreed in zone of range overlap in the Great Plains. Northern Orioles are common in open woodlands, river groves, suburban shade trees. Typical call of eastern form is a rich *hew-li;* song is a musical, irregular series of *hew-li* and other notes. Western form's common call is an emphatic *skip;* song is like eastern form's but less varied and somewhat harsher.

1st fall ♀

Scott's Oriole

♀

1st spring ♂

♂

♀

1st spring ♂

♂

Orchard Oriole

Audubon's Oriole

1st fall ♀

Northern Oriole

"Baltimore Oriole" ♀

♂

"Bullock's Oriole"

♀

"Baltimore"-"Bullock's" Intergrade ♂

♪ **Hooded Oriole** *Icterus cucullatus* *L 8″ (20 cm)*
Breeding male is orange or yellow-orange with black upper back, wings, and tail; black patch extending from lores to throat; two whitish wing bars, the upper bar broader. Forms vary in intensity of color. Males in western Texas are brightest orange; coastal California birds are palest. Texas birds show black on forehead. In all forms, winter plumage is duller; buffy-brown tips on black back form a barred pattern; compare with Streak-backed Oriole. Adult female Hooded Oriole lacks paler underparts of Northern Oriole (preceding page); bill is longer and more curved than in Orchard Oriole. Juveniles resemble adult female. Immature male shows black lores and throat by first winter. Hooded Orioles are common in varied habitats; found especially around palms. Breeding range is expanding northward on west coast. Calls include a sharp *eek* and a whistled, rising *wheet*. Song is a rapid series of throaty whistles, trills, and rattles.

Streak-backed Oriole *Icterus pustulatus* *L 8¹/₄″ (21 cm)*
Mexican species, casual fall and winter visitor to southeastern Arizona; very rare in southern California. Distinguished from winter Hooded Oriole by streaked, not barred, upper back; deeper orange head; and thicker based, straighter bill. Female is duller than male. Immatures resemble adult female, but immature female lacks black on throat. *Wheet* call is softer than Hooded Oriole's call and does not rise in pitch. Other calls resemble those of Northern Oriole (preceding page). Formerly known as Scarlet-headed Oriole.

Altamira Oriole *Icterus gularis* *L 10″ (25 cm)*
Distinguished from Hooded Oriole by larger size, thicker based bill, and orange or yellowish lesser and median wing coverts, forming a distinct shoulder patch. Lower wing bar whitish. Immatures are yellower than adults; acquire full adult plumage by first summer. Resident but rare and local in south Texas; found chiefly in groves of tall trees, willows, mesquite. Calls include a low, raspy *ike ike ike*. Song is a series of clear, varied whistles. Formerly known as Lichtenstein's Oriole.

Spot-breasted Oriole *Icterus pectoralis* *L 9¹/₂″ (24 cm)*
Mexican and Central American species, introduced and now resident in southern Florida. Adults have orange or yellow-orange shoulder patch; black lores and throat; dark spots on upper breast; extensive white on wings. Young birds are yellower overall; immatures may lack breast spots. Found in gardens, open woodlands. Florida population is apparently stable but not expanding. Song is a long, loud series of melodic whistles.

Hooded Oriole

breeding ♂

winter ♂

1st spring ♂

♀

Orchard Oriole ♀ for comparison

♂

♀

Streak-backed Oriole

Immature ♀

immature

Altamira Oriole

Spot-breasted Oriole

immature

♪ **Scarlet Tanager** *Piranga olivacea* *L 7" (18 cm)*
Bright red body with black wings and tail marks breeding
male. During late summer and fall, male shows splotchy green
and red as he molts to yellow-green winter plumage. Female is
distinguished from other female tanagers by uniformly olive
head, back, and rump; whitish wing linings. Immature male
Scarlet Tanager resembles female, but is brighter below, with
brownish primaries retained through first summer; wing coverts are black. Some immatures show faint wing bars; compare with bold wing bars of Western Tanager. Robin-like song
of raspy notes, *querit queer query querit queer,* heard in deciduous forests where Scarlet Tanager is a common summer
inhabitant. Call note, a low *chip-burr.* Winters in South America; casual migrant in the west.

Western Tanager *Piranga ludoviciana* *L 7¹/₄" (18 cm)*
Look for this species' conspicuous wing bars: upper bar yellow, lower bar pale yellow or whitish. Male's red head becomes
yellowish in winter. Note female's saddleback pattern: grayish
back contrasting with greenish-yellow nape and rump. Some
females are duller below, grayer above. Thicker bill shape
helps distinguish female tanagers from female orioles (pages
426, 428). Common summer inhabitant of coniferous mountain forests. Winters primarily from central Mexico south, but
casual to uncommon in winter as far north as southern Oregon. Rare but regular along the Gulf and Atlantic coasts, especially in winter.

♪ **Summer Tanager** *Piranga rubra* *L 7³/₄" (20 cm)*
Adult male is rosy red year round. Lacks black wings and tail of
Scarlet Tanager. First-spring males are patchy green and red;
full adult plumage is acquired in second fall. Some eastern females also show reddish coloring. In most females, plumage
varies from mustard to gold below, with darker olive tinge
above. Western birds are larger and paler; females generally
grayer above than eastern females. Song is robin-like; call, a
staccato *ki-ti-tuck.* Common in pine-oak woods in the east,
cottonwood groves in the west. Range is slowly shrinking in
the east; casual migrant north of summer range. Regular in
winter in southern California.

♪ **Hepatic Tanager** *Piranga flava* *L 8" (20 cm)*
Large grayish cheek patch, gray wash on flanks set off brighter
throat, breast, and cap in both sexes. Male retains dull red
plumage year round. Juvenile resembles yellow-and-gray female but is heavily streaked overall; immature male sometimes shows a touch of red on crown and underparts. Song
hoarse, robin-like. Call note, a single low *chuck,* easily mistak-
en for Hermit Thrush's call. Inhabits mountain forests, usually conifers mixed with oaks. Similar western form of Summer
Tanager is usually found in lower valleys close to water.

Scarlet Tanager

♀

winter ♂

molting ♂

breeding ♂

Western Tanager

♀

♀

winter ♂

breeding ♂

eastern ♀

Summer Tanager

western ♀

eastern ♀

western ♂

Hepatic Tanager

♀

♂

juvenile

Stripe-headed Tanager *Spindalis zena* L 6³/₄″ (17 cm)
West Indian species, casual visitor from Bahamas to southern
Florida. Brightly patterned male has two white stripes on black
head; chestnut collar and rump; thick bill. Female very plain,
with small white square patch at base of primaries.

Bananaquit *Coereba flaveola* L 4¹/₂″ (11 cm)
Tropical species; casual visitor from the Bahamas to southern
Florida. Note thin, downcurved bill. Adult has conspicuous
white eyebrow, yellow rump; underparts white, with yellow
breast; small white wing patch. Immature is duller; eyebrow
and yellowish rump less conspicuous.

Weaver Finches (Family Estrildidae)

Generally small seedeaters
known for their untidy nests.
Plumages range from red to
green to dull brown. One
species introduced into our
region from southeast Asia.

Java Sparrow *Padda oryzivora* L 6″ (15 cm)
Resident of Java. Introduced and breeding locally around Miami, Florida. Note massive pink bill; large white cheek patch;
red eye ring; wine red wash on flanks, belly. Immature is
brownish, with buffy-white throat and belly.

Weavers (Family Passeridae)

A large Old World family.
Two species have been
successfully introduced
in North America. Resemble
native sparrows but have
shorter legs, thicker bills.

Eurasian Tree Sparrow *Passer montanus* L 6″ (15 cm)
Old World species, introduced and now locally common in
parks, suburbs, and farmlands around St. Louis, Missouri, and
in nearby Illinois. Brown crown, black ear patch, and black
throat distinguish adult. Compare with House Sparrow's gray
crown and more extensively black throat. Juvenile has dark
mottling on crown, dark gray throat and ear patch.

House Sparrow *Passer domesticus* L 6¹/₄″ (16 cm)
Male in breeding plumage has gray crown, chestnut nape,
black bib, black bill. Fresh fall plumage is edged with gray, obscuring these markings; bill becomes brownish. Female is
best identified by streaked back, buffy eye stripe, and unstreaked breast. Juveniles resemble adult female. Abundant
and aggressive, House Sparrows are omnipresent in populated
areas. Also known as English Sparrow.

Stripe-headed Tanager

♀

♂

immature

Bananaquit

Java Sparrow

immature

juvenile

Eurasian Tree Sparrow

fall ♂

breeding ♂

House Sparrow

♀

Finches (Family Fringillidae)

Seedeaters with an undulating flight. Many nest in the far north; in the fall, flocks of "winter finches" roam south, appearing here one year, there the next.

Pine Siskin *Carduelis pinus* L 5" (13 cm)
Prominent streaking; yellow at base of tail and flight feathers conspicuous in flight; bill thinner than in other finches. Juvenile's overall yellow tint is lost by late summer. Gregarious; may flock with goldfinches in winter. Calls include a hoarse *tee-ee* and a harsh, rising *jeeaah*. Song is similar to American Goldfinch but much huskier. Found in coniferous and mixed woods in summer; forests, shrubs, and fields in winter. Winter range highly erratic.

American Goldfinch *Carduelis tristis* L 5" (13 cm)
Plumage variable. Breeding adult male is bright yellow with black cap; black wings show white bars, yellow shoulder patch; uppertail and undertail coverts white; tail black-and-white. Female is duller overall, brownish-olive above; lacks black cap and yellow shoulder patch. White undertail coverts distinguish female from most Lesser Goldfinches. Winter adults and immatures are either brownish or grayish above; male may show some black on forehead. Juveniles have cinnamon buff wing markings and rump. Common and gregarious; found in weedy fields, open second-growth woodlands, roadsides, especially in thistles, sunflowers. Song is a lively series of trills, twitters, and *swee* notes. Distinctive flight call, *perchik-o-ree*. Widely known as "wild canary."

Lesser Goldfinch *Carduelis psaltria* L 4¹/₂" (11 cm)
Entire crown black on adult male; back varies from black in birds in eastern part of range to greenish in western birds. All show white wing patch at base of primaries. Most adult females dull yellow below; except for a few extremely pale birds, they lack white undertail coverts typical of American Goldfinch. Immature male of black-backed form has greener back and lacks full black cap. Juveniles resemble adult female. Common in dry, brushy fields, woodland borders, farms, gardens. Call, a plaintive *tee-yee*. Song is a prolonged, variable series of musical notes, similar to American Goldfinch.

Lawrence's Goldfinch *Carduelis lawrencei*
L 4³/₄" (12 cm) Wings extensively yellow; upperparts grayish in breeding plumage; underparts largely yellow. Male has black face and yellowish tinge on back. Winter birds are browner above, duller below. Juvenile is streaked, unlike other goldfinches. Common; may flock with other goldfinches, but prefers drier grassy slopes, chaparral. Distinctive call is a bell-like *tink-ul*. Mixes *tink*'s into jumbled, melodious song.

Pine Siskin

juvenile

American Goldfinch

breeding ♀

breeding ♂

winter ♂

winter ♀

juvenile

Lesser Goldfinch

♀

black-backed ♂

green-backed ♂

pale ♀

immature ♂

Lawrence's Goldfinch

winter ♀

winter ♂

breeding ♂

juvenile

♪ Red Crossbill *Loxia curvirostra* L 6¹/₄″ (16 cm)

Bill with crossed tips identifies both crossbill species. Red Crossbill's dark brown wings lack the bold white bars of White-winged Crossbill. Plumage highly variable. Most males are reddish overall, brightest on crown and rump; but may be pale rose or scarlet or largely yellow. Males always have red or yellow on throat. Most females are yellowish-olive; may show patches of red. Throat of female is always gray except in small Alaska form where yellow extends to center, but not sides, of throat. Juveniles are boldly streaked; a few juveniles and a very few adult males show white wing bars, the upper bar thinner than the lower. Immatures are like the respective adult but juvenile wing is retained, along with streaks on lower belly. All birds except adult males have olive edges on wings. Subspecies vary widely in size; extremes are shown here for comparison. All have large heads and short, notched tails. Fairly common, Red Crossbills inhabit coniferous woods. Highly irregular in their wanderings, dependent upon cone crops. Distinctive call, given chiefly in flight, is a series of *jip* notes. Song begins with several two-note phrases followed by a warbled trill. Irruptive winter migrant. Breeding range is expanding southward in the east; has bred as far south as Georgia.

White-winged Crossbill *Loxia leucoptera* L 6¹/₂″ (17 cm)

Bill with crossed tips identifies both crossbill species. All White-winged Crossbills have black wings with white tips on tertials, two bold white wing bars. Upper wing bar often hidden by scapulars. Adult male is red overall, pinker in winter. Immature male is largely yellow, with patches of red or pink. Adult female is mottled with yellowish-olive or grayish; rump pale yellow; underparts grayish-olive, with yellow wash on breast and sides. Juvenile is heavily streaked; wing bars thinner than in adults. Fairly common, White-winged Crossbills inhabit coniferous woods. Highly irregular in their wanderings, dependent upon cone crops. Distinctive flight call, a rapid series of harsh *chet* notes. Song combines harsh rattles, musical warbles. Irruptive winter migrant. Range is rapidly expanding southward, especially in the west.

Pine Grosbeak *Pinicola enucleator* L 9″ (23 cm)

Large, plump, and long-tailed. Bill dark, stubby, strongly curved. All plumages show two white wing bars, sometimes tinged with pink in adult male. Male's gray plumage is tipped with red on head, back, and underparts, pinker in fresh fall plumage. Female and immature are grayer overall; head, rump, and underparts variably yellow or reddish; some females and immature males are russet. Fairly common; inhabits open coniferous woods. In winter, found also in deciduous woods, orchards, suburban shade trees. Usually unwary and approachable. Song and calls vary geographically; typical flight call is a whistled *pui pui pui;* alarm call, a musical *chee-vli.* Irruptive winter migrant in the east.

♂

juvenile

Red Crossbill

Alaska ♀

♂

typical ♀

typical ♂

immature ♂

White-winged Crossbill

♀

juvenile

winter ♂

♀

♂

russet

Pine Grosbeak

♪ **Common Redpoll** *Carduelis flammea* *L 5¹/₄" (13 cm)*
Red or orange-red cap or "poll," blackish chin. Flanks, rump,
and undertail coverts distinctly streaked, unlike Hoary Redpoll. Bill larger than Hoary's. Male usually has rosy breast and
sides, brighter than in Hoary. Both sexes paler, buffier overall
in winter. Juveniles lack red cap until late-summer molt;
males acquire pinkish breast the following summer. Breeds in
subarctic forests and tundra scrub. Interbreeds with Hoary
Redpoll where ranges overlap. Some authorities consider the
two to be a single species. In winter, redpolls frequent brushy,
weedy areas, also catkin-bearing trees like alder and birch; irruptive south of Canada. Unwary and social, forming large
winter flocks. Flight is deeply undulating. When perched,
gives a *swee-ee-eet* call. Song combines trills and twittering.
Flight call, a dry rattling.

Hoary Redpoll *Carduelis hornemanni* *L 5¹/₂" (14 cm)*
Red or orange-red cap or "poll," black chin. Frostier, paler
overall than Common Redpoll, with a smaller bill. Streaking on
rump, flanks, and undertail coverts minimal or absent. Red on
male's breast is usually paler than on Common Redpoll and
does not extend to cheeks or sides. Fairly common; nests on or
near the ground above arctic tree line; interbreeds with Common Redpoll where ranges overlap. Some authorities consider
the two to be a single species. Calls and song are like those of
Common Redpoll, perhaps slightly slower. *C.h. hornemanni,*
breeding on Canadian arctic islands and Greenland, is larger,
paler than more widespread *exilipes*. Rare sightings of *exilipes*
occur south of Canada in winter, usually with Common
Redpolls.

Rosy Finch *Leucosticte arctoa* *L 6¹/₄" (16 cm)*
Plumage variable; some subspecies were once considered as
separate species. Basically, Rosy Finches show pinkish-brown
in wings and lower body. Back of head often gray, forehead
black. Underwings largely silver; flight undulating. Juveniles
lack pink tones and gray crown. Females are duller and grayer,
especially in "Brown-capped" and "Black" forms. Winter birds
are also duller, with yellowish black-tipped bill. "Gray-
crowned" coastal forms, such as "Hepburn's" and the bird
found on the Pribilofs, show larger amounts of gray on face and
vary in size as shown. Interior "Graycrowns" can show narrower gray area on head. "Graycrowns" nest in rocks and cliffs
high in western mountains or on Alaskan tundra. "Brown-
capped" is the rosiest form; common year round in Colorado
Rockies and neighboring ranges. The uncommon "Black"
form is distinctly darker; breeds in the Great Basin, central and
northwestern Rockies. Rosy Finches winter in open country at
lower altitudes; casual in towns. Winter strays are seen in the
midwest, mainly at feeders. Unwary and easily approached.
Calls include a series of *cheew* notes at varying high pitches.

juvenile

breeding ♀

breeding ♂

winter ♀

Common Redpoll

winter ♂

exilipes winter ♀

hornemanni winter ♂

Hoary Redpoll

exilipes winter ♂

"Hepburn's" winter ♂

Pribilofs winter ♂

juvenile

breeding ♂

Rosy Finch

"Gray-crowned" interior

breeding ♀

"Black"

breeding ♀

breeding ♂

breeding ♂

breeding ♂

"Brown-capped"

♪ **Purple Finch** *Carpodacus purpureus* L 6" (15 cm)

Not purple, but rose red over most of adult male body, brightest on head and rump. Rose color, acquired in second fall, is most intense in worn plumage of summer. Back is streaked; tail strongly notched. Pacific coast form, *C.p. californicus,* is buffier below and more diffusely streaked than the widespread *purpureus,* especially in females. Adult female and immatures are heavily streaked below; closely resemble Cassin's Finch. Note that dark ear patch and whitish eyebrow and cheek stripe are slightly more distinct in Purple Finch; bill slightly stubbier and more curved. Adult lacks streaking on undertail coverts. Compare also with female House Finch. Fairly common, Purple Finches are found in coniferous or mixed woodland borders, suburbs, parks, orchards; on the Pacific coast, inhabit coniferous forests, oak canyons, lower mountain slopes. Calls include a musical *chur-lee* and, in flight, a sharp *pit.* Song is a lively, complex warbling.

♪ **Cassin's Finch** *Carpodacus cassinii* L 6¼" (16 cm)

Crimson of adult male's cap ends sharply at brown-streaked nape. Throat and breast paler than Purple Finch; streaks on sides more distinct. Red hues do not appear until second fall. Tail strongly notched. Undertail coverts always distinctly streaked, unlike adult Purples. Adult female and immatures otherwise closely resemble Purple Finch. Cassin's facial pattern is slightly less distinct; bill is slightly straighter and longer. In flight, Cassin's gives a dry *kee-up* or *tee-dee-yip* call. Lively song, a variable warbling similar to songs of Purple and House Finches. Fairly common in upper mountain forests and open evergreen woodlands. Rare along coast. Casual winter vagrant east of range and west in California.

♪ **House Finch** *Carpodacus mexicanus* L 6" (15 cm)

Male has brown cap; head, bib, and rump are typically deep red but can vary to orange and yellow. Bib is clearly set off from streaked underparts. Tail is squarish. Adult female and juveniles are brown-streaked overall; lack distinct ear patch and eyebrow of Purple and Cassin's Finches. Young males acquire adult coloring by first fall. Abundant; found in semiarid lowlands and slopes up to 5,000 feet. Introduced in the east in the 1940s, where its range is rapidly expanding, especially in urban areas. Lively, high-pitched song consists chiefly of three-note phrases; usually ends with a nasal *wheer.* Calls include a hoarse *wheat.*

Common Rosefinch *Carpodacus erythrinus*

L 5¾" (15 cm) Eurasian species seen rarely on western Aleutians and other western Alaska islands. Strongly curved culmen. Lacks distinct eyebrow. Adult male's head, breast, and rump are deep red. Females and immatures are brown-streaked above and below, except on pale throat.

440

californicus ♀

Purple Finch

purpureus ♀

californicus ♂

purpureus ♂

Cassin's Finch

♀

♂

House Finch

typical ♂

variant ♂

♀

♀

♂

Common Rosefinch

Evening Grosbeak *Coccothraustes vespertinus*
L 8" (20 cm) Large, stocky, noisy finch with big bill. Black tail and wings, with prominent white patch on inner wing. Wing linings yellow. Bill pale yellow or greenish in spring, whitish in winter. Yellow forehead and eyebrow on adult male; dark brown and yellow body. Grayish-tan female has thin, dark whisker stripe, white-tipped tail; white patch on inner wing smaller than male's; second patch, on primaries, conspicuous in flight. Juvenile female resembles adult female. Juvenile male is yellower overall; wing and tail similar to adult male. Strident call, *clee-ip* or *peeer*. Breeds in mixed woods; in the west, mainly in mountains. In winter frequents woodlots, shade trees, feeders. Winter numbers vary greatly from year to year. Range is expanding in the east.

Hawfinch *Coccothraustes coccothraustes* *L 7" (18 cm)*
Eurasian species. Casual spring stray on western Aleutians and islands off western Alaska; less frequent in fall. Big, stocky, like Evening Grosbeak, but has black throat and lores. Yellowish-brown above; pinkish-brown below. Big bill is blue-black in spring, yellowish in fall. Female resembles male, but is paler, grayer. Conspicuous white band shows on extended wing. Flight is high, fast, and undulating. Walks with parrot-like waddle. Call is a loud, explosive *ptik*.

Eurasian Bullfinch *Pyrrhula pyrrhula* *L 6¹/₂" (17 cm)*
Eurasian species. Casual migrant on Aleutians; casual in winter on Alaskan mainland. Cheeks, breast, and belly rosy red in adult male, brown in female. Black cap and face, gray back, prominent whitish bar on wing, distinct white rump. In profile, top of head and bill form unbroken curve. Juvenile resembles female, but with brown cap. Call is a soft, piping *pheew*.

Oriental Greenfinch *Carduelis sinica* *L 6" (15 cm)*
Eurasian species. Casual migrant, mainly in spring, on outer Aleutians. Adult male has greenish face and rump, gray nape and crown, bright yellow wing patch and undertail coverts. Adult female similar but paler, with a brownish head. Juvenile has same yellow markings as adults, but is streaked overall.

Brambling *Fringilla montifringilla* *L 6¹/₄" (16 cm)*
Eurasian species; fairly common but irregular migrant on Aleutians; casual fall and winter visitor to southern Alaska, with a few records in Canada and lower 48 states. White rump conspicuous in flight. Adult male has tawny-orange shoulders, spotted flanks, white belly. Head and back are fringed with buff in fresh fall plumage; these fringes wear down to black by spring. Female and juvenile duller than adult male, have mottled crown, striped nape. Bramblings may twitch tails while perched. Flight call, a nasal *check-check-check*.

Evening Grosbeak

breeding ♂

juvenile ♂

breeding ♀

Hawfinch

breeding ♂

Eurasian Bullfinch

♂

♀

Oriental Greenfinch

♂

♀

juvenile

Brambling

breeding ♂

fall ♂

♀

Index

The main entry for each species is listed in **boldface** type and refers to the text page opposite the illustration.

A musical note at the end of a common-name entry indicates that the species is included on the records that accompany this book. The number and letter after the note refer to the specific record number and side.

449

460

Type composition by National
Geographic's Photographic
Services. Color separations by
The Lanman-Progressive
Companies, Washington,
D. C. Printed and bound by
Kingsport Press, Kingsport,
Tennessee. Paper by Mead
Paper Co., New York, N.Y.

Library of Congress CIP Data

Field guide to the birds of
North America.
　Includes index.
　1. Birds—North America—
Identification. I. National
Geographic Society (U. S.) II.
Title: Birds of North America.
QL681.F53　1983
598.297　83-13262
ISBN 0 87044-472-7

You are invited to join the
National Geographic Society
or to send gift memberships to
others. (Membership includes
a subscription to the
NATIONAL GEOGRAPHIC
magazine.) For information
call 800-638-4077 toll free, or
write to the National
Geographic Society,
Department 1675,
Washington, D. C. 20036.

The Artists

Cover by *Patricia A. Topper*

Marc R. Hanson,
pages 25-37, 97-101

Cynthia J. House,
pages 61-95

H. Jon Janosik,
pages 19-23, 39-47, 103, 107-111, 121

Donald L. Malick,
pages 183-187, 191, 195-205, 229, 239-247, 263-275

John P. O'Neill,
pages 10-11, 231, 233, 295-299, 309-313, 419, 427, 429

Kent Pendleton,
pages 189, 193, 206-223

Diane Pierce,
pages 49-59, 123, 125, 129, 135, 381-417, 435-443

John C. Pitcher,
pages 105, 115-119, 127, 131, 133

H. Douglas Pratt,
pages 2-3, 225, 227, 255-261, 277-293, 301-307, 315-379, 421-425, 431, 433

Chuck Ripper,
pages 173-181, 249-253

Thomas R. Schultz,
pages 141-171

Daniel S. Smith,
pages 113, 136-139

Lee Marc Steadman,
pages 235, 237

Additional artwork by
Veronica Freeman
Betsy Reeder
Patricia A. Topper

Acknowledgments

Many people generously contributed their time and knowledge to the production of this guide. In particular we express our gratitude to Claudia P. Wilds, who played a substantial role in the initial planning for the book and continued to assist us throughout its progress, especially with the sections on shorebirds, rails, mimic thrushes, and doves.

Our thanks go also to Thomas A. Allen, Stephen Bailey, Lawrence G. Balch, Dr. Richard C. Banks, Louis Bevier, Daniel Boone, Danny Bystrak, William S. Clark, Victor Emanuel, Kimball Garrett, Freida Gentry, Daniel D. Gibson, Peter Grant, Dr. James L. Gulledge, Rebecca Hyman, Lars Jonsson, Kenn Kaufman, Lasse J. Laine, Paul Lehman, Guy McCaskie, Joseph Morlan, Betsy Reeder, Dr. J. V. Remsen, Robert F. Ringler, John Rowlett, Rose Ann Rowlett, Will Russell, Thede Tobish, Dr. John Trochet, Laurel Tucker, Nigel Tucker, Terence R. Wahl, Hal Wierenga, and Alan Wormington. We also thank the staff of the U. S. Fish and Wildlife Service's Patuxent Wildlife Research Center in Laurel, Maryland.